# Evaluating health interventions

An introduction to evaluation of health treatments, services, policies and organizational interventions

## John Øvretveit

**Open University Press**
Buckingham · Philadelphia

Open University Press
Celtic Court
22 Ballmoor
Buckingham
MK18 1XW

and
1900 Frost Road, Suite 101
Bristol, PA 19007, USA

First Published 1998

A catalogue record of this book is available from the British Library

ISBN  0 335 19964 X (pb)  0 335 19965 8 (hb)

*Library of Congress Cataloging-in-Publication Data*
Øvretveit, John, 1954–
    Evaluating health interventions: an introduction to evaluation of
  health treatments, services, policies, and organizational
  interventions / John Øvretveit.
        p.   cm.
    Includes bibliographical references and index.
    ISBN 0–335–19964–X. (pbk)  ISBN 0–335–19965–8 (hb)
    1. Medical care–Evaluation.    I. Title.
    [DNLM: 1.  Outcome and Process Assessment (Health Care)
  2.  Evaluation Studies.    W 84. 1 096a 1997]
  RA399.A1098    1997
  362.1'068'4–dc21
  DNLM/DLC
  for Library of Congress                                                97–8733
                                                                          CIP

Typeset by Type Study, Scarborough
Printed in Great Britain by Redwood Books Ltd, Trowbridge

# Evaluating health interventions

RESEARCH UNIT IN HEALTH
AND BEHAVIOURAL CHANGE
UNIVERSITY OF EDINBURGH
MEDICAL SCHOOL
TEVIOT PLACE
EDINBURGH EH8 9AG

# Contents

# Foreword

As both volume and skills in healthcare increase, there is a parallel increase in the need to evaluate the outcomes and effects of the services rendered.

In this book John Øvretveit furnishes us with timely, thoughtful and thorough guidelines for evaluation methods applied to health services.

Though high cost medicine – new technologies and remedies – are introduced at a rapid pace, they are often put to practice with little evaluation and few systematic examinations of effects. The same holds for many established treatments and services: we continue using them although their justification may be scanty. The flagrant differences in surgical interventions and types of treatment for identical diagnoses combined with medically inexplicable variations in hospitalization are but two indicators of the need for more evidence based medicine and a better scientific justification for the choices made. Clearly, the medical profession and health authorities share the responsibility for securing more informed decisions.

I welcome this book for many reasons, but first of all as a contribution to the provision of better health care for the public. Patients have a right to expect that the treatments and the services they receive are properly evaluated. Taxpayers also expect health policies and changes to organizations to be evaluated. This book will help researchers and health employees to apply evaluation methods, and thus to ensure safe, high quality and effective healthcare.

Gudmund Hernes
Minister of Health of Norway

# Preface

Most people working in the health sector use evaluations or are involved in an evaluation in some way. Yet many health practitioners, managers and policy advisors are not well equipped to use, supervise or carry out an evaluation. There is a danger that the evidence-based healthcare movement will impose a limited view of evidence. In teaching evaluation to groups which included many different professions, I found that there were few texts which gave a simple overview of the range of evaluation approaches and methods which are used in healthcare. This book aims to give such an overview. It is based on my experience carrying out evaluations as a contract researcher, and from teaching health evaluation on the Brunel University masters course in public service evaluation in the UK. It also draws on my more recent experience teaching Nordic health service practitioners and managers and carrying out evaluations of Nordic and other overseas health services and policies.

The book does not give detailed guidance for researchers who need to carry out a particular type of evaluation: there are a number of excellent books for researchers on economic, experimental and other types of evaluation which readers are directed to for more 'how to do it' details. However, the book does aim to draw researchers' attention to different approaches to evaluation which they may not have considered.

'Learning by doing' is certainly one of the more effective ways to acquire knowledge and skills. But I have found that equally effective, for me, is 'learning by teaching'. As a contract researcher I have evaluated services and policies in health and social care since 1980. Yet it was through teaching evaluation that I discovered that my knowledge of evaluation was in fact limited and specialized. I discovered a diversity of approaches which was far greater than I had imagined, and that concepts and ideas from some types of evaluation could be used in other types. I developed a respect for approaches which were different from those which I had used, and found that other evaluators had not only encountered many of the practical and methodological problems which I had faced, but had developed effective strategies to deal with them.

This discovery was possible for me because teaching a broad range of people with different needs had forced me to look widely into the subject and allowed me a certain amount of time to explore this diversity. In healthcare, this luxury of time or the resources are not available to managers and policy makers who do not have a background in evaluation or research, but who wish to use or commission an evaluation. Neither is it available to practitioners who wish to do small scale evaluations, or who increasingly need to use evaluations to improve their practice. The luxury of time is often not available to researchers who need to 'convert', temporarily or permanently, from their discipline-based research to carry out an evaluation.

Yet it is only by learning about evaluations of different interventions in health, such as treatments, services, policies, organizational interventions and educational programmes, that managers, practitioners and researchers can gain the knowledge and skills which they need, and see the richness of the subject. The aims of this book are to give a broad overview, to convey some of the enthusiasm which I and some of my colleagues hold for this multidiscipline, and to give 'beginners' a grounding in the subject.

Some texts can be disabling for those new to the subject because they are too detailed, ignore certain approaches or are preoccupied with criticizing approaches which are unfamiliar to the newcomer. There are excellent texts on specific approaches, such as experimental treatment evaluations or economic evaluation, but these can give the impression that there is only one way to do an evaluation. US texts on 'programme' evaluation give good practical guidance about how to do certain types of evaluation, but many of the examples are not from healthcare and use terms and assume contexts unfamiliar to those outside the USA. I also felt that few texts did justice to an approach in evaluation which I have termed 'developmental evaluation' or to the 'action orientation' of most evaluation projects. Neither did they sufficiently consider values. None gave the overview which I felt the people whom I was teaching needed – a diverse group of people with different backgrounds, wanting to evaluate many different types of interventions and all needing a broad introduction before they specialized.

The book does not align itself with any particular approach. In my view critics of the experimental approach often criticize what is in fact their own inaccurate caricature of the approach, and are unfamiliar with the sophisticated debates within this paradigm. Some experimental evaluators and doctors often make similar mistakes when criticizing developmental evaluation or certain qualitative methods. Each approach can inform the other and has its place: different approaches are required for the many different types of intervention which need to be evaluated in health services, and there is both plenty of room and a need for all in this new and growing field.

I want to acknowledge the colleagues who have helped, inspired and influenced me over the years: in particular, Maurice Kogan and Christopher Pollitt of the Brunel University Centre for Public Policy and Practice, Martin Buxton of the Brunel Health Economics Research Unit, David Hunter and Steve Harrison at the Nuffield Centre for Health, colleagues at the Lund Institute of Health Economics, Arja Rimpela, now Head of the School of Public Health at Tampere University, Finland, and Edgar Borgenhammer, Mats Brommels and Keith Barnard. Thanks are also due for support and humour from Barbara, Gill and Mary. I particularly wish to thank Don Berwick and Brent James for their encouragement and example over the years.

# 1 ▷ What is evaluation?

*What are figures worth if they do no good to men's bodies or souls?*

(Eyler 1979)

*Practical life cannot proceed without evaluation, nor can intellectual life, nor can moral life, and they are not built on sand. The real question is how to do evaluation well, not how to avoid it.*

(Scriven 1991)

## Introduction

This book is about how to use or make an evaluation of a health treatment, service or policy. It aims to increase your ability to carry out a simple evaluation, and to understand and appraise reports of different types of evaluations. It has a practical focus: on 'evaluation for action'; on making and using evaluations to improve people's health and the health services in which we work. It is about a multidisciplinary approach to developing evidence-based healthcare practice, as well as evidence-based management and policy-making.

This book does not argue for or against different approaches to health evaluation. Rather, it shows the need to choose a design and methods which are most suited to the purpose of the evaluation and to the type of intervention which we are evaluating. It describes a variety of approaches within the four broad categories of experimental, economic, developmental and managerial evaluations. It shows the strengths and weaknesses of each, and the different criteria by which evaluations carried out within each perspective should be assessed.

*We are in danger of replacing indifference about effectiveness with a dogmatic and narrow view of 'evidence'.*

This plural and practical approach is because our subject is evaluating health interventions of many different types. Even for an intervention of one type, such as a change to how teamwork is organized, many different evaluation designs and methods are possible. Both evaluators and users of evaluations need to know which type of evaluation could be used and the advantages and limitations of each. All need to understand the strengths and weakness of qualitative and quantitative methods and when and how to combine them.

Evaluation is not a boring subject, although some of the literature is not designed for those with attention deficit disorder: this is not a criticism of experimental evaluations, which are often well written for busy clinicians, but a criticism of the unnecessary jargon and long-winded discussions which hide a lack of substance in some evaluation writings. This book is not without its slow moments, but I hope to convey to you some of the fascinating issues and human drama within this rapidly evolving field, and to develop your understanding in a relatively painless way, but without sacrificing necessary scientific rigour. We will encounter conflicts between different views about how to study people and how to enable change, about what counts as 'evidence', about the type of explanations which an evaluation should give and about whether evaluators should take more responsibility for ensuring that action follows from their work.

*In modern healthcare it is unethical not to be concerned with evaluation, and no longer acceptable to be 'evaluation illiterate'*

Health evaluation raises questions about our own and others' values and about what we consider important in life. It involves questions about how we change clinical and managerial practice and about how governments and organizations make health policies which affect us all. We will see how evaluations are used to advance and defend powerful interests, and how the evaluator has continually to choose between the ideal and the practical. We will see how simple evaluation methods are breaking the division between research and practice, and how more practitioners are applying the methods to improve the organization of care as well as the treatments which they give to patients.

As health professionals we monitor our patients' response to a treatment and have an ethical obligation to evaluate our own practice. As managers and policy-makers we need to ensure that resources are used to the best effect and that we can explain to the public why we have made certain choices on their behalf – a public of consumers and taxpayers who are increasingly using the findings from health evaluations. We can all use evaluation principles and methods to improve our practice and how we provide our service.

## Who is the book for?

This book is for people who need to read and use evaluation reports and for those planning or making an evaluation. One group is health practitioners or researchers new to evaluation. They may be wanting to make better use of evaluations reported in their professional journals, or to evaluate their own or their colleagues' practice (self-evaluation). They may work for an organization which uses the treatment they are evaluating, or work for an organization which wants to evaluate its own service or a new policy. They may be 'external evaluators' planning an evaluation or already carrying one out. The main interest of those making an evaluation is in the phases of defining the item to be evaluated, deciding criteria of valuation and gathering and analysing data.

The book is also for managers, advisors and policy-makers who use or sponsor evaluations: they are evaluation 'users', as are practitioners and, increasingly, patients and patients' groups. Those using evaluations need to be able to understand an evaluation and critically appraise it in a short period of time, and then decide whether the evaluation suggests that they should act differently. They may ask internal or external evaluators to undertake an evaluation. Their interest is mainly in the phases of defining the item and criteria, assessing proposals for an evaluation, judging value and planning and carrying out action.

The purpose of the book is to increase evaluators' ability to make evaluations which are useful, and to increase the ability of others to make better use of an evaluation. Evaluation is becoming a more common activity in health services. The reader is almost certain to be involved in an evaluation or using at least one type of evaluation. All health professionals, whatever the position in which they work, need to understand the fundamentals of evaluation. They will need even more in the future to be able to apply findings from evaluations, and to use evaluation methods to improve their own clinical or managerial practice and the surrounding organization of care.

## How to use the book

Why are you looking at this book? What do you want from it? When I am new to a subject, I do not know enough about the subject to say what I need to know. For some this book will give you an introduction and help you to decide whether you need to know more or which skills you need, and guide you to other sources. The following gives suggestions for how different readers might make the best use of their time looking through this book. In Appendix 4 the book gives a number of learning exercises which readers can use individually or in a group to apply and work through the ideas that are covered. The first is a 'learning needs and objectives exercise' which you can use to clarify what you want from this book, or from a training course or conference on evaluation. The last section of this chapter gives a guide to all the chapters.

### Health practitioners

Health practitioners – doctors, nurses, therapists and others – might find that starting with Chapter 3 is the best way to get a simple and rapid introduction. This chapter uses an evaluation of a treatment to give an example of different evaluation designs. To gain an overview of evaluation you could continue with this introductory chapter, which will also help you to decide which chapters you want to turn to next. Do spend a few minutes on the 'learning needs and objectives exercise' in Appendix 4, after you have read some of the introduction, so that you can clarify what you want from the book. If you want to become more skilled in critically assessing an evaluation report, and learn how to understand a complex study quickly, then test and improve your skills by analysing the case examples in Chapter 4.

### Service managers

Health managers should go straight to Chapter 9 if they come to this book with a view to managing an evaluation. Chapter 9 follows a colleague who decided to buy in an evaluation of a service which she managed in order to help her to decide whether to set up a similar service in another area. Then you could finish reading this introduction, and next turn to Chapter 8 on managerial evaluation, which will be more familiar territory, and will help you decide where to go next.

### Policy makers and purchasers

'Policy makers' are politicians and their advisors, and managers with authority to make policies; for example, about allocating resources, changes to how health organizations work and measures to promote health. Purchasers and others working for organizations which pay for health services are increasingly using evaluation for a number of purposes. This chapter shows the range of approaches, and Chapter 14 considers how to make better use of evaluations of different types. You may not need to know some of the details of different designs and data gathering methods, but the discussion of economic evaluation (Chapter 6) and of quality and outcome evaluation (Chapter 13) will be of use and will help you to decide which other parts of the book to look at.

### Teachers

If you are reading this because you already run courses or sessions on evaluation, then you will be able to decide without my suggestions which chapters might be of most use. Some of this book has already been used for international distance learning courses in health evaluation. Have a look at the ten learning exercises in Appendix 4: you can use or adapt some of these for individual or group work. Teachers new to the subject might like to think about which type of knowledge and skills their students most need, and the time their students have to gain these. How many need to be able to carry out an evaluation, and of which type? How many only need to be able quickly to understand and critically assess an evaluation report?

This first chapter gives some basic definitions which help students to get orientated. I have found the models of evaluation design in Chapter 3 a quick and effective way of building students' ability quickly to read, understand and critically assess most types of evaluation report, and Chapter 4 will test and deepen their ability to do this. (Appendix 2 gives a framework which students can use to appraise any evaluation critically, and Appendix 3 gives six 'empty' design formats for them to write notes summarizing an evaluation.) After this, there are some chapters which apply to all types of evaluation, such as the one on data-gathering methods, and some which are more relevant to specific subjects. I have found debates on 'what counts as evidence' some of the most interesting teaching events: the last section of Chapter 14 is a good basis for such stimualting debates.

### Researchers

The main value of this book to researchers is to give a simple introduction to types of evaluation which they have not encountered, or to help those making the transition from pure research to decide how best to deal with the practical issues involved in making an evaluation. One question is what, if any, is the difference between evaluation and research? Chapter 9, which describes the phases of an evaluation, will help you to answer this question and to understand how a sponsor and user are thinking when they ask you to carry out an evaluation.

Newcomers may find Chapter 2, on theory, history and perspectives in evaluation, a good starting point. Then you can judge whether you need to study the description of designs in Chapter 3 by reading a case example in Chapter 4 and testing how quickly you can analyse it. You will find the discussion of data gathering methods which you have already used a bit basic (Chapter 11), but Chapter 14 will challenge you to decide what your responsibilities for implementation are, and Chapter 10 will alert you to the practical issues and politics of evaluation.

More about the contents of each chapter is given at the end of this chapter. Each chapter finishes with a list of key points, which can help those who have not read the chapter to decide if they need to. Next, we look at some basic terms and which types of 'intervention' need to be evaluated in the health sector.

## Evaluation: some basic terms

Evaluation is simple – it is something which we do all the time without thinking. We are always judging the value or importance of things, or of what we and others do. In everyday language, when we evaluate something we usually mean we judge its value. Sometimes we also mean that we look more closely before judging value: for example, we look at how we have spent our time, before then judging the value of how we spent our time. But many of us are very quick to make judgements.

More thoughtful evaluation is more complex. We are more careful to get the right information and to use it in the right way in order to reach our judgement of value. We are clearer about what is important to us: our criteria of valuation. We are also more careful about how we make a link between our judgement of value and how we could act. In systematic evaluation the usual approach is to separate the collection of information (the task of the 'evaluator') from judging value and acting (the task of the 'user' of the evaluation). Other differences from everyday evaluation are the evaluator's careful definition of what is to be evaluated, and of the information needed, as well as his or her careful selection and use of methods for collecting and analysing the information.

Systematic evaluation is also complex in that the evaluator has to know about a range of methods and approaches so as to be able to choose the best methods for the purpose of the evaluation. We do not use methods like participant observation and grounded theory to get information about the cost of home care in comparison to hospital care, but we may use these methods if the purpose is to find out how patients and carers judge or make use of these types of care. Ideally the evaluator has to be able to use a variety of methods, or at least to know which method is best for the purpose of the evaluation. Ideally those sponsoring and managing an evaluation should be able to make an independent judgement about whether other methods

**Basic terms**

*Evaluator*: the person making the evaluation.

*Sponsors*: those who initiate or pay for the evaluation.

*Users*: those who make use of or act on the evaluation.

*Intervention*: an action on, or attempt to change, a person, population or organization which is the subject of an evaluation.

*Target*: the part or whole of a person, population or organization which the intervention aims to affect.

*Outcome*: the consequences of the intervention; that which 'comes out' of it.

*Target outcome*: the change effected by the intervention on the target (the difference which the intervention makes to the target, whether intended or not).

would be more cost-effective and what can and cannot be expected from the evaluation.

In the pages to come we will continually return to the purpose of an evaluation and to the criteria for valuing something. Next come some basic terms, then a discussion of the term which we use to describe the subject of an evaluation ('an intervention'), and then we introduce the different types of intervention which are evaluated.

As a test of your understanding of basic terms, what is the 'target' of an evaluation of a primary care programme for expectant mothers? This is a trick question, because normally we talk of the 'subject' of an evaluation rather than the 'target' of an evaluation. The 'subject' of the evaluation is a primary care programme (which is the intervention) and the 'targets' of the primary care programme are expectant mothers. The point is not to confuse you, but to alert you to the fact that some reports use the word 'target' to refer to the target of the evaluation (e.g. Breakwell and Millward 1995). This book uses 'target' to describe the person or object which the intervention

**Who makes evaluations?**

*External evaluators*: researchers or consultancy units not directly managed by and independent of the sponsor and user of the evaluation.

*Internal evaluators*: evaluation or development units or researchers that are internal to the organization, and that evaluate treatments services or policies carried out by the organization or one of its divisions.

*Self-evaluation*: practitioners or teams who evaluate their own practice so as to improve it.

aims to change. It uses the term 'subject' to describe the intervention which is evaluated.

Note also that 'outcome' is the end result of the intervention and is a broad concept which encompasses a variety of consequences of the intervention, some of which are intended and some of which may not be. Many evaluations study the outcome for the targets of the intervention. In this case the outcome of the primary care programme is the effect of this intervention on expectant mothers (the targets) – whether they are changed in any way by the programme. Evaluations often measure some aspect of a patient or population before and after the intervention. Many things apart from the intervention may account for any before–after difference which the evaluation detects. 'Target outcome' here refers to the difference produced which can be attributed to the intervention. It does not refer to the before–after difference in general, just that which can be attributed to the intervention.

## What do we evaluate?

### The concept of 'intervention' (otherwise termed 'the evaluated')

Evaluations gather data for the purpose of valuing an intervention. An intervention is an action which results in a change: for example, a nurse gives a mother an information leaflet about breast feeding and the mother reads the leaflet. An intervention is something which someone does, which 'comes between' (*inter venire*) what would otherwise happen. The aim of an intervention is to produce a change, and to make a difference to people's lives.

Most evaluations examine an intervention which aims to alter the course of events so that people gain a health benefit from the intervention – people or populations are the targets of the intervention. There are also interventions to health organizations, such as a training programme, or a change to how people delegate work, or a change to how primary care personnel cooperate with a hospital and social services – in this case health personnel or organizations are the immediate targets of the intervention.

What is wrong with calling the things (or phenomena) which we need to evaluate 'interventions'? After all, most of what we do in the health sector aims to make a difference – to intervene in people's lives or in how we organize. This is true, but what about assessment or diagnostic methods which we need to evaluate: for example, a new type of brain scanning technique, or a care management assessment system? Are these 'interventions'? The purpose of many new diagnostic techniques is to help to assess a patient, but without making an intervention in the sense of directly causing a change in the patient. And what about an evaluation of whether patients from different social groups get equal access to and use of a service? Are all mothers given a leaflet about breast feeding, and one which is in a language which they can understand?

There are thus two problems with using 'intervention' to describe the different subjects of evaluations: first, not all interventions aim to change people; second, not all evaluations aim to find out if the intervention did change people. We may take for granted the value of breast feeding or the effectiveness of the programme, or not be interested in effectiveness, but be more concerned with how many mothers are reached by the programme. The purpose of some evaluations is to assess not the effect, but whether, for example, the service is provided to all equally. Using the term intervention implies that our main criterion of valuation is whether 'the evaluated' produces a change, when we may want to concentrate on other criteria of valuation such as costs or equity. We may know that the intervention has an effect but we may want to judge its value according to other criteria.

There is no real need to 'split hairs' at this stage about whether 'intervention' is the best general term to use to describe the subject of an evaluation – you will need all your energy for more important hair-splitting discussions later. The point is that by calling the subject of an evaluation an 'intervention' we imply that the thing has already made a change or had an effect. Yet it is precisely this which many evaluations try to find out. Strictly speaking, intervention means come between what would otherwise have happened and does not necessarily mean that a change was produced. To avoid the implication that a change was produced, the book sometimes uses the even less elegant term 'the evaluated' instead of 'intervention' to describe the subject of the evaluation. This term describes only the subject of the evaluation without implying any characteristics of the subject, such as whether it does intervene in someone's life and produces a change.

## Defining the subject of the evaluation and assessing effects

There are two further points to be made before we look at different types of interventions. The first is that how we define and specify the thing or phenomenon to be evaluated is of the utmost importance if we are to make a useful evaluation. By define I mean 'draw a boundary around' (*de-finire*) which includes and excludes certain other things or phenomena. In the example of the nurse and mother, what was the intervention? Do we define it as the nurse giving the leaflet? Or was it this action and the mother reading the leaflet? What do we do if the mother does not read the leaflet? Do we say that there was no intervention, or that the intervention had no effect?

In the example it was implied that the intervention was the nurse giving and the mother reading the leaflet. A plan for an evaluation and a report must precisely describe the intervention, and also specify the key elements 'inside' the boundary of the intervention: for example, specify the details of the leaflet. Some evaluations aim only to get a good description of the evaluated – to specify possibly important elements and to define what should and should not be considered part of the evaluated. Thus there may be a difference between the intended intervention and what was actually done, and we need to know exactly what was done and evaluated to be able to interpret and apply the findings.

The second point concerns which changes we look for and when we look for them. Discovering that an intended intervention does or does not produce a change in the target makes it easy to judge its value, according to one common criterion of valuation. Note, however, that there may be other types of change which may be of value – for example, the nurse may feel that she or he is doing something to encourage breast feeding and this may raise morale. Further, there is such a thing as an unintended intervention, an unplanned event or action which produces a change: evaluations looking back into the past can often discover that something a practitioner or service did had an important effect, even though it was not intended.

In summary, many evaluations try to describe or measure changes which the intervention produces in the target. They aim to collect data about how big the valued changes are, and whether there are any changes which are not valued or which are harmful. These data help others to judge the value of the intervention.

Evaluations differ in the scope of the possible changes which they investigate: they may look at one type of effect, or at many effects and at short- or long-term effects. In the example, a limited investigation is of any change in the mother's attitude. A broader one would also look for changes in her behaviour: did she breast feed, or persuade others to? Broader still would be to include studying any change to the mother's or baby's health. Evaluations also differ in the time period over which possible change is investigated. The scope and time period depends on the evaluation purpose and questions or hypothesis to be tested.

The main points are that the subject of an evaluation is an intervention, and evaluations will do one or more of the following: describe the intended and actual intervention, describe or measure its consequences, provide information for judging the value of the intervention and explain why what was described did occur.

## Evaluation defined

*Evaluation is making a comparative assessment of the value of the evaluated or intervention, using systematically collected and analysed data, in order to decide how to act.*

A slightly longer definition highlights the important features of evaluation:

*Evaluation is attributing value to an intervention by gathering reliable and valid information about it in a systematic way, and by making comparisons, for the purposes of making more informed decisions or understanding causal mechanisms or general principles.*

Let us unpack this definition and look at each feature.

*. . . attributing value to an intervention . . .*

The intervention is the thing or process of which we judge the value. The 'evaluated' that we will look at are health treatments, services, policies and interventions into, or changes to, health organizations. These subjects are very different in their nature and complexity. Some are easier to define than others. Defining or specifying what we are evaluating is important because we want to be sure exactly what it is that we are judging the value of. Even treatments can be difficult to define exactly, as we will see when we look at 'alternative' treatments such as aromatherapy and homeopathy.

Exact definition often gets more difficult as we move from biophysical systems to social systems such as services, and then to 'higher level' social systems when we are looking at a health policy such as a ban on smoking which is implemented across health and other sectors. We will see that all evaluators spend some time defining the evaluated before they start, and that the only purpose of some evaluations is to get a clearer description of an intervention.

If we are able to define the evaluated, how do we then judge its value, or 'attribute' value to it? The first point is that it is the 'users' of the evaluation who judge the value of the evaluated; that is, politicians, managers, citizens, health practitioners and others. Strictly speaking, evaluators do not judge value. They simply collect, analyse and present information. The information which they decide to collect and the way they present it is designed to concentrate on certain things which some, or all, users think are important for them to be able to judge value.

Why does the definition of evaluation include 'attributing value'? Surely this suggests that the evaluators make a judgement of value rather than just the users? We will return to the questions of the evaluator's values and whether or not the evaluator judges value in Chapters 9 and 14 – note at this point that there are different views on these questions. The definition includes 'attributing value' because it aims to encompass the whole process of evaluation and to draw attention to the part which users play in evaluations, rather than keeping this separate. I think that there is something lacking in a definition and understanding of evaluation which does not include valuation. This definition recognizes the process of valuation and this book shows how values enter into most parts of the evaluation process.

*. . . gathering reliable and valid information about it in a systematic way . . .*

This second part of the definition shows one way in which an evaluation helps users to attribute value: the evaluation presents to them information about the evaluated which is reliable and valid and has been gathered by evaluators in a systematic way for the purposes of judging value. This distinguishes evaluation from journalism, where the journalist does not use the same rigorous methods. What then is the difference between evaluation and other types of research, which also give valid and reliable information about the evaluated?

*. . . by making comparisons . . .*

Comparison is the main way in which evaluation helps users to attribute value, and, together with valuation, is what distinguishes evaluation from some other types of research. Different types of evaluation carry out different types of comparison. One type we are familiar with is where the evaluation compares one group which gets an intervention with another group which does not, to see if an intervention has any effect on the first group (the experimental controlled trial). This is a comparison of the measured state of two groups, and evaluations of this type will use different ways to try to be sure that any difference in the measured state can be attributed reliably to the intervention. Other types of comparison are to:

♦ compare the state of one or more people, populations or organizations before an intervention to their state after the intervention;
♦ compare the needs of people or populations to their needs after an intervention;
♦ compare the objectives of the intervention to the actual achievements;
♦ compare what is done to a set of standards or guidelines (e.g. audit).

We can only judge value if we make a comparison. Many evaluations use 'value criteria' to help to make the comparison, or only one criterion, such as symptom relief, cost or the number of eligible people using a service. In the two-group evaluation model the criterion is the measure used to measure the state of the two groups. In 'before and after' evaluations the criterion is the before and after measure. In the other two types above the criterion is the objectives, standards or guidelines.

Where do criteria come from? This question is important because if we can only judge value by making a comparison, and if the criterion is the way we compare, then the type of criterion we choose will shape the data we collect and how we judge the value of the evaluated. The criteria come from one or more users of the evaluation, or are predefined (e.g. established standards), and users agree to adopt them to help them to judge the value of the evaluated. Recognize, though, that people judge the value of the evaluated using many criteria, most of which are below awareness or half-formed criteria, and are different for different people and interest groups. Evaluators may help people to clarify the criteria of valuation which they want to use. This point, that an evaluation makes a limited comparison using limited criteria, takes us to the next part of the definition:

*. . . for the purposes of making more informed decisions . . .*

Examples of decisions are if or when to use a treatment, how to improve a service or whether to reduce or discontinue it. Decisions to be made may be about how to set up other similar services or whether or not to set them up, or whether to abandon, extend or modify a policy.

We need to add to the phrase '*more informed decisions*' the phrase '*than they would otherwise do*'. People do not need an evaluation to judge the value of something and to decide how to act. Very few treatments, services or other interventions have been or ever will be evaluated. Generally, mangers, practitioners and citizens go about their business as if evaluation and reports do not exist. The purpose of evaluation is to add to the information which people have and to improve the way that they judge value, so that they can make more informed decisions than they would otherwise do.

The way evaluation does this is to make clear the criteria used in the evaluation for judging value, so that people can decide whether or not to accept these criteria or how much weight to give them in making their judgement of value. It also helps decisions by giving information about the intervention and its performance in relation to these criteria. But people will decide how to act by using criteria and values not included in the evaluation, and also by making judgements about the feasibility and consequences of different actions.

*. . . or understanding causal mechanisms or general principles.*

This last part of the definition draws attention to the fact that the primary purpose of some evaluations is only scientific knowledge, and here evaluation clearly overlaps with scientific research. Medical researchers and other scientists use certain evaluation designs because they are useful for investigating cause–effect mechanisms in different phenomena and for explaining and predicting. The 'general principles' refers to the aim of most evaluations being to produce findings which can be generalized beyond the specific intervention studied – this makes evaluation more than consultancy or development work.

## Other definitions

The definition above is just one of the many definitions of evaluation. More are listed at the end of Appendix 1. For example:

> Program evaluations aim to provide convincing evidence that a program is effective. The standards are the specific criteria by which effectiveness is measured.
>
> > (Fink 1993)

This defines evaluation in terms of finding evidence of effectiveness. It is true that many evaluations examine effectiveness, but there are other ways to judge value. We also tend to find what we are looking for. Should we not have a more sceptical approach than to aim to provide convincing evidence that a programme is effective? Should not the evaluator instead assume that the programme has no effects?

Another definition of evaluation is in terms of assessing whether the evaluated achieves its goals:

> The critical assessment, on as objective a basis as possible, of the degree to which entire services or their component parts (e.g. diagnostic tests, treatments, caring procedures) fulfil stated goals.
>
> > (St Leger *et al.* 1992)

Achieving goals is also a criterion we could use to judge the evaluated, but whose goals? Those of management? Suppose meeting needs is not a goal? Both achieving goals and effectiveness are criteria we could use to judge the evaluated, but there are other possible criteria. The broader definition given at the start of this section allows us to include other types of descriptive or developmental evaluations and 'goal-free' evaluation (Scriven 1973), but also distinguishes evaluation from other activities.

## What is the difference between evaluation and 'fundamental research'?

How does the earlier definition distinguish evaluation from other activities? Evaluation is a form of research in the sense that it is a systematic investigation of the evaluated and aims to discover new knowledge. Evaluators use surveys, interviews, measuring instruments and other data gathering methods which other researchers also use. Some evaluations also use experimental design – for example, a controlled trial of a surgical technique – and these evaluations are also called scientific or medical research. The definition above gives room for traditional research within the category of evaluation by defining one purpose of evaluation to be discovering causal mechanisms, where such types of conceptualization are appropriate.

In my view it is not data gathering or study design which is distinctive of evaluation, but gathering data for the purposes of judging value, the element of comparison and the practical focus. That is, the methods are used within an overall 'process of evaluation' which clarifies the criteria which are to be used to judge value (for example, a criterion of effectiveness) and then gathers information about the evaluated against this one criterion or more criteria. Thus, it is how the methods are chosen and combined in a process called 'evaluation' that has a practical purpose which distinguishes evaluation from other types of pure research, investigative journalism and other activities. This process is termed here 'evaluation for action' and described in the following pages.

This book emphasizes the practical purpose of evaluation and makes a distinction between pure or fundamental research (the aim of which is only scientific knowledge) and evaluation (the aim of which is to help people to make better informed practical decisions). Some scientific research does not involve comparison, or does not enable people to judge the value of something or to make better informed decisions. There is certainly an overlap between evaluation and research but while most evaluation could probably be termed research of some type, only some types of research are evaluation. Because of the practical emphasis of the book, it makes a greater distinction between evaluation and some types of research than that made by other books and writings, and some do not make this distinction at all.

What is the difference between evaluation and clinical audit or quality assurance? In my view none, and later chapters consider clinical and other types of audit as one type of evaluation. Quality assurance is a catch-all term, and most quality assurance is also a type of evaluation. There are also different uses of these terms in different countries (Øvretveit 1997a). Some writers distinguish audit from research. For example, Black (1992) points out that audit uses 'evaluative research' as a basis for defining what is good quality care, and also that the data gathered in some audits are useful for some research, giving as an example the UK Intensive Care Society's database from 28 intensive care units.

I think it is useful to distinguish between audit and some types of research because there has been a tendency to redefine some research as audit in order to secure finance, and because some practitioners doing audit try to use research and outcome methods which are too sophisticated and expensive and not necessary for answering the practical questions with which they are concerned. As Black (1992) puts it, 'there is a danger of audit masquerading as research but without the necessary scientific rigour, or research pretending to be audit, but without any attempts to improve the quality of care being studied.'

My own view is that some types of audit are research and are also evaluations, but most audit and quality assurance does not and should not meet the same rigorous scientific criteria which are used in basic or pure research. The purpose is different. Audit is one type of evaluation which asks 'Are we (or they) doing things right?' Experimental evaluation (the activity which Black and some others refers to as 'evaluative research') asks, 'What is the right thing to do?' when there is no established knowledge to guide us.

---

**Definitions: different activities for different purposes**

*Basic or pure research*: using scientific methods which are appropriate for discovering valid and generalizable knowledge of a phenomenon for the purpose of contributing to scientific knowledge about the subject.

*Audit*: an investigation into whether an activity meets explicit standards, as defined by an auditing document, for the purpose of checking and improving the activity audited. The auditing process can be carried by external auditors, or internally for self-review, and the knowledge produced is specific to the service and cannot be generalized. The standards can be external and already made, or can be developed by the service providers for self-audit – in clinical audit, ideally by using scientific research.

*Monitoring*: continuous supervision of an activity for the purpose of checking whether plans and procedures are being followed (audit is a sub-type of the wider activity of monitoring).

*Review*: a single or regular assessment of an activity, which may or may not compare the activity to an explicit plan, criteria or standards. (Most audits or monitoring are also types of review. Many 'managerial evaluations' are reviews or monitoring.)

*Evaluation*: a comparative judgement of the value of an intervention in relation to criteria, for the purpose of making better informed decisions about how to act.

*Action research*: a systematic investigation which aims to contribute to knowledge as well as solve a practical problem. (Some action research is a type of evaluation. Much 'developmental evaluation' is action research.)

---

## Summary: What evaluation can and cannot do

♦ Evaluation cannot itself carry out changes, but it can give a more informed basis for others to carry out changes.
♦ An evaluation study cannot attribute value to the evaluated, but it can give information which helps others to attribute value. In selecting which information to collect the evaluator decides which information is relevant to attributing value, and excludes other possible information.

While the evaluation does not itself attribute value, the way in which it is done shapes how others attribute value.

♦ Evaluation makes clear certain criteria which others can use to judge the value of the evaluated.

♦ An evaluation study cannot include all the criteria which people will use to judge the value of the evaluated, or all the things which people need to consider in deciding how to act.

♦ An evaluation does not have to be an expensive three-year randomized controlled trial – it can simply be a description of something such as a new policy and how it is implemented.

♦ Not all health evaluations look at effectiveness – there are other criteria of valuation – but most do look for the effects of the evaluated.

## Evaluation for action

*As a result of an evaluation, someone should be better able to act or make a decision – an evaluation user should be more informed.*

As well as giving a general overview of evaluation, this book describes an approach which emphasizes the practical aims of evaluation, summarized in the phrase 'evaluation for action'[1] (elsewhere as 'action evaluation'; Øvretveit 1987a). Evaluation for action is an objective and systematic approach for making a comparative judgement of the value of an item against criteria, in order to decide how to act. The 'item' may be a defined treatment, a service or a policy (termed the 'evaluated' or the 'intervention'). Evaluation for action:

♦ recognizes the different perspectives of different groups ('stakeholders') who have an interest in the results of the evaluation and in the item being evaluated (it is politically aware);

♦ uses criteria agreed by one or more stakeholder groups (the primary users of the evaluation) to decide which data to gather and how to judge the value of the item (criterion-based);

♦ considers, at each step of the evaluation, the practical actions which the findings imply and which others might take if they were to act on the findings (an action orientation is an integral part of the approach);

♦ uses the most relevant theory and methods from different disciplines for the purposes of the evaluation, to help to decide the evaluation criteria, to gather and analyse data, and to clarify the implications for judging value and for carrying out action (multidisciplinary);

♦ covers the phases of defining the item to be evaluated, clarifying evaluation criteria, gathering and analysing data, and judging value and planning and carrying out action.

Does this mean that the purpose of evaluation is change? Certainly change is the aim of evaluation – the aim is to enable practitioners,

1 I am indebted to Steve Harrison for suggesting that evaluation for action was a better term than action evaluation, which could be confused with action research.

managers and others to do things differently and better as a result of the evaluation. The aim of evaluation, like the aim of a health intervention, is to make a difference, even if the difference is only that people continue to do what they did before, but with more confidence that they are doing the right thing or doing things right. If a change is made at all – and we will see in the last chapter that it takes more than a conclusive evaluation to produce a change – then usually people make a change after the evaluation is carried out. But it is also true that some approaches to evaluation – many 'developmental evaluations' – use methods such as action research methods to change the people or organization being evaluated while doing the evaluation.

How can you evaluate something while you are changing it at the same time? Here we touch on one of the differences between different evaluation perspectives: usually evaluations using an experimental perspective do everything which they can to ensure that the intervention does not change during the evaluation. Developmental evaluations often feed back findings to people in a service during the evaluation so that they can make immediate changes.

The main point here is that the purpose of evaluation is practical action. 'Evaluation for action' is thus a broad umbrella term for a variety of different approaches which can be used for the purpose of practical improvement. It extends beyond the phases of an evaluation study which are usually described in research-oriented evaluation texts because evaluation for action pays attention to how to assist the practical actions which could follow from the data gathering.

## What can you evaluate?

One reason for using the broad definition of evaluation discussed above is that this book is for health personnel and researchers. Most people working in the health field now need to be able to use or make evaluations of four categories of things or phenomena: treatments, services, policies and changes to health organizations. In this section we note differences in the nature of these items which, as we will see in later chapters, have implications for how we evaluate them and collect data about them. Evaluation theory and techniques for one type of intervention can draw on and contribute to evaluation theory and techniques for evaluations of interventions in other categories. This is another reason why this book considers all four categories – because there is scope for more cross-fertilization between sub-fields of evaluation in health.

Health treatments, programmes or services and policies are all 'interventions' which are used to intervene in people's lives in order to improve their health. They are all different in nature, and also have different 'targets'. There are three different 'levels' of evaluation in the sense that the target of a treatment (a part or whole of a person) is a different level from the target of a service or programme (a population), which in turn is a different level of target from that of a health policy (a large population). The breadth and nature of each of these targets are different. The targets can all be viewed as 'systems', but the 'level' of a biochemical system is different from the level of a single human being as a system, which in turn is different from a population or a service as a system.

A fourth category of phenomena which are evaluated in health is changes to how health services and health personnel work. These changes include training programmes, a new system for devolving responsibility or a personnel appraisal system. These changes are also interventions but they do not have patient or population health as their primary aim – the aim may be to save money.

Table 1.1 helps to clarify which type of design and method is best for an evaluation, and it also introduces the way in which certain terms are to be used in this book. Note that some interventions directly improve health (D) and some may aim to improve health, but act indirectly (I) – better health is the ultimate aim. They will both be termed 'health interventions' (strictly speaking, 'intended' ones). There are also interventions which do not aim to improve health directly or even indirectly, but to increase efficiency or save money (O for operational interventions).

## Treatments

The category of 'treatments' includes different therapies, such as drugs, surgical, physical, psychological and social therapies. Therapies differ in their nature: the active agent in most drug therapies is a chemical agent; in

*Table 1.1*  Different direct and indirect health interventions

| Focus or target of the intervention | Examples of interventions |
| --- | --- |
| An individual: one patient or person | *Treatment:* hernia surgery (D)<br>*Care:* voluntary worker bringing shopping for an older person just out hospital (D)<br>*Assessment or test:* an X-ray or care management needs-assessment (I)<br>*Health promotion:* advice about reducing risk factors for heart disease |
| A population: a group of patients | *Service:* a surgical service (D); a care management service (D)<br>*Programme:* a health promotion programme to encourage 'healthy living' (D)<br>*Project:* increasing community participation in the management of a health service (I) |
| A large population | *Policy:* people over 65 will be offered influenza vaccination (D); smokers will not be given certain types of heart surgery. |
| A system of care (the way a system is organized, and elements within it, such as health practitioners) | *Reorganization:* all units will have one general manager, who will report to the director; a fax communication system will be installed between the hospital discharge unit and all primary care centres (I)<br>*Payment system:* performance-related pay (O)<br>*Policy:* there will be no overtime working for the next six months (O)<br>*Training:* training in how to treat and prevent bed sores (I) |

physical therapy it is physical manipulation, usually by a physical thera-
pist. Strictly speaking we should say 'the active agent is thought to be',
because many therapy evaluations aim to find out exactly what is the active
agent, as well as to test the hypothesized effectiveness of what is defined as
the treatment. In the past most evaluations have been carried out on medical treatments which aim to cure an underlying pathology, and by using a
controlled trial design. The purpose of some treatment evaluations is to
investigate the nature of the treatment: for example, to describe a new type
of treatment such as a plant treatment used by people in Lapland for treating frostbite.

However, all health treatments have the same type of target – a person,
or part of a person. The definition of a treatment does not usually include
the organizational context within which the treatment is used. For
example, we can evaluate a new drug for hypertension or a new dressing for
leg ulcers, regardless of the setting. To some extent the boundary between
what is a treatment and what is a service is arbitrary. Very few 'treatments'
are actually single interventions like a drug treatment; indeed, many drug
treatments are not single interventions because the efficacy and effectiveness of many drugs depend on them being combined with other interventions, even if it is only information to the patient about when to take the
drug. Cancer treatments are one example of treatments which are usually
multiple, and which, at a certain point, merge into what some would call a
service. There are different views about whether some disease-prevention
interventions or health education should be considered a treatment, a service, a 'programme' or a policy. As we will see in later chapters, the way in
which we conceptualize and define the intervention has implications for
how we evaluate it.

## Services and programmes

When we evaluate a service or programme the item we are evaluating is
larger in scope and more complex than a treatment. The effects and costs
of some treatments may depend on how and where they are applied, in
which case we may define the thing to be evaluated as the treatment plus
the organizational context. A service is one or more treatments as well as
the way the treatment is given to the patient – it includes the organization
and environment of care.

Is a primary health care centre a programme, a service or both? The word
'service' is sometimes used to mean the same thing as 'programme', but a
service usually means an organization which provides a range of programmes. In the USA programme is more common a term than service, and
'programme evaluation' has grown into a large industry, mostly paid by
government to make independent evaluations of public welfare programmes. Generally speaking, a service is an ongoing organization or
institution, whereas a programme is time-limited or renewable with specific
objectives (like a project). But further to confuse things, a service can sometimes also be a policy: for example, 'case or care management' can be a service for coordinating care or it can be a policy of an organization which
marks out a general intention of that organization.

'Health care project' is sometimes used to mean a time-limited inter-national health care programme: for example, a three-year overseas aid funded child health project in a developing country. This book uses the terms 'service' and 'programme' interchangeably, with one exception: when referring to an institution which provides education it uses the term 'educational service', but the term 'educational programme' is used to describe a specific type of education and training for health personnel or patients. Evaluations of services may involve an assessment of outcomes, of processes, of inputs or of the needs of patients, populations or health personnel, and often of more than one of these dimensions of a service or of the targets of a service (shown in Figure 2.1).

## Policies, reforms and interventions to organization

Policies are directives or rules which aim to change or regulate how people behave. In this booklet we distinguish two types. The first type is health policies which have people's health as their primary and direct target: for example, health policies to increase immunization, reduce smoking or pre-vent infections.

The second type is organizational policies, such as non-discrimination, a policy to reduce waiting times, decentralization or a policy to reduce personnel overtime. These are interventions whose immediate purpose is to change how a health organization operates. Many organizational poli-cies have improving health as their ultimate purpose, and it is sometimes difficult to distinguish a 'health policy' from an 'organizational policy'. In such cases the evaluation distinguishes between the immediate effects (change to organizational functioning) and longer-term effects on people's health. We use different methods to evaluate different types of organizational policies: the policies may be local or specific to one organization, or may be regional or national and applied to many organiz-ations. Local managers often have to interpret national policies and they interpret them differently in different settings. The fact that the policy is being evaluated will influence how managers and practitioners imple-ment the policy.

Sometimes large-scale policies are called reforms, typically when a government reforms how services are administered, such as introducing patient charges or new ways for patients to change their doctor. A reform is 'a significant set of changes to the method of financing, organisation, or running of health services, or to patients' rights' (Øvretveit 1996c). Examples are the transfer of responsibility for care for the elderly from counties to communes in Sweden, the decentralization programmes in a number of African countries or the British NHS 'market reforms' of 1991. Evaluation has an important part to play in planning reforms: for example, by local 'pilot' testing, by comparative analysis of similar reforms else-where, by theoretical policy analysis or by simulation modelling. However, to date most health reforms have been driven by ideology rather than by evidence of effectiveness or other findings from evaluations.

There are also 'interventions to organization'. Examples are a training programme for health personnel, a quality assurance system or a new weekly meeting to decide collectively how to allocate patients who are referred to a service. Each of these interventions could be evaluated for the immediate effect on health personnel or for the effect on patients. These interventions to organization are sometimes called 'new policies' or 'health reforms': for example, the law requiring a quality assurance system in Norwegian hospitals is one type of intervention to organization, which could also be termed a policy or a reform.

## Health promotion

*We need more evaluations of health promotion: how do we best evaluate health promotion?*

This is an assertion and a question which is increasingly being made, but what type of intervention are we referring to? Is health promotion a treatment, a service, a policy or an intervention to organization? An intervention to promote health can be any of these. Treatments to help someone stop smoking, such as counselling, hypnosis or a nicotine patch, are all health promoting interventions. A service which gives education in schools about the dangers of smoking is another type of health promotion, as is a policy to ban smoking in public buildings, as is a training programme to train general practitioners about the best way to help their patients stop smoking. We will see later how important it is to define precisely the intervention which we are evaluating.

## Outline of the chapters

What are evaluations for? And what is the difference between experimental, economic, developmental and managerial evaluations? These are the two main questions addressed by Chapter 2. We look at the reasons for making or using an evaluation and why evaluation is becoming an increasingly important activity in health services. The chapter introduces the four main perspectives in evaluation, and discusses what we mean by perspective and how the perspective taken by the evaluator influences what the evaluation looks at, and how. It also gives a short history of evaluation and considers what we mean by 'evaluation theory' 'evidence' and explanation.

How would you evaluate a radical new treatment for sleeplessness? This question was put to me by a friend recently who was convinced that she had discovered such a treatment. It worked on her children too. Chapter 3 puts this question to readers, and takes them through six evaluation designs which they could use. The example introduces the newcomer to evaluation to some of the principles of evaluation and to some of the main concepts and terms, which are also listed in the glossary in Appendix 1.

How quickly can you make sense of an evaluation report? Test yourself and develop your skills in critical analysis by reading the summaries of evaluation studies in Chapter 4, and looking at the diagrams there which sum up the key features of the evaluations. You will learn how to draw a diagram of an evaluation, which is a powerful and quick way of getting to the heart of an evaluation report. It is also very helpful for clarifying different types of design you might use in an evaluation which you are planning.

Chapters 5, 6, 7 and 8 describe different approaches to evaluation: the experimental, the economic, the developmental and the managerial. Then Susan makes an appearance in Chapter 9: she manages a service and we follow her experience as she contracts and manages an evaluation. The point of this chapter is to describe some of the common issues and considerations in the eight phases of planning, designing and carrying out an evaluation. By taking a manager's perspective, who is also the financial sponsor, we illustrate for researchers how their proposal and work could be assessed and used.

What should you look out for when you are carrying out an evaluation, and, if you are a manager, how can you best sabotage an evaluation which might make you or your service look bad? Chapter 10 discusses some of the trade secrets, and aims to help the reader to become more 'street wise' by understanding more of the politics of evaluation. It discusses roles, responsibilities and practical issues in carrying out an evaluation, such as confidentiality, access, reporting and communication.

Chapter 11 is more sober and scientific and considers a key part of any evaluation: data gathering and analysis. It summarizes different methods, such as observation, interviewing, questionnaires, measurement and existing data sources. Chapter 12 looks in more detail at data gathering theory and concepts – it considers what we mean by 'valid evidence' for an evaluation and the different types of data which an evaluator may need to gather. It also considers how to ensure the methods are valid, reliable and sensitive, as well as questions of sampling. It gives references to further literature and guidance which are of particular use to evaluators who may not be familiar with the many methods which can be used in health evaluations. Chapter 13 turns to a type of evaluation which is increasingly common and has special significance in health services – evaluating quality. It describes concepts and methods for quality evaluations, gives examples and shows the numerous ways in which evaluation methods contribute to quality improvement.

Is it evaluators' fault that their work is often not used? Chapter 14 returns fully to the main theme of evaluation for action and looks at the weak link in the chain from initiation of an evaluation to action: the link between the evaluation findings and implementation. It considers how to increase the use value of evaluations, how to maximize utilization and the shared and distinct responsibilities of evaluators and users.

If you have not done so already, look at the learning exercises in Appendix 4 and try at least one: this book is based on and tries to encourage 'learning by doing'. While you are there, look at the other appendices, which are intended as a resource that you can use at any time.

## Conclusions

♦ Health personnel need an understanding of how to use and carry out evaluations of treatments, services, policies and interventions to organization. Using and carrying out evaluations is part of everyday work in the health sector and we all now need to be 'evaluation literate'.

♦ Evaluation is attributing value to an intervention by gathering reliable and valid information about it in a systematic way, and by making comparisons. The purpose of an evaluation is to help users to make more informed decisions, or to understand causal mechanisms or general principles.

♦ Evaluations gather data for the purpose of valuing an intervention. The data to be gathered depend on the purpose of the evaluation (e.g. to describe, to explain, to judge any effects), the criteria of valuation (e.g. effectiveness, equity, cost, autonomy), the nature of the intervention (e.g. treatment, service, policy or intervention to an organization) and the perspective taken by the evaluator (e.g. experimental, economic, developmental, managerial).

♦ 'Evaluation for action' describes a process for defining valuation criteria and for collecting information about the evaluated for the purpose of helping users to make more informed decisions. It aims to include in the evaluation the criteria of all the interest groups which are important for implementing changes. This process includes, but extends beyond, what is often reported in a scientific evaluation study.

♦ Evaluation is different from consultancy, management review and investigative journalism in having a greater emphasis on scientific rigour, in using methods which are used in medical and social scientific research, in aiming to produce findings which can be generalized and in contributing to and drawing on published theory and research. In these respects evaluation is like scientific research.

♦ Evaluation is different from pure research, although some types of research, audit, monitoring and quality assurance are also types of evaluation.

♦ Evaluation studies differ according to the following.

  ♦ The *subject* of the evaluation: a treatment, service, policy or organizational intervention.
  ♦ The *target* of the intervention: a part or whole of a person, a population, service personnel or organization.
  ♦ The *purpose*: to decide whether it works, how and why it works, whether it is worth the money, how to make it better, how well it performs (Chapters 2 and 3).
  ♦ The *user* of the evaluation: managers, clinicians, patients, policy makers, the public as payer, other scientists/researchers (Chapter 2).
  ♦ The *evaluation perspective*: experimental, economic, developmental or managerial (Chapters 2, 5, 6, 7 and 8).
  ♦ The *design*: descriptive (type 1), audit (type 2), before–after (type 3), comparative-experimentalist (type 4), randomized controlled trial (type 5) and intervention to organization (type 6) (Chapters 3 and 4).
  ♦ The *methods* for gathering and analysing the data within the broad categories of quantitative or qualitative methods (Chapters 11 and 12).

# 2 ▶ Evaluation purpose, theory and perspectives

*The purpose of evaluation is to make someone's life better. As a result of an evaluation, someone should be better able to act or make a decision which is important to him or her.*

*The perspective which an evaluator uses and the type of evaluation made should be suited to the questions of the evaluation user.*

## Introduction

One reason why evaluation can be confusing is that there are so many types of evaluation. Case–control, formative, summative, process, impact, outcome, cost–utility, audit evaluations – Patton (1980) estimated over a hundred approaches. Few books give a good overview for health personnel: many books on evaluation favour one perspective, do not say much about the others, and often describe one type of evaluation using terms which are different from those used in another book. Are all these types really different? What is the difference and when should one use one approach rather than another? These are the questions which this chapter sets out to answer by giving a simple classification of perspectives, and by describing the most common types of evaluation.

Why do we need evaluation? If there is not a good answer to this question then we cannot justify spending time and money on an evaluation which could be spent on services. This chapter starts by looking at how different groups in society could be helped by an evaluation, and at the reasons for and purposes of evaluation. Then, continuing our introductory overview, we consider evaluation theory and give a short history of evaluation in the health sector. We see from this that the scientific experimental perspective has dominated health evaluation, but that a number of other approaches are increasingly used to evaluate services and policies.

To give a framework for understanding types of evaluation the chapter introduces four perspectives – the experimental, the economic, the developmental and the managerial – each of which is described in detail in later chapters. Most health evaluations are carried out within one of these perspectives. The concept of a perspective not only helps to make sense of the variety of types of evaluation, but also highlights assumptions which are not always made clear in reports or recognized when planning an evaluation. Some of these assumptions are discussed in this chapter when we look at the critique made by some evaluators of the experimental and natural science models, and when we look at more recent approaches to evaluation in the health sector. We finish this second introductory chapter by noting a few of the more common terms used to describe evaluations, such as process, formative, pluralistic and summative evaluation.

# Why evaluate?

Why do we need to evaluate health treatments, services and policies?

## To decide resource allocation

Some health products, such as cough medicine, are bought and sold on an open market. The theory of markets is that, if there is not enough cough medicine produced for the demand, then prices will rise until demand drops or new manufactures enter the market and compete, bringing down the price. Although no markets operate like the perfect market ideal, there is a price mechanism which relates supply to demand. We know the value people give to a cough medicine from the price they are prepared to pay for it, and price acts as a mechanism which influences how much of the product is made in society.

Public health services are different. People do not pay directly for public health services, but pay through a 'third party' – a third party insurer or government decides how much of which types of services will be provided. This is because we want the types and amount of health services to be allocated according to criteria other than how much people are able to pay. We often do not know exactly how much different services cost, and the way we cost health services is different from the way we cost services in open markets. Management information systems now give us a better idea of cost and allow us to compare the resources used by certain treatments and services, but we often need special evaluation studies to find out the details of these costs, and to validate the systems.

Thus, because there is no price valuation, and because we want other criteria apart from price to decide the value of a treatment or service, we need evaluations to help to make more informed decisions about what to spend money on and how much to spend. Evaluation is increasingly being viewed as a way to help us deal more rationally and fairly with competition for limited finance between different services and between different patient interest groups, and to help to challenge or legitimate existing allocations.

## Patients' ignorance

More patients want to know all the benefits, drawbacks and side effects of treatments and want independent evaluations which they can access and understand. Patient associations are increasingly willing to finance evaluations, especially of alternative treatments. Information for patients to make better informed decisions about whether to undergo a treatment or use a service is one reason for evaluation: evidence-based patient choice.

This is certainly a good reason for evaluation, but not a justification for poor evaluation or for a report which could be misleading. Consumerism and patients' rights have created a new demand for evaluation, and for 'user-friendly' information. At its best this demand for instant and digestible information has increased the clarity of reports and information systems – examples are US schemes for giving information to patients about surgeon's outcome performance. At its worst this trend has reduced some reporting to a dangerous over-simplification of the complexities of treatment and service provision. Patients need more of the right type of information for patient choice to be real, but no information is better than partial or misleading information.

Another reason for evaluation is to counter patient or sectional interest group pressures. Considerations other than patient views should enter into decisions about treatments and services. Patient views and valuations are not and should not be the only criteria for judgement. Patients can only partially evaluate a treatment: for example, one which gives symptom relief but which does not cure the underlying pathology. Patients can only partially evaluate a health service: they cannot fully judge the quality of a service or the value for money. Without evaluation we may be too influenced by patient demands or the demands of a small group of the population who have not considered a range of features of a service or treatment, or the alternative uses of the resources.

## To improve professionals' knowledge and decisions

We know very little about what works or is cost-effective. One estimate was that 21 per cent of 126 health treatments had been evaluated (Dubinsky and Ferguson 1990), and a number of these have been found to be ineffective or of dubious effectiveness or value. This is not to suggest that more evaluation is the solution – getting practitioners to act on evaluations is the more difficult task and takes longer than carrying out a number of well designed evaluations. Rather it is to suggest that more evaluations of high-volume or high-cost procedures would save money and reduce suffering as a result of unnecessary treatment, that evaluations need to take more account of the everyday context of care and that we need better ways to enable practitioners to act on conclusive evaluations. Most important of all is a more receptive attitude on the part of practitioners and managers to evaluation, both to using evaluations and to spending more time and effort evaluating their own practice and organization of care.

## To improve managers' knowledge and decisions

Although few health treatments have been evaluated, there are even fewer evaluations of types of service organization or management technologies. It is likely that more money is wasted on changes to service organization and on new management technologies, such as some quality programmes which are ineffective, than is wasted on ineffective treatments (Øvretveit 1996b; 1997c). An evaluative attitude on the part of managers is as important as increasing the actual number of evaluations of services and management techniques. Management performance can be increased by managers learning evaluation skills and methods to use in their everyday work, and critically assessing and making a greater use of evaluations carried out by others.

Evaluation is an important tool to help managers and others to use resources in a more rational way. Demand is increasing and resources are decreasing. We need to protect the services and treatments which work and are cost-effective, and to be less influenced by those with interests in retaining services and treatments of dubious or no value. Health financiers and purchasers are using evaluations to decide and justify how they allocate resources, and the evidence-based medicine movement is having a growing impact.

### Because we have to

With competing claims on limited finance, managers and practitioners have to justify starting, expanding or stopping any treatment or service. Other competing treatments or services will be justified by reference to evaluations. Public accountability increasingly requires us to justify not only changes, but also continuing to use resources in the way in which we do: 'zero-based accountability'. The climate of reduced finance and of increasing public scrutiny means that managers and practitioners need to know if there is evidence to support the things which they do now.

Managers are required to use and carry out evaluations not only to justify how they use resources. Everything they finance and oversee has consequences, and some actions may be harmful to health. The public and the courts are less willing to accept ignorance as an excuse for the consequences of health treatments or policies. 'We did not know at the time' is less of an acceptable excuse in the information age: 'Why not?' There is an expectation that responsible public agents, including practitioners, should give more active consideration to the potentially harmful consequences of what they do.

There are now more government directives to carry out evaluations. An early example was the US Congress in 1962 requiring evaluations of certain

---

The need for managers, practitioners and others to make and use evaluations has increased since the 1980s and continues to do so. All the above reasons mean that those working in the health sector need a greater understanding of evaluation, in order to:

♦ be able quickly to understand and use an evaluation report, for example about a treatment or service they are proposing or opposing,
♦ apply the general principles of evaluation in their own work and to do more systematic service reviews,
♦ be able to initiate and manage an in-house or external evaluation of a treatment, service, or proposed change.

federally funded programmes, which was followed by many similar requirements for state and federal programmes. Since the 1980s there has been in
Europe a rapid increase in the number of local, central and European
government programmes which are required to be independently evaluated or inspected. Proposals for new regulations are also evaluated in terms
of the predicted 'cost of compliance'. Managers increasingly have to
cooperate with or initiate evaluations to meet requirements for funding or
to satisfy standing orders, and contract evaluation is of growing importance
and has become a sub-discipline in its own right.

## Better informed political decisions

Politicians often do not examine in detail the cost and consequences of proposed new policies, or of current policies. A good example was the lack of
prospective evaluation or of even small scale testing of internal market
reforms in Sweden, Finland and the UK, especially of general practitioner
fundholding in the UK. This is not to imply that all new policies should be
evaluated or that the results of an evaluation should be the only basis on
which politicians decide whether to start, expand or discontinue health
policies: just that politicians could sometimes save public money or put it to
better use if they made more use of evaluation and of the evaluative attitude.

## The purpose of an evaluation

Evaluations are thus useful to and needed by different groups in society, and
serve different purposes. A theme of this book is that the purposes of the primary user of the evaluation should decide the design and perspective of the
evaluation. Managers questions and decisions to be informed are often
different from those of clinicians, and they will usually need a different
evaluation design and approach from one which would be helpful to clinicians. Sometimes there is overlap between the needs of different users and it
is possible for an evaluation to serve a number of purposes and answer more
than one question, but this is difficult to achieve and rarely successful.

This emphasis on the purpose of the evaluation, who it is for and their
questions is not to suggest that the evaluator becomes the servant of the
user. We will see in later chapters that the evaluator plays a role in helping
to define the question, has considerable discretion in how to conduct the
evaluation and draws users' attention to issues and questions which they
have not considered but should do – giving a service does not mean being
servile. The point is that clarity about the following 'purpose questions' is
essential for a useful and valid evaluation.

- *Who* is the evaluation for?
- *What* are the questions it aims to answer?
- *Which decisions* and actions should be better informed as a result?
- *How much* resources and time are available, is it possible to achieve the
  purpose with these or should the purpose be more limited, or should
  time and resources be increased?

> **Defining the purpose of the evaluation**
>
> It should be possible to complete these sentences:
>
> The evaluation is for . . . [primary user] to answer the question(s) . . . in order that the user can make better decisions about . . .
>
> The evaluation does not aim to . . .

## Common questions for evaluations

♦ Does it work? (Is it effective, in an ideal situation (efficacy) or in most ordinary contexts (effectiveness)?)
♦ Why and how does it work? (Explanation?)
♦ What are all the effects, including unintended and long-term consequences? (Outcomes?)
♦ How long-lasting are the effects? (Outcomes sustained?)
♦ What are the costs? (Resources used?)
♦ Is it cost-effective (compared to other ways)? (Outcomes for the resources?)
♦ What do patients and carers think about it? (Acceptability, satisfaction?)
♦ Can people from all sections of society benefit from it? (Equity?)
♦ How can we improve it? (Development.)
♦ Is it meeting established standards and within regulations? (Compliance and safety.)
♦ Should we stop it, or should we do more of it? (Cut or extend?)

## Evaluation theory and history

As part of this overview of evaluation in health, we now note some of the history and theory of evaluation in the different fields of treatment, service and policy evaluation. Evaluation has become so common in the health field that it is easy to forget that, as a disciplined and systematic activity, evaluation is relatively new. It is true that we can find examples of evaluation in ancient Chinese and Greek administration, in the Church and in crafts and trades through the ages. Evaluation, in the sense of judging value and thinking about action, before or after the action and for the purposes of improvement, is as old as human consciousness. However, evaluation as we know it today only began to develop with the growth of science in the sixteenth and seventeenth centuries. The scientific revolution established a distinction between fact and value: science was to be concerned with gathering and using facts, not with judgements of value. In one sense the separation of the act of valuing from the act of gathering information laid the basis for evaluation becoming a systematic activity.

However, evaluation only became a recognized specialist activity in the second part of the twentieth century, and big business in the 1960s.

Evaluation grew out of established scientific disciplines and was stimulated by the practical concerns of society. More recently some evaluators have challenged the separation between fact gathering, which is traditionally the role of the evaluator, and valuation, which is the role of the users. They have shown the interplay between both, and also that the definition of 'problems of society' adopted by evaluators is often that of powerful groups in society seeking to maintain control.

Health evaluation has been influenced by traditional disciplines as well as by evaluation theory from programme and educational evaluation. Early health evaluation can be characterized by the predominance of treatment evaluation, which overlaps with and grew out of medical clinical and epidemiological research. The beginnings of policy evaluation can be seen in early sociology and government commissioned working groups with the task of proposing public policies for health services and for public health. From the 1960s onwards there was a growth of retrospective and prospective systematic health policy evaluation by academic units and private consultants. Together with a greater use of commercial management techniques, the 1980s saw an increase in evaluations of health services. Many evaluations were intended to inform resource allocations and decisions about new services, as well as to carry out traditional inspection more thoroughly. In the 1990s there was a greater emphasis on the use of completed evaluations in making clinical and managerial decisions in health services, and on health practitioners using more systematic methods for self-evaluation: for example, in quality assurance.

Evaluation theories and the history of evaluation have been different in the three fields of treatment, service and policy evaluation, although there has been some cross-fertilization between these fields. The following notes some of this history, after first considering what we mean by 'evaluation theory'.

## Evaluation theory

A theory is knowledge about a subject which predicts, explains or allows us to understand significant features of the subject. An evaluation theory is more than a theory about how to carry out a successful evaluation – this is a methodology of evaluation. Evaluation theory is also more than an explicit statement by the evaluator of his or her assumptions concerning the nature of the thing which will be evaluated – termed 'programme theory' by US writers in the case of service evaluations. An evaluation theory includes a theory about the item which is to be evaluated, and a theory about how to get valid knowledge of that item for the purposes of the evaluation.

Shadish *et al.* (1991) view 'programme theory' as one of the five areas which evaluation theory should cover. They propose that an evaluation theory should cover:

1 The nature of the social programme to be evaluated, including theories about its structure, functioning, how change can be made and the relation of the programme to the wider context (i.e. programme theory).

2 Which type of knowledge about the evaluated is considered valid and credible.
3 The part values play in evaluation and in making a valuation of the evaluated.
4 Ideas about the practice of evaluation and the role of the evaluator.
5 How social scientific knowledge from the evaluation can be used to improve the programme.

Few theories of evaluation cover all of these areas, and most are concerned with the fourth area of practice and methodology, or the second in the case of treatment evaluation. Cronbach *et al.* (1980) emphasize the importance of using theory about political processes, because these politics affects both the service or policy being evaluated and the evaluation process itself: 'A theory of evaluation must be as much a theory of political interaction as it is a theory of how to determine facts' (Cronbach *et al.* 1980). In common with these writers, Chen (1990) argues for 'theory-driven evaluations', which examine the assumptions and theories underlying social programmes and which develop theories about these programmes. He defines programme theory as 'a specification of what must be done to achieve the desired goals, what other important impacts may also be anticipated, and how these goals and impacts will be generated.'

Because treatments, services, policies and organizational changes are such different subjects, there are different evaluation theories about each. However, evaluation theory, in the sense of explicit statements and discussions about each of the five areas proposed by Shadish *et al.* (1991), is not well developed, with the notable exception of theories about experimental evaluations of treatments. We will see later that there is debate about natural and social science approaches within evaluation and about the role of qualitative and quantitative methods, and these debates have contributed much to developing evaluation theory. We will also see that a new field of evaluation-related theory is developing as a result of discussion about the overlap and links between clinical audit and research, and about the 'science of improvement' (Berwick 1996) and 'clinical epidemiology' (Sackett *et al.* 1991).

Later in this chapter we consider one of the theoretical debates in evaluation about how health services should be evaluated: the 'experimental–phenomenological' debate. The general point for the moment is that evaluation theories are important in that they frame what the evaluator sees, and guide evaluators' choice of which design and methods to use and how to analyse and report their findings.

## Treatment evaluation

The history of evaluation in the health sector starts with and has been dominated by treatment evaluation approaches. Medical knowledge advanced greatly as a result of both practitioners and researchers applying the scientific method and attitude in everyday settings. There is a continuum ranging from pure laboratory science to the trial-and-error experimentation and observation of doctors and others in their everyday practice. An early example was the discovery by James Lancaster in 1601 that lemon juice prevented scurvy in seamen and his subsequent 'experiment'.

Treatment evaluation had its origins in agriculture research and then clinical experimentation, and developed rapidly when the controlled trial became formalized and refined in the 1940s and 1950s. One of the earliest and most well known randomized controlled trials was of a treatment for tuberculosis – streptomycin – in 1948 (Pocock 1983; Cochrane and Blythe 1989). In addition, advances in epidemiological method and statistical recording and analysis led to important discoveries: many of these studies can be regarded as retrospective evaluations. More recent developments have been new evaluation designs for alternative therapies, simulation evaluations and meta-evaluations. Sophistication in carrying out treatment evaluations has reached a high level, as has the knowledge of different evaluation methods for different treatments. However, as we will see when considering evidence-based medicine, there is increasing debate about the limits of experimental evaluation and the appropriateness of this approach for evaluating some treatments or multi-treatment services (Chapters 5 and 14).

## Service and policy evaluation

It is a sad truth that randomized experimental design is possible only for a portion of the settings in which social scientists make measurements and seek interpretable comparisons. The number of opportunities for its use may not be staggering, but where possible experimental design should by all means be exploited.

(Webb *et al.* 1966: 6)

This view is one which is no longer held by many service and policy evaluators, but it held sway for many years. Evaluation of social programmes, services and policies began in the nineteenth century, but only really developed with an increase in the number of studies and greater methodological sophistication in the 1960s and 1970s in the USA. The reasons were money and the law. At this time the US government began to require evaluation of a variety of federal programmes. This period saw health service evaluators adapting methods which colleagues used for evaluating treatments, drawing on methodological understanding from the field of programme evaluation, and making greater use of social scientific and action research methods. The experimental paradigm was adapted for service and policy evaluations, leading to a variety of quasi-experimental designs (Chapter 5).

In the 1980s developmental and qualitative evaluation approaches came to occupy equal, if not greater, prominence as preferred methods for service and policy evaluations (Chapters 7 and 8). The number and type of evaluation and monitoring activities in health services have increased considerably since the 1980s, mostly owing to government attempts to control costs, pressures for increased accountability and new information technology. A new development has been practitioners carrying out systematic evaluations of their own services and making changes as part of quality assurance and improvement programmes (Chapter 13).

Health policy evaluation as a systematic and distinct activity is more recent than both treatment and service evaluation, and even more difficult to separate from related activities such as policy analysis. Many proposed and ongoing health policies are examined in different ways, and in relation to defined criteria such as equity, but these studies are often not called evaluations. In the 1980s there was also an increase in 'international' policy evaluation, such as cross-European studies of policies, the ambitious evaluations of the World Health Organization (WHO) 'health for all' targets and evaluations of health programmes, projects and policies in developing countries.

Evaluations of interventions to health organizations are even more recent. They have followed on from the increase in planned interventions to health organizations and systems and from the increasing range of educational and organizational development techniques for such interventions. Since the early 1990s there have been many evaluations of different types of quality assurance and quality programmes: these and other types of evaluations of interventions to organization are discussed in Chapters 7, 8 and 13.

## Evaluation theory: summary

Health evaluation has thus grown out of different traditional disciplines and backgrounds, notably medical research, epidemiology, statistics and more recently social science methods and theory. In Europe, health evaluation has not been greatly influenced by general evaluation theories and methods from the fields of programme and educational evaluation. The dominant perspectives are the experimental and the economic.

As a result of this diversity of subjects, perspectives and disciplinary backgrounds, we find disagreement between evaluators about evaluation theory and practice. Even within the field of programme evaluation, Shadish *et al.* (1991) note areas of disagreement about:

♦ the role of the evaluator;
♦ which values should be represented in the evaluation;
♦ the questions which the evaluator should ask;
♦ the best methods, given the limited time and resources;
♦ how the evaluator should try to ensure ultilization;
♦ which factors do or should influence the above choices about role, values, questions, methods and utilization.

However, there are some areas of agreement and attempts to develop a theory of evaluation. Scriven (1991) draws attention to some of the common elements in many types of evaluation and proposes that evaluation is a 'transdiscipline'. We saw above each of the areas covered by the five-element evaluation theory which Shadish *et al.* (1991) aimed to develop. After an extensive review of theories of programme evaluation, Shadish *et al.* (1991) concluded that there are four areas of agreement between theorists:

♦ evaluations are usually made within time and resource constraints, which call for difficult trade-offs;
♦ evaluators are rarely welcomed;
♦ there are limitations to any single evaluation;
♦ evaluators need to be more active in ensuring that their findings are acted on.

## Four evaluation perspectives

The evaluator views the intervention using a particular perspective. This perspective can help the user of the evaluation to see things that they may not otherwise see, and thus to make a better judgement about the value of the intervention. It can also blind users to things which they should see if they rely entirely on an evaluation which does not describe its perspective and limitations.

This book proposes that any evaluation is undertaken from within one of four 'evaluation perspectives', which some would call 'evaluation paradigms'. It does this for two reasons: first, to simplify and make more understandable the range of types of evaluation in the health sector; second, to draw attention to the assumptions which underlie different approaches to evaluation, and which are not often made explicit in an evaluation report or even in a detailed discussion of methods. In the following we consider what we mean by 'perspective', and summarize the four perspectives considered in this book. In the section after this we look at the debate within evaluation about the strengths and weaknesses of what was the dominant perspective – the experimental.

### What is an evaluation perspective?

An evaluation perspective both 'sees' and 'focuses' on certain aspects of an evaluation and on its consequences. For example, an economic perspective focuses on how many resources are used by the evaluated and the benefits produced. I use the word 'perspective' to convey three things. First, looking through a particular 'pair of glasses' allows us to see some things better than we would otherwise do. Second, we do not see some things because our perspective is selective. Third, a perspective carries assumptions about whether what we can see really exists: a perspective involves assumptions about what is valid knowledge (epistemology), about the aspects of the evaluated which are selected and about how to create this knowledge (methodology). These assumptions frame how the evaluator conceptualizes the intervention and shapes the evaluation design and the data gathering and analysis methods.

This chapter introduces four perspectives – the experimental, the economic, the developmental and the managerial – and later chapters discuss them in detail. An evaluation can be made using any one of these perspectives: each perspective can be used to evaluate any of the four categories of treatments, services, policies and organizational interventions. However, one perspective is more often used than another to evaluate one category of interventions. For example, the developmental perspective is used more often to evaluate services or organizational interventions than to evaluate treatments. Which perspective the evaluator uses depends on the purpose of the evaluation, on the nature of the evaluated and on its predicted effects, but also on the evaluator's training and disciplinary background.

The purpose of this and later chapters is not to equip you to be able to do an evaluation using one of these perspectives. Rather, it is to enable you to choose the right perspective for the item you want to evaluate, to know where to go to find out more and to understand the strengths and weaknesses of an evaluation which has been carried out using a particular perspective. The last ability is important for non-scientists, such as most managers, because many evaluation reports appear at first sight to have considered everything, and often do not spell out their assumptions or limitations.

### Experimental, economic, developmental and managerial evaluation perspectives: an introduction

*Experimental* evaluations aim to discover whether an intervention has effects, and the causes of any effects. The evaluation is designed to test hypotheses and follows the model of a scientific experiment. In the example in Chapter 1 of a nurse giving a mother information about breast feeding, the evaluation would review previous research and define a hypothesis: for example, 'information interventions of the type specified have no effect on mothers' baby-feeding practices.'

The intervention would be carefully defined and held stable by ensuring that nurses followed a standard approach. There would be an 'operational definition' of mothers' baby-feeding practices and a measure of these practices – mothers' reports of their behaviour would not be considered very reliable. Attempts would be made to control for influences other than the nurse-and-leaflet intervention which might affect the mother's behaviour. The ideal is a prospective experiment – one planned before it is carried out – because this helps the evaluator to do everything he or she can to control for influences other than the intervention. A common way of doing so is to allocate mothers in a random way to one group which get the intervention and one group which does not. This helps to increase the certainty that any changes in the measure of baby-feeding practices can be attributed to the intervention, rather than to something else.

This is a simple summary of the perspective to show some features and the difference from the other three perspectives. There are a variety of designs used within this perspective (Chapter 5), but the main point is to highlight the idea of an experiment, a defined hypothesis which is tested, maximizing control of the intervention and of other possible influences, and one or a few objective measures.

*Economic* evaluations aim to discover how many resources are consumed by using an intervention, and usually also to quantify the consequences of an intervention, sometimes in money terms. Economic evaluations share many of the assumptions of the experimental paradigm about objective measurement and controls, and are often built on experimental evaluations. For example, a common type of economic evaluation would try to quantify the resources used in the nurse-and-leaflet intervention and express these in money terms. It would try to measure the consequences of the intervention and express these in terms of the resources saved and consumed. The perspective assumes that the resources used could always be put to other uses, and tries to compare the costs and consequences of the intervention to those of other ways of using the resources.

*Developmental* evaluations are based on a different philosophy of science, with different assumptions about the nature of the intervention and about the purpose of evaluation. Developmental evaluations use systematic methods and theories within an evaluation framework to enable service providers to develop and improve their treatments, services, policies or organizational interventions. For example, in one type of developmental evaluation the evaluators might interview ten mothers before and at two weeks after the intervention, to find out what they did and what they thought about breast feeding. The findings would be reported back to the nurses and the evaluator would work with them to decide ways to improve the chances of mothers using breast feeding, and how to reach the mothers whom the nurses do not usually meet. Developmental evaluations have an immediate practical focus and involve the evaluator working with providers in an independent role to enable providers to judge the value of what they are doing and to improve what they do. Developmental evaluations may also be carried out by providers themselves for self-improvement, or in a peer review process.

*Managerial* evaluations are made for managers and supervisory boards to monitor or improve the performance of services or policies, or to check that agreed changes or projects were implemented as intended. Their purpose is to ensure accountability, value for money and performance improvement. For example, one type of managerial evaluation might involve evaluators sending mothers a short questionnaire to find out how many mothers report being given a leaflet, and whether they breast feed or not. It might also try to gather information about which social groups in the area are most likely to have contact with the nurse. Many managerial evaluations in health compare actual activities against procedures and standards which are thought to ensure safety, efficiency, effectiveness and equity. They are usually done by people working for health service organizations, although external evaluators may be used to help to create systems for audit or for performance management evaluations.

This summary is simplified and emphasizes some of the differences between the perspectives, yet there are many things which are common. Each aims to gather information about the intervention and, in these examples, information about the effects. Each gathers this information in a systematic way using data gathering methods which are established within the perspective, and the data help users to judge the value of the intervention. Each faces and has ways of dealing with ethical issues: the ethics of withholding an intervention where there is some knowledge that the intervention is of some benefit; the ethics of quantifying and comparing the value of breast feeding to alternative uses of the resources; the ethics of contacting mothers and asking them about breast feeding; and the ethics of reporting to management evidence about whether health personnel do or do not follow a policy. There are other similarities which we will see later in the more detailed discussion of each perspective, which will also show the variety within each perspective.

Table 2.1 summarizes the differences between these perspectives, and Table 3.1 shows examples of evaluations from each perspective and the designs which they use.

*Table 2.1* Differences between four approaches to evaluation

|  | *Primary users* | *Purpose* | *Focus of study* | *Methods* | *Evaluator role* |
|---|---|---|---|---|---|
| ***Experimental*** | Scientists and, in time, health practitioners | Discover evidence of effect and causes | Outcomes | Hypothesis testing; measurement of outcome; control and quantification of variables; statistical analysis | Independent, external, detached, scientist |
| ***Economic*** | Managers, policy makers | Calculate resources used and benefits | Inputs, activity, outputs and outcome | Quantitative and specialist measures of outcome | Independent, external, detached, scientist |
| ***Developmental*** | Managers and people working in the service | Help providers to improve in the short term | Process | Primarily qualitative | Independent, collaborative or self-evaluation |
| ***Managerial*** | Managers and supervisory boards | Accountability and performance management | Inputs, process and outputs | Quantitative and qualitative | Inspectorial, detached, quasi-independent |

## The perspectives debate in evaluation – evidence and explanations

The following two questions characterize the 'experimental versus phenomenological' debate within health evaluation:

*How can you properly evaluate a service without objectively measuring outcome and controlling for influences on the outcome apart from the service?*

*How can you properly evaluate a treatment without investigating patients' subjective experiences, recognizing that the statistical average obscures important effects on some individual patients, and that the treatment should be varied and tailored to each patient and that treatment and context cannot be separated and controlled?*

One question the reader will need to consider is: 'Are the perspectives actually different scientific paradigms which are incompatible, or is it possible to combine elements of each perspective?' In this section we consider the social science critique of the experimental perspective and the positivist conception of 'facts' and 'evidence'. This shows some of the theoretical debate within health evaluation, debate which has arisen most recently in relation to the ideas put forward within the evidence-based medicine movement about what constitutes evidence of service effectiveness and which is further discussed in Chapter 14.

We noted above that treatment evaluations are usually performed using the experimental and economic perspectives. In the past twenty years the economic perspective has increasingly been used to evaluate services, and,

---

**Dimensions of evaluation**

*Purpose*: the dimension of self-development versus inspection and accountability (this is one of many dimensions of purpose).

*When the evaluation is undertaken in the evolution of an intervention*: for a mature service or completed intervention, or for an intervention in a developing stage, or for a possible change, service, or treatment yet to be implemented.

*Predominant focus*: inputs, processes, outputs (how many?) or outcomes (what changes or effects?).

*Scope*: comprehensive–limited.

*Methods*: qualitative–quantitative.
*Evaluator role*: self-internal–external independent.

*How often*: one special evaluation–frequently and routinely.

---

more recently, policies and health promotion programmes. Attempts were made to use the experimental perspective to evaluate services and policies, and some still believe that this should and can be done. However, many have questioned the feasibility and the appropriateness of the experimental perspective for evaluating services and policies. The 'social science critique' has not only led to the creation and acceptance of different approaches for evaluating services and policies, but has even challenged the pre-eminence of the experimental perspective in evaluations of some types of treatments such as alternative therapies (Johannessen *et al*. 1994).

## The critique of natural science models for social evaluations

There is a history of debate within evaluation science which mirrors the debate in social sciences about using natural science methods for studying social phenomena. In evaluation there are four different strands to the debate. First is how or whether to evaluate using an experimental model where we think about the intervention as an experiment – the 'design debate'. Second is the debate about the status of 'facts': do 'facts' have an independent objective existence or are they socially created? Part of this debate is about using qualitative methods for data gathering: for example, the relevance and validity of reporting measures of patient satisfaction or patients' comments – the 'subjective data debate' (Chapters 11 and 12).

Third is the debate about scientific method: is the task of the evaluator to follow the hypothetico-deductive method and to propose hypotheses about the intervention which one then attempts to falsify by deductive tests, or to build up information about the intervention inductively from a series of observations, or some mixture of the two? Fourth is the debate about the proper aims of evaluation and about how people, populations and organizations should be regarded. Should they be evaluated as entities capable of self-reflection and transformation? This is the 'philosophical debate', which also underlies the first two debates.

Are causal explanations possible when the subject of study is people who can reflect on and attribute meaning to phenomena? In what sense is what we do caused or determined if we can become aware of the 'causes' and act differently, possibly as a result of an evaluation? These questions will sound familiar to anyone who has sat through 'the philosophy of the social sciences'. In evaluation the phenomenon of 'reflexivity' applies both to the targets of the intervention, such as patients, and to the people who are carrying out an intervention, and both may be the subject of an evaluation. In the earlier example, the nurse–mother intervention is not an intervention to an entity which only operates according to physical and chemical laws: both nurse and mother are conscious beings, have choice and attribute meaning to breast feeding and to the information leaflet in many different ways. The concepts of cause and effect have some application, but they ignore certain important characteristics of the mother and the nurse and have limited relevance for understanding or judging the value of the intervention. What is lost by confining the study of effect to a single or a few objectively verifiable behavioural measures? Would doing so help to understand the value of this intervention to Muslim women and children?

Some evaluators view the natural science model as the ideal, and seek to approximate it in their evaluation designs, building modifications to accommodate for the problems of control and bias and using techniques of single, double or triple blinding. The experimental approach has been successful for evaluating many medical treatments, and has been applied with adaptations for quasi-experimental evaluations of social interventions. Some evaluators, however, reject this model, proposing that evaluation should not and cannot study either the evaluated or its effects using natural science methods, and should not seek to explain the effects using the same types of causal explanations as the natural sciences. They make this argument not just for evaluations of social entities or polices, but also for evaluations of many conventional and alternative treatments (Johannessen et al. 1994). These criticisms are considered in the discussion of the strengths and weakness of experimental evaluation in Chapter 5.

*Our individual and social existence is both determined and can be determined by us*

Many evaluators take a midway position. Human beings are determined in two senses: we may not like it but we are subject to the operation of physical and biological laws, yet with determination and effort, we can also become conscious of these influences and sometimes overcome them, or at least make accommodations to them. A midway position also recognizes that the evaluation approach to take depends on the type of item you are evaluating and the purpose of the evaluation: if the evaluation is of a national policy and the purpose is to help to adjust the policy during implementation, then some elements of the experimental approach can be useful, but data gathering should involve qualitative as well as quantitative methods. A few argue that the evaluated should be viewed as a system, and that methods for conceptualizing, studying and intervening in systems should be used.

The main point here is that the majority of evaluators working within the developmental perspective do not just have a methodological preference for qualitative methods. They have different views to those of experimental evaluators about the purpose and rationale for evaluation, and work within phenomenological and other paradigms which are common in the social sciences. Note, however, that developmental evaluations also include a small sub-group of evaluations which use experimental principles, but use qualitative methods, seek information about a number of types of outcome and accept providers' and beneficiaries' accounts (subjective data) as valid insights into and data for valuing the evaluated.

In fact there is a fine dividing line between quasi-experimental evaluations and some developmental evaluations, as some of the latter do attempt to get evidence about outcome, but do so without the rigorous controls or techniques to reduce bias of the full experimental evaluation or of the single-case experimental design. We can think of a spectrum of developmental evaluations, ranging from those close to the experimental paradigm to, at the other extreme, those working with phenomenological and naturalistic methods. The latter aim to give service providers or policy makers regular feedback which they can use to change and improve a service or intervention. They often aim to change the evaluated while the evaluation is being made (Øvretveit 1987a). These types of evaluations are at the other end of a spectrum of 'control' from the end where experimental randomized controlled trial (RCT) evaluations would be placed. They often do not evaluate a service against objectives or criteria, but aim to help the service or others to develop such objectives or criteria. It is the collaborative, practical, direct and immediate working with service providers, but with the evaluator in an independent role, which distinguishes the developmental evaluation from other types.

There are three main points to be made in summary. First, there are different and strongly held views within the field about how to evaluate health interventions, and these differences will be discussed further in the chapters to come. Second, this book holds that there is a place for all perspectives. Which you use depends on the purpose and questions to be answered, and on what would be of most help to and credible with the users of the evaluation. The 'evaluation for action' approach outlined in Chapter 1 gives a framework within which an evaluation using any of the perspectives can be carried out. The third point is to note that this 'live and let live' approach is not shared by many evaluators, and this is especially apparent in debates about interventions on the boundaries between a treatment and a service, as, for example, in some combined cancer treatments. Evidence-based medicine is now on the attack to regain some of the ground lost to social scientists, who have made inroads into service evaluation, after more or less winning the policy evaluation ground.

The next section of this chapter notes some of the different labels to describe approaches to evaluation. Table 2.2 summarizes the distinctions made in this chapter and in Chapter 1 about different types of intervention and different perspectives in health evaluation.

## Types of evaluation

The categories of four perspectives and of four types of intervention were developed to help make sense of the many different types of evaluation in

*Table 2.2*  Examples of evaluations of different types of interventions using different evaluation perspectives

|  | *Experimental* | *Economic* | *Developmental* | *Managerial* |
|---|---|---|---|---|
| *Treatment* (diagnostic 'interventions' are also included in this category) | Controlled trial of a new surgical technique compared to a conventional treatment | Costs and effects of a surgical technique compared to a drug therapy for the same condition | Feedback to service providers of patient experiences and satisfaction with a new treatment | Assessment for managers of the impact on services and on patients of a new treatment |
| *Service* | Controlled trial of the effectiveness of a community-based psychiatric emergency service compared to a hospital service | Evaluation of the cost, savings and effects of a psychology service in a general practice | Description for service providers of their organization of care and of different perceptions of the strengths and weaknesses of the organization | Audit of a service's compliance with regulations for quality assurance |
| *Policy* | Quasi-experimental comparison of the effects on patients of GP purchasing (fundholding) compared to non-purchasing practices | Cost and effects of a new nationwide health screening policy for people over 75 | Feedback to policy makers of the progress in implementing a policy, in order that policy makers can make 'mid-course corrections' | Assessment for managers before a proposed policy is implemented of the likely effects and implications |
| *Intervention to organization* | Controlled trial of a method for teaching critical appraisal of clinical literature to medical students | Economic evaluation of the costs and savings of retraining staff for multiskilled working | Independent feedback to staff of the effects on other services of their change to to opening hours and referral arrangements | Evaluation for management of the impact of changes to junior doctors' hours of working |

the health sector (Table 2.1). Like any model it has its limitations, one being that there are approaches to evaluation which do not fit well into this model and which cross-cut the categories. Another model is given in Figure 2.1 to show some terms which are used to describe different types of evaluation. The next section of the chapter gives a brief summary of these different types of evaluation, many of which fall into the 'developmental' or 'managerial' categories. The terms are sometimes referred to in an evaluation report or in general discussions of evaluation and form part of the vocabulary of evaluation.

In the following we start with types of evaluation carried out before an intervention: for example, a 'feasibility evaluation' of the costs and benefits

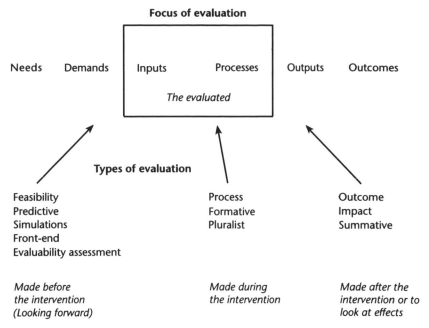

**Figure 2.1** The focus of different types of evaluation
Note: This is a rough guide only

of starting a new service. Then we note those which concentrate on the process of an intervention: for example, those carried out to evaluate a policy or programme as it is being implemented. Then we note those which look at impact and finally those which combine an examination of needs, inputs, processes and outcomes.

## Evaluability assessment

An assessment of an intervention which is carried out to decide whether or not to make a full evaluation is called an evaluability assessment. Such an assessment clarifies the intervention and its boundaries, the main evaluation questions and the main components of the item to be evaluated. It enables management to define more precisely the objectives of the service and to agree which they want evaluated. An evaluability assessment reports the different possible ways in which the item could be evaluated and the costs and benefits of different evaluation designs (Wholey 1977, 1983).

## Front-end, *ex ante* and feasibility evaluation

Before implementing an intervention, people may want an assessment of its possible consequences and costs: for example, a new policy to pay general medical practitioners to run stop-smoking clinics, or a new information technology system. These studies are sometimes called appraisals and are carried out for an intervention which is being proposed, or for a new or not widely applied intervention. They differ from an evaluability assessment in that they do not look at the possible ways of making an evaluation, but at the possible consequences of the intervention.

## Modelling and simulation

Have you ever used a computer spreadsheet to change income or expenditure figures so that you can see what the effects of these 'interventions' would be? If you have, then you have made one type of simulation, or modelling evaluation. Economists frequently use mathematical models and computers to simulate different interventions or changes to policy. Some economic evaluations assess, before an intervention is used, the costs and consequences of introducing the intervention, usually by comparison with existing services or policies. An example is Barer's (1981) use of simulation models to calculate the savings in Canada of providing all primary care through community health centres. Methodologies for these types of assessments are described in HERG (1994).

Simulations are becoming an increasingly important type of evaluation – for example, to simulate drug and treatment interventions – especially where experimentation is not possible for ethical or other reasons. One project used simulation to investigate the impact of four types of quality improvement techniques for premature labour and delivery hospital services. Evaluations of new hospital buildings are also made using virtual reality equipment: patients and health personnel 'walk around' the simulated buildings and give their judgement ratings about the selected features which are being evaluated.

## Multi-attribute utility evaluation and decision analysis

Multi-utility evaluations are used to help people choose between different options. They are a type of simulation technique. They use group decision analysis techniques to make explicit the criteria of valuation used by decision makers, and to compare systematically the performance of the options on these criteria. This approach has been used within health services by managers to evaluate computer systems before purchasing a system, and to develop a quality assessment system and assess the performance of the service (Øvretveit 1992b). It is an especially useful technique when there is no time to gather data and when decision makers need to organize their subjective judgements to make a decision about alternative courses of action, but when there are many considerations which need to be brought together. The method is described in Edwards and Newman (1988) and in Øvretveit (1992a, b).

## Formative evaluation

Formative evaluation is one type of 'developmental evaluation'. The purpose of a formative evaluation is to give information and assistance to the people who are able to make changes to an intervention so that they can make improvements. Usually the people are service providers, and the evaluator works closely with them, sometimes helping them to review and clarify aims, and regularly giving them feedback and information. The information can be about outcomes (e.g. reporting back patients' perceptions), but it is often about aspects of the treatment process or of the service operation and about differences between intentions and everyday practice.

Evaluators working in this mode tend to have a preference for qualitative methods. Formative evaluations also give a description of the evolution of the intervention, but, because the evaluator has usually had some influence on the evolution of the intervention, this description may be of limited use to other services. They are best suited to services in an early developmental stage, in a crisis or in transition, but this approach can also be used to develop treatments such as some social therapy treatments or alternative medicines. Formative evaluations are one type of action research (Hart and Bond 1996).

> Evaluation may be done to provide feedback to people who are trying to improve something (formative evaluation); or to provide information for decision-makers who are wondering whether to fund, terminate, or purchase something (summative evaluation).
>
> (Scriven 1980)

## Process evaluation

As the name suggests, this focuses on the 'process' of the evaluated, and is mostly carried out on services and programmes, as well as to evaluate the process of policy implementation. Process evaluations are different from formative evaluations in that they only look at process, whereas formative evaluations may also gather data about outcomes. The aim of process evaluations is to give people external or internal to the service an understanding of how a service operates and of how the service produces what it does, rather than an understanding of what it produces. This is useful where people want to set up a similar service elsewhere (replicate it), or know that it is effective but want to know why it is, and where experimental methods cannot be used. Preferred designs are case study and descriptive designs, and the methods are usually interviews and document analysis. Particularly important in making process evaluations are hypotheses about strengths and weakness, as well as the theoretical perspective used to conceptualize the process. Tracer or patient-pathway mapping methods are sometimes used (see Chapter 11).

## Implementation evaluation

These evaluations are made to evaluate how well or the extent to which a treatment, service or policy was implemented. This is a form of 'audit' evaluation because the evaluated is compared to a model of an intended policy or service, and information is gathered about the extent to which the evaluated differs from what was intended. This is one form of managerial evaluation and is increasingly used by financial donor organizations to evaluate health programme implementation in developing countries.

## Summative evaluation

Scriven (1967) defined and distinguished summative evaluations from formative evaluations in terms of the purpose of summative evaluations being to help decision makers to decide whether to continue a service or policy. The aim is to give decision makers an assessment of the effects and efficiency of an intervention – to 'sum it up'. The focus of summative evaluations is on outputs and outcomes, and on resources employed, and they are usually done for management or those external to the programme, rather than for service providers internal to the programme.

## Outcome or impact evaluation

These are terms used for any evaluation which concentrates on discovering the outcomes or wider impact of a treatment, service or policy (Rossi and Freeman 1993). An outcome evaluation would certainly be part of a summative evaluation, might be part of a formative evaluation, but would not be an element in a process evaluation. Robertson and Gandy (1983) make the following distinction between outcome and process evaluation:

> Outcome evaluations attempt to assess the effects produced by policies or programmes, and the extent to which such results measure up to programme 'goals' . . . The purpose of process research is to identify – normally through the use of 'soft' methodologies like participant observation – what seem to be the most important elements contributory to the outcome of a given programme . . . This kind of research is therefore reliant on description and inference from observation, in order to build up a sensitive composite picture of the functioning of the programme.

## Pluralistic evaluation

What constitutes success? Many evaluations, especially of services and policies, help users to judge the value of an intervention by gathering information about the success of the intervention. Some outcome or impact evaluations have been criticized for adopting one view of what is a valued outcome, often the view of those in power. Pluralistic evaluation investigates the views of different interest groups about what is success and their views of the extent to which the intervention was a success. A good example is an evaluation of a day hospital for older people with mental health problems by Smith and Cantley (1985), who note that, 'Pluralistic evaluation offers an ethnography of the way the services function and an explanation of the processes involved (in terms of the pluralistic interests of participating groups) as well as (somewhat complex) conclusions about the success of the services on a range of criteria.'

## Meta-analysis

Meta-analysis is an evaluation of other reported evaluations or research. Some meta-analyses combine results from different research studies by assessing the quality of the conclusions, and then combine the conclusions using weighting and other techniques. A criticism of this method of combining studies to express the value of a type of intervention is that the studies are qualitatively different. St Leger *et al.* (1992: 178–9) give a short summary and note their reservations. A meta-analysis can be made using a panel of judges, or by reanalysing the original data from studies with a similar design.

Another type of meta-evaluation is to assess and select reported research, and to do so for a particular purpose. Three examples are: as a method of evaluation (for example, to evaluate clinical trials of homeopathy; Kleijnen *et al.* 1991); as a method to review previous research as part of an evaluation study (e.g. Cummings *et al.* 1989); and as a method used by clinicians to assess previous evaluations of a treatment in order to inform their clinical practice in relation to one case (e.g. in evidence-based medicine; Rosenberg and Donald 1995; Gray 1997) or for formulating guidelines. Guidance for making a systematic review of the clinical effectiveness of treatments are given in NHSCR&D (1996), and in papers available from Cochrane Centres in Denmark, the UK and Canada (Sheldon and Chalmers 1994).

## Health project evaluation (e.g. in developing countries)

How would you evaluate an AIDS programme in Kenya? There are many examples of overseas-financed health projects in developing countries. Health projects are schemes to improve health or prevent illness in defined populations and are usually time limited. New techniques and evaluation designs are being used to assess and improve the impact of these projects and a field of expertise is developing which is termed 'health project evaluation'. These techniques include a number of methods summarized under the heading 'rapid appraisal', needs surveys and data gathering methods suited to developing countries. Some consider the WHO 'Health for all 2000' programme to be an international health project (WHO 1994). The techniques used to evaluate this programme are of particular interest because of their breadth and scale, because of the changes which WHO made after its first evaluation in 1988 and because WHO is financed by the governments whose progress on the targets is being evaluated by WHO.

*Table 2.3*  Perspectives most often used to evaluate different types of intervention

|  | *Experimental* | *Economic* | *Developmental* | *Managerial* |
|---|---|---|---|---|
| *Treatment* | Often | Often | Rarely | Rarely |
| *Service* | Sometimes | Often | Often | Often |
| *Health programme or project* | Sometimes | Sometimes | Often | Often |
| *Policy* | Rarely | Sometimes | Often | Often |
| *Reform* | Never | Rarely | Sometimes | Sometimes |
| *Intervention to organization* | Sometimes | Sometimes | Often | Often |

## Conclusions

♦ Table 2.3 shows the different perspectives and the different categories of interventions, noting which perspective is most often used to evaluate which types of intervention.

♦ Health evaluation is a broad and heterogeneous subject and field of activity: many different types of interventions are evaluated, there are different perspectives to evaluation and a variety of designs, and evaluations are carried out by people with different disciplinary backgrounds who are employed by different organizations.

♦ We need to evaluate health interventions to help patients to make more informed choices, to give a better basis for professional and management decisions, to help decide how best to use scarce resources, to assist policy making and implementation, and to account for the use of public finance and improve service performance.

♦ The perspective, design and methods used in an evaluation should be determined by the purpose and questions to be answered, and should be credible to the users and help them to make more informed decisions. There are no good or bad evaluations, just those which are more or less suited to the purpose and questions to be answered.

♦ It remains to be seen whether a distinct 'transdiscipline of evaluation' (Scriven 1991) with a body of 'evaluation theory' (Shadish *et al.* 1991) will develop, but there is certainly a rise in the number of multidisciplinary evaluations in the field of health and a greater understanding of the methods of different disciplines.

♦ Although evaluation is a practical applied discipline, two orientations exist within the field: an academic-scientific orientation which is more influenced by the research and theory of established disciplines, and a practical 'service' orientation where the evaluator is more concerned to give practical tangible assistance to users in the short term.

♦ The four most common health evaluation perspectives are: experimental, economic, developmental and managerial. Each perspective involves a set of assumptions about how to conceptualize the item to be evaluated and about what constitutes valid knowledge about the evaluated and about ideal strategies for gathering this knowledge, and each has preferred methods for data collection and analysis (Table 2.4).

♦ Experimental evaluations aim to discover whether an intervention has effects, and the causes of any effects. The evaluation is designed to test hypotheses and follows the model of a scientific experiment (Chapter 5).

♦ Economic evaluations aim to discover how many resources are consumed by using an intervention, and often also to quantify the consequences of an intervention, sometimes in money terms (Chapter 6).

♦ Developmental evaluations use systematic methods and theories within an evaluation framework to enable service providers to develop and improve their treatments, services, policies or organizational interventions, often while the evaluation is being done (Chapter 7).

♦ Managerial evaluations are made for managers and supervisory boards to monitor or improve the performance of services or policies, or to check that agreed changes or projects were implemented as intended. Their purpose is to ensure accountability, value for money and performance improvement.

♦ Some of the more common terms used to describe types of evaluation are formative, process, summative, outcome or impact evaluation, pluralistic and implementation evaluation. Most of these are used to describe service or policy evaluations.

*Table 2.4*  Types of health evaluation within the four main perspectives (described in Chapters 5 to 8)

---

1 *Experimental* (Chapter 5)
   1.1 Controlled trial – randomized
   *Quasi-experimental*
   1.2 Controlled trial – non-random controls (e.g. matched)
   1.3 Self-controls – time series (or 'longitudinal')
       (a) Group tested before and after the intervention
       (b) Single-case experimental
   1.4 Retrospective case control
   1.5 Observational (cross-sectional or longitudinal)*

2 *Economic* (Chapter 6)
   2.1 Costing
   2.2 Cost-minimization
   2.3 Cost-effectiveness
   2.4 Cost–utility
   2.5 Cost–benefit

3 *Developmental* (Chapter 7)
   3.1 Descriptive social research
   3.2 Action evaluation
   3.3 Self-review

4 *Managerial* (Chapter 8)
   4.1 Standards and regulations compliance
   4.2 Goal or plan compliance
   4.3 Efficiency
   4.4 Needs effectiveness

---

*Note*: Observational studies are not, by definition, experimental studies. These types of observational study are classified here within the experimentalist perspective because such studies share the assumptions about facts and methods which characterize this perspective.

# Six designs

*What is 'in the box' and what was compared?*

*What are the criteria for evaluation and where do they come from?*

## Introduction

Even if we have grasped the basics of experimental randomized controlled trial design, we may find ourselves in a management job where we have 30 minutes to decide how to respond to the recommendations of an evaluation into a nurse training programme, which used qualitative methods and a retrospective case study design. Many health personnel need to be able to understand quickly, and sometimes to carry out or manage evaluations of a variety of interventions: health promotion programmes, treatments, health reforms, organizational changes and educational programmes, to name a few. There are many different approaches and technical terms, even for evaluating one of these types of interventions, and the same terms are sometimes used by different writers to mean different things.

This chapter is for people new to evaluation. Its purpose is to introduce some basic concepts and designs, and to do so in a way which does not further confuse the beginner. It aims to be simple, but not simplistic. It uses an example treatment, asks who might be interested in the treatment and their questions, and considers how we might evaluate it in order to illustrate general concepts and ideas in evaluation. The chapter gives a 'basic diagram' and uses it to describe six types of evaluation design which we could use to evaluate this treatment. This diagram is useful for making sense of a particular evaluation which we have to understand quickly, and for seeing some of the differences between approaches. The chapter ends by looking in more detail at the issues involved in evaluating the example treatment and at the same time introduces other basic concepts, such as dependent and independent variables and confounding factors. Chapter 4 gives examples of evaluations and encourages the reader to decide which of the six designs was used in each example.

### An example intervention

A friend of mine thinks that evaluation is 'a lot of fuss about nothing'. She and her children use a particular 'therapy' because they know it works. It is a therapy which modern medicine has never encountered and her challenge to me was, how would you evaluate it? I knew that I was being 'set up' and that this was going to be an argument not just about evaluation but about medicine in general, the state of health services and probably men's attitudes to feelings as well. She called Kerstin, her older daughter, to bring 'the therapy' to me, which Kerstin did reluctantly because she knew a long and boring adult discussion was about to begin.

Kerstin produced a small box, inside of which lay a small woman doll about 2 cm long. She began to get serious when I laughed and patiently explained to me that this was a special doll from Guatemala, and, if you told your doll your worries then your worries would go away. Kerstin's mother explained that when she or her daughters had trouble sleeping, they put the doll under their pillow and they found that they could sleep better. 'We know the value of our Guatemalan dolls, and they work for us, but I bet your scientific evaluation methods would say that they do not. How would you evaluate our dolls, then?'

I will not tell you how the discussion went, but I will ask you to test what you know about evaluation on this example. We have an intervention, which we can call 'Guatemalan doll therapy' (GDT). We could evaluate its effects on reducing worries – after all, that was what Kerstin claimed. Let us keep it simple and evaluate it as a way of helping with sleeplessness, because this is easier to measure.

## Interest group perspectives

'How would you evaluate it, then?' was the challenge. In the situation above, I instinctively reached for the academic's answer when needing time to think: 'It depends.' A moment's thought and I realized that this was the right answer, because the starting point for any evaluation is to clarify for whom we are evaluating the item. We need to understand their questions and the decisions which they need to make which cause them to seek a systematic evaluation. As described in Chapter 2, the purpose of evaluation is to help people to make better informed decisions – we need to understand what they need to know for them to act differently. People in different social roles have different questions which relate to the decisions they have to make in their social roles.

We could evaluate an intervention like GDT from six different perspectives, each with a different set of questions and different actions which would follow from an informed answer to the questions. Normally we would design our evaluation to answer the questions of one or more interest groups or 'users' of the evaluation, and we would use a different design for different questions.

In the example, we will not take the perspective of Kerstin's mother and sisters: they believe GDT works, and their theory that it reduces sleeplessness is built on their experience. But other people who do not sleep well have questions which they would like answered before they are prepared to go to the trouble of getting a doll and trying it for themselves. We can call people who go to a health service for help with their sleeping problem 'patients'. Patients' questions are 'does it work?', and if it does, 'how well does it work?' They may already use other therapies, and, if GDT 'works', they may want to know how well it works in comparison to sleeping pills or other common sleeplessness strategies, like counting sheep or salmon jumping up a stream.

If we were doing an evaluation only for this interest group or from their perspective, we would then pursue things further with these 'evaluation users'. We would try to focus on the most important questions by looking at whether answers to each question would lead people to act differently or not. This would help us to separate the 'interesting questions' from those of real consequence for their lives, and to focus on the latter. We would also define the criteria which they use to judge the value of the therapy: for example, reducing sleeplessness, effort involved and no side effects. We would use these criteria of valuation to decide which outcome variables to measure and data to gather.

If we were to use an experimental perspective, we would also translate patients' questions into 'theories' or hypotheses to test: for example, 'Using GDT has no effect whatsoever on sleeplessness.' But all of this is jumping ahead to later parts of the chapter. It may be that other patients would feel that their answers would be satisfied by a detailed description of how Kerstin, her sisters and mother use GDT and of their experience. At present, however, we need to decide whether the patient's perspective is the only one we will take in designing the evaluation. Who else would have an interest in an evaluation of GDT for sleeplessness? Who else might be 'users' of the evaluation and what questions would they want the evaluation to answer?

A second set of potential users are healthcare workers whom people with sleeplessness consult for help, such as nurses or doctors. If you were a doctor or nurse who had heard about this therapy, what questions would you have of an evaluation of GDT? What would you need to know which would make you act differently? Because doctors and nurses understand their patients' concerns, we would expect them to have similar questions to patients, but they would want stronger evidence than a detailed report of one family's experience: 'Does it work for all patients with this problem?' They will also have questions about side effects, about long-term effects and about interactions with other therapies which some of their patients might be undergoing.

A third interest group is managers, such as managers of primary health care centres or of a health financing agency. What questions would they have of an evaluation of GDT? 'How much does it cost?' and 'How much could it save us?' are probably their main questions. They would also want answers to questions like those raised by the doctors, if only to give a credible explanation to healthcare workers about why they were, or were not, supporting the introduction of GDT therapy in their service – they expect patients' groups to demand it and expect healthcare workers to criticize them for trying to save money. They are also interested in possible risks, because their service might be blamed for giving a treatment which could cause harm.

A fourth interest group perspective which we could take in the evaluation is that of politicians. Politicians have to make choices about how much money to allocate to different purposes, and justify these choices. Their social role also requires them to be sensitive to and respond to the wishes of the people they represent. They also want to be re-elected and want to look good to the section of the population on whose vote they depend.

They have similar questions to patients, doctors and managers, but with a different emphasis and priority: they are concerned about cost-effectiveness because they will have to defend their decisions, but they also want to know, 'How many people want it and which people?' If they are also responsible for social and educational services, they will want to know if there are any extra costs or benefits for these services and possible wider effects.

A fifth interest group are scientists and health researchers. Their questions are, 'What is already known about this or similar therapies?', 'What are the effects?' and 'Why do any effects occur – what are the causes of any effects?' An evaluation for this group would require a different, and probably more costly, design from that which would answer the questions of other groups.

Last but not least is the sixth group which evaluators have to bear in mind: journalists and 'the media'. In theory they represent the general public, who have questions about the best use of their money as taxpayers. In practice they are looking for a good story and for drama. This group is not an interest group with a perspective in the same way that the other groups are in that there is less commonality of interest. However, evaluators need to consider their questions and how the media might use the evaluation, especially if one or more of the media are sponsoring the evaluation.

---

**Stakeholder perspectives**

We can evaluate an item on behalf of one or more of the following perspectives and interest groups:

- patients or possible patients;
- health practitioners;
- managers;
- politicians;
- health researchers and scientists;
- the media.

Implementation of the results of an evaluation is more likely if the evaluation has paid attention to the concerns and questions of interest groups which can support or oppose changes. These are the six groups which are often significant in any action following an evaluation study. There will be different sub-interests and perspectives within each group.

---

There are other interest group perspectives which the evaluation might take, such as those of drug companies, social security departments and employers. However, the main point highlighted here is that the perspective which the evaluation takes decides which questions it will aim to answer and the type of design which is best for answering them, given the time and resources available.

## Defining the question and the intervention

Before considering six different designs, we need to note some other points which are raised by the above discussion. The first is that if the evaluation were to take only one perspective then to decide the design we would clarify the key questions and decisions, the user's criteria for valuation (e.g. reduction in sleeplessness, effects for the costs) and the criteria for comparison (e.g. to other therapies), and relate these to a hypothesis to test, that is if we were to use the more common type of experimental design.

The second point is that the evaluation may be sponsored by one group, but they may want perspectives other than their own to be considered. For example, an evaluation may be sponsored by a grant-giving body which wants an evaluation from both a scientific perspective and a patient perspective. The evaluator may have to guess the questions of concern to these interest groups and propose to the sponsor how the evaluation will answer these questions. He or she may have to convince the sponsor that these are important questions to these interest groups, and that answers to these questions would have consequences for how people in these groups acted.

A third point is that the evaluator will usually have to prioritize one, two or three key questions which the evaluation will set out to answer. This is not easy even with one group, but with more perspectives to consider, choices will have to be made about which perspectives and criteria of valuation to give priority. However, evaluators also have a duty to draw sponsors' attention to the questions which others have and which an evaluation might be able to answer – we may be able to persuade our sponsor to accept a design which allows us to answer others' questions as well.

Note also that we are here considering a treatment. The same concepts and principles also apply to services, policies and interventions to organization: for example, in designing an evaluation of a service providing GDT, or a local or national policy to provide GDT as an alternative to sleeping pills, or a programme to train health personnel how to prescribe GDT.

Let us return to the question, 'How would you evaluate it?' When faced with this question by Kerstin's mother, I was able to explain that it depended on whom I was doing the evaluation for. I then wanted to start talking about how we could tell if it worked or not and to use some evaluation concepts, but I could see things were getting too abstract. I decided to do what many people do when asked how they would evaluate this treatment – go straight to talking about evaluation designs and to leave the explanation of technical terms until later.

## What is in the box?

Using the paper and coloured pen which Kerstin put on the kitchen table, I drew the 'basic diagram' shown in Figure 3.1. This shows the intervention to be evaluated inside a 'box'. This 'box' represents the treatment, service,

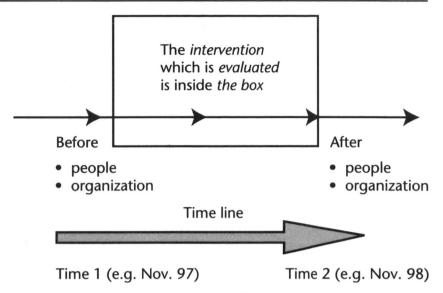

**Figure 3.1** The basic drawing of an evaluation design (if you cannot draw it, then it is not clear or understood)

policy or organizational change to be evaluated. The 'box boundary' defines what is and is not evaluated. I explained to Kerstin that the box is the 'doll therapy'. The arrow shows people who do not use the doll before, and then they use it and are inside the box, and then stop using it and move outside of the box.

'Why do people go inside the box?' asked Kerstin. 'They just do,' I said, but this did not satisfy Kerstin's mother. 'Well, it is to show that people "go through" the intervention. In the evaluation business we say that they are the "targets" who are "exposed" to the intervention.' Kerstin looked troubled. 'Why do people stop using the doll when it works?' 'So that we can find out if it works.' 'Why . . .' 'They just do,' I interrupted, asking Kerstin for another piece of paper so that I could draw different designs.

## Six evaluation designs

How would you evaluate Guatemalan doll therapy? Most readers have ideas about how to carry out an evaluation. Consider which of the following six types of design is closest to your design, and whether any of the others are better. Remember that the best design depends on the nature of the thing which we are evaluating, whether the design will answer users' questions and how many resources and how much time we have to carry out the evaluation. Imagine that we are doing the evaluation for a patient's organization, and they want to know whether GDT works, will wait 12 months to know and will pay $25,000 for the evaluation.

### Descriptive (Type 1)

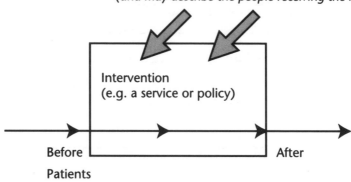

Evaluator observes and selects features
of the intervention, which he or she describes
*(and may describe the people receiving the intervention)*

Intervention
(e.g. a service or policy)

Before                                                                    After

Patients
or population

- ♦ *Questions answered by this design*: What is it? What happens?
- ♦ *Purpose of this evaluation design*: to produce both a good description of the intervention which is being evaluated, and of 'important' features of the 'environment' surrounding the intervention, so as to enable users to make a more informed judgement of the value of the intervention.
- ♦ *Most often used for*: developmental and managerial evaluations to describe the key features of services, policies or intervention to organization, and some simple consumer satisfaction descriptions. A description of the resources used by a service can be a simple economic evaluation.
- ♦ *Key points*: the evaluator does not just observe and describe, but is influenced by concepts and theories to decide what to describe and how to conceptualize the intervention. If the description uses explicit standards and criteria to decide what to describe, then it is a type 2 audit design. If the description involves a before–after comparison, then it is a type 3 outcome evaluation (see below).
- ♦ *Strengths*: needs few resources, can be done in collaboration with service providers and people receiving a treatment, and can clarify objectives and highlight problems.
- ♦ *Weaknesses*: can be ignored as unscientific, biased or trivial. Depends on the skill, knowledge and credibility of the evaluator and the theoretical perspective which he or she uses to select and conceptualize what to describe – a descriptive evaluation by a health economist would be different from one done by an anthropologist or psychologist.

In the GDT example, GDT would be in 'the box' and the evaluation would be to describe it, to describe how patients used it and their experiences. Of all the six designs my first choice of design for an evaluation of GDT would be such a descriptive design, using observational and diary data gathering methods (Chapter 11). This is because I am not sure exactly what the therapy is and what type of outcome I might look for. The 'patients' have given a rough description of the therapy, but I would want to find out more about exactly how people used it and about other things in 'the context' which might be important.

Sometimes a descriptive design is of most use to managers who are remote from a service and who ask for an evaluation. After discussion it becomes apparent that they do not have the time or money for an outcome evaluation and actually only want a description of 'what is really happening' by an independent observer. Another reason to do a descriptive evaluation of an existing service or policy is to give a precise description which allows other people to set up a similar service or to carry out a similar policy. It may also be premature to try to judge the value of something if there is not an agreed and explicit description of it.

Can we really call a simple description like the type 1 design an evaluation? Some would say not, but sometimes when people want something evaluated they are often unsure exactly what it is they want to evaluate, what its aims are or what questions they want answered. Evaluators are sometimes too quick to propose a sophisticated and expensive design when more consideration of the user's concerns and questions would show that all they need is an independent description, which then helps them to judge value.

Sometimes users want 'an assessment' of a group of people, either a partial assessment, for example of their blood pressure, or a more global assessment, such as quality of life. Assessments of this type are sometimes called evaluations: for example, a 'student evaluation'. These are measurement exercises and we could categorize them as one type of descriptive evaluation – a description of the state of the targets of the intervention after the intervention. Knowing what people think of an intervention can also give us one source of information to help to judge its value.

Descriptive evaluations can be used to describe a new or unfamiliar treatment, but are more often used to describe a service or policy which is unclear or which is in the early stages of evolution. For services, 'the box' is both processes (service activities) and inputs (the health personnel, their equipment etc). These evaluations can give a description of what a service does (process), what it is for (objectives) and who does what in the service, the inputs to the service and the context within which the service operates. They can be used to give a general description of outcomes, but are not suitable for evaluating effectiveness. Often their purpose is to describe and conceptualize a service so as to give service providers or policy makers a basis for thinking about improvements.

Descriptive evaluations may or may not describe the costs of a service. They can be 'retrospective' and done after a service has been changed or a policy carried out (e.g. many 'summative' evaluations), or 'concurrent' and done while a service is operating or a policy being implemented (e.g. many 'developmental' or 'formative' evaluations).

## Audit (Type 2)

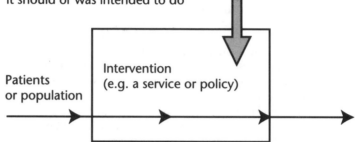

- ◆ *Questions*: did the intervention follow procedures or achieve objectives set for it?
- ◆ *Purpose*: to judge the value of what people are doing by comparing what they do with what they are supposed to do.
- ◆ *Used for*: managerial monitoring of services operation and policy implementation, simple economic audits, developmental self or peer review exercises and some types of quality assurance and clinical audit.
- ◆ *Key points*: like descriptive evaluation, but describes the intervention in comparison to intended objectives, procedures or standards which are usually specified in writing. The audit may be carried out by external evaluators (e.g. visiting peers) or by the service providers themselves, using established standards.
- ◆ *Weaknesses*: depends on having a clearly specified set of standards, procedures or objectives, or on creating such a set as part of the evaluation. Does not help to judge the value of the intervention, but just whether people 'follow orders' – there is an assumption that if people follow procedures then they are doing something of value, but the intervention may be ineffective or inappropriate.
- ◆ *Strengths*: few resources needed, can be done quickly, good for self-evaluation, usually of some use, can help to understand why a service or policy fails or succeeds and can sometimes give knowledge which can be generalized. If standards are evidence-based, this can be a cost-effective method for improving practice.

This design is often used in audits of clinical, financial, organizational, regulation compliance and contract matters, and for evaluations made for aid donors of health programmes in developing countries. Audits assume that, if the service providers follow the standards, then a beneficial outcome will follow, but this may not have been proven before. This evaluation design does not discover effects or possible causes, but it can be used to audit outcome or performance: for example, how well a service complies with patients' rights, guarantees or charters. Checking whether practitioners are following treatment guidelines is one type of audit evaluation. However, the term 'clinical audit' also describes clinicians first deciding which guidelines and criteria to use: where their decision is based on evidence of effectiveness, then the audit has more value.

A financial audit compares how the service spends money and operates its accounts with established standards for accounting. It assesses whether financial procedures were followed in the service and whether money was spent as intended, and may also assess whether the service achieved financial objectives which were already defined: for example, a 6 per cent return on capital.

Other types of audit evaluations are of services: for example, a quality assurance audit using a set of quality standards, or a policy audit to check whether people are complying with a policy. The King's Fund organizational audit (Brooks 1992) and quality award assessments (Øvretveit 1994a) are methods for auditing service organizations against standards and criteria which experts believe are important for producing a good quality service. Audits may be retrospective or concurrent, and may or may not consider costs.

Some would not consider audits to be a type of evaluation because the design does not aim to evaluate the effectiveness of the intervention, but to evaluate whether people carry out procedures, achieve objectives or meet standards. 'Monitoring' is certainly a better term to describe many of the activities which use this design, but this book takes a broad view of evaluation and includes audits as one form of evaluation. One reason for so doing is because information about whether people or services meet specifications or objectives is an increasingly important way to judge the value of what they are doing, where specifications and objectives are based on evidence about what is effective. Generally the value of audits depends on the validity of the guidelines, standards, procedures or objectives, and whether these are derived from evaluations carried out using other designs.

An audit evaluation would not be suitable for evaluating GDT because none of the interest groups want to know whether people do or do not follow a defined procedure for carrying out the treatment. Some experimental evaluations audit people's compliance with a defined treatment procedure during the evaluation, so as to increase the controls in the evaluation. In this instance, an experimental evaluation of GDT might use an audit within the larger evaluation to check whether patients follow the instructions for using GDT, and whether health practitioners follow the guidelines for giving instruction about using GDT. An audit evaluation might be suitable for evaluating a new policy which introduced GDT and GDT guidelines into a primary health care service. Chapter 8 considers these types of design in more detail, as they are the most common designs used in managerial evaluations.

## Before–After (Type 3)

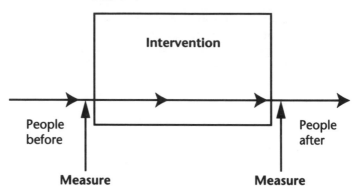

Measure                                   Measure

- ◆ *Questions*: What effect? What difference does the intervention make to the target?
- ◆ *Purpose*: to help to judge the value of an intervention by comparing the state of people or organizations before with their state after the intervention (outcome measurement).
- ◆ *Used for*: discovering limited or broad changes in people undergoing treatment, services and organizational interventions, in simple quasi-experimental, economic, developmental and managerial evaluations.
- ◆ *Key points*: the before–after comparison may be of single measured states before and after (e.g. blood pressure, or the expenditure of an organization), or of many features of the target which are collected before and after (e.g. patient expectations and experiences, physical measures, providers assessments of 'patient progress', patient income losses). In both cases, the before–after comparisons are based on theories about the possible effects of the intervention.
- ◆ *Weaknesses*: cannot give conclusive objective evidence of effects because, if there are effects, these may have been caused by things other than the intervention (the many possible 'confounding variables' are not controlled), or by selecting subjects who would show these effects over time anyway.
- ◆ *Strengths*: can be small scale and relatively quick. They can be designed to use few resources if the evaluator selects a small number of subjects, makes one or a few simple 'before' and 'after' measures and makes the measurement soon after the intervention.

For many this design is the first recognizable evaluation design so far, because it looks at outcome, or rather the difference which an intervention might make to the target. However, those who take this view would also be dissatisfied with how this design tries to discover the effect of the intervention: how does the design prove that the difference is due to the intervention and not to something else, or even that the difference would not have happened anyway without an intervention?

The evaluation compares a group of patients before and after an intervention. In a quasi-experimental before–after type 3 design, the subjects are selected, then measured, the intervention is given as if it was an experiment and the subjects are measured afterwards. There would be a hypothesis about the intervention's effects, and one or a few specific objective measures which were logically derived from this hypothesis, such as blood pressure, cholesterol levels or quality of life.

Before–after designs used within a developmental perspective will use questions about possible effects rather than hypotheses: examples are the designs sometimes used in service evaluations. They will collect a variety of data about and from the subjects before and after, and sometimes during their exposure to the intervention. Such designs differ from type 1 because although some type 1 designs might describe the state of people after receiving the service, type 1 designs do not compare before and after states (i.e. outcome).

Many evaluations using this design do not measure just once before and once after, but repeat the measure at different times. For example, an evaluation of light therapy for seasonal affective disorder used a measure of depression at two-week intervals during the month before and the month after the treatment (Dam *et al.* 1993). For some variations of this design the diagram is slightly misleading in suggesting that people 'pass through' a service and that the treatment or service stops: this does not always happen. Sometimes people continue receiving the treatment or the service. Examples are medication for hypertension, interventions for chronic disorders and home care services. For these, the diagram shows that a measure is taken before they start and then at periods after first receiving the treatment.

This design could be used to evaluate GDT, but the time limit of one year and the budget for the evaluation of $25,000 would mean a limited study without the detailed attention to controls which would be necessary for this type of evaluation (Johannessen *et al.* 1994). It could give 'suggestive' but not conclusive findings and might be misleading or misinterpreted by the media, even when the evaluator takes care to point out the limitations. These 'quasi-experimental case control' designs are discussed in more detail in the next chapter.

## Comparative-experimentalist (Type 4)

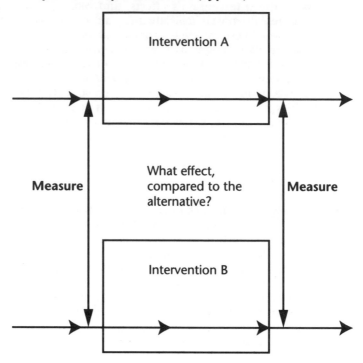

- ♦ *Question*: what effect, compared to a similar intervention?
- ♦ *Purpose*: to judge the value of an intervention in comparison to a similar one, using a before–after 'outcome' comparison.
- ♦ *Used for*: economic and quasi-experimental evaluations of services, of interventions to services and sometimes of treatments and policies.
- ♦ *Key points*: like type 3 outcome evaluation, but compares the outcomes of two groups undergoing different interventions. Variations are (a) where one 'intervention' 'B' is a placebo; (b) a retrospective design (e.g. some comparative evaluations of services); (c) a comparison of end states only, rather than the before–after change (outcome).
- ♦ *Weaknesses*: expensive, and can be even more difficult than type 3 designs to prove that the effects were due to the interventions alone (unless one is a placebo).
- ♦ *Strengths*: if made with care, such evaluations can suggest which of the two interventions is more effective or cost-effective, and are suitable where it is unethical or impractical to treat only one group.

Unlike type 3 designs, this design compares two interventions, but it does use the type 3 before–after outcome comparison. It is a common design for evaluations of treatments or services: for example, where a new treatment or service is started at one site which people want to compare with a traditional treatment or service at another site. An example is a comparison of the health state of patients before and after a new rehabilitation technique for stroke patients compared to conventional rehabilitation.

Evaluations with these designs are carried out according to experimental principles, with hypotheses to test and with different methods for controlling for influences other than the interventions, such as patient characteristics (age, sex, severity of illness, duration of previous illness etc.). A common control technique is 'matching' the characteristics of the people experiencing each intervention to try to exclude influences which might affect outcome other than the intervention. This is, however, a far less satisfactory means of control than selection and then random allocation to two groups (type 5).

One version of this design is like the controlled randomized experiment design (described next as the type 5 design), but in the type 4 design the control group goes through a similar or comparable intervention rather than a placebo. An example is where evaluators compare groups of subjects which get different treatments, such as a cost-effectiveness study of drug therapy compared to surgical therapy.

The design, like the type 3 design, can be used to make use of opportunities to create a 'natural experiment': for example, to make a retrospective evaluation where there are records or measures already available. Within the experimental perspective, prospective designs are preferred because they allow the evaluator to arrange beforehand for better experimental controls and more rigorous hypothesis testing. Note that some people may 'drop out' (not complete the intervention) – we consider the significance of these and other factors for assessing the results in Chapters 5 and 12.

One variation of the design is where intervention B is a placebo, but the more powerful type 5 designs are more often used. Some type 4 evaluations only use an 'after' measure and compare the two groups to see if there is any difference in the end state of people receiving the two interventions. An example is patient satisfaction with a computer information system compared to a physician giving the information. It costs more, but is more common, to have 'before' measures too, so that a comparison of the change which occurs in both groups can be made (the outcome). When evaluating a service, a policy or a change to organization, we can increase our certainty that the intervention has the effect we think it does by comparisons with other services or places which do not have the same thing.

Comparative outcome evaluations of this type can give some objective evidence of the effect of the intervention compared to another one, but they take longer and use more resources than type 3 designs. The cost and time required increase with more subjects (which calls for more time and care matching subjects), with more complex measures (e.g. quality of life measures), with more than one 'after' measure and with measurement some time after the intervention.

As a design for our example GDT intervention, this design has a certain appeal – it would be interesting to compare GDT to sleeping pills and or other treatments. However, the money and time budget would not allow for many controls and only allow us to carry it out for a few subjects, which would make the conclusions of little value to scientists and to our sponsors.

The difference between type 4 and type 3 designs is that two interventions are compared. The differences between type 4 and type 5, which we consider next, are that patients are not randomly allocated and the type 4 usually compares two similar interventions. The controls in type 4 are therefore fewer than for the type 5 full experimental design.

### Randomized controlled experimental (Type 5)

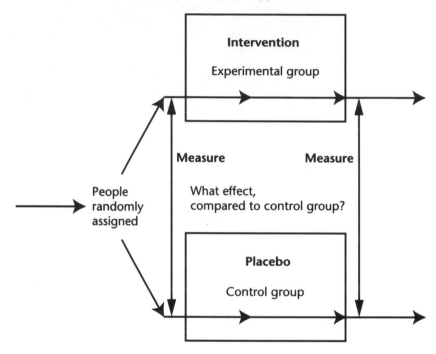

- ♦ **Question**: what effect, compared to a control group?
- ♦ **Purpose**: to compare one group that receives an intervention with another group that does not, but that is in all other possible respects the same.
- ♦ **Used for**: experimental and economic evaluations to gain 'conclusive' evidence of the effect of a treatment or service on one or a few measures of the health state of a group of patients.
- ♦ **Key points**: like type 4, but the people selected are randomly assigned to a control (placebo) and an intervention group. This evaluation is able to reduce the number of possible explanations for any differences between the outcomes being due to things other than the intervention.
- ♦ **Weaknesses**: expensive, takes time, needs evaluators with experience, skill and statistical expertise to produce credible results, often does not examine patients' subjective experience and may mask extreme effects on some individuals in the group average.
- ♦ **Strengths**: gives more reliable and valid information about the effect of the intervention than the type 3 simple outcome evaluation and the type 4 non-random, non-placebo comparison. The results from a well conducted evaluation using this design have high credibility with most clinicians.

This design is the 'classic' evaluation design, which many think of for a 'proper' evaluation of a treatment or a service. The idea behind this design is to create two groups which are exactly the same in all respects apart from the fact that one group received the intervention. The design can rule out many alternative explanations for a change which is detected in the targets, and can give evidence of causal mechanisms.

The second control group do not 'get nothing', but receive an intervention called a 'placebo' – some estimates are that 30–40 per cent of patients will show an improvement without any intervention (Benson and McCallie 1979). There is much debate within the field about the best placebo for different types of intervention, such as for psychotherapy, and about the validity and ethics of using a placebo.

Type 5 designs are prospective and called 'experimental' because the evaluator intervenes to create a change and studies it using similar principles and controls to those used by a natural scientist in a laboratory.

Strictly speaking, the comparison is between the two groups, not between the intervention and nothing, and the 'experiment' tests a hypothesis, not the intervention *per se*. The result of the evaluation is a tested hypothesis, not a tested intervention. A typical hypothesis is that the subjects undergoing the intervention will (or will not) differ from the controls on a measured characteristic. These points are discussed together with other details in Chapter 5, such as how previous research is used to decide the hypothesis and to decide which other variables to control for, the selection criteria for subjects, reducing biases in selection, sample size, drop outs, randomization, statistical techniques, such as significance tests and confidence intervals, and generalizability.

'You get what you pay for' is one response to the criticisms of the cost of evaluation designs of this type. Another is 'If it's worth doing, it's worth doing well.' The evidence about an intervention which is produced by a well conducted design of this type has a much higher certainty than that of any of the other designs. However, the evidence is limited to the effect of the intervention on one or a few measures of the target – most evaluations of this type only measure one or a few outcomes. Further, the conclusions might not be generalizable from the carefully controlled subjects and setting to other settings – the high 'internal validity' can mean a lower 'external validity'. These and other criticisms are discussed in Chapter 5.

The full design is not suitable for many service and policy evaluations because of the difficulties of controlling for extraneous variables, and the service or policy itself often changes. Whether service policy and other evaluations should try to approximate to this design is another matter, which is considered in Chapters 5 and 7. It is not suitable for our example treatment evaluation of GDT because of the budget and time constraints, and because the intervention and our theories about it are not yet well enough defined for a design of this type. At this stage a magnifying glass is more useful than sophisticated experimental equipment.

### Intervention to a health organization (Type 6a): Impact on providers

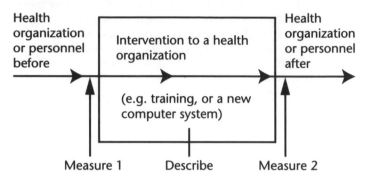

◆ *Question:* what is the effect of an intervention to a service on health personnel or organization?
◆ *Purpose*: to help to judge the value of an intervention to a service by comparing the state of health personnel or of organizational functioning before with the state after the intervention (outcome measurement).
◆ *Used for*: discovering the effect of a policy, a training or organizational development programme, a reorganization or other changes to organizational functioning in simple quasi-experimental, economic, developmental and managerial evaluations.
◆ *Key points*: the data to be gathered before and after depend on the user's questions and future decisions, the objectives of the intervention and any theories about how the intervention may affect health personnel or organization – common methods are surveys, observation and measures such as personnel work stress. Before and after data could be costs, as in an economic evaluation of the effect of an intervention on the service costs.
◆ *Weaknesses*: as with type 3, it is difficult to be sure that any effects on health personnel or organizational functioning which are detected are only due to the intervention and not to other influences. It does not consider the effect on patients – if a change to health personnel or organization is detected, how does this change affect patients?
◆ *Strengths*: cheap, quick and usually better than nothing, as long as the limitations are spelled out. More useful when another evaluation has already discovered how the intervention or its outcome affects patient care.

## Intervention to a health organization (Type 6b): Impact on patients

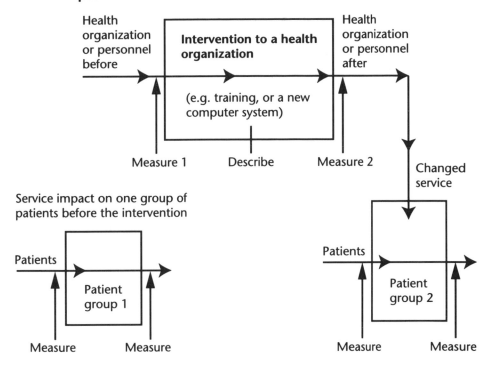

Health organization or personnel before

**Intervention to a health organization**

Health organization or personnel after

(e.g. training, or a new computer system)

Measure 1    Describe    Measure 2

Changed service

Service impact on one group of patients before the intervention

Patients

Patient group 1

Measure    Measure

**Service before**

Patients

Patient group 2

Measure    Measure

**Service after the intervention**

- ◆ *Question*: what is the effect of an intervention to organization on patients, and on health personnel or organizational functioning?
- ◆ *Purpose*: by comparing patient outcomes before and after the change, the design can help to judge the value of a change to organization or of other interventions to a service.
- ◆ *Used for*: evaluations of training programmes, quality assurance and other interventions intended to improve patient care, in a quasi-experimental, economic, developmental and managerial evaluation.
- ◆ *Key points*: the two patient groups before and after need to be carefully matched to increase the probability that any difference in outcome between the two groups is due to the intervention. Variations of this design involve comparing two or more services receiving the intervention and the effects on the patients of these services.
- ◆ *Weaknesses*: difficult to match or control for patient characteristics between the two before and after patient groups. The measures chosen to study the effect of the service on patients might not detect important benefits or disbenefits produced by the intervention.
- ◆ *Strengths*: there is an increasing need to assess how changes to health organizations affect patient care, whether or not this is the primary aim of the change or intervention. This design and variations on it allow an evaluation of the impact on patients and on health personnel.

**Making sense of an evaluation**

To understand an evaluation report, and to decide a design, it helps to draw a diagram with:

◆ a 'box' around what was evaluated;
◆ any before and after measures, and when they were made;
◆ the timescale, and the number of people involved.

Ask of the report:

◆ What was in 'the box'?
◆ What were the comparisons?
◆ What were the criteria of valuation and the data gathering methods/measures?

## Six designs: summary and concluding points

These six models of design are useful for people new to evaluation to see some of the different types which are possible. It is helpful when reading an evaluation to try and draw it in this way: to draw the 'box' and the type of design to show the essential features. Most evaluations use one of six types of design.

◆ Descriptive (type 1): a description of features of the intervention or implementation process.
◆ Audit (type 2): a comparison of what is done against specified standards or objectives.
◆ Before–after (type 3): the 'before' state of targets of the intervention compared to their 'after' state.
◆ Comparative-experimentalist (type 4): a comparison of the before and after states of two groups of people who received two different interventions.
◆ Randomized controlled experimental (type 5): a comparison of a defined before and after state of people who were randomly allocated to an intervention and to a placebo.
◆ Intervention to a health organization (type 6): the before and after states of a health organization or personnel after an intervention to service operation (6a), or the impact on patients of such an intervention (6b).

We can see that different designs would answer different questions, and that some designs are more expensive and take longer than others – whether the extra time and cost is worth it depends on for whom we are doing the evaluation and their questions. An evaluation does not need to be an experimental randomized controlled trial (RCT) or comparative design to be useful – it depends on whom the evaluation is for, their questions and their criteria of valuation. An RCT may be too expensive, and take too long for some users, may not be practical or may be unethical. Evaluations are to help people make better informed decisions than they would otherwise do. However, for inexpert users of evaluations who cannot assess the limitations, a poorly designed and conducted evaluation is worse than none at all because it may be misleading.

To discuss the strengths and weakness of these designs in more detail, as well as principles of evaluation, we need to consider some basic concepts which were implied or used in the above descriptions. The next section describes these concepts and lays the basis for the more detailed discussions of the designs in the coming chapters.

---

**Considerations in designing an evaluation**

♦ Which user perspective(s) to take.
♦ Which decisions and actions could be informed by the evaluation: what do people need to know to act differently, or to do with more confidence what they do now?
♦ The users' criteria of valuation.
♦ The criteria of comparison to be used in the evaluation.
♦ The questions which the evaluation aims to answer.
♦ Hypotheses about the effects of the evaluated, and about features of the evaluated which may cause predicted effects.

---

## Design concepts

In summarizing the different designs we relied on the idea of a 'box' which contained or drew a boundary around what we were evaluating. We also touched on the idea of measuring the state of people before and after getting the intervention. The following looks at these and other ideas in more detail and introduces the technical terms which are used in many evaluations. The reader is invited to ask whether these concepts are relevant to all types of evaluation – I think they are, but some evaluators would say that they are only relevant within the experimental perspective.

### 'The box', or 'specifying the evaluated'

It is not possible to evaluate something properly unless you clearly define what it is that you are evaluating. A precise definition of the evaluated is necessary for others to repeat the evaluation and, for those making an experimental evaluation, to ensure that the intervention remains stable or constant while it is being evaluated. If we did not define GDT as including putting the doll under the pillow then we might find that 'it' works for some people and not for others, when in fact different people were using different interventions. It is also difficult for others to decide how to act unless the evaluated is clearly defined. People could read a report about Guatemalan doll therapy which had not defined exactly what was evaluated and might then take decisions which were not justified. Misunderstandings or uncertainty about exactly what had been evaluated are particular problems with service or policy evaluations.

There are three aspects to defining the evaluated. The first is drawing a boundary around what is to be evaluated which excludes things that are not to be evaluated. (This idea comes from systems theory, which can be used to conceptualize the evaluated as a system.) The second is describing what is inside the boundary: the key features of the evaluated which are thought to be significant in some way, usually because these features might cause or influence the effect. The third is defining whether the evaluated is stable or not ('consistent'): for example, whether the same doses of a drug are given at the same times. In service or policy evaluations it is common that the service or policy changes or is changed in some important way while the evaluation is being made – in this case part of defining the evaluated is describing how it changed.

These ideas were simplified in the diagrams above in one of the most important concepts in evaluation – the concept of 'the box'. The box is the boundary we draw around the evaluated. This boundary defines what we are evaluating as within the box – everything outside the box is not evaluated. Some treatments are easy to define and draw a box around, especially drug treatments. But even then we will need to include within the box specifications about when and how the drug is taken, because we may already know that it is only effective if it is taken at certain times and in certain doses. What we specify in the box is connected with our or others' theory about what it is which causes the effects or what is important about the evaluated. The box also includes any specification inside the box about whether the evaluated changes at all during the evaluation (the third aspect above). Usually it does not, or we control or constrain the changes. If we expect changes, one strategy is to try to redraw the boundary more 'narrowly' to exclude the things that change, so that what we evaluate stays constant.

In the example of GDT, what are we evaluating? What do we put in 'the box'? Is the evaluated the doll, and only the doll? Is our entity 'bounded' – can we draw a clear boundary about the thing we want to evaluate? We certainly have to specify that the doll must be put under the pillow of the person who has trouble sleeping, but does he or she have to put it under the pillow? How should we describe the therapy and what will our description include and exclude so that we know what to put in the box and what to leave out?

*Can you make an evaluation of something if you cannot put it in a box in this way?*

The short answer is yes, but you have to make a special kind of evaluation. If we or our sponsors have problems specifying the item to be evaluated, we may need to do a type of evaluation which aims to describe and understand the item. The first evaluation design – the 'descriptive evaluation' – helps to specify the item and to decide what is inside and outside the box. Specifying services and programmes is usually even more difficult than for treatments. It may not be easy to define what it is which we want to evaluate and to draw a box around it. For example, in a type 4 evaluation of day surgery compared to conventional 4–7-day surgical treatment, do we include within the box the care at home provided by community nurses or other carers (Russell *et al.* 1977)?

Later we will see that the challenge posed by alternative medicine is not to the medical profession, but to the conventional evaluation paradigm and to 'box thinking'. For the moment we will use the concept of 'the box', but recognize that many things which we want to evaluate do not have clearly defined or agreed boundaries. Indeed, this may be one reason why we are asked to evaluate it – to help to describe and define it more clearly.

## Dependent and independent variables

Dependent and independent variables are two terms which are frequently used in evaluation reports. Such reports can be confusing if the reader does not understand these terms. A quick way to remember what they mean is to remember that the dependent variable is the outcome of the intervention. Independent variables are what might cause the outcome. This helps the newcomer to evaluation (and to medical research) to remember these terms, but is not an accurate definition.

To be more precise we need to look more closely at an experimental evaluation design, where these terms are most often used, and at statistical analysis. In our GDT example we will first consider outcome and outcome measurement (the dependent variable) and then we will consider the independent variables (things that vary). To keep it simple we will take the patient's perspective, and take ability to sleep as a key criterion of valuation. There are different measures which we could use: hours slept uninterrupted each night, or the number of times waking from sleep and hours awake at each occasion.

If we choose hours slept as our measure, we could say that we have a theory that the hours slept would vary according to whether or not we used the intervention. The outcome which can vary (sleep) is called the 'dependent variable'. We call it a 'dependent variable' because we hypothesize that its variation will depend on other variables, such as the intervention and characteristics of the people involved in the evaluation. The dependent variable is the outcome which we predict will be affected by the intervention.

In the type 5 design there is a control group (which did not get the intervention, or rather got a placebo intervention) and an experimental group (which got the intervention). We assume that the intervention is stable and does not vary. For example, in the GDT example, we assume that the intervention – GDT – can be defined and described in a box, and that everyone in the experimental group got the same therapy. The evaluation then compares the measured outcome of the two groups to see if there is any difference and looks for explanations for the difference. The independent variables are participation in an experimental and a control group, and other characteristics which might vary and explain or predict the outcome.

In practice it is difficult to control possible explanatory variables. The person who is 'taking' GDT may have a cup of coffee before going to bed, and not have coffee on other nights. This 'variation' to the circumstances of the experiment may affect the outcome, as may many other factors which we chose to put outside the box as not being an integral part of GDT. All these possible influences on the outcome are called 'confounding variables' or 'confounding or extraneous factors', and experimental evaluations try to predict what these might be and to stop them varying (control them) or to make adjustments for them.

Finally, note that we do not have to set up an experiment to try GDT and then run it to evaluate GDT (prospective evaluation). One way is to look into the past to find evidence of the effectiveness of GDT (retrospective evaluation). We could do this by interviewing people who have used it in the past, or by looking at diaries which people might have kept or records of their sleeping.

### Summary of terms

*'The box'*: the boundary we draw around the evaluated to define what it is we will evaluate. It includes inside the box a specification of the key features of the evaluated (e.g. a definition of what is and what is not GDT).

*Dependent variable*: one effect we think might depend on the intervention – the outcome (e.g. sleeplessness).

*Independent variable*: a variable which might explain the outcome. The independent variable is what statisticians call any variable which they want to assess for its possible effect on the outcome variable (e.g. being a member of an experimental group).

*Control group*: a group of people who do not get the intervention (e.g. those not using GDT).

*Retrospective evaluation*: looking into the past for evidence about the intervention (e.g. looking back in time to find out what effect GDT had on people).

*Prospective evaluation*: designing an evaluation and then collecting data while the intervention is happening, and usually also before and after the intervention (e.g. doing an experiment by getting people to use GDT and then looking at the results).

*Criteria*: the comparisons against which we judge the evaluated – often effectiveness is one such criterion (e.g. sleeplessness).

*Operationalize*: convert something general (e.g. a criterion) into something specific, usually into something which we can measure (e.g. a measure of amount of sleep, such as a diary record).

*Outcome measure*: a measure of an important predicted effect of the intervention on the target person or population (e.g. a measure of amount of sleep, or of how long awake).

### Do you live longer if you pray?

Francis Galton hypothesized in 1883 that, because it was 'their profession to pray', clergymen would live longer than other members of society. His chapter on the 'Objective efficacy of prayer' reported his finding that the average recorded age of death, in the records of a mixed population which he considered, was 68.14 for lawyers, 68.74 for those in 'trade and commerce' and 69.49 for the clergy (doctors were lowest at 67.31).

As one of the first statisticians, Galton was careful to consider a wide sample and to take 'reliable records' covering a number of years from 1758 to 1843. He notes confounding factors, emphasizing that account should be taken of 'the easy country life and family repose of so many of the clergy'. His conclusion was thus that 'the prayers of the clergy for protection against the perils and dangers of the night, for protection during the day, and recovery from sickness, appear to be futile.'

Was this really an evaluation of the efficacy of prayer, as Galton suggests? If it was an evaluation at all, what did Galton evaluate? If we think of this as an evaluation, what would we call the dependent and the independent variables? What were two of the confounding factors?

(In 1939, in *Science and Everyday Life* it was reported that 'For a long time Anglican clergymen headed the list [of the long lived], but they are now twelfth out of 200, though they still delay their departure for a better world longer than clergy of other denominations.')

## Conclusions

- ◆ Health practitioners, managers and researchers need to understand basic evaluation terms and types of design. Evaluation can be confusing because there are many different approaches and because evaluation reports often assume a background knowledge of the approach used in the report.

- ◆ An evaluation can be made to inform one or more of six interest groups: patients, practitioners, managers, politicians, researchers and scientists, and the media. One or more of these interest groups may be the financial sponsor of the evaluation. To decide the design, the evaluator needs to clarify who will be the main user of the evaluation and their key questions.

- ◆ If we have few resources we can only do an evaluation from one perspective and even then we have to focus on a limited number of questions, or just one.

- ◆ If we have more resources we can seek to answer questions posed by more than one perspective. But we may find that the design we need to answer properly questions posed by one group (e.g. managers) means that we cannot use a design which answers the questions raised by another group (e.g. scientists).

- ◆ Some evaluations do not make it clear whom the evaluation is for, and which 'user perspective' they adopt in designing the evaluation.

- ◆ Design is always a balancing act or trade-off. Inexperienced evaluators are sometimes too quick to decide design before working through purposes, questions and perspectives. However, we cannot define these without some consideration of possible designs and the answers they could give: planning is an interaction between the possible design and the questions and purposes.

♦ Ideas which are fundamental to many types of evaluation are: the operational measure of outcome, the hypothesis about what produces the outcome, an open mind about all the things which might affect the outcome and the idea of control – control of the intervention, and control of things other than the intervention which might vary.

♦ Most evaluations use one of six types of design: descriptive (type 1), audit (type 2), outcome (type 3), comparative (type 4), randomized controlled experimental (type 5) and intervention to a service (type 6).

♦ Nearly all the six designs are used by each of the four evaluation perspectives, but each perspective tends to make more use of one type of design (e.g. the type 4 design is common within the economic perspective). Table 3.1 gives examples.

♦ Each of the six designs has been used to evaluate nearly all of the different types of health intervention: treatments, services, policies and organizational interventions.

*Table 3.1*   Evaluation perspectives and designs – example evaluations of different types of interventions

| | *Experimental* | *Economic* | *Developmental* | *Managerial* |
|---|---|---|---|---|
| *Type 1: Descriptive* | Descriptive evaluations are not undertaken within the experimental perspective, although some clinical case studies might be considered as an evaluation | Cost description of day and inpatient care (Marks *et al.* 1980) | A patient satisfaction survey of an information service (e.g. Greenhalgh *et al.* 1996). Evaluation of a psychogeriatric day hospital (Smith and Cantley 1985) | Managerial assessment of the performance of hospitals in a region in India (Mahaparatra and Berman 1994) |
| *Type 2: Audit* | Audit evaluations are not undertaken within the experimental perspective (but many clinical audits draw on findings from experimental evaluations) | UK Audit Commission assessment of GP fundholders' compliance with financial and other regulations | Rapid assessment of an African district health system (Nordberg *et al.* 1993) (case example 6) | Managerial audit of compliance with law to report patient injuries (Odegård 1995). Quality assessment of health facilities in New Guinea (Garner *et al.* 1990) (case example 7) |

*Table 3.1* Continued

| | Experimental | Economic | Developmental | Managerial |
|---|---|---|---|---|
| *Type 3: Before–after* | Quasi-experimental study of light therapy as a cure for winter depression (Dam *et al.* 1993) | Imaginary example: costs to patients and employers of managing a chronic condition (e.g. asthma), before and after receiving a new treatment or care package | Reporting to staff patients' expectations compared to their experience after the service (Babakus and Mangold 1992) | Prescribing exercise (Lockwood 1994) (case example 2) |
| *Type 4: Comparative experimentalist* | Quasi-experimental comparative study of traditional and alternative cancer services (Bagenal *et al.* 1990) | Comparative costs and effects of using a clinical psychologist in primary care (Robson *et al.* 1984) | Facilitated peer review comparison of two similar services for people with a learning disability (Øvretveit 1988) | Comparison of IT systems for management purchasing decisions (Keen 1994) |
| *Type 5: Randomized controlled experimental (RCE)* | Randomized controlled trial of a community-based discharge team compared to conventional hospital discharge (Townsend *et al.* 1988) | Cost and effectiveness of drug to reduce cholesterol levels (SSSSG 1994). Evaluation of costs and effects of influenza vaccine (Nichol *et al.* 1995) (case example 4) | Feedback to physicians afterwards of the results of an RCT in which they took part which evaluated methods they used for helping patients to stop smoking (Wilson 1992) | Randomized controlled trials are rarely undertaken of services or policies from the management perspective because of difficulties in arranging controls and randomization, and the length of time taken. |
| *Type 6: Intervention to a health organization*<br><br>*(a) Impact on providers* | Quasi-experimental evaluation of the impact on surgical services of media publicity about high hysterectomy surgery rates (Domenighetti *et al.* 1988). RCT of impact of reading material on clinician's care (Cohen *et al.* 1985) | Economic evaluation of a training programme for treating leg ulcers (Pearce 1996) (case example 5) | Impact on health providers of organizational audit in a Swedish hospital (Edgren 1995). Impact on doctors and middle managers of hospital quality management programme (Øvretveit 1996b, 1997b, 1998) | Evaluation of UK NHS reforms in one region (Appleby *et al.* 1994). Meta-analysis of evaluations of the impact on GPs of changes in GP payment systems (Scott and Hall 1995) |
| *(b) Impact on patients* | Quasi-experimental evaluation of the effect of quality assurance on patients and personnel in a mental health service (Sinclair and Frankel 1982) | Cost to patients before and after and other effects of a change in payment system to doctors (Auditor General 1991) | Feedback to staff and patients of the effect on patients of changes to team organization in a community mental health centre (Øvretveit 1994b) | Evaluation for managers and government of the effect on patients of a UK GP fundholding scheme (by the UK Audit Commission) |

*Note:* 'Case examples' refers to the summaries and analyses of evaluation case examples given in Chapter 4.

# Seven evaluation case examples

*It takes skill and practice to make sense of evaluation reports. The value of the report to you depends on your ability to assess it critically for your purposes. Once learned, these skills of analysis are a valuable asset, and also a good basis for designing or managing an evaluation.*

## Introduction

After this chapter you will be able to understand and analyse an evaluation more quickly than you can now. As well as being useful in its own right, this skill is a good foundation for designing and planning an evaluation of your own. Chapter 3 introduced six types of design, which we will now use to analyse and understand 'case examples' of different types of evaluation. We consider evaluations designed to answer the following questions.

- Is prescribing exercise of value to some patients? (A quasi-experimental evaluation of a 'treatment', case example 2.)
- What is the value of substituting nurse practitioners for doctors in primary care? (An experimental evaluation of a service, case example 3.)
- Does influenza vaccination work, and, if it does, is it worth the cost? (An experimental–economic evaluation of a treatment, case example 4.)
- What is the value of giving leg ulcer treatment training to community nurses? (A managerial evaluation of an intervention to a service, case example 5.)
- How can one best assess a district health system in Africa to give the information which managers and planners need? (A developmental evaluation of services and decentralization policy, case example 6.)
- Do health facilities in New Guinea meet defined standards of quality? (A managerial evaluation of services, case example 7.)

The first part of the chapter gives a 'warm-up' example and then the case example summaries of different evaluation studies. The second part of the chapter gives my analysis of each of these case examples. You can use two methods to analyse the examples: the first is a simple method which involves drawing a diagram of the design. The second method is a more detailed analysis. Both are demonstrated in the first case example 'warm-up' summary.

The purpose of this chapter is to test and develop your skills to analyse an evaluation. It also illustrates some of the variety of types of evaluation and the strengths and weakness of each for its purpose. By reading the summaries and by trying to draw the design you can 'learn by doing', and possibly also learn from your mistakes by comparing your analysis with the analysis given later in the chapter.

## Analysing case examples of evaluations

The first is an imaginary case example which is then used to illustrate the 'simple' and then the 'detailed' methods of analysis. The chapter then gives summaries of real evaluations for you to analyse and draw a diagram using one of the 'empty formats' in Appendix 3.

My summaries only give the main points from the published reports because their purpose is to illustrate types of design, and for you to practise carrying out an analysis. You will find when you make an analysis that you are assessing both the adequacy of the report and the design and conduct of the study. Some of your criticisms will be about the report, and some will be about the design and how the evaluation was carried out. This often happens in 'real life'; for example, where the report does not clearly describe certain important features of the study and you cannot tell whether the conclusions are justified because the methods used were not fully described.

---

**Simple analysis of an evaluation**

For the evaluation in question, decide:

1 **Intervention? What was evaluated?** (*Describe the intervention: what is 'in the box' and what is 'outside the box'; the box 'contains' the intervention.*)

2 **Comparisons? What were the comparisons?** (*For example, before and after; what was done compared to what was intended; one treatment or service compared to another or a placebo.*)

3 **Measures? What were the measures, or the data which were gathered?**

4 **Criteria? What were the criteria of valuation?** (*What criteria were used to judge the value of the intervention – these may be implied and not explicit.*)

5 **Design? Which of the six designs did the evaluation use?** (See Appendix 3 or draw your own diagram.)

(Appendix 2 gives a framework for making a more detailed analysis.)

---

### Case example 1 ('Warm-up'): Does Guatemalan doll therapy work?

Extravagant claims have been made for Guatemalan doll therapy as a cure for sleeplessness and other ailments, but there is little reported evidence of effectiveness. Concern was raised by Astra and Littlejohn (1993) that the use of this treatment might delay diagnosis of underlying depression, which could be further exacerbated if the treatment failed. In the evaluation reported in this paper, twenty patients from a primary health care centre in Bergen, Norway, were selected for treatment using this method. The patients were all members of the Norwegian West Coast Sleeplessness Society, which sponsored the evaluation.

The treatment consisted of patients telling their worries to a 2 cm long Guatemalan doll purchased from a distributor in Gothenberg, Sweden. The patients were instructed to tell their worries to the doll for no less than five minutes just before bed, and afterwards to place the doll under their pillow as described in the instructions given with the doll. They were instructed to do this every night for four weeks. The length of uninterrupted sleep was measured over a five-day period before the treatment, and then during the fourth week of treatment for a five-day period. The method of measurement and recording was the patient noting the time of uninterrupted sleep in a diary in the morning.

The findings were that seven patients slept longer on average during the five days in the fourth week of treatment than they did for the five days before treatment. All seven slept longer than six hours uninterrupted on each night. Over the five days before treatment three reported less than four hours' uninterrupted sleep for two nights and four reported less than five hours' uninterrupted sleep for three nights. No significant difference in uninterrupted sleep was reported by the ten other patients for whom measures were available.

The study shows that some benefit was reported by seven out of seventeen patients and that Guatemalan doll therapy might be a cost-effective treatment for some types of sleep disorders.

Try working through the 'simple analysis' questions shown earlier. Before turning to my analysis later in Part II of the chapter, decide which type of design was used, and draw the details of the evaluation in the 'empty format' for that design given in Appendix 3. Once you have done the 'simple analysis', the 'detailed analysis' is much easier. You can try this using the 'framework for a detailed analysis' in Appendix 2, and compare your analysis to the one I did.

### Case example 2: What is the health value of prescribing exercise?

The following is a partial summary of Lockwood (1994). A country-wide evaluation of similar schemes was published by Jackson (1997).

A national fitness survey in the UK in 1991 showed the health problems of inactivity, and a number of studies have reported the health benefits of increased exercise. However, health practitioners have not found it easy to get people to take more exercise. In this study GPs referred patients to one of two local health centres for a 'prescription' of a ten-week gym exercise programme. Patients paid £1.50 per session at the Selby centre and £1 at York, and could also use other facilities, such as the swimming pool. Patients were offered reduced rates for joining the gym after the programme to encourage their continued attendance at the centre: 50 per cent did so at Selby and 67 per cent at York. The only health service financing was £300, which was used to pay for a heart monitor for each of the two centres.

Thirty-six patients took part in the Selby scheme and 108 in the York scheme. The evaluation made a number of physical measures of each patient before and after the ten-week programme, and asked each patient to fill in a questionnaire at the start, at the end and at three and six months after the end of the exercise programme. The findings show a significant reduction in percentage body fat, body mass index and systolic blood pressure, and increases in peak flow. Overall, 91 per cent reported benefiting from the scheme and many reported improvements in self-confidence, feelings of well-being and lower levels of stress. Nine per cent reported that they did not benefit.

The number of patients completing their prescription and joining the gym (67 per cent at York) suggests that GPs are powerful motivators for change, and that this scheme is a good way to covert previously sedentary individuals into regular exercisers.

If you decide which design this evaluation used and carry out the 'simple analysis', you can compare your ideas with the drawing and analysis given later in this chapter.

### Case example 3: The value of substituting nurse practitioners for doctors in primary care

The following is a summary based on Spitzer *et al.* (1974). A related study on how physicians and nurses were affected is reported in Spitzer *et al.* (1973).

In Canada nurses can take specialist training to become 'nurse practitioners', which allows them to become 'co-practitioners' with primary care doctors and to 'share the physician's responsibilities for the continuing care of patients'. This study set out to discover the costs and effects of substituting nurse practitioners for doctors in two family practices in a suburban Canadian town.

After two years of not being able to accept new patients, two family practices decided to try to reduce the demands on the family doctors by assigning patients to nurse practitioners. Families were selected for the evaluation on the basis of one family member having been in contact with either practice over the past 18 months. The families were assigned to either the 'conventional' service with a family doctor and a conventional nurse, or a service where the nurse practitioner was the first point of contact. In all, 1058 families were allocated to the 'conventional service' and 540 families were allocated to the 'nurse practitioner service' which comprised two nurse practitioners. Patients were sent letters explaining the study and patients in the nurse practitioner group were asked to make appointments with their new named nurse instead of their usual doctor.

Four types of measures were made: measures of mortality, patient functioning, quality and costs. Similar mortality was found in both groups of patients, and also similar physical, social and emotional functioning in both groups when measured before and one year after the start of the experiment. The method used to measure functioning ('health status') was a 'special questionnaire instrument'. A follow-up survey found that 97 per cent of patients in the conventional group and 96 per cent of patients in the nurse practitioner group were satisfied with the health services received during the experimental period.

Two methods were used to assess the quality of clinical judgements. The first was to track care using ten 'tracer' indicator conditions which show the effects of the choice of treatment. The second was to assess how 13 common drugs were prescribed. A peer group from the same area set criteria for adequacy of patient management of these ten tracer conditions and 13 drug prescriptions – these criteria were not made known to the nurses or the doctors in the experiment. The findings were that quality of care as defined by these measures was similar for the doctor and nurse practitioner services.

Costs and productivity were compared before and after the one-year experiment by comparing gross revenue, volume of services and number of families under care. The actual revenue dropped by 5 per cent because the practices could not get reimbursement for the clinical services given by the nurse practitioners under the Canadian national insurance system. A 9 per cent rise in income would have resulted if these services had been reimbursed, due to a rise of 22 per cent in families under care and the extra volume of services which was possible. The study shows that nurse practitioners provide a similar quality of care and are cost-effective from the point of view of society, but are not financially profitable for doctors.

Carry out the simple analysis and decide which design this evaluation uses – then compare your ideas with the drawing and analysis given in this chapter.

### Case example 4: Does influenza vaccination work, and, if it does, is it worth the cost?

The following is a partial summary of Nichol et al. (1995).

Between 10 and 20 per cent of the population suffer from influenza every year, which causes significant mortality and morbidity in all age groups. Vaccination is recommended for people in high-risk groups, but this study investigated whether vaccination for healthy working adults would be cost-effective.

Volunteer subjects were recruited from the Minneapolis–St Paul area in the USA through advertisements and other methods, and were screened for eligibility in the trial according to age, participation in full-time employment, not having serious medical conditions or previous vaccination. Questionnaires were given to those taking part in the trial to find out their health status, demographic characteristics, number of children, whether they smoked and amount of sick leave during the past six months. Subjects were randomly assigned to the vaccination treatment or to a placebo: 424 subjects were assigned to vaccination and complete data were available on 409 subjects after the trial; 422 subjects were assigned to the placebo and complete data gathered on 416 subjects afterwards. Checks after randomization found that there was an even distribution in both subject groups of the measured characteristics which might have influenced outcome.

In addition to the data gathered after screening for eligibility, data were gathered from five repeated telephone interviews which were conducted after the vaccination or placebo over the 'influenza season' from December to the end of March 1994. At the first call 7–14 days after injection, subjects were asked about any side effects and, at each further call, whether they had experienced an upper respiratory illness (URI), whether they had taken sick leave (absenteeism) and about recent visits to the doctor (visits). Checks on subject blinding made at the final interview found that subjects identified whether they had received a placebo or vaccine at a rate which was slightly better than chance (57 per cent on average).

Side effects which subjects reported to be associated with the vaccination were the same or larger for the placebo group for nearly all categories apart from 'arm soreness' (e.g. 14.4 per cent of the placebo group reported headaches compared to 10.8 per cent of the vaccine group). Other findings were that, in the vaccine group, episodes of upper respiratory illness were considerably lower (105 per 100 subjects compared to 140 per 100 placebo subjects), absenteeism rates were lower (70 days per 100 subjects compared to 122 days per 100 placebo subjects) and doctor visits were lower (31 visits per 100 subjects compared to 55 visits per 100 placebo subjects). The economic analysis based on these outcomes found that the combined direct and indirect cost savings averaged $47 per person, $6 of this being direct savings on medical costs. Although relying on subjects' self-reports, the study shows that influenza vaccination of healthy working adults results in significant health and economic benefits.

### Case example 5: What is the value of a programme to improve the leg ulcer treatments provided by community nurses?

A summary of Pearce (1996):

It has been estimated that, in the UK, community nurses spend 25–50 per cent of their time treating leg ulcers, but it is thought that some of the treatments given could be more effective. A small group of nurses at an NHS community health service trust reviewed the literature and concluded that nurses were not following best practice for effective treatment of leg ulcers. A training programme was devised for the nurses at the trust which was based on recent research and included education on assessment, seminars on bandaging techniques and use of wound care products, as well as sending nurses recent publications on wound care.

The nurse development officer who was running the project and also evaluating it gathered data about nurse activity before and after the training programme. Data were gathered on the number of patients visited by nurses in the trust, the number of visits made each week, the amount of direct nurse–patient contact time and the wound care products used. The costs of products were calculated from these data and from data on direct nurse–patient contact times. Data were collected from the caseloads of 11 nurses and converted into a percentage of the overall workload.

The findings were that, in April 1995, before the training programme, the total number of patients with leg ulcers who were visited by the trust nurses numbered 80, and these patients made up 13 per cent of the nurses' caseload. In total there were 294 visits per week and the average cost per patient per week for wound care products was £24. By December, and after the training programme, it was found that the number of patients with leg ulcers had dropped to 56, and these now made up 8.6 per cent of the caseload. The number of visits per week had dropped to 171, and the average cost per patient was £16.50.

On the basis of these figures, it was estimated that the annual saving to the trust resulting from the training programme was £50,000 (cost of wound care products saved £28,800, and saving on nurses' time £11,200). The evaluation showed that training in recent research-based knowledge changed nurses' practice, resulted in more effective care and reduced visiting time and prescribing costs.

### Case example 6: Describing a district health system to give African managers and planners the information they need

A summary of Nordberg *et al.* (1993):

Managers and health planners need descriptions of health systems and of population needs in order to manage and plan health services, especially in countries which are decentralizing health management. Some external descriptions have been carried out, notably in Tanzania and Ghana, and WHO has proposed a number of indicators which could be used in such descriptions. This study set out to describe a district health system in Kenya using a method based on rapid assessment principles. Its secondary aim was to make recommendations about practical methods which could be used for descriptive evaluations of health systems and population needs in developing countries.

The subject of the assessment was a health care district in rural Kenya with a district hospital, health centres, community health workers and traditional healers, as well as church mission hospitals and clinics. Three data gathering methods were used to create the description: a self-administered questionnaire given to head personnel of each health facility, structured interviews with these personnel and a review of written reports and records at each facility, although the last were found to be of limited use for the evaluation. The questionnaires gathered data about manpower, physical facilities, finance, activity, service programmes, contact with local leaders, decision making authority and problems and plans. The interviews followed up items covered in the questionnaires and in addition explored such areas as local community involvement, job satisfaction and frustration, and information systems.

The findings were analysed and results were published in a project report which was made available to local managers and planners. The evaluation described the physical facilities in the district and details, including equipment and transport, estimated populations served and some of the problems perceived by the managers interviewed. Recommendations for future simple monitoring systems were given. As well as giving a broad and independent descriptive picture of the health system which was of use in future planning and management, the study gave a stronger voice to local health managers and accelerated the decentralization process. From this one description it is possible to make a number of recommendations for improving services in similar districts. The study also gives a basis for devising self-monitoring and external evaluation methods which use few resources and can be carried out quickly, and which are necessary for decentralized management and more equitable plans.

### Case example 7: Do health facilities in New Guinea meet defined standards of quality?

A summary of Garner *et al.* (1990):

Developing countries are increasingly using and adapting quality methods to ensure and improve the quality of their services. Some, notably Indonesia, are using their national quality programme to assist their decentralization programmes. To monitor these programmes, government, regional and district managers need simple methods for assessing the quality of services which they are responsible for. This project carried out an external evaluation of the quality of health facilities in Papua New Guinea to provide managers with this information.

Health facilities in rural New Guinea are provided at three levels: aid posts for populations of between 500 and 3,000, health sub-centres for populations up to 10,000 and health centres serving up to 20,000. The study audited 76 of a total of 469 centres between March 1987 and August 1988. The study was influenced by a 1988 WHO report on quality assessment in primary health care, and created the standards of quality used in the evaluations in discussion with local experts. A set of standards was developed for rapidly assessing the quality of service, and included standards of the physical facilities, personnel performance, level of supervision and availability of essential drugs and equipment. In addition standards were developed to probe the performance of the centres in providing three procedures: child immunization, obstetric emergencies and febrile convulsions in children.

Data about each centre were gathered to judge their performance in relation to each of these standards. The data gathering methods used were observation, interviewing and assessment of ten patient records, carried out in a visit which lasted 'several hours' to all of the 76 centres by four data collection teams. The data from the patient records for auditing the three procedures were assessed by two different clinicians against national standard treatment protocols.

The data from the visits were analysed and the final report showed the centre's quality performance in a number of areas. The results were summarized in terms of the percentage of centres meeting the defined standards for infrastructure, outpatients, inpatients, obstetrics, maternal and child clinics, pharmacy and supervision. For example, 80 per cent of centres met the standard of 'usually a qualified nurse during outpatient clinics', 60 per cent had 'fridge cold, clean and working well' and 10 per cent had 'no fridge'. The evaluation found poor quality of inpatient records, which made it impossible for clinician assessors to judge compliance with treatment protocols. Misuse of antibiotics was common, and it was also found that the number of medical staff was strongly associated with higher quality scores for meeting standards.

Although the study sacrificed depth of assessment for breadth of coverage in visiting 16 per cent of the country's centres, it was able to assess the variations in quality between centres and areas. These and other data provided useful information for planning, although they gave little information about actual clinical performance, such as accuracy of diagnosis and appropriateness of treatment. The study shows that simple quality audits of health facilities have an immediate impact on quality owing to the 'police car effect', as well as providing useful information for management, and provides a test of methods which others can adapt for similar purposes. Evaluations of financial and activity performance in health systems need to be complemented with evaluation of quality, and this quick, simple and cost- effective audit approach gives one method for carrying out such evaluations.

## Part II: Analyses of the evaluation case examples

The 'warm-up' example is analysed first, using the framework for a simple analysis shown at the start of this chapter. Then a detailed analysis is given of the same example showing in full the questions in the 'Framework for analysing an evaluation' to illustrate how to use the framework given in Appendix 2. The other case examples which follow are summarized using the simple analysis framework.

### Case example 1: A simple analysis of an evaluation of Guatemalan doll therapy

#### 1 What was evaluated?
(Describe the intervention – what is 'in the box' and what is 'outside of the box' – the box 'contains' the intervention?)

*Telling worries to a 'Guatemalan doll' for at least five minutes before bed, and putting the doll under your pillow.*

## 2 What were the comparisons?

(e.g. Before and after? What was done compared to what was intended? One treatment or service compared to another or a placebo?)

*Length of sleep of ten people before and after three weeks of starting the treatment.*

## 3 What were the measures, or the data which were gathered?

*Length of uninterrupted sleep as noted by patients in their diaries in the morning.*

## 4 What were the criteria of valuation?

(What criteria were used to judge the value of the intervention? – these may be implied and not explicit)

*Not stated explicitly, but the criteria for valuation appear to be uninterrupted sleep, harmful effects and cost, although data were only gathered about the first.*

## 5 Which of the six designs did the evaluation use?

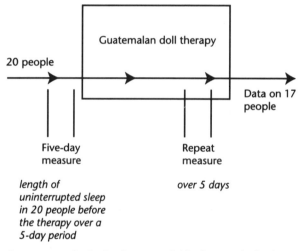

**Case example 1:** Design type 3 ' before and after' comparison of change in one measure.

## Case example 1: A detailed analysis of an evaluation of Guatemalan doll therapy

**Title:** *An evaluation of Guatemalan doll therapy*

**Type of evaluation:** *design type 3 (before–after); type of intervention, treatment; evaluation perspective, experimental.*

### 1 Target of the intervention

Who or what does the intervention which is evaluated aim to change? (e.g. patients, population, providers)

*People who have difficulty sleeping.*

## 2 Description of the intervention

Are the elements of the intervention precisely described, and the boundaries of the intervention defined? (What is 'in the box', and what is not evaluated?)

*Telling worries to a 'Guatemalan doll' for at least five minutes before bed, and putting the doll under your pillow.*

## 3 Users

Who was the evaluation done for, or who might be users of the evaluation?

*The Norwegian West Coast Sleeplessness Society, people who have difficulty sleeping, general medical practitioners and other health professionals, health researchers, health managers.*

## 4 Value criteria and perspective

Are explicit criteria used to judge the value of the intervention, or are these implied? What are the criteria used to judge the value of the intervention? From whose perspective is the intervention evaluated ? What are the comparisons which are used to judge the value of the intervention?

*Not described in the short summary. Implied that if the treatment helps people to sleep uninterrupted for longer, then it is of value. Implied that a harmful effect could be desperate actions taken by people who found that the treatment did not work. Costs were also mentioned. Thus the criteria for valuation appear to be uninterrupted sleep, harmful effects and cost.*

## 5 Evaluation question(s) or hypotheses for testing

*None were given in the summary. The evaluation appears to answer the question, 'Does GDT lengthen uninterrupted sleep in patients who have difficulty sleeping?' It does not answer the more general question 'Does GDT work?'*

## 6 Type of evaluation design

Note in the diagram:

Data-gathering or measures of *the target* of the intervention:

♦ any measures or data gathering of *outcome*, and when and how often these were made (timing and frequency)
♦ any *'before'* measures or data gathering, and when and how often these were made (timing and frequency)
♦ any measures or data gathering of the target *during* the time the target received the intervention?
♦ how many people or providers (targets) began undergoing the intervention and how many people completed? (any 'drop outs'?)

What else was measured or data-gathered about? (e.g. about health workers, or about the intervention?)

*Type 3, outcome 'before and after' design – see the diagram shown in 'simple analysis' above.*

## 7 Data sources and collection methods – details

From whom or what did the data come (data sources), which methods were used to collect data from these sources and what did these data describe?

*The patients noted in diaries in the morning for how long they had slept uninterrupted.*

### Validity

Are valid connections made between the criteria of valuation and the things about which data are collected? (discussion of 'operationalisation' of concepts). How good are the measures as representations of the phenomena or things they are supposed to measure? Did the study use accepted techniques for ensuring validity for the data gathering method which was used?

*The criteria of valuation were not given. If one criterion is uninterrupted sleep then the measure was valid. But the report also implies more general criteria for valuation, such as help with sleep problems or sleeplessness. Uninterrupted sleep is only one type of sleep problem, so the measure is not a valid measure of sleep problems apart from difficulty staying asleep. The connection between the measure and sleeplessness was not discussed in the summary.*

### Reliability

Would others using the same methods get the same results?

Could there be errors in the data (systematic bias or random) introduced by the data gathering method or design? What is the general reliability of this method, and what precautions were used in the evaluation to ensure and maximise reliability (e.g. interviewer training)?

*Patient self-reports, even written near the time, are not very reliable. No other data were gathered to correlate with patient self-reports, or to find out if any patients forgot to record the time in the morning and filled it in later by guessing. The summary does not describe the data gathering method in detail, such as how the patients were instructed to measure the time and record it. Data were not available for three patients, and no explanation is given – they may have dropped out of the study because they found no benefit, which would bias the results. No explanation of how the patients were selected for the study was given – if volunteers were requested they may have been sympathetic to the method and this could bias towards favourable results.*

### 8 Validity of conclusions

Did the evaluation prove that the intervention did or did not make any difference to the targets of the intervention, if that was one of the purposes of the evaluation?

Is there sufficient evidence to support the conclusions?

*It is reported that 'no significant differences were reported by ten patients in uninterrupted sleep', but the criteria of significance were not given. The resources used were not described and so there is no evidence about costs, and no comparisons with other treatments or with a placebo. The limitations of data collection, validity, reliability and of the design do not really justify even the modest conclusion that 'Guatemalan doll therapy might be a cost-effective treatment for some types of sleep disorders.'*

9  **Practical conclusions and actions resulting from the evaluation**

*Not stated or discussed in the summary. This report might persuade some people or health workers to try the treatment, but the concerns about possible harmful effects remain unaddressed by this study.*

10  **Strengths and weakness for the purpose**

Is it clear or implied who is the actual or intended users of the evaluation?

Is it clear which decisions and actions the evaluation is intended to inform?

Strengths and weaknesses of the *design* for the purpose

Was there bias in the sample, in selection before, and in the population measured after (i.e. drop outs)?

Would the study have detected possibly important unintended effects?

What changes might the evaluation itself have produced which reduce the validity or reliability of the findings?

Strengths and weaknesses of the data gathering methods/measures for the purpose?

Were all the limitations described?

Were the conclusions justified by the results?

Could some people be misled by the report?

Would the conclusions be credible to the audience for the evaluation (users)?

Were there any unethical aspects?

Could the purpose have been achieved with fewer resources or in a shorter time?

**Strengths**

*As a simple and low cost evaluation for a patient's association, the evaluation does have some strengths, but the purpose of the evaluation is implied rather than stated. The strengths are that objective measures were attempted of one type of outcome (uninterrupted sleep), which have some validity, and the findings could support a proposal for a more rigorous evaluation.*

**Weaknesses**

*It is not stated clearly whom the evaluation is for or its purpose. No clear questions or hypotheses were set. The decisions or actions which the evaluation could inform are implied rather than stated in the conclusion. The treatment is not well defined and other causes of interruptions to sleep are not controlled. It would have been possible to define a hypothesis for this type of study, which would have strengthened and focused it: for example, 'use of GDT has no effect on length of uninterrupted sleep over a five-day period, four weeks after the treatment is started.' Bias may have been introduced in the selection of patients and in the group for whom data was available, but no details were given. The sample size was small. No attempt was made to discover harmful effects, or whether any effects were sustained with or without the treatment. The summary did not describe the limitations of the design or of the data gathering methods. It is not clear what the evaluators consider a 'significant difference' in uninterrupted sleep in ten patients. The size of the difference in uninterrupted sleep for the seven patients who benefited was not clearly presented.*

## 11 Other comments

*The evaluation is of some use even though it has many weaknesses. It is difficult to see how it could have been done better with the same time and resources without knowing the purpose, which has to be inferred. It also raises interesting questions about how to design an evaluation which would be more conclusive and have more credibility with health professionals, if more finance were available. Should the possible effect of the treatment on other types of sleep problems be investigated? Should patients be interviewed to discover their views of the treatment? How would such a design control for other possible causes or explanations of interruptions to sleep? Can and should a placebo be used to control for some factors? Some of these questions can best be answered by clarifying the purpose of a future evaluation, but there are some questions which might not be answerable by using an experimental evaluation technique for evaluating this type of treatment.*

Which additional comments would you make, under any of the 11 headings? Which of my comments do you disagree with – there is one 'deliberate mistake' (a comment which is not correct). Make two assessments: first, in relation to an ideal evaluation, without worrying about limits to time and money; second, in relation to the time and money which was available, whom the evaluation was for and the purpose of the evaluation.

## Case example 2: What is the value of prescribing exercise?

### 1 What was evaluated?

*An exercise programme at community sports centres, where GPs referred patients and gave a general prescription for exercise. The summary does not give the details of the exercise programme. In fact two separate schemes were evaluated, one at York and one at Selby.*

### 2 What were the comparisons?

*Before and after measures of physical characteristics of people who were referred, as well as patients' views. The two schemes were not compared – at least not in the summary report.*

### 3 What were the measures, or the data which were gathered?

*Continued attendance at the centre after the programme, measures of body fat, body mass index, systolic blood pressure and peak flow rates before and after. Patient answers to questions were also gathered before and at intervals after, but these data were not described in detail, apart from '91 per cent reported benefiting from the scheme, and 9 per cent reported that they did not benefit, with many reporting improvements in self-confidence, feelings of well-being and lower levels of stress.' The summary did not say at what time after the programme these reports were made.*

**4 What were the criteria of valuation?**
*Not stated explicitly, but the criteria for valuation appear to be whether people continued attendance, changes to physical characteristics thought to reduce risks of ill health, 'patient' satisfaction and cost.*

**5 Which of the six designs did the evaluation use ?**

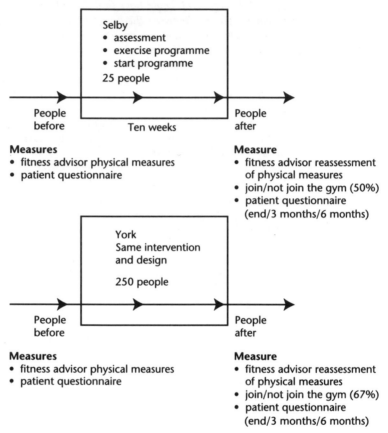

**Measures**
- fitness advisor physical measures
- patient questionnaire

**Measure**
- fitness advisor reassessment of physical measures
- join/not join the gym (50%)
- patient questionnaire (end/3 months/6 months)

**Measures**
- fitness advisor physical measures
- patient questionnaire

**Measure**
- fitness advisor reassessment of physical measures
- join/not join the gym (67%)
- patient questionnaire (end/3 months/6 months)

**Case example 2:** Prescribing exercise, type 3 design.

## Case example 3: What is the value of substituting nurse practitioners for doctors in primary care?

For simplicity, the summary described patients being allocated to either a conventional or a nurse practitioner service – in the actual study patients were randomly allocated. However, because a full type 5 randomized controlled trial design was not used, the summary and the analysis below show a type 4 comparison design (see Spitzer *et al.* 1973, 1974 for full details).

**1 What was evaluated?**
*Two nurse practitioners providing first contact and continuing care in a family practice.*

**2 What were the comparisons?**
*Between a nurse practitioner service and a conventional doctor–nurse service. Before and after measures of functioning, quality and costs.*

**3 What were the measures, or the data which were gathered?**
*Mortality rates during the one year of the experiment. Household surveys of health status, which included physical, social and emotional functioning. Three measures of the quality of care: patient satisfaction, management of ten 'tracer conditions' and prescribing of 13 common drugs (compared to peers' criteria for these items). Total income to the service, volume of care and new patients registered.*

**4 What were the criteria of valuation?**
*Death, health status, quality of care and costs.*

**5 Which of the six designs did the evaluation use?**

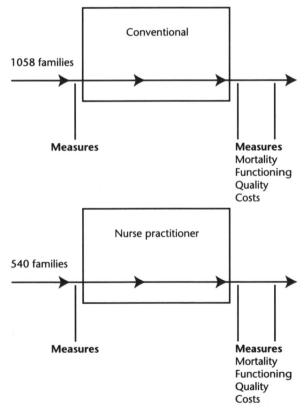

**Case example 3:** Nurse practitioner, type 4 design.

### Case example 4: Does influenza vaccination work, and, if it does, is it worth the cost?

**1 What was evaluated?**
*Influenza vaccination for working adults.*

**2 What were the comparisons?**
*Vaccinated group compared to placebo group.*

**3 What were the measures, or the data which were gathered?**
*Self-reports to questions given over the telephone at five intervals over a three-month period, about side effects, upper respiratory illness rates (URI), sick leave from work and number of visits to the doctor, as well as calculations of the direct and indirect costs and savings of vaccination.*

**4 What were the criteria of valuation?**
*Side effects, illness, days off work, doctors' time, loss of income to the patient and medical costs.*

**5 Which of the six designs did the evaluation use?**

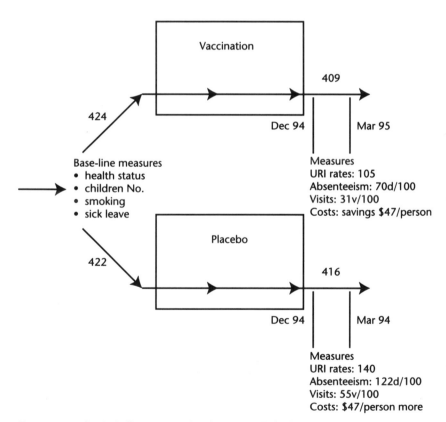

**Case example 4:** Influenza vaccination, type 5 design.

### Case example 5: What is the value of a programme to improve the leg ulcer treatments provided by community nurses?

**1 What was evaluated?**
*A training programme on how to treat leg ulcers, based on a review of recent research on the subject.*

**2 What were the comparisons?**
*Nurse activity and costs before and after the programme.*

**3 What were the measures, or the data which were gathered?**
*Number of patients visited, percentage of patients in nurses' caseload with leg ulcers, total number of visits per week, average prescription cost and cost of nurse–patient contact time per week.*

**4 What were the criteria of valuation?**
*Fewer patients visited with leg ulcers, lower costs.*

**5 Which of the six designs did the evaluation use?**

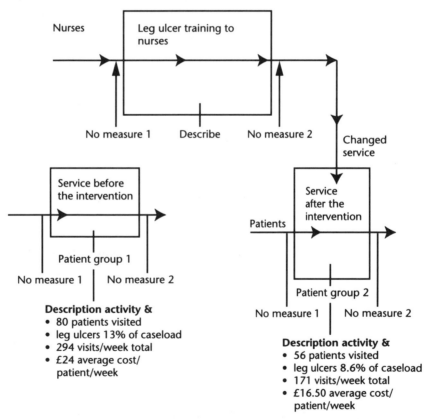

**Case example 5:** Training for nurses in leg ulcer treatment, type 6b design.

### Case example 6: Describing an African district health system

**1  What was evaluated?**
*The facilities, services and organization in a rural Kenyan district health system.*

**2  What were the comparisons?**
*There were no comparisons in the usual sense, such as with other districts or in relation to preset standards. If there were any comparisons it was the external evaluators' ideas of what should be described and was important compared to the health system which they found in action.*

**3  What were the measures, or the data which were gathered?**
*Data were gathered from questionnaires completed by heads of each facility in the district, interviews with each head and written records and reports. Few data were collected on population health needs.*

**4  What were the criteria of valuation?**
*Not stated explicitly, but the criteria for valuation appear to be those of the evaluators, who were also influenced by previous published research. These include whether certain equipment is present, how the services cooperate and relate to local communities and the views of heads of service. It is difficult to define the criteria of valuation used without seeing the full report and without carrying out a detailed analysis.*

**5  Which of the six designs did the evaluation use?**

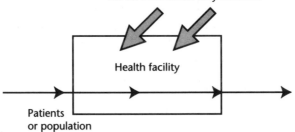

**Case example 6:**  Description of an African district health system, type 1 design

### Case example 7: Do health facilities in New Guinea meet defined standards of quality?

**1 What was evaluated?**
*Health centres serving populations of up to 20,000 in rural New Guinea (76 of them).*

**2 What were the comparisons?**
*Each centre's facilities and performance were compared to defined standards and protocols. Comparisons were also made between centres in terms of their performance on these standards and protocols, and this showed wide variation across the 76 centres.*

**3 What were the measures, or the data which were gathered?**
*The data gathering methods were observation against checklists and interviews by the visiting team. In addition, ten patient records were used by two clinicians to assess a centre's performance in relation to national protocols for three procedures. This assessment was not possible for inpatient services because of the poor state of patient records.*

**4 What were the criteria of valuation?**
*The general criteria of valuation were not stated explicitly, although it is said that the evaluation was influenced by WHO guidelines. However, from the standards and assessment methods it appears that the criteria of valuation are the presence or absence of certain equipment and facilities, compliance with protocols and adequacy of supervision. Clinical performance, outcome or patient satisfaction were not criteria used for judging value in this particular quality evaluation.*

**5 Which of the six designs did the evaluation use?**

Quality standards and protocols

**Visiting evaluators** compare health centre facilities and activity with specified standards

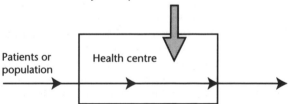

Patients or population

Health centre

**Case example 7:** Quality audit of a health centre, type 2 design.

# Experimental evaluations

*First, and most satisfactory, is experimental design. It is a sad truth that randomised experimental design is possible only for a portion of the settings in which social scientists make measurements and seek interpretable comparisons. The number of opportunities for its use may not be staggering, but where possible experimental design should by all means be exploited. Many more opportunities exist than are used.*

(Webb *et al.* 1966: 6)

*How do you know if you are an instinctive experimental evaluator? When someone proposes a change, while others are thinking about what this will mean, your first thought is, 'A change – this is an opportunity to do an experiment!'*

## Introduction

Experimental evaluations are the most common approach for evaluating simple and complex treatments. For a time they were also considered the ideal approach for evaluating services, policies and organizational interventions, which within this perspective were treated as 'social experiments' to be evaluated. An understanding of the principles of this perspective is essential for all evaluators and users of evaluation. This is not to say that the principles and standards of proof within this perspective should be applied within other perspectives, but the concepts of the experimental perspective do help to illuminate issues within other perspectives, and raise questions which proponents of other approaches need to answer.

The purposes of this chapter are to describe the different designs used within this perspective and their strengths and weaknesses, to enable the reader to assess an experimental evaluation or a proposal for one and to show where to go for more details of particular approaches.

Experimental evaluations apply the principles of scientific method to evaluate an item or intervention. They do this by thinking of the item to be evaluated as an experiment to test a hypothesis. For example, a common approach is to hypothesize either that the intervention has no effect (the null hypothesis) or that it does have an effect. The evaluation tests this hypothesis by measurement to discover any effect, and by a design which excludes other things which could have an effect.

Ideally the 'experiment' is prospective – it is planned and then run, with people being measured, then given the intervention and then measured – rather than retrospective, where the evaluators try to look at what happened in the past as a historical experiment. Some writers do not refer to the retrospective, comparative or case studies described below as experimental because an intervention is not planned and then done like an experiment (e.g. Fink 1993). Here we classify such studies within the experimental perspective because they apply the same scientific-experimental assumptions and similar techniques: strictly speaking they are not planned experiments, but they would like to be. Normally these retrospective studies are called 'observational' studies.

The first type we consider is the randomized controlled trial, which involves a concurrent comparison group (the type 5 design shown in Chapter 3). Then we consider quasi-experimental approaches such as those which compare two interventions (type 4 design), and those with longitudinal self-controls (type 3 design) and historical case evaluations with controls. Finally, we look at 'observational' evaluations carried out within this perspective, such as some longitudinal and cross-sectional observational evaluations, and summarize by way of a checklist for assessing experimental evaluations.

## The randomized controlled trial (RCT)

There are different experimental evaluation designs, but the most well known and the one which exemplifies the principles most clearly is the randomized controlled test or 'trial' design (see the type 5 diagram in Chapter 3). There are five features to this approach. The first is that the evaluator reviews previous knowledge about the item to be evaluated. The aim is to define the hypothesis to be tested by building on previous knowledge. This review helps the evaluator precisely to specify the intervention which previous knowledge suggests has the effect, and to focus on what type of effects would be predicted if the intervention does have an effect: for example, a drug for cancer therapy for an 'x' diagnosis, administered at 'y' time and in a 'z' way. The review also helps to identify other possible factors or variables which could influence the measure, and knowing these helps to create the design and controls. This careful building on previous established knowledge and seeking to extend it by further testing is consistent with the classical model of science.

The second feature is careful selection of people for the trial: this includes deciding how many people will take part, which people to exclude and the practical ways to select them. This is a type of 'filtering' which is done before the selected people enter the trial (shown in the diagram for type 5 designs in Chapter 3; these and other details are discussed in Chapters 11 and 12). The third feature is a design with one 'experimental group' (or organization or area – the 'experimental site') which gets the intervention, and one group which does not get the intervention, termed a 'control group' or 'control site'. If too few people are in each group then any difference may be due to chance rather than intervention, so the design considers the number of people which need to be involved. The fourth feature is that people are allocated randomly to the experimental group and the control group: that is, they have the same chance of finding themselves in either group.

Randomization is important. The intervention is one of many things which may affect the outcome: for example treatment outcomes are often different for men and women, smokers and non-smokers, or for older and younger people. In many patient groups there is a 'spontaneous improvement' over time. Random allocation with large enough groups, and which has been preceded by careful selection, aims to ensure that the characteristics of people which could affect outcome are evenly distributed between both groups, so that any outcome differences between the two groups can be attributed to the intervention. There are many characteristics which we do not know about but which might affect outcome – random allocation means that we can control for these as well. We use 'matching' when we cannot randomize – this is discussed in 'Non-randomized controlled trials' below.

People get better when they feel cared for, regardless of the medicine. A 'significant improvement' was reported in up to 40 per cent of patients with angina, severe postoperative pain, or cough when they were given assurance and a non-active pill (Beecher 1955, see also Benson and Epstein 1975 and Benson and McCallie 1979). While the effectiveness of 'tea and sympathy' and 'tender loving care' are well known to health workers, and these are recognized interventions, they do prove a problem for experimental evaluators. An early recognition of this problem was a note by a well known experimenter, Benjamin Franklin, who wondered in a letter to a colleague whether the improvements in his patients might not have been from the electric shocks he was giving them, but from 'the exercise in the patients' journey, and coming daily to my house, or from the spirits given by the hope of success, enabling them to exert more strengths in moving their limbs' (Franklin 1941). Thus, to find out if an intervention is effective we do not compare it to nothing. One way of controlling for 'experimental effects' is to give the control group a 'placebo' intervention rather than nothing.

A characteristic which could affect outcome is that a person knows that he or she is in a control group or an experimental group. 'Single-blinding' is when the people in the control and the experimental group or site do not know which group they are in. 'Double-blinding' is where both the subjects and the people giving the intervention do not know which is the control group and which is the experimental group. 'Triple-blinding' is where even the evaluators do not know who is in which group until the experiment is over. ('Ethical blindness' is where evaluators do not tell subjects or caregivers that they are taking part in a pre-planned evaluation.)

The fifth feature of the RCT design is that the evaluators use one or a few objective, valid and reliable data gathering methods to collect evidence about people before and after the intervention and placebo. These measures are usually but not always of objectively observable and measurable phenomena, such as physiological or behavioural changes, rather than ratings or reports by the subjects of their subjective states. (Chapter 11 discusses these measures and other data gathering methods.) Previous guidance for RCTs has proposed that a single specific outcome measure is used, but more RCTs are using more than one outcome measure.

RCTs often compare one intervention with a placebo, rather than two interventions because they assess 'absolute effectiveness' rather than 'comparative effectiveness' of treatments. This book follows convention in defining RCTs in this way, but note that some include trials which compare two interventions: for example, Cochrane's original conception was of assessing a new treatment compared to an existing one using randomization rather than matching (Cochrane and Blythe 1989).

An example of an RCT which also illustrates the use of both qualitative and quantitative methods and which takes a medical, economic and social perspective is a study of day and traditional hernia surgery (Russell *et al.* 1977). More details and examples can be found in the publications discussed in the penultimate section of this chapter.

One feature of experimental design is statistical analysis. Different analyses are performed to judge the significance of the results '$P$' values and 'confidence' intervals are discussed in Chapter 12 with regard to data analysis.

In summary, the main features of an RCT design are:

- the intervention (the hypothesis) and the necessary conditions for the intervention are specified and controlled;
- the intervention is compared to a placebo (or sometimes to a conventional treatment);
- bias is reduced by random allocation of people to experimental and control groups, careful selection for the trial and a large enough number of people;
- one or a few measures of possible effects (outcomes) are used;
- the measures are usually of objectively observable or measurable change, rather than of subjective states and subject reports.

---

**Five features of a randomized controlled trial evaluation**

1 Review of previous knowledge to specify the hypothesis to be tested.
2 Selection of people or sites for the test or 'trial'.
3 An experimental and a control group (or site) of sufficient numbers.
4 Random allocation of subjects to each group.
5 Measurement of outcomes in both groups.

---

## Strengths and weaknesses of RCTs

*Is it better to know a little for certain, or more, but not for sure?*

The aim of randomized controlled trials is to try to get irrefutable proof about whether or not there is an effect, and to exclude all possible explanation of the cause of the effect apart from the cause being the intervention. There is no doubt that the RCT has great strengths as an approach to evaluation (Cochrane 1972, Cochrane and Blythe 1989). However, an RCT is expensive and has many practical problems, even for simple treatments. The US Congressional Office of Technology Assessment estimated that 10–20 per cent of clinical interventions have been evaluated by RCTs (Eddy and Billings 1988). Among other issues, this raises the question of how many interventions can or should be evaluated in this way. There are also criticisms of this approach as an appropriate model for evaluating alternative therapies, and for evaluating services and policies. Some of these criticisms apply to all experimental evaluations and to the perspective in general. The ten main criticisms are:

*The intervention and its context*

1 Problems in specifying the intervention: some treatments and many services cannot be precisely specified, especially when new, and 'premature' specification may exclude something which causes the effects. For example, to evaluate an alternative therapy, the way in which an intervention has to be specified in order to carry out an RCT may force the evaluators to exclude or ignore some features of the therapy. It may be necessary to gain a better understanding of the intervention and develop theories about it before considering whether or how it could be specified for an RCT evaluation. RCT supporters, however, argue that carrying out an RCT is a good way of working towards a specification, because showing no effects under the RCT conditions does not pretend to prove that other conditions and combinations would have no effect, but it does give some certain knowledge.

2 Problems of control: difficulties in excluding influences other than the intervention and in keeping the intervention stable. If the intervention is long term, then the chances increase of other factors combining with the intervention to have an effect, or of these factors weakening the effect of the intervention ('confounding' factors or variables). In a laboratory it is easier to ensure that the same intervention is consistently applied ('standardization') and to exclude other factors. But in practice settings and in organizational evaluations this is usually not possible (Øvretveit 1997c).

*The subjects (or 'targets')*

3 Problems creating controlled experimental and control groups: it is difficult in practice to ensure that true randomization has been done. The latter problem applies even more to control techniques for 'matching', discussed below with regard to non-randomized trials. People will have different general health conditions and their diagnoses will vary, and this can result in important differences between experimental and control groups, even in large samples and with careful preselection. People should know that they are taking part in an evaluation, even if they do not know if they are in the control or experimental group, and this knowledge may affect outcome (the 'Hawthorne effect'). In the case of services or policies it is not possible to conceal from people that they are getting or not getting a service, or the type of service (e.g. living in a private or public home for older people).

*The effects and outcomes*

4 RCTs often concentrate on a few measurable outcomes and ignore others, such as patients' experiences. The scientific paradigm of the

experimental evaluation excludes effects and outcomes which cannot be measured, but which may be important. What is a valid measure of the outcome of psychotherapy? Surely effectiveness measures of psychotherapy are different for each person? If we narrow our focus to measures of symptom relief, we do not discover effects such as feeling and being more autonomous, more confident and trusting, and preventative effects against future stress-related breakdown. Both the scope of the outcomes and the type of outcome considered may be limited in this type of evaluation.

5 Some outcomes and impacts may take time to become evident, but, to minimize confounding factors, many RCTs measure outcome a short time after the intervention.

### Other criticisms

6 The findings of the evaluation might not generalize to other settings. The conditions of everyday practice are different from the conditions under which the evaluation was done. If the evaluation proves effectiveness, it may be difficult for clinicians to ensure that the intervention is always carried out in the way it was done in the evaluation.

7 The statistical techniques for analysing and presenting the results (in simple terms, the probability of the hypothesis being true or false) traditionally show averages and do not show possibly important effects for a few individuals – averages may mask important 'outliers'. However, one technique used by clinical psychologists presents the before and after scores of individual patients on a scatterplot, thus showing individual changes. While this technique is not suitable for large samples, it is one of a number of techniques which have been developed to meet the criticisms of methods used in RCT and other experimental evaluations.

8 Ethical issues: even if it is suspected that the intervention has an effect, is it fair to withhold its possible benefits from the control group?

9 The costs and resources: planning and doing a valid RCT is extremely expensive and it takes time before the results are available. Evaluating a new drug costs between $70 million and $145 million and can take between five and eight years. Given that the results of RCT evaluations are often not conclusive and may be of limited usefulness, is it justified to spend a large amount of resources in this way? The resources could be used for other purposes, the evaluated may be only of potential benefit to a few and there may be less expensive alternative evaluation designs.

10 Reductionist science: it is said that the traditional natural science approach is to account for phenomena at the lowest level of investigation (e.g. explaining disease states in terms of biochemical elements). Experimental evaluations have been criticized for being predisposed to reductionism and for seeking causes in the smallest elements. This may or may not be true for some evaluations, but perhaps a more valid criticism is that traditional experimental evaluation design is not well suited to investigating social systems or the complex way in which some interventions may work in interaction with subjects or their environment. 'There are only atoms – everything else is mere social work' (an anonymous research biologist).

## Summary

Some of these criticisms are well founded for some experimental evaluations, and do rule out RCT as an appropriate design for evaluating some types of intervention. However, it is important to distinguish between three types of criticism: criticisms of the data gathering and analysis methods which are often used, the criticisms of types of design and the criticisms of the experimental perspective. For example, although most RCTs have traditionally not used subjective patient reports, many more are now using such data gathering methods – a criticism of a preference for some types of data gathering method is not a valid criticism of the design principles or of the perspective.

A well designed RCT with careful controls can discover whether or not an intervention has an effect and the size of the effect, but can also identify causes of the effect if there is one. There are not many things in life more certain than the findings of a meta-analysis of a number of high-quality RCTs which shows that the RCTs came to the same conclusions.

---

### Some terms used in experimental evaluations

*Control group or control site*: a group of people or an organization that does not get the intervention. The evaluation compares it to the experimental group or site, which gets the intervention. People are randomly allocated to either group, or, if this is not possible, the control group or site is 'matched' with the experimental group.

*Randomization*: allocating people in a random way to an experimental or a control group.

*Matching*: ensuring that people (or organizations) in the experimental and control groups (or sites) are the same in all the characteristics which could affect the outcome of the intervention given to the experimental group or site.

*Cohort*: a group of people, usually sharing one or more characteristics, who are followed over time.

*Confounding factors or variables*: something other than the intervention which could influence the measured outcome.

*Randomized controlled trial*: an experiment where one group gets the intervention and another group gets a placebo, and people are assigned to each group in a random way.

*Placebo*: something which people think is an intervention, but which has no known 'active ingredient'.

*Single-blinded trial*: the people (subjects) in the control and experimental groups do not know which group they are in.

*Double-blinded trial*: neither the subjects nor the service providers know which group is the experimental and which is the control.

An important issue is whether evaluators should use the RCT as an ideal from which they reluctantly diverge. In my view all evaluators and users of evaluations should know and understand the basic principles of RCT, even if they do not know the details of some of the methods, such as the different statistical techniques. We need to know how to assess a reported RCT evaluation to decide whether and how to act. Further, RCT design confronts issues which arise in most types of evaluation, such as recognizing possible bias and controlling for bias, attention to measurement and data collection, careful specification of the item to be evaluated, care in attributing changes to possible causes and issues of replicability and generalization. All these issues need to be addressed in most types of evaluation.

We now turn to two other categories of evaluation carried out within the experimental perspective: quasi-experimental and observational evaluations.

## Quasi-experimental and observational evaluations

We have noted that the experimental perspective and designs are most often used for treatment evaluations, and touched on the problems of using this approach to evaluate services, policies and health reforms. Other evaluation designs are used where conditions do not allow randomization and a full RCT, but where evaluators still want to work within the scientific experimental paradigm and to test hypotheses about interventions (Cook and Campbell 1979).

Campbell and Stanley (1966) first used the term 'quasi-experiment' to describe evaluations which used experimental principles and which tried to create experimental conditions, but where randomization and other controls were not possible. Their argument was that RCT design was not possible for many social interventions and programmes, but that experimental principles should still guide how the evaluator approached the design and conduct of an evaluation. Below we consider the most common types: the non-random controlled trial; the comparative trail; the longitudinal evaluation with 'self-controls'; the historical case–control evaluation, and observational evaluations using experimental principles.

First, here are two examples of quasi-experiments with some controls. A study which shows that useful results can be obtained from evaluations which fall far short of the basic experimental criteria is that of Hoey *et al.* (1982). In this study nurses in a morning clinic offered influenza vaccine to patients, and a comparison was made between the morning vaccination rates and the afternoon rates with the traditional physician approach. Some factors were controlled for over the six-week trial, which found that the traditional approach led to 2 per cent of 348 patients being vaccinated compared to 52 per cent of the 435 'morning patients'. Another is an observational cross-sectional study in the US of variations in rates of use of treatments for 123 surgical and medical patients (Chassin *et al.* 1986).

### Non-randomized controlled trials (concurrent comparison group)

As the name suggests, these tests or trials are like RCTs, with an experimental and a control group and other controls, but people are not randomly assigned to either group (e.g. same variation of the type 4 design shown in Chapter 3). If evaluators cannot randomly allocate, or they are evaluating an organizational intervention, then they use 'matching' to try to ensure that the experimental or control groups or sites are the same in all important respects. In this way evaluators try to ensure that the measured effects can only be attributed to the intervention because they have tried to control for other possible causes of the effects. A variation of this design is where two interventions are compared, rather than one intervention and a placebo (e.g. a drug treatment compared to surgery).

Matching is better if made before the intervention by assessing people for the characteristics and then allocating them in a matched way to experimental or control groups (pre-selection or prospective matching). 'Paired matching' is a version of this, where a person (or site) is selected for one group, and then someone (or site) is selected for the other group that has the same characteristics as the first person (or site). The control possible in 'retrospective matching' is usually less because evaluators look back in time at the characteristics of the people (or sites) in the experimental and control groups, compare the groups and use statistics to assess whether the differences in outcomes are due to the intervention or other characteristics. 'Group matching' is trying to ensure that each group contains on average the same number of people with the same characteristics.

Is your new treatment better than your old treatment? One way to find out is to create an experimental group of patients receiving the new treatment, and compare outcomes to those from a control group made up of matched patients who received the old treatment (a concurrent experimental group, compared to a historical control). Note, however, that Sacks *et al.* (1982) found that studies using historical–current control techniques were four times more likely to report a 'significant improvement' with a new therapy than were studies with concurrent randomized controls.

### Longitudinal experimental evaluations using 'self-controls'

In these designs groups or individuals act as their own controls over time. Only one group of subjects gets the intervention, but in other respects the intervention is treated like an experiment (e.g. the before–after type 3 'outcome' design in Chapter 3). The evaluation is planned and a 'before' or 'base-line' measure is made. Then the group gets the intervention and an 'after' measure is made. The evaluators consider to what extent the difference between the before and after measures can be attributed to the intervention. Without a control group it is not possible to be sure that changes, if any are found, would not also occur to a greater or lesser degree in a group which did not get the intervention. These are sometimes called 'prospective cohort studies'.

A variation which is sometimes possible is the 'cross-over' design. One group gets intervention A and one group gets intervention B, then the groups switch and get the intervention which the other group would get, with a measure of change before switching. Surely both groups get the same overall intervention, but in a different sequence? True, but this design produced some interesting findings when both groups received eight sessions of behavioural/cognitive psychotherapy and dynamic psychotherapy. It made it possible to compare outcomes in both groups before changing therapies, and then after the second set of eight sessions. It also allowed evaluation of a combined therapeutic approach which had been thought to be effective and avoided the practical and ethical problems of using a placebo or no-treatment controls in a clinical setting (Shapiro and Firth 1987).

## Single 'target case' experimental evaluation

In this variation, an intervention is made to a single 'target case' (one patient or one organization), and before and after measures are made, with the aim of finding proof for or against the intervention causing the change in the measure. This design has some similarities to the clinical case study in traditional medicine, but the controls and measures are more rigorous (Barlow and Hursen 1994). One version which is suitable for some treatments is where the intervention is made to the patient and then withdrawn, and this cycle is repeated with measures made before and after the intervention: the ABAB . . . or 'reversal' design (Johannessen 1991). This version depends on the patient's condition reversing to an original state, and this assumption may be questionable. In randomized single target case experimental design, the evaluator does a 'before' measure, then randomly assigns a treatment (which may be a placebo) and then does an 'after' measure. Designs like these have been used in evaluations of alternative medicines.

Note that 'case study' can refer to three very different types of research. It is most commonly used to refer to a method of traditional applied clinical research where one patient is observed in a 'clinical descriptive case study'. The second is the 'single target case experimental evaluation', which was just discussed, where an intervention is made to one patient or one organization (the target or subject) and the effects are studied – this has more rigorous controls than an observational clinical case study. The third type of case study is also an evaluation design, but considers the

---

**Myths about experimental evaluations**

- the RCT is the only design used for experimental evaluations;
- if you cannot control it, you cannot use an experimental design;
- experimental evaluations do not use qualitative data or investigate patients' subjective experience;
- experimental evaluators hold that the only way to evaluate a service, policy or health reform is to carry out an RCT;
- there are no good RCTs of alternative or complementary therapies.

intervention as the case, not the patient or target exposed to the intervention. This is the 'descriptive case study evaluation', shown as the type 1 design in Chapter 3, where the intervention is described, and sometimes also the effects of the intervention, but there is no attempt to control or use experimental methods.

Yin (1989) refers to this type in his definition of a case study as 'an empirical inquiry that investigates a contemporary phenomenon with its real-life context, especially when the boundaries between phenomenon and context are not clearly evident'. In Chapter 7 we consider the last type in more detail when looking at developmental evaluations.

## Historical case–control evaluations (retrospective)

Case–control evaluations are retrospective. Evaluators find people or organisations which exhibit a characteristic ('cases'), and then try to find out what caused the characteristic. They do this by comparing the people or organizations to others which do not have the characteristic, but are in other respects the same (the control group or organization(s)). They differ from experimental and quasi-experimental studies in that people are selected for the study group because they show the outcome characteristics which the evaluation is interested in – they are not selected so as to be subjected to the intervention or control and then measured. Some historical 'cohort' studies are of this type although 'cohort' should really only be used to describe a prospective 'forward-following' study of a group.

This is not a real experimental evaluation because it is looking back over time, but case–control evaluations do follow the principles of prediction and of control to minimize for bias, and are considered in this section as a quasi-experimental approach. They can never indicate as strongly as RCTs or even experimental comparative control can that the difference was due to a particular cause, but they can show associations or lack of evidence of associations and suggest possible causality. Case–control evaluations depend on good historical documentation and statistics as well as expert statistical analysis. They sometimes use data which were reported in other research, or from service case records.

Strictly speaking, any experimental or quasi-experimental approach should be prospective, where 'the experiment' is run after the design is made. This fits most closely with the natural science experimental model, where a prediction or hypothesis is made and the experiment or intervention is run to test the hypothesis. In this way the experiment can be designed to maximize the control of possible variables and influences and ensure accurate measurement. Purists argue that retrospective evaluation – where evaluators look back in time to find out the effects of an intervention – should not be termed 'experimental' because the evaluator does not have the same controls, and call these case–control studies 'observational' studies. However, retrospective evaluations are often done using the same experimental principles and, with statistical and other techniques, can approach the controls used in prospective experimental evaluations.

## Observational evaluations (cross-sectional or longitudinal)

The last types of quasi-experimental evaluation which we consider here are other observational studies. These typically give a description of variations of practice or of use of new technology across areas at one time (cross-sectional) or of variations over time (longitudinal). Some descriptive case studies which use experimental principles fall into this category. Hypotheses about the case(s) to be observed are specified, the case(s) are carefully selected to be representative or to exemplify features which allow generalization, the observation is done, and the results are analysed and presented. Some prospective cohort studies are called 'observational evaluations' (e.g. Fink 1993). Note that observational studies are not usually described as experimental, but are considered here as falling within the experimentalist perspective.

---

**The main types of evaluation within the experimental perspective**

*Full experimental*

1 Controlled trial – randomized.
   (comparing an intervention to a placebo or an alternative treatment)

*Quasi-experimental*

2 Controlled trial – non-random controls (e.g. matched).
   (comparing an intervention to a placebo or an alternative treatment)
3 Self-controls – time series (or 'longitudinal')
   (a) group tested before and after the intervention;
   (b) single-case experimental.
4 Retrospective case–control (historical).
5 Observational (cross-sectional or longitudinal).

---

# Where to find out more and examples

We do not know whether having a baby in hospital is safer than having one at home. Should a controlled trial be carried out to find out? This was a question discussed in a fascinating debate published in the *British Medical Journal*, and which illustrates many of the issues, strengths and weaknesses of RCTs and of other designs (Volume 312, pp. 753–7, 23 March 1996). Part of the discussion drew attention to the importance of clearly defining the question:

> To ask whether there should be a trial of home versus hospital delivery puts the cart before the horse, by proposing a method before deciding on the question to be answered.
>
> (Macfarlane 1996)

For a simple overview of RCTs, two of the best introductions are Newell (1992) and St Leger *et al.* (1992). For more details and examples, a good general text is Holland (1983), and both simple and more sophisticated methods for carrying out a clinical trial are discussed at length in Pocock (1983) and Schwartz *et al.* (1980). A useful short paper on how to assess experimental evaluations is that of Fowkes and Fulton (1991), and the excellent short book by Crombie (1996).

For quasi-experimental designs, there is a useful discussion of how to investigate causal relations in Sechrest *et al.* (1990). Quasi-experimental evaluations for services and policies are described in a US text by Cook and Campbell (1979). Case control designs are discussed in detail by Schelesselman (1982), and a paper by Sasco *et al.* (1986) discusses their use in evaluating screening programmes. Longitudinal and single-case quasi-experimental designs are discussed in Guyatt *et al.* (1988), Aldridge (1988) and Johannessen (1991), and single-case research designs in Kazdin (1982). There are similarities between these methods in the case of individual patients (Guyatt *et al.* 1986) and the methods of continual improvement, where the 'case' is the organization of care (i.e. the intervention) (Berwick 1996). Yin (1981, 1989) discusses how single-case study design can be developed to give a more rigorous evaluation method.

Some of the most interesting discussions of experimental evaluation can be found in writings about evaluation designs for alternative or complementary health care. The best general overview is to be found in Mercer *et al.* (1995). Patel (1987) gives a shorter analysis and designs for homeopathy are discussed in Kleijnen *et al.* (1991). Both believers and 'new age' evaluators will not be disappointed by a collection of papers in Johannessen *et al.* (1994), and the discussion of the technical, logical, moral and philosophical critique of controlled trials in a short paper by Heron (1986).

*When is a placebo not a placebo? When it is a psychotherapy placebo.*

Does psychotherapy work, and if so which type is best? These and other more specific questions have been answered in different ways, in another evaluation subject area where paradigm and methodological battles have been fought for many years. One even-handed overview of psychotherapy evaluation, which examines most of the methodological issues and also attempts a meta-analysis, is by Smith *et al.* (1980). While it is dated, the issues it covers are as relevant as ever to the 'to trial or not to trial' debate, not least because it also considers evaluation of drug therapies for mental illness. Written by statisticians, it gives a painless and readable exposition of the methodological issues and findings in one branch of evaluation, which has relevance for most other treatment and service evaluations. An interesting anthropological discussion of the 'placebo effect' can be found in Helman (1994).

## Should we act on this RCT? Twelve questions for assessing an RCT

Practitioners and managers need to assess the scientific validity and practical implications for their service of a relevant RCT or quasi-experiment before acting. The following gives a simple questions checklist of the requirements which an RCT of a treatment should meet. Many are also relevant for assessing quasi-experimental evaluations of services, programmes and policies.

1  Is the intervention precisely defined?
2  Is the hypothesis stated and will confirmation or disconfirmation give unambiguous evidence of the effects of the intervention?
3  Can you tell which patients were excluded and which diagnostic criteria were used to select patients for the trial
4  Are patients in normal settings likely to be similar in important characteristics to those in the trial? (One criterion for judging generalizability of the evaluation.)
5  Was the size of groups large enough to show that the difference found was greater-than-chance?
6  Was allocation to groups random and blinded? Were subjects, health-care workers and evaluators blind with regard to who was in each group, until after all the data were returned?
7  How do we know that all experimental patients took the full treatment (how many 'drop-outs')?
8  How valid, reliable and sensitive were the outcome measures, were they done at a sufficiently long time after the intervention and, if the time was long, what other confounding factors might have influenced outcome?
9  Were the statistical analyses valid and were the assumptions noted?
10 Does the report list and assess all possible confounding factors and variables?
11 To what extent can we generalize the results of this experiment to our service and patients?
12 Was the evaluation ethical, and if not, should or can we ignore it?

## Conclusions

♦ All the approaches to evaluation described in this chapter follow traditional experimental scientific principles. This is most clearly demonstrated in the RCT, which treats the intervention as an experiment, measures effects and controls for other possible explanations using methods such as standardization, a control group and randomization.

♦ Experimental evaluations aim to discover whether an intervention has effects and the causes of effects, by using an experimental design to test a hypotheses and to exclude other explanations for the effects, and by using methods to minimize sources of error and bias.

♦ Prospective trials are interventions designed to test a hypothesis. Retrospective 'experimental' evaluations do not change anything but look at what happened in the past as if it was an experiment, to test a hypothesis about the posited historical 'intervention': they are usually termed 'observational' studies.

♦ The different types of evaluation carried out within the experimental perspective are the randomized controlled trial (single-, double- or triple-blinded) and quasi-experimental and observational evaluations (Box 5.1 gives a summary).

♦ The experimental perspective has traditionally used one or a few objective measures of outcome, but more RCTs and many other quasi-experimental designs are now using subjective data from patients and quality of life measures.

♦ The experimental perspective involves a set of assumptions about how to conceptualize the item to be evaluated, and about how to create valid knowledge through experimental designs. Evaluators working within this perspective sometimes do not accept that evaluations made from another perspective give valid or useful knowledge, or that such studies should really be called evaluations.

♦ The experimentalist perspective addresses issues which need to be considered in most types of evaluation, such as recognizing possible bias and controlling for bias, attention to measurement and data collection, careful specification of the item to be evaluated, care in attributing changes to possible causes and issues of replicability and generalization.

# 6 ◆ Economic evaluation

*They could tell us the cost of everything, but we still had to decide the value of the service.*

*The point of valuing something in money terms is so that we can easily compare its value to something else. This reminds us that we could spend the money on other things. But to express the value of different things in one measure, such as money, we make many assumptions and ignore features which are difficult to express in these terms.*

## Introduction

Although it is a 'younger brother' to experimental evaluation, economic evaluations has now made its own home and achieved recognition in the health sector. Economic evaluations are the second most common type in the health sector, and are often combined with or built on to experimental evaluations. The economic perspective is used to evaluate treatments, different services and policies, health reforms and health projects, as well as interventions to health organization. Some understanding of the principles of economic evaluation are important even for those who will never carry out or use an economic evaluation. Most health evaluations need to pay attention to the resources used by and consequences of an intervention. Many economic concepts and ways of thinking are helpful in designing an evaluation study and also in deciding how to act on the findings.

Are they unethical? A surprising question, but economic evaluations can raise strong passions. There are those who argue that not to look at the costs of an intervention is irresponsible because it ignores how the money could be spent on other things. Yet there are those who oppose 'reducing everything to money' – different interventions cannot be compared or valued in 'simplistic' terms, and doing so hides the assumptions of the calculations behind apparently objective and precise figures. And it is true that, after following the relentless logic from calculating the costs of nurses' time through to the value of a year of life expressed as a number, we seem to have missed something along the way – it all makes perfect sense, but it feels senseless.

Economic evaluations can make it easier for people to avoid the painful and complex work of weighing up all the considerations in judging the value of an intervention. But they can also give information about the use of resources which is essential for making judgements of value and which we as health workers and as citizens increasingly need to consider – they can force us to confront the unthinking choices which we often make and would rather not make consciously. This chapter will not equip you to carry out an economic evaluation, but it will introduce you to the concepts and principles of the economic perspective, and to the main types of economic evaluation studies: cost-description, cost-minimization, cost-consequence description, cost-effectiveness, cost-utility and finally cost-benefit – the last being a term which is incorrectly used to describe almost any economic analysis. The chapter will also sensitize you to the assumptions underlying different types of study, because there is virtually no one working in the health sector who does not now need to be able to assess the strengths and weaknesses of an economic evaluation.

### The economic perspective

Economists are philosophers of scarcity. The economic perspective focuses on how many resources are used by an intervention and on the consequences of the intervention which can be quantified. Yet to define the economic perspective in this way is to leave out the most important assumption of the perspective, which is that the resources used by an intervention could always be put to other uses, or rather that the resources are being withheld from other uses. This is the concept of 'opportunity cost', which lies as the heart of the economic perspective, and which forces us to recognize choices.

Thus a more accurate definition of economic evaluation is 'the comparative analysis of alternative courses of action in terms of both the costs and consequences', where the alternative could be no action (Drummond *et al.* 1987). The consequences include the effects on a patient or on the beneficiary of the intervention. Sometimes 'consequences' include resources which are saved or used as a result of the intervention by patients (e.g. travel costs), their families, a health service and society.

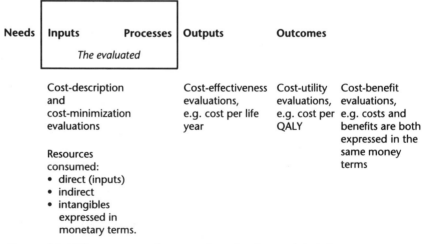

**Figure 6.1** Different types of economic evaluation and their focus

Economic evaluations differ in the ways in which they assess costs and consequences and in what they include and exclude as costs and as consequences (the scope of the evaluation). Figure 6.1 uses a time diagram to show the different types of economic evaluation underneath the aspect of the intervention's inputs, outputs and outcomes which the type of evaluation focuses on.

## Cost-description and (cost-minimization evaluations)

*How much does it cost, and which is the least expensive?*

Cost-description and cost-minimization evaluations only calculate the resources used in interventions ('inputs'), and usually quantify these resources in money terms. This makes it easier to compare the total resources used by different interventions. Examples are cost-description evaluations of inpatient care compared to day care: Marks *et al.* (1980) report retrospective costing of a range of procedures, including 'breast biopsy and partial mastectomy', finding that inpatient costs for the latter were on average $210, compared to day patient costs of $26.

Note that many cost evaluations only describe the costs of one intervention, and are thus termed 'partial' evaluations because they do not explicitly compare the intervention with one or more alternatives (i.e. they use design types 1, 2 or 3 (Chapter 3)). In economic evaluation, 'description' usually means description of one intervention and not a comparison: for example, a cost description of the resources consumed by a new drug treatment for asthma, or a nursing service, or a new personnel overtime policy. A 'cost-consequence description' is also a 'partial' economic evaluation because, although it considers consequences as well as costs, it does not compare the intervention with alternatives. However, there is an implicit comparison because the costs of the one intervention are expressed in money terms and this invites comparisons with other uses of the money, although many of these other uses may not have been so precisely costed.

Cost description is similar to what many of us do when we calculate the costs of a proposed or past action. But it involves two things which we do not usually do when looking at the cost of, for example, a holiday. First, cost description calculates accurately the cost of all resources consumed by the health service: for example, the cost of all staff time and materials, electricity, administration and other 'overheads'. Second, it often lists a range of other costs, such as to other welfare services, to patients and relatives and to society, as well as the 'intangible costs'. The resources used which are described depend on the perspective of the study: the three most common are the health service, the patient and the societal perspective. It is the duty of the professional evaluator to draw attention to the perspective taken and to note the resource uses which are important to other perspectives.

We note that this simplest of economic evaluations makes many assumptions about how to quantify the resources consumed by one intervention, and, if two or more are compared, how to equate and compare the resources consumed. There are assumptions about what to include in the cost of 'overheads' (is training included?) and in the costs of capital and rate of depreciation. There are questions about how broad the scope of the costing should be: should it include environmental costs? Economists have different views about which costs should be considered as direct, indirect and intangible, and about the breadth of scope of costing. A technique called 'sensitivity analysis' is useful because it allows us to vary an assumption to see how it affects the results of the study: for example, a graph which shows how varying the costs charged for 'overheads' affects the total cost of an intervention. However, we should really call calculating costs 'economic valuation', so that we remind ourselves that it is not a technical value-free procedure, but involves many assumptions.

Cost-minimization evaluations are more complicated than cost descriptions because they aim to find the lowest cost alternative. They assume that the consequences of the alternatives are the same, or that the differences are unimportant. Examples are cost-minimization evaluations of conventional or short-stay treatments, of comparable outcome drugs, of home and hospital treatment, of day compared to inpatient treatment and of private and public services. Like cost-description evaluations, cost-minimization includes assumptions about costing inputs, but also assumptions about outcomes which may or may not be valid, even if previous RCTs have show insignificant differences in outcome.

The number and type of assumptions increase dramatically when we move from quantifying inputs to quantifying the consequences of an intervention, and then to comparing alternatives with different outcomes. For example, is the time of an unemployed person to be costed as the same as that of a highly paid person? What is the cost of suffering when waiting for a treatment (a 'non-resource use consequence')? How should we compare the value of a benefit now to receiving that benefit in five years time – what 'discounting' formula should we use? This leads us to the three most well known types of economic evaluations: cost-effectiveness, cost-utility and cost-benefit.

## Cost-effectiveness evaluations

*If we compare the effects of each intervention on a single, simple measure, which intervention gives better value for money?*

Cost-effectiveness evaluations quantify both the costs of one or more interventions and the effects. These evaluations use one all-embracing measure of effect as a way of comparing alternatives – effects are often quantified in terms of number of lives saved, or life years or disability days which are gained or lost, or cases detected in a screening programme. Where only one measure of effect is used it is easier to compare which of the alternatives has the greater effect on the one measure and to compare the costs of the alternatives for their different single effects. The art is to decide which single outcome measure most captures the value of the results of the intervention. We can see that some of the weaknesses of this approach are similar to those of experimental trials which concentrate on one measure of outcome.

An example is a Swedish evaluation of a drug to reduce cholesterol levels, which also builds on an RCT evaluation (SSSSG 1994). The RCT found in the experimental group 30 per cent less total mortality and 42 per cent less coronary mortality five years after the treatment (all patients in the trial already had heart disease). Jonsson's economic evaluation took life years gained as the measure of effect, and estimated how many fewer hospital days the treatment resulted in and the cost of this. Taking these costs and the lives saved (treating 100 patients with the drug for five years would save four deaths which would otherwise occur), he estimated that the cost of the treatment and the savings meant that each life year gained cost between $6,500 and $8,500. Note that in this case the costings do not include indirect costs, nursing home costs or effects other than mortality. Note also that in economic terms the decision whether or not to invest in the drug depends on a concept of an acceptable cost-effectiveness ratio – as a 'rule of thumb' one life year gained for less than $13,000 is considered by some in Sweden as cost-effective.

Cost-effectiveness evaluations of services, educational programmes or policies, however, are rarely able to build on an RCT evaluation. Often we cannot be certain that the effects will result from the intervention. This is a particular problem for some non-treatment health care programmes such as health promotion schemes. However, these evaluations are becoming more popular for interventions other than treatments. Managers and policy makers increasingly need to know, in the precise terms that cost-effectiveness evaluations can give, the likely costs of the expected effects of new programmes or proposed changes. They need this information to justify starting or withdrawing programmes, and to face their more sophisticated critics who often already have cost-effectiveness information for similar interventions.

## Cost-utility evaluations

*How much well-being do different interventions produce in relation to their cost?*

Knowing that a treatment on average increases the quality of life by $x$ years only allows crude comparisons between the treatment and another treatment or nothing. It does not allow comparisons between the quality of life produced by treatments, which are important comparisons to make in healthcare. Cost-utility evaluations quantify the effects of the evaluated in terms of how people value the effect, rather than in simple terms of lives or life years saved. The technical term for the value or usefulness of something to a person is 'utility'. Most cost-utility studies use one or more quality of life measures (Bowling 1992): the most well known measures of utility are the 'quality adjusted life year' (QALY) and the 'healthy day equivalent' (adjusted for quality of life).

Cost-utility evaluations allow comparisons across healthcare programmes, allowing us to compare heart transplantation with ante-natal screening with stopping-smoking programmes. We will see that some question the validity of these comparisons, but the point for the moment is that in cost-effectiveness evaluations comparisons are limited to treatments where the effectiveness measure can be meaningfully compared – number of lives saved is not a good outcome measure for comparing a liver transplantation programme with hospice care.

A cost-utility evaluation will calculate the cost of the interventions (or nothing), calculate the utility of the effects (how much value people give to the effect they get) and then show how much it costs to get the effects for each intervention (or none). The value of effects – for example, the value of being able to return to work three months earlier, or of being able to walk – are not thought up by the evaluators but are based on valuations made by ordinary people using special techniques. The simplest is nine boxes with box 1 as the 'worst imaginable health state' and box 9 the 'best imaginable health state', or variations of this, such as a 'thermometer' with 100 as the best state and 0 the worst. Another is the 'time trade-off': would you rather be healthy for five years and then die, or live for 15 years with, for example, less mobility and recurring pain (i.e. a defined sub-optimal health state)? If you have a clear preference to live longer, would this preference then apply to ten years, or seven? The aim is to find out the person's valuation of health states by reducing the time until the person has no preference between the alternatives.

A third method is the standard gamble, where a person is asked to choose between a state of poor health (which is defined) for $x$ years, and a treatment which involves a chance of death or of being restored to full health. Would you rather not take the treatment if you had a 50 per cent chance of death? What about a 10 per cent chance? The chances are changed until the person is indifferent between the two alternatives. These and other techniques are summarized in Richardson (1992) and in more detail in Brooks (1986). These techniques are of interest not just because they help us to understand some of the assumptions underlying cost-utility studies, but because they are methods which help people to express their personal valuations of different 'health states' and as such can be used in different types of evaluation. Knowing the value which people give to different health states helps clinicians and others to judge the value of an intervention and to make more informed decisions – and, to some extent, more democratic decisions.

Cost-utility evaluations using QALYs can compare the number of QALYs which could be expected if resources were used in different ways; or, expressed in a different way, the different costs to get one quality if the resources are used on different treatments. The following – from the SMAC (1990) Report on Cholesterol Testing – gives an illustration of the kinds of comparisons which have been suggested:

| Intervention | Cost per QALY produced (£) |
|---|---|
| Hospital haemodialysis for kidney failure | 19,000 |
| CABG (moderate, one vessel disease) | 16,400 |
| Cholesterol drug treatment | 13,500 |
| Heart transplant | 6,700 |
| Kidney transplant | 4,000 |
| CABG (main vessel disease) | 1,090 |

|                                        |       |
|----------------------------------------|-------|
| Hip replacement                        | 1,030 |
| Cholesterol lowering diet programme    | 176   |

These comparisons are only possible if you accept the assumptions and quantification methods underlying cost-utility evaluations, which are many (Hunter 1992; Smith 1992; Gerard and Mooney 1993). Criticisms of QALYs include: that they are based on the values of small populations; the small number of interventions which have been studied using this approach; technical flaws; a bias to giving greater value to duration of life than to life itself, and to valuing the young; that QALYs do not distinguish between life-enhancing and life-saving treatments and try to equate them; and the impact which QALY-based allocation would have on traditional rights of access to health care. Yet, without other information, these comparisons are increasingly being used to make resource allocation decisions. There is nothing wrong with doing so, as long as the assumptions and limitations are known and other information is also used.

## Cost-benefit evaluations

*Is the benefit of the intervention greater or smaller than its cost when both are measured in money terms?*

You may remember hearing about compensation awards by law courts: to the farm-labourer who lost his hand, or to a person who was still conscious during surgery. We may wonder how they judge these values: in fact in non-jury cases there are detailed methods for 'fairly' calculating the value of a hand, or of a damaged business reputation. But how should we in the health services judge the monetary value of restoring health or function? How do economic evaluators assess the benefits and express these in money terms, as well as the costs of one or comparable interventions?

Cost-benefit economic evaluations quantify the effects of an intervention in monetary terms. Thus, rather than expressing the effects of a treatment as lives saved, or in quality of life units, the typical cost-benefit evaluation expresses the effects in terms of money value. These evaluations show that spending $x$ money will result in benefits worth $y$ money, and give an easily understood idea of the 'value for money' of the intervention.

For example, the Swedish National Road Administration calculates the cost of different measures to reduce road accidents and compares these costs to their average 'cost per casualty' for a fatality ($550,000 total, which includes $60,000 for healthcare costs, net loss of a worker's production, and 'costs owing to property damage and administration' plus $490,000 as 'human value' costs (i.e. 'non-resource use consequences')). The reader will be comforted to know that the costs of 'severe casualty' are about one-seventh of these costs (in 1989 values).

Unlike in the other types of evaluation, both inputs and the outputs are quantified in the same (monetary) terms. Cost–benefit evaluations also make it possible to compare the value of the effects of different interventions in monetary terms. This involves assumptions that different effects can be quantified and reduced to the same unit of money value.

'How much would your household be willing to contribute each year in taxes to a helicopter ambulance service?' This question comes from a Norwegian study which used a technique that is being explored as an alternative to QALYs for measuring the benefits of healthcare: the 'willingness to pay' technique (Olsen and Donaldson 1993). The aim is to get people to say how much they would be prepared to pay for a particular treatment or service, which is described together with its benefits and risks, usually assuming that they would pay through taxation. The advantages are that people use a familiar unit of measure – money – and bring into their valuation of the intervention a sense of what they would have to give up by not having the money. The more complicated versions of this technique ask how much people would pay for a number of services. In the study cited, people were in fact prepared to pay significantly more for helicopters and heart operations than for hip replacements. While this method for quantifying benefit in money terms does make greater use of ordinary people's valuation, the techniques used are not without problems (Olsen and Donaldson 1993).

---

**Definition of types of economic evaluation**

*Cost-description*: measurement of the costs of one thing, or of more than one, in a way which allows an explicit or implicit comparison of costs. (A 'partial' evaluation looks at only one intervention and does not make an explicit comparison.)

*Cost-minimization*: assumes that the differences in outcome produced by the alternatives are not significant, and calculates the cost of each alternative with the purpose of discovering which is the lowest cost.

*Cost-effectiveness*: the effectiveness or consequences as shown on one measure, for the cost (e.g. lives saved, cases of diseases avoided or years of healthy life). No attempt is made to value the consequences – it is assumed that the output is of value. Used to compare the different costs of using different ways to achieve the same end result.

*Cost-utility*: considers the utility of the end result to the patient for the cost. Often uses the QALY measure, where extended life is at the expense of side effects. Measures consequences in time units adjusted by health utility weights (i.e. states of health associated with outcome are valued relative to each other). More complex than cost-effectiveness.

*Cost-benefit*: an attempt to value the consequences of a programme in money terms, so as to compare the assessed value with the actual costs. A range of benefits are valued in money terms. Concerned with how worthwhile an end result is for the cost.

Cost-benefit evaluation methods are also used to assess interventions to organization and for investment appraisals of proposed building or service schemes. An example is evaluation of information technology (IT) systems: cost-benefit analyses can be carried out to predict the costs and benefits of a system, or retrospectively to evaluate the actual costs and benefits. However, economic evaluations of IT systems, like evaluations of other types of intervention to organization, face problems in isolating the effects of the system from other changes which might have occurred. There are also the familiar problems of defining what is in 'the box' – is the IT intervention the hardware, or the training as well? In many cases the IT system does not just automate a manual system, but changes the whole way work is carried out. Neither the intervention nor the context is likely to be stable (Keen 1994).

## Strengths and weaknesses of economic evaluations

It is important to distinguish the strengths and weaknesses of the economic perspective in general from the different strengths and weaknesses of each type of economic evaluation. Criticisms of QALYs are not criticisms of the economic perspective or of types of evaluation such as a cost–minimization study. The above aimed to give an impression of how the economic perspective is applied in evaluation, and of some of the assumptions of different types of economic evaluations. Not all economic analyses are evaluations, but most are because they involve an explicit comparison, or the implicit comparison of the 'do nothing' opportunity cost: describing the resources used – often in money terms – invites us to think of other ways of spending the money.

All economic evaluations attribute value to an intervention by using systematically gained information about the resources used, and by comparing the intervention to nothing at all or to other uses of resources. Many also gather information about effects and use outcome measures to measure effectiveness or benefit. Many assess effects other than those for the patient, but studies differ in the scope of their effects assessments and in whether they take a health service or societal perspective. Economic evaluations differ in how narrowly they define costs and benefits, and in the accuracy and the validity of their measures. The purpose of most economic evaluations is to compare the cost-benefit or utility of the intervention with other uses of the finance. Some meta-studies draw together a number of evaluations of the same intervention to produce a synthesis evaluation, but there are technical problems in combining studies in this way.

From an economic perspective, healthcare funders have to maximize the benefit they can get from the total sum they have to spend. They need information about costs, and about outcome performance to decide benefits, and this information needs to be about both national averages and potential local providers. Buxton (1992) proposes that funders should only finance 'new' treatments on condition that the provider evaluates them, and that funders should be prepared to contribute to the cost of evaluation.

Economic evaluations are often combined with or built on to experimental evaluations. The economic analysis may be perfect, but any weaknesses in the experimental design will invalidate any practical conclusions (HERG 1996). Economic evaluations, in common with other types of evaluations which express results in quantitative terms, may give an impression of objectivity which is not justified, and which can mislead even experts. There are many assumptions about how to quantify costs, including which costs to exclude from the calculations. There are assumptions about how to quantify health consequences for individuals (e.g. just years of life or quality of life, and which aspects of quality?), about when to measure consequences and about which consequences to exclude (e.g. effects on relatives, costs for other services). There are assumptions about how to make valid comparisons of the effects of intervention when the effects of each intervention are expressed in the same units, such as quality of life units.

Where there is no other basis for resource allocation decisions, managers and politicians are increasingly using cost-utility or other economic analyses. Few detailed cost-utility evaluations have been carried out on interventions other than treatments, in part because economic evaluators have tended to develop methods which focus on individuals, such as utility to individuals. There is great scope for applying utility quantification and costing to interventions such as health promotion and educational programmes for patients, citizens and healthcare workers. (Three papers in one volume of *Health Education Research* consider the role of health economics in the evaluation of health promotion (e.g. Craig and Walker 1996), and Haycox (1994) describes a methodology for estimating costs and benefits.) The fact that many economic evaluations have concentrated on the costs to health services and on individual-based valuations does not mean that the perspective cannot take a societal view. As we increasingly consider the many influences other than health services on health, and seek the cooperation of other sectors to improve health, we should also consider the social costs and benefits of health treatments, services and policies in judging their value.

Whatever the drawbacks, the discipline of economic evaluation, like that of experimental evaluation, directly confronts many issues and involves assumptions which arise in most types of evaluation. Even if an evaluator or a user of evaluation is not involved in an economic evaluation, it is important that he or she understands issues such as those involved in quantifying resources and consequences and is aware of the detailed and through examination which health economists have given to these issues.

Most evaluators need to give a description of the resources used by the item which they evaluate. They also need to describe in their proposal how much resource the study they propose will use and the costs, as well as expected benefits and possibly savings, that could result from the evaluation. Will it ultimately be a 'cost-free evaluation'? The theories developed by economists about how to quantify resources, and criticisms of the methods economists use, need to be understood by all evaluators and users of evaluations.

### Further reading and examples

More details can be found in the best introductory book on health economic evaluation (Drummond *et al.* 1987) and in an excellent review of cost-
utility methods and assumptions given by Richardson (1992). 'Is
rehabilitation cost-effective?' is a question which McKenna *et al.* (1992)
seek to answer in a review of nine studies, which also discusses different
approaches and their application in such programmes. 'How can we prove
health promotion is cost-effective?' suggests a less than neutral evaluative
attitude, but it is a question increasingly put by frustrated health promotion practitioners: the discussions in Tolley *et al.* (1996) and Craig and
Walker (1996) are a good starting point, and Haycox (1994) describes a
possible methodology for estimating costs and benefits.

## Conclusions

- ◆ Economic evaluations are used to evaluate treatments and services, and
  for prospective evaluations of health policies, but less often for organizational interventions.

- ◆ All economic evaluations help others to judge the value of an intervention by gathering information about the resources consumed by an
  intervention, expressed as costs. Many also gather information about
  the consequences of the intervention.

- ◆ Some economic evaluations will only consider a limited set of resources:
  for example, those consumed by one health service and those which are
  easily calculated. Others take a broader view of the resources consumed,
  show costs to society and note 'difficult to quantify' costs.

- ◆ Full economic evaluations quantify the consequences of an intervention
  as well as the costs, and also compare two or more alternatives, even
  though one alternative may be the 'do nothing' option or placebo.

- ◆ Cost-description and cost-minimization evaluations describe only the
  costs of the intervention. Cost-effectiveness studies use one measure of
  effectiveness, such as lives saved, and compare the cost and effectiveness
  of interventions.

- ◆ Cost-utility evaluations assess the utility or value of health states produced by different interventions for the cost. They allow comparison of
  different interventions used in different health services.

- ◆ Cost-benefit studies value both the resources consumed and the consequences of an intervention in money terms, thus allowing easy value for
  money judgements

- ◆ All economic evaluations make technical and value assumptions when
  they quantify costs and consequences. These are usually stated but are
  sometimes only understandable to economists: for non-economists, the
  precise quantification may obscure the values underlying the study.

♦ Economic evaluations share similar positivist epistemological assumptions to those of the experimental paradigm about what constitutes a fact and how to gain valid knowledge of facts.

# Developmental evaluation

*Two views about non-experimental approaches to evaluation:*

*Far better an approximate answer to the right question, which is often vague, than the exact answer to the wrong question, which can always be made precise.*
(Tukey 1962)

*Many short-term or applied social science evaluations can be worse than useless and give misleading 'evidence' without describing the methods. They present the evaluator's personal prejudices or the political opinions of pressure groups as if they were objective assessments. We are in danger of exchanging a narrow view of what is a fact for a view of facts as what is said by who shouts the loudest. There is plenty of room for prejudice after the evaluation, not as part of it.*

## Introction

At work, most health personnel live in the moment. They have little time to read and analyse an evaluation report, or to wait years for a thorough study to give conclusive findings, and few have time to do an experimental evaluation. This is not to suggest that evaluation research does not have an impact on clinical and managerial practice: experimental and economic evaluations do improve health care over the longer term, and are increasingly being incorporated into everyday practice. However, there is also a need for evaluations which have a more immediate and practical use, and which use fewer resources and take a shorter time to complete. There is also a need for evaluations which take a more flexible approach to deciding and collecting the information which users need to judge the value of an intervention, and which pay more attention to the subjective experience of patients, health personnel and others who are affected by a health service or policy.

The 'developmental' perspective is a term used by this book to describe a view of people and organizations which brings into focus their feelings and perceptions, and which uses different social scientific methods to evaluate interventions. One approach informed by this perspective aims to describe the intervention and the people who use it in order to give evaluation users different information to judge the value of the intervention. Another approach aims to change the intervention while evaluating it – to exploit the self-transforming capability of people and organizations which is emphasized by the developmental perspective, rather than to control for and exclude this ability of the human beings under investigation.

Developing an intervention while evaluating it is heresy to many experimental evaluators. It just does not make sense. How can you evaluate something which you are changing? Surely the aim is control, not change? The developmental perspective in evaluation grew out of a critique of natural science methods applied to social phenomena and of the experimental and economic perspectives, and has now become an established alternative. For many working within this perspective, the point is not just to show the problems of applying experimental approaches to evaluate services and policies – we saw in the previous two chapters that there are in fact many quasi-experimental designs which can be used to evaluate services and policies. For them the point is not to adapt the experimental perspective, but to adopt a different perspective. This is one which is founded on different assumptions and views about the purpose of evaluation and about the nature of the subjects which are to be evaluated.

There are three distinct approaches. One draws on a social research tradition and uses descriptive and non-experimental case study designs and a variety of data-gathering methods, and the evaluators keep a 'respectful distance' from the intervention ('descriptive social research evaluation'). Another approach draws on an action research tradition, and aims to change the intervention while carrying out the evaluation, with the evaluators working closely with users, providers and patients ('action evaluation'). A third approach is 'self-evaluation': health personnel themselves use systematic methods to judge the value of what they do, so as to make better informed decisions.

*In one sense we are all developmental evaluators now – the question is how well we do it and how to do it better.*

Developmental evaluations are usually carried out to evaluate health services, or interventions to health services, as well as certain health policies, rather than to evaluate treatments. This chapter and the next will argue that, although both developmental and managerial approaches are influenced by and draw on the experimental and economic evaluation perspectives, they are not a 'second-best' or less rigorous form of evaluation but are appropriate for their different purposes. Those using this approach do, however, need to pay more attention to describing their methods, demystifying the approach and answering the often legitimate criticisms made by experimental evaluators about validity, reliability, replicability and generalizability.

In this chapter we discuss the perspective and describe the two main approaches of social research and action evaluation. The third – self-evaluation – is discussed in more detail when we consider quality evaluation in Chapter 13. We also note specific types of evaluation which show features of the developmental perspective, such as formative, illuminative, social analytic, process and pluralistic evaluation approaches. The purpose of this chapter is to enable you to explain the features of the 'developmental' perspective and of approaches informed by this perspective, to assess the strengths and weaknesses of a 'developmental evaluation' project or proposal for one and to judge when a developmental evaluation project is needed. It does not enable you to carry out such a project but gives references to other texts which would help you to do this.

## Developmental evaluations

How can you help users to judge the value of an intervention when you do not treat it like an experiment or calculate costs? This question is put jointly by evaluators using an experimental and economic perspective to those working within the developmental perspective. Behind the question are assumptions: that a sceptical and objective experimental approach produces valid knowledge (define your hypotheses and test them, ideally trying to falsify them), and that knowledge can be accumulated by building on previous experimental evidence; that the focus should be on measurable effects and on costs; that careful attention to data gathering using valid and reliable methods produces facts; and that this then provides evaluation users with the information which is most useful for them to judge value and to decide how to act.

The first response is that experimental and economic evaluations are often not possible, especially for services, policies, health reforms and many interventions to organizations. These 'interventions' often change, are ill-defined, have multiple and contradictory objectives and have a variety of effects, some of which cannot be predicted or imagined. Such evaluations usually take too long, cost too much, give only partial information and involve practical and ethical problems – if they can be done the findings often arrive too late to help decision makers.

The second is that these perspectives carry assumptions about what constitutes valid information about an intervention, and about how to produce this information. For some users and the questions which they ask, these assumptions are appropriate – users such as clinicians trained in medical scientific research techniques. For other users, such as many health personnel, patients, managers and policy makers, valid information includes an understanding of patients' and professionals' experiences and perceptions. This and other types of information can help these users to judge the value of an intervention, and may be more helpful to them for deciding how to act than limited information about outcomes and costs. In what sense is this 'subjective' information less certain or less valid than information about costs or objective measures of blood sugar or cholesterol levels? This second response to the question arises from a view of patients and health personnel as meaning-creating subjects, whose views are valid and who are capable of transforming themselves through self-reflection.

Neither of these responses answers the question. The third response is disarmingly simple and infuriates some experimental evaluators, but it catches the spirit of the developmental perspective. How do you help users to judge value? You work closely with them and other stakeholders to decide which information they think would be of most help, and when it would be of most use. You work with them to get the best balance between time, money and the detail, reliability and validity of the information. You keep giving them information as it becomes available.

A fourth response is given by some evaluators, who feel that the argument is unnecessary. This response draws attention to the many developmental evaluations which use not only quantitative methods, but also experimental principles. Within a developmental framework, evaluations have used before–after designs (type 3), comparative designs (type 4), hypothesis testing and small scale experiments, even if these designs and data gathering methods might not meet the same rigorous standards as those used in a full experimental or economic evaluation.

In fact the developmental perspective informs three different evaluation approaches. The first are evaluations like those just mentioned, which use experimental designs and ideas but within a developmental perspective, often feeding back the findings while the evaluation study is being done or where service providers themselves carry out the evaluation – these are 'pragmatic experimental' evaluations. The second type are developmental evaluations which do not use experimental principles but do contribute to changes in the intervention while the evaluation is being carried out, and as part of the evaluation design. The evaluation is itself an intervention to the intervention which is being evaluated – these are 'action research' evaluations. The third are descriptive 'case study' evaluations which do not aim for change during the evaluation, use a variety of established social science research methods and give their feedback and reports after gathering and analysing the data – the 'descriptive social research' evaluations. Before looking at what all have in common and defining this perspective, we need to consider some examples (see Table 7.1).

## Examples of developmental evaluations

An example of a descriptive social research evaluation which did not aim for change during the evaluation is that of the UK 'resource management experiment' (RM). This was a government initiative to involve doctors in budgeting and managing hospital services, which was initially introduced at six sites. The evaluation used traditional social science methods and

*Table 7.1* Three types of developmental evaluation with different approaches to change

|  | Changes as part of the evaluation | No change during the evaluation |
| --- | --- | --- |
| *Social research evaluations* (descriptive case study methods) | Some social research evaluations provide interim reports. | Researchers usually try to minimize their influence on the service or intervention while they carry out the evaluation. Results are more likely to be generalizable. |
| *Active evaluations* (action research methods) | The purpose of the evaluation is to change the intervention while carrying out the evaluation. | Action evaluators rarely wait until the end of the evaluation to feed back results, or take steps to minimize their influence |
| *Pragmatic experimental evaluations* (quasi-experimental methods within a developmental framework | Some developmental evaluators will use quasi-experimental methods and feed back information as the evaluation proceeds. | Some service providers run small scale experiments as part of their service quality improvement project. |

treated the sites as six different case studies which were compared to each other and to the objectives of the initiative (Packwood *et al.* 1991). This evaluation was an example of a descriptive developmental evaluation which could also be classified as a managerial evaluation.

One purpose of the evaluation was to assess whether RM had succeeded in 'involving doctors in management' – a criterion of valuation derived from the objectives of the initiative. The methods used by the multidisciplinary evaluation team were interviews, participant observation of meetings, collection of data about financial costs and questionnaire surveys. The evaluation was 'summative', so it did not involve feeding back results to the sites until the study was over. The evaluation itself did not introduce change while it was being done. An interesting assessment of the 'payback value' of this evaluation is given in HERG (1994): in the concepts of this book this assessment is in fact an economic evaluation of a developmental evaluation of an intervention to organization produced by a government policy.

An example of an action evaluation is a project to develop a new integrated health and social service primary care team in Northern Ireland. In this project the evaluator worked with the team to define and evaluate the options for team organization, and then to establish a team quality assessment system. Rather than evaluating the quality of the team's service and reporting this back to the team, the evaluator worked with members of the team to help them to define quality criteria which were based on patients' views gathered from focus group meetings (Øvretveit 1991a). The team then developed simple surveys and measuring instruments which they used routinely to find out what patients thought about the service.

## Defining the developmental perspective

The developmental perspective has a longer tradition within educational evaluation than in the health sector. The following captures many of the features of the perspective.

> The basic emphasis of this approach is on interpreting, in each study, a variety of educational practices, participants' experiences, institutional procedures, and management problems in ways that are recognisable and useful to those for whom the study is made. The Illuminative evaluator contributes to decision-making by providing information, comment, and analysis designed to increase knowledge and understanding of the programme under review. Illuminative evaluation is characterised by a flexible methodology that capitalises on available resources and opportunities, and draws upon different techniques to fit the total circumstances of each study.
>
> (Parlett 1981)

There are many different types of evaluation within this category, but what they all share is a pragmatic developmental aim, a flexible approach to choosing methods and a close and continual link between the emerging findings of the evaluation and practical action. Although there are exceptions, the features of many developmental evaluations are as follows.

♦ *Local*: done for and with people in one service unit, but with the aim of also producing general descriptions and knowledge which are of use elsewhere.
♦ *Close collaboration*: between the evaluator and service providers and sometimes patients during all stages of the evaluation.
♦ *Continual feedback*: applying emerging findings from the evaluation to practice during the evaluation process.
♦ *Of single or a few cases*: the case being a service, organization, patient or personnel who are the target of the intervention, using case study techniques but not case–control designs.
♦ *No controls*: no attempt to control the evaluated or to create experimental and control groups, but may compare case study sites.
♦ *Non-experimental design*: the evaluation is not designed as an experiment to test a hypothesis (but parts of the evaluation may aim to test providers' or others' hypotheses).
♦ *Inductive*: concepts and theories are often built up inductively out of the data which the evaluator gathers.
♦ A preference for *qualitative techniques* such as interviewing and documentary analysis.

Evaluations of this type are made when the item to be evaluated is difficult to specify or is likely to change while the evaluation is being carried out. Evaluators are often asked by sponsors to evaluate a service or policy which is poorly defined, or where there are different views about what the service or policy is, or about its objectives. It may be premature to start developing evaluation criteria until the item is defined more clearly – this is one reason why an evaluator may choose a developmental approach to evaluation using a descriptive type 1 design (Chapter 3).

Developmental evaluations are more often carried out to evaluate interventions such as services and policies, rather than treatments. However, an increasing number of evaluators are using this perspective to evaluate alternative therapies, rather than the experimental perspective (Johannessen *et al.* 1994). The evaluators do not try to make the item to be evaluated into an experiment, but seek to evaluate it by describing it, and by trying to deepen understanding of what it is and how it works.

Developmental evaluations may be made by external evaluators employed by an agency other than the one being evaluated, and with a social science background, often influenced by action and participatory research methods. They may also be carried out by people internal to the organization, or self-evaluations may be carried out by health personnel for service and self-improvement. The latter are more likely to use quasi-experimental designs, but within a developmental paradigm (Berwick 1996).

## Descriptive and action-evaluation

What is the difference between the different approaches to evaluation within this category? Which type of developmental evaluation is best for which circumstances and questions? The following first considers the two most common sub-categories: descriptive social research evaluations using case study methods, and action-evaluations using action research methods. Then we consider approaches which involve one or more features of the developmental perspective, such as 'qualitative', 'illuminative', 'responsive' and 'real-time' evaluation.

## The difference between experimental and descriptive case study evaluations

The case study is an established way of generating knowledge within many disciplines. In clinical medicine the 'case' is an individual patient. Detailed discussions of this 'observational' method of research can be found in psychotherapeutic and psychiatric research texts. 'Case study' is also used in a second sense to describe one type of experimental evaluation: where an intervention is made to one patient (the target) and the effects are studied. Such 'single target case' experimental evaluations have more rigorous controls than the observational clinical case study. A similar approach can be used to study the effect of an intervention on one organization as 'a case' – the case is not a patient but an organization (Yin 1989). 'Experimental case evaluations' are designed to test a hypothesis and to create causal explanations, often by adopting the null hypotheses that an intervention has no effect and by using controls. The approach is deductive – a hypothesis is derived and the whole evaluation is designed around testing the hypothesis.

Case study evaluations within the developmental perspective are carried out in a different way to case study evaluations within the experimental perspective. There is usually no attempt to control carefully for other variables or to hold the intervention constant. The evaluation is of one or a few 'cases', which can be randomly selected or selected to exemplify special features; for example, one or more organizations or patients who have undergone a planned or unplanned intervention. The approach is inductive and naturalistic. Developmental evaluations thus use a non-experimental case study approach and methods which have been developed within social sciences for case study research.

The danger of the case study approach is that it may become merely an extended anecdote without evaluative relevance (Cheetham *et al.* 1992).

## Descriptive social research evaluations

One example of a descriptive social research evaluation is reported in St Leger *et al.* (1992). This is a study of a UK Chinese health information centre. The study examined and reported different views about the objectives of the centre, together with details of activity and financial data gathered specially for the evaluation. The reports were checked and rechecked by staff working in the service. St Leger *et al.* (1992) also discuss 'testimonial evaluations', which are really a method for seeking and recording people's reflections on their experience of a service, or of being part of a change process. This method is often used in developmental evaluations, especially to give tangible examples, and is discussed further under 'interview data gathering' in Chapter 11. St Leger *et al.* (1992) also describe a study made by nurses working in a day surgery unit, who assessed patient satisfaction and other features of the service for the purposes of improving it.

Other examples of larger scale, longer and more extensive descriptive social research evaluations in the UK are those of the NHS Management Advisory Service (Brunel University 1984; Henkel 1991), of the NHS clinical audit programme in four therapy professions (Kogan and Redfern 1995) and of the NHS total quality management programme (Joss and Kogan 1995). The last is of interest because the evaluators studied a number of hospitals and services, but also looked at two comparable non-health organizations which had introduced quality programmes.

One approach is to use 'rapid appraisal' methods to give evaluation users a qualitative picture of the health and other problems of people in a defined community. This approach draws on the views of selected 'informants' in the community and involves testing hypotheses which emerge as the research proceeds (Ong 1993).

Many descriptive social research evaluations aim to describe the inputs and processes of the evaluated, its boundaries, the context, and often also the outputs. Evaluations of this type are useful to service providers for giving them an independent 'mirror' which they can use in reviewing and improving their service. They are also useful for managers and policy makers who want an independent description of the operation of a service, and one which also answers any specific questions they may have. They can be used to get an independent description of a new treatment, especially one which is not well defined or understood, such as some social, psychological or alternative therapies. They can also be used as a study preliminary to an experimental or other type of evaluation, or to do an 'evaluability assessment' (Wholey 1977, 1983).

Although descriptive evaluations often do not give measures of outcomes or effects, they are useful for quick feedback, use few resources and can be used when a service or policy is undergoing change. Both the quality and usefulness of evaluations of this type are very dependent on the skills of the evaluator, and on the theory and models which they use to select what to describe. Some descriptive evaluations start off with a clear model or theoretical perspective which they then use to select what to describe and to guide data gathering. Some work inductively, seeking to build models out of the data to describe key features of the evaluated – descriptive evaluations using grounded theory are an example of this approach. These qualitative approaches are described in more detail in Chapter 11.

## Action-evaluation

Action-evaluations aim to change the intervention while evaluating it, although the dividing line between descriptive and action evaluation is not absolute. For example, the evaluation of the Chinese information service above might be classified as an action evaluation, because interim reports were checked by staff and this would have produced changes before the evaluation was finished and the final report produced.

An example of an action research evaluation is a study of a community mental health service (Øvretveit 1994b), sponsored by the board of the centre, where the users were the board, health personnel and clients of the centre. The aims were to discover and report to the board and staff working at the centre answers to three questions: how much multidisciplinary working and client participation occurs and how could both be improved; what are the strengths and weaknesses of the centre; and how can the cost-effectiveness of the centre's services be improved?

These questions were derived from criteria of valuation which were discussed between the evaluator and the sponsors. The evaluation compared the centre's achievements against intended objectives, and activities against standards and norms using data gathered from interviews and service documents. The evaluation involved reporting back findings in workshops, describing the changes which were made and developing different models for future working. The final report also included an assessment of the needs of the population and information about how far these needs were being met by the centre.

Another example was a project to evaluate the quality of a 'family aid service' which gave practical assistance to people with learning disabilities and their families. In one type of action evaluation the evaluators would collect service users' and others' assessments of the quality of the service. They would report these assessments back to the service personnel, and work with them to clarify the implications and options for change. The action evaluation reported by Øvretveit (1988) took a different approach: the evaluator developed a suitable quality assessment system and trained the service personnel to apply it to their own service. The service providers gathered clients' assessments of the service and then decided which changes to make. A degree of objectivity and critical assessment was introduced by having colleagues from a similar service involved in each other's quality assessment. The report describes the system which was developed, the standards and objectives which the service personnel developed and revised in collaboration with clients, carers and their colleagues in a similar service and the measurements which service personnel and their colleagues used to evaluate the quality of their own services. Another example is the 3-year action-evaluation of the Norwegian TQM programme (Øvretveit 1996b, 1997b, in press).

We can define one type of action evaluation as 'working with providers to analyse and judge the value of what they are doing through gathering data and deciding and carrying out improvements'. Action evaluations can also be carried out for users other than providers – for example patients or patients' associations – and to help them to develop their organization or services. They can also be carried out by providers themselves, as part of their everyday work or as a special project (Hart and Bond 1996). One feature is the close collaboration between the evaluator and providers (or users) to design the project and its focus, to decide criteria and measures, to collect measures, to judge value and to decide and plan action. Another is analysis: to help providers to reflect on what they do, to give them an external view and to help them to conceptualize their service and work. The help to decide and carry out improvements is provided by reporting analyses and data, working with providers to define the practical implications and to clarify options for action.

The main features of action evaluation are as follows.

♦ The subject is one or a small number of services or intervention(s).
♦ Continual collaboration and frequent feedback.
♦ Criteria and comparisons are those useful and meaningful to providers.
♦ Usually short term.
♦ Change while the evaluation is being done.
♦ No controls or experimental design.

## Developmental evaluation approaches

Many developmental evaluations use a case study approach, and concentrate on a single case or small number of cases. However, there are different ways of carrying out developmental evaluations, and the following notes some of the more common approaches, many of which have been used in health settings.

### Pluralistic evaluation

Success is a pluralistic notion. It is not a unitary measure.
(Smith and Cantley 1985: 173)

A study which showed the value of developmental evaluation in the health setting and which put forward the 'pluralistic approach to evaluation' was that of Smith and Cantley (1985). The study was of a new day hospital for older people with mental health problems, with two objectives: to describe the services and the factors which were 'most influential' in its development, and to explore conceptual problems in evaluating new services of this type. It considered how different groups defined success: nurses, psychiatrists, GPs, social workers, and patients' relatives. These criteria were patient flow, clinical cure, integrated services, impact on related services, support to relatives and quality of services.

The study provides a critique of the 'predominant mode of evaluative research – experimental, rationalist and objectivist', a detailed account of the practical and methodological issues involved and the findings, and defines features of 'pluralistic evaluation', which include:

♦ identifying the main stakeholders in the intervention;
♦ understanding and describing the interpretations which different parties make of events and of the agencies in which they are involved, especially of what constitutes 'success';
♦ documenting the strategies which each party uses to advance its interests;
♦ the use of a variety of data sources and methodological triangulation (see Chapter 11).

By defining and assessing 'success' according to the views of different interest groups, this approach is more able to remain neutral and independent. However, as Smith and Cantley themselves acknowledge, understanding and representing these views is not of itself an evaluation, and it also produces 'somewhat complex conclusions about the success of the services on a range of criteria'.


## Qualitative evaluation

We noted that developmental evaluations make a greater use of qualitative methods for data collection than other approaches to evaluation. However, some evaluators have more than a preference for qualitative methods: they propose a distinctive approach to evaluation which can be characterized as 'qualitative'. As outlined by Greene (1994), qualitative evaluation exemplifies some of the features of the developmental perspective: case study design (a) concentrates on meanings by looking at context and pays less attention to generalizability; (b) relies largely on qualitative methodology; (c) recognizes the influence of the evaluator on the inquiry; and (d) aims for increasing the practical understanding of a programme.

Patton (1980) stops short of proposing a distinct approach to evaluation, but describes how qualitative methods can be used more often within existing evaluation approaches.


## Illuminative evaluation

Illuminative evaluation also exemplifies features of the developmental perspective, and has been used mostly in the field of education (Parlett and Hamilton 1976). The aim is to 'interpret practices, participants' experiences, institutional procedures and management problems in ways that are recognizable and useful to those for whom the study is made.' Qualitative methods are often used, such as ethnographic methods, but within a paradigm which is different from the natural science experimental paradigm:

> Its primary concern is description and interpretation rather than measurement and prediction. It stands unambiguously within the alternative anthropological paradigm. The aims of illuminative evaluation are to study the innovatory program: how it operates; how it is influenced by the various school situations in which it is applied; what those directly concerned regard as its advantages and disadvantages.
>
> (Parlett and Hamilton 1976: 144)

Such kinds of evaluation are difficult to replicate, in the sense that another evaluator could repeat the methods and come to the same conclusions. They can be criticized for not having sufficiently well defined designs and methods – the approach emphasises the flexible selection of methods according to the subjects and opportunities which arise. An overview of this approach is given in Parlett (1981), and the methods described in detail in Parlett and Dearden (1977).

## Responsive evaluation

The use of qualitative methods and also close collaboration between the evaluator and users are highlighted in another approach which falls within the developmental paradigm: responsive evaluation. Stake's (1975) description of the practical features of this approach show clearly the differences in assumptions and methods from those of experimental evaluators, but also the systematic nature of the approach:

> To do a responsive evaluation, the evaluator conceives of a plan of observations and negotiations. He arranges for various persons to observe the program, and with their help prepares brief narratives, portrayals, product displays, graphs, etc. He finds out what is of value to his audiences, and gathers expressions of worth from various individuals whose points of view differ. Of course, he checks the quality of his records: he gets program personnel to react to accuracy of his portrayals; and audience members to react to the relevance of his findings. He does most of this informally – iterating and keeping a record of action and reaction. He chooses media accessible to his audiences to increase the likelihood and fidelity of communication. He might prepare a final written report, he might not – depending on what he and his clients have agreed on.
>
> (Stake 1975)

This approach to evaluation shares the assumptions of phenomenological and similar approaches in the social sciences: studying people who are experiencing the intervention in natural situations without external controls or manipulation, understanding the meanings people give to events within a specific context, as well as feeding back information and expecting and noting reactions or how people incorporate the information into their actions.

## Real-time evaluation

Real-time evaluation is an approach used by the Tavistock Institute Evaluation and Development Review Unit in the UK to review health, educational and social services. It grew out of the action research methods pioneered by the Tavistock in the 1950s. This approach studies the intervention over a 'life cycle' and assumes change. More than this, the evaluation itself is 'formative', and 'shapes' the intervention while the evaluation is being done. Many of these studies do look at outcome, but give more attention to the process of implementation, with the aim of linking any outcomes to specific actions.

The philosophy of the evaluators is to involve service providers in the evaluation and to create conditions for them to learn and to develop a common understanding about the service. They use a systems perspective to show how the service is influenced by and itself influences the environment in which it operates. Stern (1990) defines evaluation in a way which is compatible with this approach: 'Evaluation is any activity that throughout the planning and delivery of innovative programmes enables those involved to make judgments about the starting assumptions, implementation processes and outcomes of the innovation concerned.' This approach is described in more detail in Stern (1993).

## Social analytic evaluation research

A related approach which also builds on an action research tradition as well as psychoanalytic theory and methods is social analytic evaluation research (Øvretveit 1984, 1987a). The focus of this approach is organization, and the aim is to work with service providers and managers to describe current organization, document different views about aims and about the effectiveness of organization, and provide an analysis of further organizational options for pursuing different aims. The evaluation component is making explicit views about aims and values, and assessing current organization against these aims and values. One example is an evaluation of a community mental health centre (Øvretveit 1994b).

## Facilitated peer review

In these types of developmental evaluations, the evaluator helps practitioners or service providers to develop a method to review their own practice or service, and then helps them to use the method to do a review. In these types of developmental evaluation, the evaluator's role is not to describe or report back their findings, but to enable others to do their own evaluation and to develop their own criteria to do the evaluation. These evaluations differ from peer review audit (described in Chapter 13) in that the practitioners or service providers do not use a ready-made auditing system of standards and criteria, but are helped by the evaluator to develop their own and to decide the process they will use to do the review.

An example is facilitated peer review evaluation, developed by Heron for medical general practitioners (Heron 1979), and for managers (Heron 1981). Another is a facilitated peer review evaluation of a service for everyday assistance to people with a learning difficulty (Øvretveit 1988), and for primary health care (Øvretveit 1991a).

## Continuous improvement self-evaluations

These types of evaluation are a form of developmental evaluation, but are done by service providers or practitioners themselves. The theories and methods come from the field of quality improvement (Deming 1986). Service providers use a specific framework to define the item to be evaluated, to guide their collection of data, to analyse the data and to decide and implement changes. Associated with this approach are a set of methods, or 'quality tools', which providers use in a systematic way to evaluate and change their service and to develop their knowledge of how it operates. A short summary is given in Berwick (1996) and in Batalden and Stoltz (1993).

## Strengths and weaknesses of developmental evaluations

We need to distinguish the strengths and weaknesses of the perspective from those of particular evaluation approaches which are informed by the perspective. This book used the term 'developmental' to describe a perspective which brought into view people's feelings and perceptions and their ability to change through becoming conscious of their circumstances.

The strengths of this perspective for evaluating health interventions are that it reveals patients' experiences and uses methods for including this dimension within evaluations. This perspective has also had an impact on experimental and economic evaluations which have traditionally ignored subjective outcomes that are difficult to quantify. It also brings into view providers' and other stakeholders' views and gives methods for gathering these views and building up a broad picture which can help evaluation users to judge the value of an intervention. These are strengths not just for evaluating polices and services and for explaining processes over time, but also for evaluating treatments, especially combined treatments for longer-term and chronic health conditions.

When we turn to specific evaluation approaches which are influenced by this perspective we need to distinguish between descriptive social research and action evaluation. The strengths of descriptive social research evaluations are that they allow a flexible research strategy which can gather and explore different views about the intervention and about the history of an intervention. Because they do not use experimental design they can be used to evaluate an intervention which is changing, such as many services and policies. They draw on a tradition of social research with well developed methods and designs, such as the case study, which can be described and replicated and which are becoming more understood and valued by users of evaluations. If the 'case' is well selected and described, then the findings can be generalized.

A weakness of this approach can be that the results are difficult to assimilate and use to inform action: many users do not have time to read through long reports of qualitative findings, no matter how richly they convey the lived experience of patients. Another is that the explanations of effects, where they are given, are of influences, not causes, and do not carry the certainty or specificity which some evaluation users want or are used to. Results are not summarized in a standard way on one page as a graph or numbers in a table with confidence intervals. Often users are faced with many pages of text, sometimes reporting raw data with little analysis, and users are invited to draw their own conclusions from the 'novel' which lies before them. To paraphrase one doctor, otherwise sympathetic to this approach, 'The report was a long treatise of sociological waffle – it did not help me or the management team to decide whether to set up another service like this.'

Some of the strengths and weaknesses of action evaluations are similar to descriptive social research, but there are the additional strengths that the results are practical and more immediately useful to service providers, and are available during the evaluation. They are quicker, cost less, produce immediate benefits and are under closer control by users than descriptive social research evaluations and experimental and economic evaluations.

They are not only suitable for interventions which are changing, but are of most use when users or providers wish to influence these changes by drawing on systematically gathered information.

The weaknesses of action evaluations are that they are often not replicable or generalizable, and are rarely published. Their success greatly depends on the research and consultancy skills of evaluators, their knowledge of the service, credibility with service providers and clients, their ability to work flexibly, in ambiguity and without structure and their ability to use different data gathering methods. They cannot give objective and conclusive evidence of effectiveness because the intervention is changed. Compared to experimental evaluations, the techniques for reducing bias are poor and it is often difficult for external assessors to see how the findings were arrived at, and whether the findings were not the subjective preoccupations of the evaluator which were 'imposed' on the data. The data may be misleading if the limitations of the design and data collection methods are not described in ways which users can understand. One otherwise excellent 45-page published evaluation report gave the following three-sentence description of the evaluation methods, with no further references: 'The evaluation used a variety of methods to explore how key players saw the Carers Impact process and the changes achieved. A detailed confidential report was written to each fieldsite and distributed to the team and task force group. More general summary reports which identified common themes were written at different points during the programme' (Unell 1996).

A theme of this book is that the strengths and weaknesses of an evaluation approach depend on the purpose which the evaluation is to serve, the questions to be answered and the type of intervention to be evaluated. Generally, both social research and action evaluations are useful when:

♦ the objectives of the intervention are unclear;
♦ the boundaries of the intervention are unclear;
♦ there is continual and complex change in the intervention;
♦ there is uncertainty about the effects of the intervention;
♦ there is uncertainty about what causes or influences any effects;
♦ users want some improvement quickly.

But not when the intervention is stable and users want limited but certain information about effects in order to compare its value to the alternatives. Action evaluations are usually not appropriate when:

♦ users want to assess effectiveness without changing the intervention;
♦ users want knowledge which applies to other services or interventions (generalizable).

## Conclusions

♦ The developmental perspective describes a view of people and organizations which brings into focus their feelings and perceptions, and which uses a variety of social scientific methods to evaluate interventions.

- The developmental perspective in evaluation does not treat the intervention as if it were an experiment, but it does use designs which are also used by experimental evaluations, and scientific techniques such as comparison and hypothesis testing.

- Developmental evaluations often concentrate on one or a few 'cases', such as a service, an area or an organization where a policy is in operation. The way in which the case is studied is different from the way in which cases are studied in an experimental evaluation.

- There are three main approaches: descriptive social research evaluations, action evaluations and provider self-evaluations.

- Descriptive social research evaluations use case study methods to describe the intervention and the people affected by it, in order to give evaluation users a variety of information to judge the value of the intervention. Such evaluations do not intervene in the intervention which they evaluate.

- 'Action evaluations' use action research methods to change the intervention while evaluating it, and give frequent feedback to service providers. They tend to use qualitative and multiple methods, aim for service provider reflection and self-development rather than accountability and inspection, and seek out providers' explanations and accounts as well as those of beneficiaries and other interested observers so as to help to understand and review the intervention.

- Developmental evaluations may also be carried out by providers themselves for self-improvement, or in a peer review process, and sometimes use quasi-experimental techniques to run tests on changes to organization before introducing them (see Chapter 13).

# 8 ▸ Managerial evaluation

*Evaluation is increasingly used to serve managerial purposes, and a distinct field of 'managerial evaluation' is emerging as evaluators adapt traditional methods and create new ones to help with their routine management work and with special management and policy decisions.*

## Introduction

Evaluation as a tool of management and as a routine management activity has become increasingly common, and more recently has been encouraged by the 'evidence-based healthcare' movement. New information technology is opening up many more possibilities, but this technical sophistication is often not matched by the evaluative skills of managers, or by evaluators' understanding of the needs of managers. One aim of this chapter is to highlight some of the differences between this and the three other perspectives in evaluation, so that both managers and evaluators may choose the most appropriate designs and methods for their purposes.

The 'managerial perspective' describes a perspective taken by evaluation exercises and studies in health services which concentrates on the needs and concerns of managers and policy makers. The aim is to enable managers and policy makers to judge the value of activities and interventions and thus better to fulfil their task. This usually means that the information has to be gathered quickly and presented in a way which is easy to use in management decision making.

Examples are inspections of hospitals or nursing homes, special studies of service performance, evaluations of whether programmes or projects were implemented as intended and projects which help to set up routine monitoring systems. Evaluation is also becoming a recognized phase within 'the management process' and a 'built-in' part of new programmes and projects. Many researchers would not consider a phase in the management process or these special studies to be evaluation, because neither produces casual explanations or aims to contribute to scientific knowledge. They are defined as evaluations in this book because they do involve the systematic collection of data for the purposes of judging the value of an activity in order to decide how to act.

Like developmental evaluations, managerial evaluations are completed quickly (in anything from a few days to one year), and can be used to improve service efficiency or quality. They are often carried out by people working for health service organizations and inspection agencies, using a design which compares the evaluated to a set of established procedures, standards or objectives (a type 2 audit design). However, unlike developmental evaluations they are carried out specifically for managerial and supervisory purposes, using standards and procedures for comparison, and usually routinely gathered measures and official records. It is this inspection role, and the purpose of helping managers and managerial boards to make immediate decisions by giving timely and practical information, which distinguishes managerial from developmental and other evaluations.

Does taking a managerial perspective in evaluation mean that an evaluator unquestioningly designs and carries out the evaluation to serve a specific managerial purpose? Are accuracy and scientific certainty in data gathering sacrificed for the sake of getting some information quickly? Are simple practical recommendations more important than laying out the details of the data, with all their limitations and uncertainties?

> *Is the evaluator a 'managerial policeman' or 'police car', whose presence is more important than the information he or she gathers?*

The simple answer to all these questions is no. Yet we will see in this chapter that the more detailed answers depend on whether the evaluator is internal to the organization, or contracted in by management, or carrying out an evaluation which is intended to be of general use to many managers. The answers depend on the needs of the management users, the intervention to be evaluated and the time and resources available.

Why do managers carry out and use evaluations? The chapter first describes the purposes of managerial evaluation and gives examples. It distinguishes monitoring from needs-effectiveness evaluations, and then considers different types of managerial evaluations. The last part of the chapter concentrates on a subject central to many managerial evaluations – performance evaluation – and how this can be undertaken routinely or in special studies.

## What is the managerial perspective in evaluation?

The managerial perspective in evaluation is a set of assumptions and values which underpin most but not all managerial evaluations.

It views health interventions from the point of view of health service funding bodies, health managers and their concerns and tasks. In general the management perspective is concerned with two things: ensuring that things are done properly, and trying to use available resources to the best effect.

In the past, evaluations carried out within this perspective have tended to view health organizations as rational mechanisms for implementing policy, with simple and uncontested objectives. Judging the value of a policy or a service thus involves collecting facts which enable managers to assess the extent to which objectives have been met or standards and procedures complied with. In recent years there has been a recognition that there are competing interest groups which hold different views about what is a fact and about the value of different policies and services. Some managers have found these 'pluralistic' or social research evaluations of use for evaluating services and policies and for designing new services and policies. However, many managerial evaluations take the traditional perspective, and are different from other types of evaluation in that their sole purpose is to give managers or their employing organizations information for judging the value of current or proposed services, policies or other interventions.

The category of managerial evaluations includes routine and special types of evaluation carried out for managers and supervisory boards at different levels of the health services and of government. Managerial evaluations generally serve as a mechanism for accounting to the public for the way in which money is spent and for the way in which health services are conducted. They are carried out for a variety of purposes: to protect the public by identifying unsafe activities, to ensure standards are met, to improve performance and value for money, to ensure that agreed policies and projects are carried out as intended, for contract monitoring or evaluation and to speed or improve the implementation of policies or projects.

They are usually carried out by quasi-independent government inspectors – for example, Norwegian county public health departments or UK public health directorates – by government-contracted inspectors or consultancy firms, or by specialist staff internal to a service with an inspection role. A manager or public body may also use an external independent evaluator to help to create and test a system, which managers then use for routine internal monitoring and performance management. Organizations financing health services or programmes may use their own staff or external agencies to evaluate the performance of the recipients of the finance, as is increasingly the case with donors of overseas development aid for health services (Engelkes 1993; Forss and Carlsson 1997).

Having made this distinction between managerial and other types of evaluation, it needs to be pointed out that it is not an absolute distinction. Some developmental evaluations can be classified as managerial evaluations, and some descriptive social research evaluations are carried out to provide management with new insights rather than immediately useful practical recommendations (e.g. Smith and Cantley 1985; Ong 1993). Note also that managers sponsor economic and even experimental evaluations where these are needed for management decisions, but such evaluations are not 'managerial evaluations' because they follow different designs and methods with different criteria of validity and allow generalizations and causal explanations. The general point, however, is that while managers and public bodies have and will continue to make use of experimental and economic evaluations, a distinct approach to evaluation is developing, undertaken by distinct institutions or internal units with their own methods, which we term here 'managerial evaluation'.

## Why has managerial evaluation developed into a distinct sub-discipline?

Managerial evaluation is a relatively recent activity in public services. Financial auditing – which some consider a type of managerial evaluation

– has a long history in public services. However, during the 1980s most European governments significantly increased their use of evaluation for managerial purposes: this trend started in the USA in the 1960s. Referring to the UK, Henkel (1991) observes that:

> Government had identified evaluation as a significant component in its strategy to achieve some key objectives: to control public expenditure, to change the culture of the public sector and to shift the boundaries and definition of public and private spheres of activity. . . . Several changes occurred. New evaluative institutions and practices were installed, based on new assumptions about the knowledge and expertise they required, the values they should endorse and the authority they would carry. . . . In particular, government emphasised the technical and instrumental purpose of evaluation by reducing the influence of service-orientated professionals and installing management criteria and expertise.
>
> (Henkel 1991)

Why do managers, public health authorities or financing agencies carry out evaluation? First, to ensure that policies or directives which were democratically agreed by public representatives are carried out. In this instance the concern is not whether the policy is effective – either this was considered before the decision was made to implement the policy, or it can be assessed once the policy has been implemented. A second reason is to assess whether a service or policy is reaching the people for whom it was intended ('uptake' or 'access'). This is a limited type of effectiveness evaluation which is sometimes viewed as part of the quality of a service, and is examined in 'impact evaluations'.

A third is to assess whether finance and effort is being used on existing services and policies in the way intended and according to standards of accounting and personnel conduct which are laid down for public services ('probity'). A fourth reason is to enable service managers to improve their use of resources by reviewing activities and comparing their services to others ('performance management' and 'comparative competition'). A fifth reason is to enforce safety standards and reduce the risks of harm coming to patients or health personnel from unsafe equipment, buildings or practices ('risk reduction'). Where managers and public authorities have purchased or contracted out services, evaluation has been used for all of these five purposes. Managers are increasingly using external or in-house units to evaluate contractors before contracting out services, for contract monitoring and at contract renewal times (Demone and Gibelman 1989).

Do managers and governments really need to use evaluation designs and methods for these purposes? The short answer is that managers think that they do. Managers have established internal units to carry out monitoring and evaluation and these units have adapted evaluation methods for their purposes. Managers themselves increasingly make use of evaluation designs, methods and principles in their own work. Managers also contract external evaluations for specific purposes and have found them useful. However, the answer to the question really depends on what we mean by evaluation design and methods and on being more specific about exactly what managers' needs and questions are. The rest of the chapter considers examples and different types of managerial evaluation as a way of answering this question.

## Examples of managerial evaluations

Managerial evaluations cover a broad range of subjects and methods. Examples of managerial evaluations are: financial auditing, special 'value for money' studies and comparisons of similar services by government auditors or inspectorates, routine inspections of safety, inspections of compliance with various regulations, internal or external monitoring of projects or policies which were directed by higher bodies or agreed for implementation by management, contract evaluation and some quality assurance programmes.

Many countries have quasi-independent evaluation and monitoring organizations which undertake managerial evaluations of public services. In Sweden, the National Board of Health and Welfare has powers to carry out uninvited inspections and evaluations of any health service in the country. Recent special evaluations have included an unpublished comparison of mortality rates in 15 hospitals, and a comparison of outcome and quality of trauma services in small and large hospitals in two counties. Two other studies were of levels of medication in nursing homes, which found wide variations after controlling for diagnosis and severity of illness, and a comparison of four services which performed operations for congenital heart problems – this study contributed to decisions about centralizing services. In these and other works the Board makes use of a wealth of data which are regularly reported by most Swedish health services, some of which are required by law to be reported (e.g. adverse events; Odegård 1995). Another example is the Australian Auditor General investigation into the effects of reducing GPs' fees and of removing items from the country's Medicare Benefits Schedule (Auditor General 1991).

In the UK, the National Audit Office and the Audit Commission are two such national organizations which traditionally undertook financial auditing and other types of monitoring, but which have both extended their activities into short-term practical evaluations. Three recent Audit Commission studies were:

♦ An audit of hospital medical staffing, which found that junior doctors were working more than the permitted 56 hours per week in one-third of the investigated hospitals.
♦ A study of GP fundholding (purchasing budgets), which found problems in how budget sizes were decided, that savings made by budget holders usually led to higher costs elsewhere in health and social services, that the only true savings were from more rational prescribing. GPs did make more appropriate referrals, had lowered their costs by switching providers and had encouraged more day surgery. The overall savings up to 1995 were £206 million, but the costs of the system had been £232 million.
♦ A study of the implementation of the UK 1993 community care legislation, which found significant variations between local authorities in

the number of people they had assessed for care, their eligibility criteria and the way they had implemented the legislation, devolved budgets and contracted services. As a result of this study and finding that the costs of authority-managed care homes were often higher than those of private ones, the Audit Commission then went on to 'help' local authorities to do a detailed study of their costs to 'ensure that they are getting value for money'.

This third study raises a question about combining inspection with development in evaluation. Some types of evaluations can be carried out either within a managerial perspective for monitoring and accountability or within a developmental perspective for self-improvement. Examples are certain quality assurance evaluations, such as 'organizational audit', which is discussed in Chapter 13. This audit process was created for developmental purposes but is now also used for inspection for accreditation. Managerial evaluations sometimes try to combine inspection and self-development: they are commissioned by management and primarily for management purposes, but also aim to enable service personnel to self-review and improve. However, combining inspection and accountability reporting with the developmental philosophy is difficult and does limit the amount of trust and involvement which many health personnel are prepared to give (Odegård 1995). This tension between external inspection and internal development, which is common in evaluation, is discussed in Chapter 13 in the context of quality evaluation.

An example of one type of managerial evaluation which also had a developmental component is described by St Leger et al. (1992). This was a study carried out by the UK national social service government inspectorate which examined how social workers dealing with child abuse were supervised. The aim was to identify good practice and give guidelines as well as a method for self-inspection. The inspectors compared practice with ideal standards which were derived from consulting with experts, and used this comparison to formulate a set of general guidelines and recommendations. St Leger et al. (1992) emphasize the importance of the background knowledge of the inspection evaluators, who were all trained social workers, and their close collaboration and credibility with all parties. This appears to have been important in reducing the tension between the inspection and development aims of the evaluation.

Another example is a system for evaluating the quality of residential homes for elderly people developed by the UK Social Services Inspectorate (SSI 1989). This project undertook a managerial evaluation of a number of homes, but its primary purpose was to produce a system which agencies could use to make qualitative evaluations of the performance of homes for management purposes such as contract monitoring. The project involved close cooperation between the government social services inspectorate and practitioners in county social services department, and the system, 'Homes are for living in' is now regularly used for routine audits. This example also shows that managerial evaluations are not always quantitative in form – the audit system gives guidelines for assessors to evaluate the home's ability to respect residents' dignity, choice and fulfilment, and other difficult to measure but valued features of care.

All the above were evaluations carried out by organizations with a national or regional remit. However, management teams are increasingly commissioning external evaluations to help the team with a variety of decisions and plans. Examples are evaluations of an organization's current information or communication systems, in order to decide whether the systems are being used to the best effect and how they could be improved (Keen 1994), or evaluations of a service's business strategy. Other examples are evaluations of the performance of a department where there are questions about expanding or reducing the size of the department, and evaluations of a quality programme or quality system (see Chapter 13).

## Types of managerial evaluations

We saw from the above examples that managerial evaluations are carried internally or by independent organizations, for different purposes and using a variety of methods. Having distinguished managerial from other types of evaluation (while also recognizing some overlap) we now look at the differences between types of managerial evaluations. This helps to make sense of the variety within this sub-field and to see the different methods and designs which are most suited to each purpose. First we look at the difference between monitoring and needs-effectiveness evaluations, and then note other differences between managerial evaluations, such as the frequency, duration, scope, subject and level of the evaluation.

### The difference between monitoring and needs-effectiveness evaluations

Some professional evaluators do not consider some of the activities which this chapter has classified as managerial evaluation to be 'real evaluation' at all. While it is true that none will win a Nobel Prize, they are increasing in sophistication and drawing on and adapting methods from other types of evaluation for their more immediate practical purposes. While this book rejects the absolute distinction between monitoring and 'real evaluation', it is useful to distinguish between different types of management evaluation which have different purposes and thus require different methods. Below we distinguish between three activities: routine administrative monitoring, monitoring evaluations and needs-effectiveness evaluations.

Examples of routine administrative monitoring are regular hygiene inspections of hospital kitchens, regular financial audits or a manager's deputy collecting reports on 'patient incidents'. These are a routine and established part of the managerial process – they are considered a form of evaluation according to the definition used in this book because they involve a comparative assessment of the value of an intervention in relation to defined criteria. Managerial monitoring evaluations, however, are not routine and are special studies conducted by external agencies. The three Audit Commission studies noted above are examples: they take the statements of standards or procedures which the intervention or policy should be meeting, and compare these to what people do. 'Implementation monitoring' is similar, but takes a description of intended objectives and plans, and monitors what is achieved against these intentions. These evaluations may also make recommendations or even propose revised standards or new timetables for plans.

However, none looks at effectiveness and at whether the intervention meets the needs of the people for whom it is intended. They assume that if service providers meet standards or achieve objectives then the needs of those served will be met. Alternatively, they aim to assess aspects of the service or policy which are not related to meeting needs: for example, whether finance was used properly, or whether a programme to achieve efficiency savings was carried out.

The extent to which needs, rather than standards or objectives, are met is a subject examined by 'needs-effectiveness' managerial evaluations. These are evaluations which assess the needs of the people to be served by an intervention and compare these with the actual outcomes of the intervention. Many experimental and economic evaluations do this, which in turn can help to set or revise standards and objectives. However, during the 1990s, managerial evaluations began to pay more attention to outcomes and effectiveness, in addition to, and sometimes instead of looking at inputs, processes, outputs and efficiency, which were their traditional subjects. Although not meeting the highest scientific research criteria, outcome

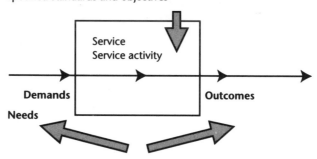

Specifications of standards, procedures or objectives

**Monitoring evaluation** compares service activity with specified standards and objectives

Service
Service activity

Demands                                    Outcomes

Needs

**Needs-effectiveness evaluation** compares needs with outcomes, to judge if the service standards and objectives are the right ones to meet priority needs

**Monitoring question:** are operating requirements being met?
**Needs-effectiveness evaluation question:** are these the right operating requirements to meet needs?

**Figure 8.1** The difference between 'monitoring evaluations' and 'needs-effectiveness evaluations'

assessment is now possible for managerial purposes because of new information technology and because experimental evaluations and other research have developed validated outcome measures which can be used routinely and at low cost (e.g. the Short Form-36, Nottingham Health Profile and General Health Questionnaire: Bowling 1992; see also Bardsley and Coles 1992). The differences between monitoring and needs-effectiveness evaluations are represented in Figure 8.1.

---

**Three types of managerial evaluations are:**

- ◆ routine administrative monitoring, such as regular management reviews, hygiene inspections of hospital kitchens or financial audits;
- ◆ special monitoring evaluations, which are specific studies, usually externally conducted;
- ◆ needs-effectiveness evaluations, which assess the extent to which a service is meeting patient or client needs.

---

## Differences between types of managerial evaluations

The three types of managerial evaluations described above differ in their purpose, timescale and sophistication. Some are concerned with checking that established standards, regulations and directives are followed (compliance). Others are less concerned with compliance and more with how well resources are used, which includes efficiency and sometimes the effectiveness of an intervention. As with all evaluations, the design and methods used depend on the purpose. If the purpose is to assess compliance then there is no need for a lengthy and expensive needs-effectiveness evaluation.

Managerial evaluations also differ in terms of the aspect of the service or policy which the evaluation considers and the scope of the evaluation. Some are limited to looking at, for example, the costs of one or more services ('inputs'), or to looking at service processes such as how different services select patients for a particular treatment. Others may be more comprehensive and aim to assess needs, inputs, process and outcomes.

Another difference is in the 'level of the evaluation'. An evaluation can be carried out for managers or managerial boards at a national level, or a regional or sub-regional level (Table 8.1). Case example 7 in Chapter 4 described a national audit of the quality of health centres in New Guinea, and case example 6 a descriptive evaluation of a district health system for African district managers and government planners. Level of evaluation can also refer to the level of the entity which is evaluated: an evaluation of a department in a hospital is an evaluation of a lower-level entity than an evaluation of the whole hospital or of a regional health system.

We can place different types of managerial evaluations in terms of the primary purpose of the evaluation, and in terms of the level of the evaluation (Table 8.1). Doing so shows that different evaluation methods and approaches will be needed for each type.

Some managerial evaluations are carried out at an international level. One example is the WHO evaluation of different governments' progress on the 38 regional targets for the 'Health for all by 2000' strategy (WHO 1994). Each member state provided national evaluation reports, with information about its performance on the targets and a 'situational assessment'. Another example is evaluation reports of the health service programmes in developing countries which were funded by donors of development aid:

Engelkes (1993) gives a summary of 83 such evaluations for donors, some of which were done by donors' internal staff and some by external evaluators. Engelkes notes problems which are common in many types of evaluations:

> Many evaluators complained about a lack of baseline data, and about the project objectives being too vague or too ambitious to use as criteria of evaluation. Insufficient time to carry out a thorough evaluation

*Table 8.1*   Purpose and level of a managerial evaluation

| Level of evaluation | Purpose of evaluation, to check (examples) | | |
|---|---|---|---|
| | *Was the scheme implemented as planned? Were standards met?* | *Efficiency (Waste avoided? Use of resources?)* | *Effectiveness (Objectives met? Needs met?)* |
| 6 National | Do all hospitals have a quality system? | Have quality systems improved efficiency? | Have quality systems enabled services to meet needs better? |
| 5 Regional | Are procedures for vaccination being followed in the region? | Are vaccinations being carried out in the most efficient way? | How many people in a defined target group need to be and have been vaccinated? |
| 4 Area authority | An area authority wants to know if all hospitals are meeting new regulations for discharging patients | How much time are community nurses spending on travel and could this time be reduced without affecting quality? | An area authority requires an evaluation of the extent to which a child health service is meeting the needs of all the needs of all the children in an area |
| 3 Hospital | Hospital management needs to check whether policies for overtime are being followed | A hospital management team wants to know how efficiently each department is managing its bed utilization | Are we seeing the people most in need of our services and meeting their needs? |
| 2 Hospital division or primary healthcare grouping | | | |
| 1 Hospital department or primary healthcare centre | Are personnel following regulations for recording and communications? | Could we communicate more efficiently? | Do our communications and systems get and give us the information we and others most need? |

*Note:* level of evaluation is in terms of (a) the user (the *management level* for which the evaluation is being carried out); or (b) the subject (the *level of the entity* which is evaluated – its size and scope).

study was also often mentioned as a constraint. Few of the evaluated projects has in-built systems for evaluation and monitoring, although at the formation of projects these had often been planned.

(Engelkes 1993: 73)

---

**Management evaluations differ in terms of:**

♦ whether the aim is to check compliance, efficiency or effectiveness;
♦ the frequency and the time taken, ranging from routine short-term monitoring to special detailed needs evaluations;
♦ limited or comprehensive, ranging from examining one aspect of the service or policy to comprehensive assessments of inputs, processes and outcomes;
♦ the level of the entity evaluated or for which the evaluation is carried out.

---

## Measuring performance

How do you evaluate the performance of a health service or health system, such as a primary care centre, a rehabilitation unit, a health promotion service, a purchasing organisation or a district health service in a developing country? What is the difference between measuring and evaluating performance? These are questions addressed by this and the next section. Health service performance measures are a controversial subject. Two opposing views are:

*It is better to have no measures at all than misleading measures.*

*Even bad measures are better than none because the people measured then have an incentive to propose better measures – this is the only way to get good measures.*

A key question is: 'What is a "good" measure of the performance of a particular service, programme, or system?' Generally, there is no single measure of performance and 'good' measures depend on what we mean by performance, which takes us back to one of the themes of the book – the need to define the value criteria for an evaluation. This will be different for different interventions, although one thing will be common – that there are many different views about performance. First we consider existing performance measures which are used for evaluating health services and systems, and the criticisms which have been made of them for these purposes. Then the next part of the chapter looks at what we mean by performance and considers the two categories of compliance and efficiency-effectiveness performance evaluation. The reader is invited to ask, in the following review of measures, what are the underlying values and assumptions about what we mean by the performance of a health service. Are the measures really measures of performance, or just of what is easy to measure?

## Performance measures and indicators

Many health organizations and health systems routinely collect a variety of types of data which they, their financing bodies or government use to monitor and measure performance. National and local government in many countries requires providers to collect basic data about activity, such as the number of people served, and providers themselves add to these 'basic data sets' to monitor their own performance. We noted earlier that different levels of organization collected different data to assist management work at each level.

Performance measures give direct measures of aspects of performance, such as efficiency. Performance indicators are less direct, and are intended to alert managers' attention to or suggest areas for further examination. They are more like 'tin openers' than direct 'read-out dials'. Examples are the 145 health performance indicators created in the UK in 1985.

In 1989, the UK introduced a new set of indicators, which now total some 2,500, and include performance in relation to Patient's Charter standards (DoH 1991b) and hospital league tables. In 1994, the latter listed 470 hospitals and trusts with their performance figures against 23 standards, together with a 'star rating' of between one to five. The standards included the percentage of patients seen within 30 minutes of their appointment time, and within five minutes of arrival at an emergency department, the number of patients not admitted within a month of the second cancellation of their operation, the percentage of day case surgery in four types of operation and the percentage of patients admitted in eight specialities within three and twelve months of the decision to admit. The chief executive of the 'top performing' UK NHS Trust commented that, 'Really these tables just measure one aspect of the work. We look forward to the day when we can measure outcome as well and hopefully show that we are as good on quality' (Chief Executive of Halton General Hospital, reported in *Health Services Journal*, 4 July 1996: 11).

Performance measures are often ratios which involve a comparison: for example, the number of day surgery cases compared to the total number of surgical operations. Some are 'efficiency' ratios which relate inputs to outputs, such as operations performed per surgeon. Many are 'contributory' or 'indirect' ratios which are easy to collect and thought to impact performance but are not performance measures in themselves, such as number of nurses per bed. There are few which relate needs to outcomes (needs-effectiveness ratios). An important but much criticized index is the UK NHS 'efficiency index', which is published every year as a single number for each provider unit and district. This index is a ratio of the change in activity and the change in spending over one year (Appleby 1993).

Performance indicators have been criticized for their inaccuracy, for lack of relevance to clinicians and to small services, for inviting misleading comparisons, for giving information about performance which is beyond management control and for not stimulating 'averagely performing' units to do better (Roberts 1990), as well as for ignoring outcomes and effectiveness. Their use for evaluating the performance of British NHS purchasing authorities is described in Ham and Woolley (1996), and of general practice in Majeed and Voss (1995).

The Swedish National Board of Health and Welfare produces statistics which allow comparisons of counties and hospitals, and there are similar systems in Norway and Finland. More attention has been paid to outcome measures and outcome evaluation in the USA, where state governments have collected and published hospital mortality rates and in some cases measures of physicians' performance (e.g. PHCCCC 1992; Øvretveit 1996a). Here sophisticated systems have been developed to adjust for illness severity and case mix, and these meet some of the criticisms of using crude mortality data for assessing performance. Measures of outcome are to be introduced into the UK hospital league tables data set.

Although limited, these data are useful for managerial evaluations and for other types of evaluation – the methodological issues involved in using existing data sources are discussed in Chapter 10. An example of what can be done with limited data was shown in a performance evaluation of hospitals in the Andhra Pradesh region of India. This evaluation added to routine hospital statistics and found similar lengths of stay, but also wide variation in turnover rate and bed occupancy, even after making allowances for inaccurate data (Mahaparatra and Berman 1994). WHO also proposes health policy indicators (WHO 1981: 19–24), which were used as a basis for the evaluations of the WHO 'Health for all by 2000' programme (WHO 1994).

*How could managers and governments improve performance measures?*

There is no lack of answers to this question, many of which are not very practical. The answer which this book gives should be easy for readers to predict, and may be becoming repetitive for some: it depends on for whom and which purposes the measures are intended. We are here interested in measures for managerial evaluations of services and policies at different levels of a health service. A general answer is given by Schyve (1995), who lists some of the characteristics of a 'good performance measure' which were used in the US Joint Commission's search for methods to measure organizational performance in their accreditation process.

◆ Relevance: does it measure something important?
◆ Reliability: is it collected accurately and completely?
◆ Discriminatory power: does it help to identify real variation among processes or outcomes?
◆ Risk adjustment: are the measures adjusted for uncontrollable factors (e.g. for patients' severity of illness) when comparisons are to be made?
◆ Validity: is the measure useful for its purpose (e.g. to improve performance, to choose a health care organization)?

In summary, the aim of performance measures is to capture the essential features of performance of the particular service so that managers and others can make comparisons over time or between services. Different measures will be required for different services, and, for the same service, managers at different levels will require different measures. Performance measures are a compromise between the information which is easy and inexpensive to collect and the information which would be ideal. Up to a point, the more information and the more detail about performance the better, but beyond that point the added value of the extra information declines and more detail becomes positively unhelpful (see Figure 8.2).

---

**Types of performance information include:**

- activity (e.g. occupancy rate, turnover rates);
- costs/resource consumption (e.g. unit costs, bed day costs, diagnostic-related group or equivalent costs);
- inputs/structure (e.g. number of staff, grade of staff, opening times);
- process (e.g. waiting times, quality indicators, satisfaction with 'hotel' facilities);
- outputs (e.g. the number of patients treated, or personnel trained);
- Outcome (e.g. mortality, morbidity and symptom reduction, satisfaction or resources used).

---

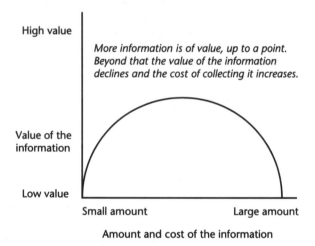

*More information is of value, up to a point. Beyond that the value of the information declines and the cost of collecting it increases.*

**Figure 8.2** The 'information value arc': the relation between the value and the amount of information.

## Performance evaluation

Florence Nightingale made the following comments about mortality rates:

> If the function of a hospital were to kill the sick, statistical comparisons of this nature would be admissible. As, however their proper function is to restore the sick to health as speedily as possible, the elements which really give information as to whether this is done or not, are those which show the proportion of sick restored to health, and the average time which has been required for this object.
>
> (Nightingale 1863)

Performance evaluation always raises questions such as, what do we mean by performance? performance for whom? what constitutes good and poor performance? is the 'amount of cooperation' with other services or professions part of performance or part of process? is performance only in relation to results or does it include process? The multiple objectives of public health services make it difficult to establish a few clear criteria of effectiveness. Many of the performance measures noted above are based on unacknowledged assumptions about the meaning of performance. These measures have been criticized for orienting managers towards saving money or 'looking good' on the measures, rather than 'doing good' and being effective, which is more difficult to measure.

What do we mean by performance? Perform means to carry out or accomplish something, and performance is the manner in which something functions. For a service which you know, would you agree with the following definition of health service performance? 'Performance is the amount made or produced or done in relation to the resources used to make or produce or do it. It is output per unit of input' (Harper 1986). To my mind this is a definition of efficiency. It captures one aspect of performance but does not include effectiveness and other aspects of performance which many people would want to include. The point here is not to put forward my definition of performance, but rather to show that evaluating performance means recognizing different perceptions of performance and being conscious about the criteria of performance which we are using. When evaluating performance we may use existing statistics or performance measures, such as waiting time or cost per day, but we should do so because we choose the measure as one which gives the best data in relation to the criteria of valuation we are using to evaluate performance. The criteria of valuation we use need to be explicit.

This book defines evaluation as 'a comparative assessment of the value of an intervention, in relation to criteria and using systematically collected and analysed data, in order to decide how to act.' To evaluate the performance of a service or system we need both clear criteria and a clear idea of what we are comparing the intervention with. One comparison which is often used in performance evaluation is 'now', compared to the same service in the past (e.g. number of day patients treated this year compared to last year) or compared to other services. This is sometimes called 'relative performance'. Another is 'absolute performance', which is performance now compared to an ideal (e.g. number of day patients treated compared to the number which were clinically possible to treat as day patients). A third is a comparison which takes account of the surrounding conditions, so-called 'contextualized performance': for example, the number of day patients treated per surgeon or compared to services with dedicated day surgery units.

The criteria used in a performance evaluation depend on the type of service or system at which we are looking, and for whom the evaluation is being made. Here we can only note some general criteria which are frequently used in performance evaluations. One set of criteria for national health programme evaluation, which is also suitable for health system evaluation, are those proposed by WHO (1981): of relevance to needs and priorities, adequacy, progress, efficiency, effectiveness and impact.

A set of criteria which gives a basis for service evaluation is the 'famous five' performance criteria (Øvretveit 1996d):

> **Performance definitions**
>
> 1 *Economy*: fewest resources or lowest cost (inputs).
> 1 *Productivity*: amount produced (output).
> 3 *Efficiency*: amount produced for the input (input/output).
> 4 *Effectiveness*: how well the service achieves the desired results (the change effected in the target, objectives met or needs/outcomes).
> 5 *Quality*: the degree to which the service satisfies patients, meets professionally assessed requirements and uses the fewest resources within regulations (requirements met).

Note that there are other definitions of each of these terms, and that there are many sub-types of each. For example, efficiency as defined above is normally termed 'technical efficiency', but there are at least four other types. Input mix efficiency is the extent to which the mix of care inputs reflects costs – we can improve input mix efficiency by substituting lower cost labour. Market efficiency (or output mix efficiency) is the degree to which the outputs of a service reflect consumer preferences. Horizontal target efficiency is the extent to which the service reaches all those who need it. Vertical target efficiency is whether the service is targeted to those most in need. I consider the last two to be aspects of effectiveness, and some see them as aspects of quality. The evaluator will need to agree with the users as to what will be meant not only by 'performance' but also by more specific terms such as 'efficiency' and 'effectiveness'. The words are just the starting point for discussions about exactly which information is required and is feasible to collect.

## Two categories of performance evaluation

The following summarizes many of the points made in the chapter by describing two broad categories of performance evaluations, according to the different criteria and comparisons which are used in each. The first is 'compliance evaluation' and the second is 'efficiency/needs-effectiveness evaluation'.

### Compliance evaluations: inspection and many audit evaluations

These include routine administrative monitoring activities and special monitoring evaluation studies, carried out to check compliance with standards and procedures, and to uphold regulations, as well as to check the implementation of directives or programmes. Together, these are the most common types of managerial evaluation in health services.

Financial audits are routine administrative monitoring carried out by external auditors to check the descriptions and records of the service about how the service spent money, and to check that money has been spent in the ways intended. Examples are the UK Audit Commission studies and studies by the National Accounting Office, as well as studies by the Swedish National Board of Health and Welfare and the US National Accounting Office. Some studies look at how well finance was controlled and plans were followed in major projects, such as computerization and hospital building schemes.

Many types of 'accreditation' fall within the category of 'compliance evaluations'. Accreditation is giving a credit for meeting standards, and is carried out by independent inspectors who assess a practitioner, a training scheme or a service against established standards. If the standards are met, the accreditors award a certificate showing that basic standards have been met, or give a licence to practise or operate. The primary aim is to ensure that minimum standards are complied with and to protect the public.

Some quality audits are carried out for local or higher-level managerial purposes. An example is the UK King's Fund organizational audit process, which also attempts to fulfil a developmental as well as inspection and quality assurance role. These systems are discussed in Chapter 13. Some medical and clinical audits are primarily to check compliance with established standards and guidelines, and are undertaken for management control purposes rather than clinician improvement purposes (Pollitt 1987, 1990, 1992).

Other types of inspection activities fall on the boundaries between routine administrative monitoring and evaluations, such as inspections of private nursing homes, or checking fire regulations and health and safety at work regulations. Another type of compliance evaluation is 'goal/plan performance evaluation' – the criterion of valuation is the extent to which a service meets its objectives or realizes its plans. The comparison is between what was planned and what has been achieved. Achieving objectives is sometimes classified as effectiveness, but in this book effectiveness is only whether needs are met. This is because the objectives of a service typically include objectives other than meeting needs. I have evaluated one service which did not specify meeting needs as one of their objectives.

### Efficiency and needs-effectiveness performance evaluations

A second category of management evaluations considers how well resources are used, rather than whether the service complied with established standards. They assess efficiency and sometimes look at effectiveness in terms of whether needs were met. In the past, performance management evaluations were primarily concerned with efficiency (outputs per input), but they are increasingly trying to assess needs-effectiveness, although this may only be practical on a routine basis for some services or for high-volume, high-cost or high-risk treatments (Øvretveit 1996a). Rapid appraisal is a practical method of data gathering for needs-effectiveness performance evaluations (Nordberg *et al.* 1993; Ong 1993).

Note that the terms 'performance management evaluation' and 'value for money evaluation' can both be used to refer to efficiency only, to effectiveness only or to both effectiveness and efficiency evaluation. 'Audit evaluations' are carried out to assess compliance, and sometimes efficiency, but rarely consider effectiveness.

Finally, it is worth noting a useful distinction between three types of performance evaluation, in terms of the comparison made between the item evaluated and the chosen standard. 'Absolute performance evaluation' compares the evaluated against an absolute or ideal standard: for example, the actual number of complaints compared to an ideal of none, or the percentage of the population vaccinated compared to an ideal 100 per cent. 'Comparative performance evaluation' compares the performance of the evaluated to the performance of the something which is similar: for example, a primary healthcare centre achieves an 87 per cent immunization rate compared to the regional average of 79 per cent or its own 82 per cent rate last year. 'Relative or contextual performance evaluation' assesses the performance of the service or intervention in the context of the local circumstances – it assesses how well the evaluated performed, given the circumstances at the time and given the starting point or base-line measure. Such evaluations often look at trends over time for the same service.

---

**Two categories of performance evaluation**

1 Compliance performance evaluation

   (a) Standards/regulation performance evaluation
   *Value criterion*: extent to which the service complies with higher level regulations and policies.
   *Examples*: a managerial quality audit of health facilities (e.g. case example 7 in Chapter 3), an audit of a day surgery unit in relation to standards for personnel supervision and equipment.
   *Evaluation design*: type 2, audit

   (b) Goal/plan performance evaluation
   *Value criterion*: extent to which the objectives are met or plans fulfilled.
   *Example*: evaluation of progress at each stage of a project to open a new day surgery unit, and/or whether the unit meets objectives set for it once in operation.
   *Evaluation design*: type 2, audit

2 Efficiency and needs-effectiveness performance evaluation

   (a) Efficiency performance evaluation (usually design type 1: descriptive)

   *Value criterion*: how many people are served or units produced in relation to the resources used (measured by unit costs).
   *Example*: evaluation of number of people served by a day surgery unit in relation to the costs, usually compared to other day units or in patient care.
   *Evaluation design*: usually type 1, descriptive

   (b) Needs-effectiveness performance evaluation (usually design type 3 or 4: before–after)
   *Value criterion*: extent to which the service meets patient or population (or staff) needs.
   *Example*: evaluation of the extent to which a day surgery unit meets the needs of patients eligible for day surgery procedures.
   *Evaluation design*: type 3 or 4, 'before-after'

## Strengths and weaknesses of managerial evaluations

Managerial evaluation was a growth business both within and outside public services in the 1970s and 1980s, owing to government concern to control expenditure, increase value for money, assure quality and increase the accountability of public service to the public as consumers and as tax-payers. These evaluations are usually made by government-employed but independent evaluators and may be routine or special evaluations. They use or create a variety of statistics about service activity and performance, which are also used for other types of evaluation (e.g. economic evaluations).

Many researchers and professional evaluators do not regard some of the activities described in this chapter as evaluations, but rather as administrative monitoring. They point out that these activities are more limited than other types of evaluation in their scope, use of methods and timescale. Managerial evaluations do not seek to discover cause-and-effect mechanisms, and rarely consider needs and outcomes, because this takes time and calls for complicated evaluation designs. Consequently, these 'monitoring mechanisms' do not contribute to scientific theory about the workings of the evaluated, and are often based on unproven assumptions about how the standards which are used for monitoring relate to outcomes – that people could be 'doing things the right way' but 'doing the wrong things', and may be efficient but ineffective (e.g. the difference between 'monitoring' and 'evaluation' shown in Figure 8.1).

However, the routine activities and projects considered in this chapter do use systematic methods, they are replicable and objective, they use comparison (e.g. the actions of people or services are compared to a set of standards, procedures or comparative indicators) as well as explicit criteria and they also involve valuation of the activities. Managerial evaluations are increasingly drawing on theories and methods which are used in experimental, economic and developmental evaluations, and are adapting these approaches for everyday monitoring and improvement purposes. Examples of this increasing sophistication are to be found in the use of economic models and economic evaluation techniques by government financial auditing departments in their special value for money evaluations, and in more attention being paid to outcome measurement.

Managerial evaluations are thus incorporating the more practical techniques and designs which have been developed and tested in other fields of evaluation. Examples of this 'managerial technology transfer' can be found in the methods used in studies made by the Swedish National Board of Health and Welfare and the UK's National Audit Office and Audit Commission. At the same time, what were once special managerial evaluations, such as special costing studies or performance assessment studies, are becoming routinized in management information systems and in routine performance management reporting.

Both routine and special-subject managerial evaluations are becoming more refined in their design and methods. The number of these evaluations and the amount of time spent on them are increasing as health services are required to account for their activities and to become more efficient. Most service managers and practitioners are already involved in one or more types of these evaluations, and need to understand the strengths and the limitations of this approach to evaluation.

## Conclusions

♦ Managerial evaluations are carried out for managers, supervisory boards and health financing agencies to monitor or improve the performance of services, or to check that agreed policies, projects or changes were implemented as intended.

♦ From the manager's perspective, evaluation is a method for the rational implementation of objectives. Managers need to assess the extent to which the objectives of a programme or project are achieved in order to decide the next steps, and need assessments of performance and of processes in order to decide how to improve. If people know that they are being evaluated, this in itself may improve performance.

♦ Managers and public bodies are making more use of evaluation for the purposes of accountability, enforcing safety standards, reducing risks, checking whether plans and polices are implemented, reviewing and replanning, ensuring 'probity', assessing patient access to services, performance management and comparative competition.

♦ Many managerial evaluations compare actual activities against procedures and standards which are thought to ensure safety, efficiency, effectiveness and equity. They are carried out by managers or their deputies or by people working for independent or quasi-independent organizations.

♦ There are three different types of managerial evaluations. Routine administrative monitoring is a regular and established part of the managerial process. Monitoring evaluations are special and sometimes externally conducted evaluations. Needs-effectiveness evaluations assess the needs of the people to be served by an intervention and compare this to the actual outcomes of the intervention for these people.

♦ Managerial evaluations are undertaken at different levels of organization, and for different purposes, and may be limited or comprehensive in their scope.

♦ In the past the focus of managerial evaluations has been on ensuring that 'things are done properly', rather than on evaluating whether 'the right things are done' in terms of assessing whether the objectives set for a programme or activity are the right ones in the first place.

♦ Many governments and services establish performance indicators and measures, which are used in routine and special managerial evaluations. The measures have been criticized for measuring what is easy to measure rather than what is important, being based on questionable assumptions about what is good and bad performance, and directing managers' attention to looking good rather than doing good.

♦ Performance evaluations may be classified as compliance evaluations, which check whether people or services are meeting regulation, standards or implementing plans as intended; or as efficiency or needs-effectiveness evaluations, which examine how well resources are used.

♦ Managerial evaluation will continue to develop in sophistication with new information technology, and as a way to respond to pressures for increased accountability and efficiency. Methods for routine outcome evaluation are already being used and will become more widespread. Health programme and health system evaluation is becoming more common in developing countries as a tool to ensure that scarce resources are used to the best effect.

# Planning and managing an evaluation

*'Goodness!' Susan breathed a sigh of relief as she put down the telephone. It was the chairperson of the local branch of the 'Mental Health Now!' association again, asking about what plans there were to open a new mental health centre in the south of the county. Susan had at least been able to satisfy the chairperson that the question was 'still under active consideration', but as the manager of the mental health service she knew that she would have to do better than that, and was herself not really satisfied with the situation.*

*She knew that most patients, carers and general practitioners were pleased with the centre in the north of the county, which had been open for 18 months. But there had been so few services to that area before. The plan had been to open another centre in the south soon after, but the building costs of the centre in the north had been over-budget and it was proving more expensive to run than had been thought. More importantly, there were a number of problems that raised questions about whether a similar centre in the south was such a good idea.*

*She had been thinking for some time about whether there were lessons to be learned from the northern centre which could help to plan a better centre in the south. Possibly a different model was worth considering. Then she remembered what her colleague had said about evaluation: perhaps an evaluation was a way to move this issue forward. Perhaps her new assistant could do it, or should she get the people she had met at the university seminar to do it. She picked up the phone again: 'Alex, can you get me the latest current budget figures for this year?'*

## Introduction

*The ambitions of evaluators and the expectations of sponsors are only exceeded by their disappointments with the limitations of the results of the evaluation.*

*The evaluator serves, but is not a servant of the user.*

The purpose of this chapter is to help people to plan and manage an evaluation. It is for managers and others who need to assess proposals and to supervise an evaluation. It aims to help to judge a proposal, to check that evaluators have predicted the likely problems and to decide if the evaluation can answer the questions posed. It is also for practitioners and researchers new to the subject. It notes some of the issues to consider in planning and making an evaluation, and lays a basis for the more detailed discussion of practical issues for evaluators given in Chapter 10.

There is no one way to plan and make an evaluation. Why, then, does this chapter describe 'phases' in planning and doing an evaluation? The reason is that many evaluations follow a similar general sequence. A framework of phases like the one described helps evaluators, sponsors and others new to the field to see some of the tasks which need to be done, and helps with the work of planning an evaluation. After describing these eight phases, the chapter then discusses some of the issues which evaluators and sponsors need to consider. These include deciding which 'user' perspective to take, which decisions the evaluation aims to inform, the criteria of valuation to be used, the part values play, how to define the item to be evaluated and its objectives and how to link these considerations to evaluation design. The chapter finishes by showing how decisions about these issues set the parameters for the evaluation design, and by giving a checklist for assessing a proposal or a finished evaluation.

To illustrate the conceptual discussion, we will be following Susan's progress in starting and managing a small external evaluation of a mental health centre. The chapter concentrates on planning and carrying out evaluations of services, policies or interventions other than treatments. Some of the phases described are slightly different for experimental evaluations of treatments: for details about planning these types of evaluations the reader is referred to introductory texts such as Fink (1993) and Breakwell and Millward (1995), and texts on clinical research such as Pocock (1983).

To introduce the content of the chapter, the following lists items which need to be considered in planning an evaluation and in deciding the design and methods to use.

♦ *The nature of the intervention to be evaluated*: is it well defined and understood (structured), or unclear and little known (unstructured); is it stable or changing?
♦ The *size and scope* of the evaluated and its boundary limits: how large is the size or scope of the treatment, service, policy or change and what is the level of the system to be evaluated?
♦ The clarity of the *purpose* of the intervention evaluated: does the evaluated have clear objectives, are the objectives measurable, is there consensus about objectives?
♦ The nature and level of the *target* of the evaluated: is the target biophysical, an individual person, a population or a group of people in a work organization?
♦ The scope of the *effects* of the evaluated on the target: if the evaluation is to look at the effects, will it look at one effect or a broad range of effects, and at which time(s)?
♦ *Perspectives and value criteria*: which user perspectives will be used and what are the criteria of valuation to be used in the evaluation?
♦ *Data required*: which data are needed which follow from these criteria, and when and how often are these data to be collected?
♦ *Timing*: when do the results need to be available to have the maximum influence on decision making? Are interim results needed or possible?
♦ *Resources*: what money, time and skills are available for the evaluation, those of both the evaluators and any collaborators? Are the resources fixed or negotiable? Are there existing data which can be used?

A final introductory and practical point. Planning is about deciding how best to use resources. A mistake which all evaluators have made is to underestimate the time and skills needed for an evaluation. When you are beginning an evaluation it helps to have some idea of the time available, and to look ahead at the phases listed below; then to draw a pie chart with 'pie slices' for each of the eight phases, which shows an estimate of how much time to allocate to each phase. This forces the evaluator to recognize the time constraints and to prioritize by allocating percentages of the total time to each phase.

## Phases in an evaluation

Designing an evaluative investigation is an art . . . general recommendations on evaluation can mislead; evaluations should not be cast into a single mold. For any evaluation many good designs can be proposed, but no perfect ones.

(Cronbach 1980: 1–2)

Many evaluations run through the following phases, although not necessarily in a precise chronological sequence. Each phase is discussed in more detail below.

1 *Initiation*: acting on a felt need to make a judgement of value about a treatment, service, policy or change, by looking at the options for making a self-evaluation, or an internal or external evaluation. The initiator may be an evaluation user, a sponsor or an evaluator.
2 *Formulation and proposal*: deciding whom the evaluation is for and which user perspectives to take, the primary questions and decisions it is to inform, the criteria for valuation and the comparisons which will be used in the evaluation.
3 *Reviewing knowledge*: discovering and reviewing what is already known about the evaluated, or about similar things.
4 *Finalizing details of design and methods*: Finalizing design and the details of which data gathering methods to use, how to use them and how to analyse the data to give information about the criteria.
5 *Data collection*: gathering and recording data using qualitative or quantitative methods, or both.
6 *Data analysis and reporting*: analysing the data, and reporting what was discovered about the evaluated in relation to the criteria.
7 *Judging value and deciding action*: users judge value and decide what to do by drawing on the evaluation findings as well as other data, and by considering the options open to them.
8 *Evaluator self-review*: the evaluator or evaluation team review the lessons for them from the evaluation, and consider any methodological innovations or improvements which they developed during the evaluation.

### 1 Initiation

The phase of initiation is where a person or people feel a growing need to make a judgement of value about an existing or proposed intervention or service. It describes someone taking action to start a formal evaluation. Initiators of non-treatment interventions are often managers who want to judge the value of a new or existing service, a new way of organizing or an intervention such as a training programme. Initiators may also be national professional or patient organizations or government departments, which issue a general invitation to submit proposals or directly contact known evaluators. Evaluators can also initiate evaluations by seeking a sponsor. Initiators can be user-evaluators, such as practitioners who want to examine in some detail the value of an intervention to their own or their colleagues' practice, or to review their own organization. Examples of the latter may be a new treatment or a way of organizing a service, and the evaluation may be to judge value by searching the literature, or by making a small scale experiment.

---

**Roles in many types of evaluations**

*Evaluator or evaluation team*: the person or people making the evaluation.

*Users*: the people who will use the evaluation to make better informed decisions.

*Financial sponsors*: those paying for the evaluation (which can be one or more users).

*Supervisor*: the manager or group overseeing the evaluation (which can be a committee of users, sponsors or a contract manager and expert advisors).

---

An important milestone in all evaluations is a contract between the evaluator and sponsor about what the evaluator will do. This also applies to 'in-house' evaluations, where a manager assigns an evaluation task to one or more of the staff. Contract agreement can follow a lengthy discussion about options and details, or it may be an agreement to carry out initial explorations in order to decide whether to make an evaluation or to help to formulate a detailed design.

*Susan telephoned her colleague, Michael, about whether to set up an evaluation of the mental health centre. He answered quickly. 'Susan, I'm not an expert on evaluation – I only inherited this task of managing these people who were doing an evaluation of a training programme for our nurses. If I knew then what I know now, we would have got much more out of that evaluation than we did. It was helpful, but it would have been even more helpful if I had been in on the planning stage. From what you say Susan it does sound like an evaluation could help you. You could get one of your staff to do it, and at least you would have control and get regular reports. But people would not talk openly to them, and their report would not carry much credibility with the pressure groups and psychiatrists. I think you should go outside, but before you do, think about what you want and when you want the report. Some of these people think we are made of money, and they don't seem to operate in real time like we do.'*

## 2 Formulation and proposal

In large scale evaluations and where the sponsor is clear about what is wanted, the sponsor will select an evaluator and a design from a number of proposals submitted. Some sponsors are not clear what they want and use the many proposals submitted to them to clarify what they want evaluated and the questions they want answers to.

Usually the sponsor and the selected evaluator will then negotiate further details in a planning phase. They will explore and negotiate the final purposes, design and details of the evaluations before a formal contract is agreed. Evaluators often have to help sponsors who know little about evaluation to define their questions and to educate them about what evaluation can and cannot do. A section later in this chapter gives concepts for helping this initial formulation phase.

Sometimes the evaluator needs to carry out a feasibility assessment to find out more about the item to be evaluated and to give the sponsor proposals for different types of evaluation, including not doing an evaluation. Giving sponsors a set of choices like this helps them to clarify what they want from the evaluation and to understand more about evaluation.

> At least the psychiatrists would talk to them, thought Susan after closing the door behind the people from the local university. She had one other group to meet: full-time evaluators from a local private consultancy which she had used before to do option appraisals on converting the local hospital. But she had been able to get into a dialogue with the university people and they had been helpful in clarifying the purpose of the evaluation. She had a good feel for them. She could see how she could work with them and that they would be able to move around the service without drama. They would be a lot less expensive too. What was Michael talking about when he said that they did not have their feet on the ground? They all wore watches, even if one had a Mickey Mouse watch with a red strap.

The end result of the formulation phase should be an evaluation plan which describes:

♦ *who* the evaluation is for;
♦ the *purpose* of the evaluation, and the one or more *questions* it aims to answer;
♦ *what* is to be evaluated;
♦ the evaluation *design*;
♦ the *methods* used to gather and analyse data (see 'data collection' below);
♦ a *time plan* of activities and milestones;
♦ the *resources* to be used and the budget.

## 3 Reviewing knowledge

This is one of the tasks in the early stages of an evaluation, even if a limited review was carried out in the previous formulation phase. The purpose is to find out what is already known about the evaluated, and to see if or how others have made similar evaluations. In most cases it will be a review of scientific and published literature, and also finding out if there are any relevant internal service documents which have described or reported the evaluated, and reviewing these. Descriptions of how to search computer and other databases for relevant published research are given in some research methods texts, such as Edwards and Talbot (1994) and in Gray (1997). Evaluators can also make use of a meta-analysis or review, and may themselves need to carry out such a review. How to assess or carry out such types of review is discussed in NHSCR&D (1996), and briefly in St Leger *et al.* (1992).

## 4 Finalizing details of design and methods

After finding out what is already known about the evaluated and looking at how others have designed and made evaluations, the evaluator often needs to revise his or her own plans for data collection. The urge is always to rush into data collection, but even a small amount of time and thought at the final planning stage saves more time when collecting data and analysing it.

*There had been arguments in the evaluation team. Alan was always talking about how important ethics were in doing an evaluation, but did this really mean going back to the sponsor to get agreement to every small change? No, the time had come to start the interviews, but it had been right to delay starting until the team had rethought how they were going to record and analyse the data. An earlier study they had found had used a method for grouping the topics which came up in interviews – changing their strategy to use this method would make data analysis much easier. And Alan had been right about going back to the sponsor to get them to get together information which the sponsor already had about people's needs in the area and about the costs of the service in the north area. But there was still the question of exactly what they should say at the start of each interview about confidentiality.*

*'It seems OK to me', said Susan at the end of the final planning meeting with the evaluation team, 'and I appreciate your coming back to me and taking me through exactly what you aim to do now that you have worked out the details. But I have to say that there are limits to how much time my assistant can devote to getting the information which you want, especially about costs – I suspect we simply do not have some of the data you are asking for. Also, I need to write a letter explaining to people who you are and what you are doing. What shall I say in my letter about confidentiality – if we have total confidentiality how can you do a report to us which gives evidence about the views of different groups?'*

## 5 Data collection

In the phase of data collection the evaluators use methods to gather quantitative or qualitative data, and may use existing data sources such as patient medical records and service documents and statistics. Chapter 11 describes methods such as observation, interviewing, questionnaires, surveys, measurement and using existing data. The following list contains issues to consider in planning which data to collect, and how and when to collect the data.

♦ How large should the *sample* be, and how should the sample be selected (e.g. for credibility, for statistical validity)?
♦ How to get *access* to the people to be interviewed or to service documents and records.
♦ *How often and when* do the data need to be collected (e.g. before the intervention, how long after, follow-up)?
♦ How will data be *recorded* in order to make analysis easier?
♦ Should there be a small pilot test of the data gathering methods (e.g. if making a survey)?
♦ Is there a need for *expert* advice or for a specialist to undertake some of the data collection?
♦ What does *previous research*, which has used this method, teach us about how to maximize validity and reliability, and have the methods we plan to use been validated?
♦ How do we get *cooperation* from service personnel and patients?
♦ What is the best way to *introduce* ourselves as evaluators to different parties? Do we have to be careful about what we say so as to minimize biasing what people might tell us?

*As it turned out they had not completed all the interviews in the time they had assigned. The other problem was that the manager's assistant had not been able to get all the costing information needed or the information about needs in the south of the area. The only thing they could do was to make estimates, and point out in the report that these were informed guesses. But the time had come for the evaluation team to think about how to present the findings to the service personnel. It was important to be diplomatic, but they had to tell the truth.*

## 6 Data analysis and reporting

A task which is often neglected when one is planning an evaluation is to look ahead to how data will be analysed, and then drawn together in a report in a way which will answer the evaluation questions. The dividing line between data collection and data analysis is arbitrary, because data collection often involves a recording method which is itself a form of analysis, such as a pre-structured set of questions for an interview.

In planning an evaluation, evaluators need to think about how they can best communicate their findings. What are the questions which their audience will have? How do evaluators convey the certainty and the limitations of their findings? By considering early on how to present their report, evaluators may then look at the data analysis methods and may decide to use different methods which give more direct answers to the original evaluation questions and to those which their audiences may raise. Methods for data analysis are discussed in more detail in Chapter 11, which also gives a checklist for assessing the quality of evidence presented in an evaluation report. Ways to communicate findings are discussed in Chapter 10.

## 7 Judging value and deciding action

The task of judging the value of the evaluated and of acting is not the task of the professional evaluator but the task of 'users' of the evaluation. If the evaluation was well planned, then the findings of the evaluation will help users to make better decisions than they would have made otherwise. More accurately, we should talk not of users judging value, but of changing their value judgements. Many will have already made some valuation of the evaluated – the information from the study aims to help them to make more informed judgements of value.

Although judging value is not a task of the evaluator, it is a phase in the overall 'evaluation for action' process, and one which evaluators and users need to plan for if the evaluation is to be of maximum use to users. Evaluators need to recognize that there will be pressure on them to judge value and to make specific recommendations for action. The role of evaluators is to help users to incorporate the evaluation information into their value judgements, but to stop at this. They do this by reminding users about the criteria of valuation which the users formulated at the start of the evaluation, and by making clear how decisions were made about which information to collect and which things were not to be studied.

Evaluators need to make clear the limitations of the evidence, what the evidence does and does not conclusively show and how the evaluators think that this relates to the decisions to be made. They need to explain clearly problems which arose during the evaluation and affected the evidence, such as poor response rate to questionnaires, patient 'drop-out' rates and any changes in the intervention which was evaluated. Some of these issues and predictable problems should have been thought through when the evaluation was designed. Looking ahead to how the users will judge value and act helps evaluators to plan the design and other details of the study.

As well as making sure that the findings are well communicated, there are certain methods which evaluators can use to help users to integrate the findings of the evaluation into their decision making process. One method is to use multi-attribute utility analysis to help users to structure their judgements (noted at the end of Chapter 2). A later section of this chapter looks at values and valuation in more detail.

*'Does this mean we should cancel our plans for a new centre in the south? If 64 per cent of the patients that you spoke to said there were delays in arranging day-care, and with the problems in interprofessional working, it seems to me you are saying that we should not go ahead with a similar centre for the south. This is your recommendation, is it not?' asked the chairperson of the local branch of the 'Mental Health Now!' association.*

*'What you do is your decision,' Alan replied, on behalf of the evaluation team. He paused. His presentation of the evaluation results had gone well, but there were concerned faces in the audience. They wanted clear answers. 'All our study shows is that a certain proportion of service personnel and patients thought there were problems and we reported these to you. You have also seen the building costs and an estimate of the running costs. It is stretching the evidence to say that the centre in the north is not good value*

*for money, which is what one of the audience said – we did not do a proper cost-benefit study because we were not asked to. There are some problems, as you see from our study, but the study evidence is something which you have to consider, along with other factors, in making your decision. You have to weigh all this up. Perhaps I could say a bit more about who we did and who we did not interview, and what we found out about people's needs in the south.'*

*Afterwards, Susan wondered whether the evaluation had made things more complicated. But, she thought, the evaluation team were right, it was a complicated issue to decide which type of service would best serve the people in the south area for the limited resources they had. She and the planning committee now had to put the evaluation findings together with other factors, like the new consultant psychiatrist's ideas and the new government policy. Now that the evaluation was over, perhaps she could persuade one of the evaluation team to join the multi-agency planning committee for the new service in the south . . .*

## 8 Evaluator self-review

The final phase is where evaluators or teams spend time reviewing what they have learnt from the evaluation. One aim is to draw lessons on how to conduct future evaluations and for self-development as an evaluator. Evaluation is a young science and also a more practical and political activity than other types of research. Learning and development for many evaluators has been from reflecting on their practice and relating this to theories of evaluation (e.g. Shadish *et al*. 1991). Evaluators should compare what happened during the evaluation to their original plan and proposal, as well as consider the strengths and weaknesses of their methods and what they might be able to use in future evaluations.

Other aims for a review are to consider the contribution which the evaluation could make to evaluation theory and methodology, as well as whether findings about the evaluated could be generalized and would be of interest to other evaluators and health service personnel. There are many reasons why evaluators rarely allocate time to carry out a review, but the plan and timetable should build in time and finance for a review, and record agreements with the sponsor about publication rights and whether sponsors or others would be able to veto publication of any details, as well as who should deal with any requests for copies of the evaluation report.

## Issues and concepts in evaluation planning and design

*What is the purpose of the evaluation? What exactly will we evaluate? What do we need to know so as to be better able to judge its value?*

In this section we consider in more detail questions and issues which arise in an evaluation and which it is useful for sponsors, evaluators and other parties to consider in the planning stages. The section first looks at the questions of whom the evaluation is for and which decisions it aims to inform. Then we look at values in three senses: those of the users and how to define the users' criteria for valuing the evaluated; then the values which are embodied in or intrinsic to the intervention which is to be evaluated (e.g. some alternative therapies) ; finally, the values of the evaluator. The section then discusses the questions of how to define the intervention to be evaluated, and how to define the objectives of the evaluated. In many evaluations, evaluators need to work with sponsors and stakeholders to answer these questions, and here we consider concepts and models which help to find answers. Sponsors need to give some thought to these questions in order to decide whether to do an evaluation, to prepare for discussions with evaluators, to judge proposals and then to manage an evaluation.

## Who is the evaluation for?

Both evaluators and sponsors need to be clear which people the evaluation is intended for (primary users), and who will or could make use of the evaluation (secondary users). There are often many audiences who are interested in the results of a health evaluation, and many who will change what they would otherwise have done as a result of the evaluation – making such a change is one definition of 'use' followed in this book. This is true of even seemingly specialized evaluations of specific treatments (e.g. some drugs), where the primary users are other researchers and clinical specialists, but where patients and patients' organizations also find out about and make use of the evaluation.

Some approaches to evaluation assume that the evaluation is only for those who pay for the evaluation, or for management. However, there are two reasons why evaluators need to bear in mind different possible users of the evaluation, their questions and their decisions which the evaluation could influence. First, by considering how others could use the evaluation, it may be possible to make small changes to answer their questions and to increase the value of the evaluation to a wider audience. Where the evaluation is paid for out of public finance, both the public sponsor and the evaluator have a duty to consider the range of possible audiences and users.

The second reason is to make implementation or change easier. The evaluation may indicate that changes are required, or no changes where there are already pressure groups demanding a change. By looking ahead to the change or no-change consequences of the evaluation, it is possible to think about the questions which those who can block or assist change would want the evaluation to address. If one takes the view that evaluators have some responsibility for practical action, which is the view taken in this book, then it is important to anticipate how the evaluation could be used by different parties who can gain and lose from the findings. Confronting the 'politics of evaluation' with sponsors can also reveal whether the request for evaluation is genuine, whether it is a delay tactic or whether a decision has already been made – these issues are discussed further in Chapter 10.

Having clarified whom the evaluation is for, we need to define what their questions are and prioritize these, as an evaluation will not be able to answer all of the questions raised by users.

## Which decisions should the evaluation inform?

The purpose of evaluation is to enable people to make more informed decisions than they would otherwise do. If an evaluation does not make people act differently, then it is a failure. This does not mean that an evaluation should always lead to change – it could give information which reduces people's doubts about the value of the evaluated and causes them not to change anything when they might have otherwise made a change.

Most evaluations should start by understanding the choices and decisions which users face about the evaluated. What are the alternatives open to users, and how do they currently value the evaluated? Is there a 'decision window' – a period of time during which a decision will be made, and which sets the time when the results of the evaluation have to be presented if they are to affect the decision? If there is, the evaluator will need a timetable which works back from this decision period and the time available will shape the type of evaluation which can be undertaken.

It may seem that the practical actions of users are of no concern to the evaluator. Yet it is only by understanding what users need and want from the evaluation that the evaluator can properly design the study. The proposition here is that the best way of planning an evaluation is to work back from the decisions in the future which users want to or could make, and to look at which information they lack that could be collected in time to help them to judge value and to make a more informed decision.

One way to proceed is to identify the questions which users have about the evaluated, and then to ask 'why?' to each of these questions to find the practical decisions and behaviours which relate to the questions. Evaluations should then focus on one or two of the key questions and decisions. This means deciding their priority: for example, by listing and ranking questions in order of importance using the group nominal technique discussed in Chapter 11. A better method for prioritizing may be to relate questions to practical decisions – this helps to eliminate the many 'interesting' questions with no, or less, consequences for action. In experimental evaluations of treatments, clarifying users' questions is still important, but the evaluator is more constrained. The design should build carefully on previous research and test a specific hypothesis.

## Which criteria of valuation?

The criteria for an evaluation are the dimensions which people use to judge the value of the evaluated. Many people judge value in terms of effectiveness – this is a dimension or criterion. Another criterion might be the cost to a specific health service. Criteria are what enable users to judge the value of something.

How do evaluators decide the evaluation criteria? The answer is that they do not – sponsors and users decide criteria. Evaluators can help users and sponsors to list and define their criteria when they are unclear or uncertain which to use. There are two ways to do this. The first is to go to the decisions which the evaluation is to inform and to consider which criteria of value would help in making the decision or in choosing between the alternatives. For example, should an organization financing a health programme in a developing country increase, decrease or terminate its financing? The criteria of valuation of the health programme which could help to make the decision include the effectiveness of the programme in meeting needs and its geographical availability – listing these and other criteria help the users to decide if they have not done so already. The second method is to look at the comparisons which people make to judge value – the comparisons may be in relation to an ideal or to another similar thing. For example, the health programme costs and evidence of effects could be compared to those of other programmes in other countries, or the comparison could be to nothing – to estimates of what would happen if the programme was withdrawn.

It is the use of value criteria and comparisons which distinguishes evaluation from other activities. The importance of defining criteria is that criteria provide the link between the users' questions and concerns and the data which the evaluator needs to gather and the measures to use (Table 9.1).

*Table 9.1*  Some examples of the link between criteria, measures and comparison

| Example criteria | Example measures | Comparison |
| --- | --- | --- |
| Effectiveness | Objectives achieved within a set time. Needs met. | Objectives compared to actual achievements. Needs compared to needs actually met. |
| Costs | Resources used represented in money terms. | With other uses of the money. Intended costs compared to actual ('within budget'). With other similar services. |
| Equity | Proportion of different eligible populations served. | Actual coverage compared to intended equitable coverage. |

In this book the term 'criterion' is used to describe a general dimension for making a comparative judgement of value, such as efficiency. Note that the term 'criterion' is sometimes used to describe something more specific, such as the cost per unit of output (in this book this is a 'measure') or 'the cost per unit of output is less than $55' (in this book this is a standard – expressed as a level to be achieved on a measure). In this book criteria are general, and standards are precise or operationalized criteria (Øvretveit 1992a).

The importance of clarifying the users' criteria of valuation is not just to decide which data to gather. It also clearly marks out the role of the evaluator: in professional evaluations, evaluators do not judge value, but confine themselves to data gathering and presentation. This meaning of evaluation as a process to which the evaluator contributes is different from the two common meanings of the term evaluation: 'to ascertain or measure the amount of something', and 'to give value (attribute) to something or to judge value'. In professional evaluations, it is not the evaluator who judges the worth or value of the thing evaluated, although evaluators can influence in many ways the valuation which others give. These questions of values and valuation are discussed in more detail in the next section. First, consider two views about values in evaluations:

> *The value neutrality of science is a myth, but nowhere is this more apparent than in the supposedly value-free 'science' of evaluation. The values of the evaluator and of many other parties enter into all parts of an evaluation study, and are often not recognized. A value-free evaluation is an oxymoron.*

> *The importance of the value-neutrality of the evaluator cannot be stressed too highly, and although difficult, must remain as an ideal to be striven for if the evaluator is to have credibility and her findings are to be taken seriously.*

## Values and valuation

This book shares the more common view among evaluators that a good evaluator does not judge the value of the evaluated: her task is to help others to make better informed judgements. Values and valuation lie at the centre of evaluation but are not often considered. Here we distinguish value issues in:

- the way users and others judge the value of the evaluated;
- the way values enter into the evaluation process;
- the values embodied in or inherent to the service, policy or intervention being evaluated;
- the values of the evaluator and how they affect the evaluation.

Evaluators need to be clear about their views in relation to all of these, and about the strategies which they use to minimize the influence of their own values or to make clear how their values influence the evaluation.

### How users judge value

The view taken here is that evaluators do not judge value – their task is to help users and stakeholders to judge the value of the evaluated. They can do this in three ways: first, by helping users to specify their dimensions of value which are to be incorporated into the evaluation study (this was discussed above in relation to criteria); second, by collecting information about these dimensions of the evaluated and providing it to users; third, by helping users to draw on both the evaluation information and other information to arrive at a systematic judgement of value.

Some evaluators see their role as strictly limited to the second task. This may be possible if users or sponsors are clear about their dimensions of valuation and about how they will use the results of the evaluation. More often, evaluators influence the way in which users structure their judgements of value, rather than only 'inputting' information into a process for judging value which is independent of and pre-exists the evaluation.

### Values embodied in the evaluated

Another value issue is whether it is the task of evaluators to make explicit the values of the service, change or programme which they are evaluating. This does not refer to the formal statements of the values of the service or policy, but to value assumptions which are unstated or unacknowledged and may be the opposite of the stated values.

Some evaluators propose that 'value explication' is an important role of the evaluator. The view taken in this book is that it depends upon whether explicating values in this way will help users to judge the value of the evaluated and to make better informed decisions. Often the explicit values of the service providers are less important than the actual results and effects, and there may be conflicts between the values and ideals of a service or policy and what it actually achieves.

### The values of the evaluators

Early approaches to evaluation in the 1960s stressed the idea of a value-neutral evaluator, and the parallels with the idea of the value-neutral scientist. Evaluators should not let their personal values intrude into their independent and objective search for the facts. Later approaches in the 1970s and 1980s reflected the debate in the social sciences about facts and value and the critique of some simplistic positivist 'vacuum cleaner' theories of data gathering. They gave greater recognition to the values of the evaluator, in some cases to argue for greater sensitivity to personal values so as to make them explicit and to help others to judge if these values had biased the findings.

Another approach was to argue for value-committed or value-driven evaluation, where the evaluator promotes certain values or the interests of particular groups. An example is House (1980), who argues that evaluators should advance the interests of the disadvantaged and justifies this by reference to Rawls's theory of justice. Whichever view evaluators take, it is their duty to state their position so that users are in a better position to decide how to use the evaluation findings.

We now turn to two problems in planning many evaluations: defining the intervention and defining the objectives of the intervention.

## What is to be evaluated? Defining the intervention

This may appear a simple question to answer. Sponsors and other users sometimes feel that the evaluator's wish to define precisely and exactly what is to be evalauted is an over-concern with detail. However, when planning an evaluation it is always necessary to spend time agreeing a precise definition of the intervention to be evaluated.

In the case of treatment evaluations, a clear definition of the treatment is necessary to decide the design and controls. Where some treatments are thought to have an effect and where it is not clear how the effect is produced, the sole purpose of the evaluation may be to establish a clearer definition of the treatment by excluding different variables which could account for any effects. Previous research is important in helping to decide hypotheses about possible cause and effect and where to draw the boundary around the intervention so as to define it more precisely (see the discussion of design in Chapter 3).

In evaluations of services, policies or organizational changes, the sponsor and user often play a greater part in defining the evaluated. Sponsors may not have a clear idea of exactly what they want evaluated: for example, 'We need to evaluate the changes which we introduced here last year.' Even if sponsors know what they mean, other people may have different understandings about what is referred to by the name the sponsor gives to the evaluated. For example, people have different ideas about where the boundaries of a service begin and end – for some 'the primary healthcare team' may include social workers, for others it may not. Different understandings are common in the case of national policies or directives which are interpreted differently at local levels, and when the evaluated is a change to a service rather than a service. Because different groups may have different views about what is and is not part of a treatment, service, policy or change, the definition of what is to be evaluated often depends on whom the evaluation is for.

Evaluators will always need to define the evaluated more precisely than the initial descriptions given to them. They usually need to work with sponsors and possibly others to do this, so as to avoid possible misunderstandings about exactly what sponsors want evaluated. The concepts described in Chapter 3 help to specify the evaluated: the concepts of 'the box' and 'the boundary' around it, which excludes what is not to be evaluated, and the concepts of input, process, outputs and outcomes.

Sometimes a preliminary or a sole purpose of the evaluation is to specify something: an $x$, which is vague and understood in different ways, such as 'the organizational development programme' or 'the total quality management strategy we have been pursuing for the past three years'. In these cases the concepts of the box and of inputs, processes and outcomes can be used to help different parties to articulate what they understand by $x$ and then to compare these different understandings using a type 1 descriptive evaluation design (see Chapter 3). The question of how to define the evaluated is related to the question of how to define the objectives of the evaluated.

## Defining the objectives of the intervention

Most services, changes and policies have objectives, and one approach to evaluation is to compare these objectives to what has been achieved by the service, change or policy. The question of the objectives of the evaluated is the last of the planning questions which we consider in detail in this chapter. First, we look at how to define objectives, and then at whether we need to – the 'goal-free evaluation' approach.

At first sight this looks a simple way to do an evaluation: to judge the value of the evaluated in terms of the degree to which it meets or falls short of the objectives. Thus a service, policy or intervention would be valued highly and viewed as a success if it achieved its objectives. Criticisms of this approach are that it assumes that the objectives of the service, change or policy are the right ones, or are valuable and valued. Other criticisms are that this approach ignores conflict about objectives, and that there may be many different and competing objectives: examples are the many and ambiguous objectives of Norwegian health services (Olsen 1995), the British NHS (Øvretveit 1994d) and Swedish health services (Axelsson and Svensson 1994). We return to these criticisms shortly, but first we consider a problem in designing evaluations of this type: the problem of abstract and unmeasurable objectives.

There are three ways to find out the objectives of a service, a change or a policy – what we will call 'the objectives of the evaluated'. The first is to look for written statements of objectives, and then evaluate what is done against these face value objectives. The second is to ask the head of a service and others what the objectives are. The third is to look at what the service does and to infer objectives.

Evaluators can proceed in one of two ways. The first is to work with selected individuals to agree which objectives to evaluate the service or policy against, and which measures to use as an indication of success or failure in achieving these objectives. The second way is for the evaluator independently to define objectives and what to use as measures by using one or more types of statements of objectives, and to use these statements to justify the inferred objectives (e.g. Øvretveit 1994b, 1996b).

### Ordering objectives at different levels of abstraction for an evaluation

In most cases evaluators will be working with objectives at different levels of abstraction. There are two sets of concepts which help to clarify objectives in order to decide which measures to use to get evidence of reaching or falling short of the objectives.

The first is to order the objectives in a hierarchy according to the time target stated or implied by the objective. The most general objectives do not have time targets but are ongoing – sometimes called 'values' or 'principles'. At the level below are long-term or strategic objectives with anything between five and ten year time targets. The theory of levels of work calls these 'level 5' objectives and proposes that organizations need other objectives with two to five year time targets ('level 4' objectives) one to two year time targets ('level 3'), one month to one year time targets ('level 2' objectives) and up to one month time targets ('level 1' objectives) (Rowbottom and Billis 1977; Jaques 1989).

*You know when people are new to evaluation – they are surprised or complain when they discover that the service has no objectives, or vague statements of aspiration, or many conflicting objectives.*

The second set of concepts come from a general theory of purpose (Kinston 1995). These concepts can be used in a similar way to order objectives in a hierarchy, and to make sense of the many terms which people use to describe the purpose of a service or policy. The simple version of this framework describes five levels of purpose. At the highest and most abstract level 5 are 'social values', which are general ideals or statements of need which the service, change or policy aims to meet. A lower and qualitatively distinct level of purpose (level 4) is a statement of 'principal object' which defines the distinctive identity of the service, change or policy, such as its core purpose or mission. Both level 4 and level 5 objectives are general and are needed to unify and inspire people around an agreed purpose. Level 3 objectives are the internal priorities which specify where the emphasis will lie between a number of valid aims, and which aims are more important than others. These can often be quantified: for example, in terms of the proportion of total resources allocated to different objectives. Level 2 objectives, or 'strategic objectives', define outcomes and directions – they are the specific things which further the level 4 principal purposes. 'Tactical objectives' are the level 1 objectives which specify detailed results to be pursued and timescales.

Both these sets of concepts are useful to evaluators and to others to clarify the objectives of the evaluated. Note that the second framework is also useful for clarifying the objectives of the evaluation exercise itself. An evaluation proposal will need to state the general and specific objectives of the evaluation. This 'purposes framework' helps evaluators to order the different statements which they need to make, and to check if any statements at one or more levels are missing – the theory of purpose predicts that the evaluation will encounter problems if it does not state objectives at each level of purpose.

> *The evaluator's question 'What are your objectives?' has a simple answer when put to most service managers or policy formulators: 'To survive the evaluation.' Most services have unclear, confusing and changing objectives and it is a naive evaluator who seeks to persuade management to accept objectives which managers think might show the measured performance of the service to be poor.*

### Problems with the evaluation-by-objectives approach

We saw above ways to deal with the 'problem of unmeasurable objectives' for a service, change or policy: to use different methods to find or specify objectives. But is this 'evaluation-by-objectives' approach fundamentally mistaken? Although it appears a simple approach to evaluation, in practice there are many problems.

♦ A service or policy which has only one stated objective will usually state this objective at a high level of abstraction. This statement then has to be operationalized in order to carry out an evaluation.

♦ Most services or policies have more than one stated objective. If the objectives are at different levels of abstraction, we often find that one at a lower level does not follow from one at a higher level – it is not derived from or linked to the higher-level objective (i.e. it is inconsistent). If the objectives are at the same level they are often conflicting, or it is unclear which is a higher priority.

♦ Stated objectives are often different from the objectives which people know about or which they pursue in practice.

♦ Often stated specific objectives are 'look-good goals', not the ones which are likely to show up poor performance.

♦ Lower-level objectives are always disputed by different groups within the organization (goal conflict), or different groups pursue different objectives.

♦ The stated or 'in-practice' objectives of a service or policy often change while the evaluation is being done.

♦ The objectives may not be related to needs.

Evaluators using the evaluation-by-objectives approach recognize these problems and use techniques like those described above to sort out and define objectives and to decide valid measures. But, if they do this in collaboration with the people in the service or those implementing the change, then they introduce a change to the evaluated by their work of specification. Alternatively, if they independently derive and specify measurable objectives, then they have to justify their inferences and recognize any value assumptions which they have introduced. Either way, the evaluation is not a simple collection of data which conclusively show the degree of success of the intervention in achieving objectives.

### Is 'evaluability assessment' an answer?

Wholey (1977) accepts these problems, and proposes 'evaluability assessment' as a solution (otherwise called by Wholey 'exploratory evaluation' or 'accountability assessment' and by Horst 'preassessment of evaluability'). Evaluability assessment is a method for forcing managers or policy makers to define objectives for which they are willing to be held accountable. Wholey argues that 'ambiguous objectives should not be rendered unambiguous by an evaluator; that, we believe, is a management or policy question.' Evaluability assessment asks a set of questions about the evaluated and uses the answers to work with management to create an 'evaluable programme'. For Wholey, 'evaluability assessment answers the question, not whether a program can be evaluated (every program can be evaluated), but whether the program is ready to be managed for results, what changes are needed for results-oriented management, and whether evaluation is likely to contribute to improved program performance' (Wholey 1983).

### Goal-free evaluation

However, evaluability assessment does not fully answer the criticisms of the evaluation-by-objectives approach, which include having to import too many assumptions about the evaluated and imposing an inaccurate rationalist model of service or policy processes. In common with some early US approaches to programme evaluation, it holds a simplistic view of organizations and organizational goals which ignores organizational politics, and acts as an instrument of management in assuming or imposing a single interest group's definition of objectives.

An alternative approach proposed by Scriven is 'goal-free evaluation'. This approach is not just to ignore any stated objectives, but for evaluators to isolate themselves from people working in a service and seek to discover any effects which the service or policy has had. The evaluator should look for any need which is met by the evaluated, and judge the value of the evaluated in terms of the social needs it meets, regardless of what the stated objectives are. Evaluation, then, should discover the effect of the evaluated and match these effects 'against the needs of whom they affect'. For Scriven (1973), 'In evaluation, blind is beautiful. Remember that Justice herself is blind, and good medical research is double blind.'

This is a different value position for an evaluator from the seemingly more neutral value position of adopting the objectives of the service or programme without questioning the value of these objectives. Strictly speaking, the approach is not so much goal-free evaluation as 'effect discovery' and relating effects to needs to arrive at a judgement of value.

### Needs-based evaluation

A needs-based approach to evaluation has its own problems, not least the problem of defining needs, which is as difficult and as value-laden as defining objectives. For example, which of the many definitions of health needs will the evaluation adopt: medical illness, capacity to benefit from a health service, restriction of normal mental, physical and social functioning, impaired well being, expressed need, normative need etc.? Most methods are costly and time-consuming and many are only suitable for research projects with many resources and skills. Edwards (1996) reviewed community-based needs assessments which had been carried out for London health purchasers, and noted weaknesses in not defining more limited population groups, in not having clear objectives for the assessments or sufficient concern for validity, especially in priority setting exercises which involved local people. The most successful were those which examined a particular area, service or disease in order to give specific ideas for improvements, and those which used primary epidemiological research.

Evaluators who use needs as a comparison and criterion will find that there are a range of methods for assessing the health needs of individuals (e.g. Bowling 1992, 1995) and of populations – the latter are described in most introductions to epidemiology or health planning, and for primary health care in Wilkin et al. (1992). One approach is to use already collected information about needs in the population, as discussed in the section on existing data in Chapter 11. Another is to use national norms of the average incidence and prevalence of categories of illness in the general population, and adjust this for the characteristics of the target population (see Øvretveit 1994b) for an example of an evaluation which used this as one criterion of valuation). For evaluators who want to carry out a direct needs assessment, one method to consider is a sample survey, as described in Chapter 11. Another is to use a mixture of methods like those used in rapid appraisal designs, including interviews, surveys and collaborating with communities to collect secondary data (e.g. Ong 1993).

## Linking planning questions to evaluation design

The issues discussed in this chapter need to be considered before evaluators can decide the best design and methods for an evaluation. Evaluators also need to know the strengths and limitations of different designs and methods in order to advise sponsors about which questions can be answered and what an evaluation can and cannot do. The following summarizes the above in a list of the key considerations when one is linking the evaluation questions and purposes to the design and methods to be used:

---

### Designing an evaluation: questions to ask

♦ *What* is to be evaluated? (The boundary definition of the evaluated.) Might the evaluated change during the evaluation?

♦ *Constraints*: what are the *time frame* and the *resources* (money, time, skills, existing data)?

♦ Do the users/sponsors need help to focus their questions?

♦ Which *value perspectives* could and will be included in the evaluation?

♦ *Who* is the evaluation for (main user)?

♦ Who will pay (financial sponsor)?

♦ Whose *criteria* of valuation are to be used and what are these criteria (external criteria (e.g. national standards), managers', service funders', patients', referrers' etc.)?

♦ What are the *evaluation questions* and why is each important (discard those that do not relate to a possible decisions and action)?

♦ Which *decisions* could the user make which would be more informed as a result of the evaluation?

♦ Are the *objectives* of the thing to be evaluated defined? Do objectives and criteria need to be formulated? Can progress in achieving the objectives and success/failure be measured? Are there conflicting objectives or differences in view about objectives? Will the evaluation need to spend time formulating/agreeing the objectives of the thing to be evaluated (how much of the evaluation is developmental in helping to define objectives)?

♦ What are the *comparisons*? (With a similar service, to nothing, before and after? Existence of comparators and their willingness to be involved, costs, the feasibility of a control group of patients.)

♦ Do service providers/managers want help or feedback *during* the evaluation?

♦ Which *data* does the user need to make a more informed decision?

♦ Always consider *alternative explanations* for the findings, and if possible anticipate these explanations and design the evaluation to exclude them.

---

This list should not be taken as implying that planning and designing an evaluation is a question of following a simple sequence, which starts with specifying the evaluated. Certainly planning and designing non-treatment evaluations is often more like immersing oneself in a sea of questions to find where the current is taking one. There is a dynamic between each of the different areas and questions noted above – the answer to one question limits the options for the answers to another. There is also a dynamic within one area: for example, the amount of resources available for the evaluation. Sponsors may be able to find extra resources if they believe that extra information or a more rigorous design make a significant difference for the decision which they have to make.

## Assessing an evaluation

*Susan paused to look at it again. The proposal for the evaluation of the mental health centre had fallen out of the file when she was putting it away with the final report. There is not much point reading this now, she thought as she looked over the time plan in the proposal. But it was lunch time and her first afternoon appointment was cancelled. As she looked at the time plan she began to see what the proposal had missed. She knew her manager was interested in what she had learned about using evaluations, and she began to make notes for their next meeting. She did a checklist which he and others could use to assess proposals. It looked a bit like the sort of thing that the university people would do, but no matter.*

Take an evaluation proposal and ask the evaluators: if you had half this time and money what would you propose? If they cannot prioritize at this stage, then be warned that they will have more difficulty doing so as the data build up in the middle of the evaluation. Unless evaluators are very experienced, their ambitions are likely to exceed what they are actually able to deliver.

Proposals should address these areas. For assessing a completed evaluation, substitute the past tense.

1 *Users*: is it clear who are/will be the main users of the evaluation? Are any significant user perspectives not included?
2 *Decisions*: is it clear which decisions the evaluation aims to inform? Are evaluation questions listed which relate to the decisions which users want to make?
3 *Definition of the evaluated*: is the item to be evaluated clearly defined (bounded), and is there agreement or consensus among users about what is and what is not to be evaluated? If not, is there a plan to construct and validate a clear specification of the evaluated?
4 *Objectives of the thing being evaluated*: does the evaluation deal adequately with problems in defining the objectives of the evaluated (i.e. objectives not being well defined, or conflicting objectives)? How does it address these problems? Are intermediate objectives inferred?
5 *Outcomes*: does the evaluation gather information about how people might be affected by the evaluated, and how well does it measure this (patients/carers, or personnel if it is an evaluation of an organizational intervention such as a personnel policy; apply 'criteria for measuring outcomes', scope, time, sample, attribution etc.)?

6 *Unintended effects*: will the methods used to gather data about process and outcome be likely to discover important consequences which were not expected or intended?

7 *Resources/costs*: will the evaluation give information about the amount of resources consumed by the intervention (time, money and other resources)? Does it quantify the resources used by patients, carers, other services or other organizations and people, and should it do so? Does the evaluation design get the balance right between examining a limited area in depth and rigorously, and examining a broad range of outcomes and issues?

8 *Data-gathering methods*: are these clearly described and justified as the most cost-effective for the purpose? Are a sufficient number of methods used for the purposes and resources available (e.g. triangulation)? Does the evaluation note the limitations of the methods and of the data collected?

9 *Reporting:* how will the results and implications for the decisions to be made by the users be communicated to them? Will the presentation and report make the limitations of the evaluation clear? Will there be any restrictions to access or publication of the results, and are these justified? Who will translate the findings into behavioural guidelines or action implications?

10 *Could a better evaluation be proposed within the resource, time and other constraints?* Does the proposal list possible and probable problems, and the strategies to minimize the effect of these on the evaluation?

Other checklists for assessing proposals for different types of evaluation are given in St Leger *et al.* (1992: Appendix B) (mostly for service and policy evaluations). For assessing evaluation designs and completed evaluations there are: the 'Economic evaluator's survival guide' in Chapter 8 of Drummond *et al.* (1987), which is also relevant for many non-economic evaluations; 'Review criteria for assessing program evaluations', Appendix C in DHHSPHS (1995); eight methodological criteria in Daley *et al.* (1992: 138–9); The 'Program Evaluation Standards' give standards for educational evaluations (JCSEE 1994) which are useful for any evaluation. One study applied these standards to 277 evaluations of Swedish overseas aid projects: 82 percent lacked an adequate description of methods, and 99 percent any analysis of reliability and validity (Forss and Carlsson 1997). More detailed methods for assessing completed experimental evaluations are described in JAMA (1993), Mercer *et al.* (1995) and Rosenberg and Donald (1995).

## Conclusions

♦ Many evaluations follow a similar sequence of eight phases in the planning and the conduct of the evaluation, although there are some differences between experimental and inductive developmental evaluations in the sequence.

♦ These eight phases are: initiation; formulation; reviewing knowledge; finalizing design; data collection; data analysis and reporting; judging value and deciding action; and evaluator self-review.

♦ This framework of phases helps people new to evaluation to see the issues to be considered, alerts them to possible problems and gives a background for assessing proposals and negotiating a contract. It also reminds evaluators of the need to plan how their time is to be used and of the need to relate the choices which they make in each phase to choices in other phases.

♦ When planning and making an evaluation, evaluators, users and sponsors need to consider whom the evaluation is for, the decisions it is to inform, the criteria of valuation to be used, how to deal with user and evaluator values and how to specify the evaluated and its objectives.

♦ The steps in many types of evaluations are as follows.

1 Clarify whom the evaluation is for: who is asking for and/or paying for the evaluation and who will be the main users of the findings?
2 Clarify the decisions and action that could follow from the evaluation: what do they want the evaluation for?
3 Clarify the evaluation criteria: how do users judge value? Which other perspectives do they want included? Which perspectives does the evaluator think should be included? What are the criteria of valuation?
4 Define the intervention, the questions to be answered and the purpose of the evaluation.
5 Design and plan the evaluation.
6 Collect data which will allow users to judge the value of the evaluated.
7 Analyse and report findings which allow users to judge value and to make better informed decisions.

# 10 ◀▶ The practice and politics of evaluation

*The evaluator is not the judge, neither is she the jury, the defence or the prosecution. She is the humble detective, but is often treated like a policewoman or executioner.*

*An evaluation is never scientific enough for the losers, nor practical enough for the users.*

*A colleague's advice: 'If you want a friend, get a dog. Don't be an evaluator.'*

## Introduction

Evaluators sometimes feel that they are everyone's enemy and no one's friend. Evaluation is not an enterprise for the thin-skinned or the politically naive. Traditional discipline-based researchers who have inadvertently 'strayed' into an evaluation are sometimes shocked at the practical problems, the indifference and also the hostility which they encounter. Their aim, after all, is honourable: a sensible and commendable search for the truth and to make the world a better place. Yet they find that their knowledge of the logic of science has not prepared them for the many practical and political issues which arise. Evaluators do not work in a laboratory, and whatever their ideal about the neutrality of the evaluation, many others do not see them or their work as neutral. They find that they also need to understand the logic of politics, in order to be able to carry out an evaluation and to maximize the chances of the findings being implemented. This is not to suggest that sophisticated research skills and attention to detail are not important. Rather, in addition to both scientific scepticism and sensitivity, evaluators also need a cynical 'street awareness'. 'Forewarned is forearmed' is the motto of this chapter.

This chapter looks at the practical problems of carrying out an evaluation. First we note problems which commonly arise in evaluations and which both users and evaluators need to know about, such as how a service or policy may change while it is being evaluated. Then we look at roles and responsibilities in evaluation to help to consider who is responsible for dealing with, foreseeing or preventing these common problems. The last part of the chapter turns to the practice of evaluation and considers issues such as confidentiality, communicating findings and gaining cooperation from service providers. It also discusses the 'politics of evaluation', which need to be understood by evaluators, sponsors and users in order to carry out and act on an evaluation. We return to the subjects of responsibility for action and change and the limits to the role of the evaluator in the last chapter when we look at increasing the ultilization of evaluations.

## Common problems in evaluation

*The key to happiness in evaluation is an attitude of cynical scepticism which expects the worst – the chances of being disappointed are lower.*

*You plan an evaluation, and then life happens.*

*If we had only known before that this would happen, we would have designed the evaluation differently.*

The evaluator needs ingenuity and a pessimistic attitude to design an evaluation, and resourcefulness and persistence to carry one out. Sickness, acts of God or other unforeseeable problems occur in most evaluations. How the evaluator deals with these unforeseen problems can be as important to the scientific validity of the results as the technical design and methods which were decided in the planning stages. In the unpredictable there are also opportunities, such as the chance to create a natural experiment. Technical knowledge has to be combined with a practical sense of what could happen and what is realistic in the situation. There are predictable problems which are common in most types of evaluation. The following notes these, some of which were touched on in the discussion of planning and design in Chapter 9.

### Carrying out an evaluation: the common hazards and challenges

In designing and making an evaluation both evaluator and users should be aware of the following common problems.

*The boundaries*: of the evaluated are always 'fuzzy' or redefinable. Chapters 3 and 5 noted that it is sometimes difficult to define the intervention precisely, and that the boundary between the intervention and its environment may not be clear. In practice it is a good policy for evaluators to assume that the item which they are asked to evaluate will not have clear boundaries, even if sponsors and others think that it does. The words used to describe the treatment, service, policy or intervention are only a starting point, which sketches out an area that then needs to be precisely specified for the evaluation to be undertaken. One purpose of some evaluations is to establish the extent to which the item which is thought to have some effect is actually part of a larger constellation of factors: for example, whether the effectiveness of the chemical agent in a drug is only due to its combination with other factors. Evaluators should approach all evaluations with a questioning attitude towards where the boundaries of the evaluated lie: knowledge of systems theory can help to decide where to draw these boundaries (Emery and Trist 1969; Senge 1992).

*Stability*: the evaluated keeps changing or will not stay still. In experimental evaluations of treatments the intervention is held constant, but in service and policy evaluations the intervention usually changes while the evaluation is being undertaken. There may be cuts to finance, a sudden crisis which requires a major change or personnel may leave, all of which can significantly change the boundary of the evaluated or its internal character. This is not a problem for developmental evaluations, which are often undertaken to contribute to the change, but it is a problem for other types of evaluation. Even where experimental evaluations use methods to hold the intervention constant, the chances of unexpected change increase with the length of time of the evaluation. Evaluators and users should expect the unexpected and consider strategies for detecting changes in the evaluated and for deciding how to deal with these changes.

*The objectives* of the evaluated are unclear, not measurable without intermediate objectives and assumptions or conflicting, or there are competing views about objectives. The 'objectives problem' is common, even for some treatments, and becomes apparent as soon as evaluators give serious thought to how to measure effectiveness or how to judge the 'success' of a service or intervention. Chapter 9 considered strategies for specifying evaluatable objectives, and the option of a needs-based 'goal-free' evaluation approach.

*Other variables* become significant or apparent. During the evaluation, new influences may arise which begin to have an effect on the outcome variable, but which were not expected, and make it more difficult to attribute any changes in the outcome to the evaluated (the 'problem of attribution'). For example, a service may have a three-year health promotion programme which aims to improve diet and exercise, and reduce work stress in a community. One year into the programme the main local employer closes, making 30 per cent of the community redundant, which changes family incomes, gives more 'free time' but increases stress for both unemployed people and those remaining in work. How do the evaluators of the health promotion programme respond to this change? Could or should they have predicted something like this and build such possibilities into the design? Can they use this as an opportunity to do a natural experiment?

*Prior information*: there are no measures or information about the target of the intervention before the intervention is made (e.g. about patient's health before the treatment, or about organizational performance before the change). The absence of 'base-line data' is a common problem and one which either reduces the design options for the evaluation, or means that the evaluation will be more costly and take a longer time if it has to first establish a set of base-line measures. Sponsors may not be aware of the lack of prior information, of the poor validity of this information or of the time it would take to get such measures before introducing a change.

*Comparability*: not comparing similar things, or the situational factors surrounding the things being compared are different. An example is using mortality rates to compare the outcomes from treatments at two hospitals, but without adjusting for case mix. A problem which sometimes arises is that sponsors want an evaluation of two types of service which appear to be different only in one major respect: for example, in how teamwork is carried out. However, after starting, the evaluation finds that the services or their surrounding context are in fact very different, and hence significant conclusions cannot be drawn about differences in, for example, costs and outcome being due to the single factor.

*Effect of the evaluation* on the intervention being evaluated (the 'police car effect'). This is a different problem from the placebo effect, which is the effect on the people who are the targets of the intervention of believing that they are receiving an intervention, whether or not they receive it. Where people are part of the intervention rather than the targets of it – for example, service personnel or people who implement a policy – their awareness that the service or policy is being evaluated can change their behaviour. They may perform better or worse than they would otherwise do because they feel not only that they are under scrutiny, but that the evaluation may have good or bad consequences for them. This is not a problem for some developmental evaluations which aim to create or exploit a 'Hawthorne effect', but for experimental evaluations it introduces a further variable which is not always possible to control for by 'blinding'.

*The outcomes* may be too broad or too long after to be unambiguously attributable to the intervention. This is the last of the more common practical problems in evaluation which we note here. Outcome problems often occur in evaluations which choose to consider a multidimensional outcome, such as quality of life, or outcomes some time after the intervention, such as

---

**Common problems in evaluation: a summary**

*Fuzzy boundaries*: the boundaries of an intervention are always 'fuzzy' or redefinable.

*Wobbly interventions*: the intervention keeps changing and will not stay still. (Consider strategies for detecting changes in the evaluated and for deciding how to deal with these changes.)

*Ghostly goals*: the objectives of the intervention are unclear, not measurable without intermediate objectives and assumptions or conflicting, or there are competing views about objectives.

*Gate-crashing confounding variables*: during the evaluation new influences begin to have an effect on the outcome variable, which were not expected and make it more difficult to attribute any changes in the outcome to the intervention.

*Prior information*: no measures or information about the target of the intervention before the intervention is made (e.g. about patients' health before the treatment, or about organizational performance before the change).

*Chalk and cheese*: not comparing similar things, or the situational factors surrounding the things being compared are different.

*Police car effect*: The effect of doing an evaluation on the people being evaluated.

*Distant outcomes*: may be too broad or too long after to be unambiguously attributable to the intervention.

those of a health promotion programme. It may only become clear in retrospect that other variables could have produced the outcome. This is an important consideration in deciding design (discussed in Chapters 3 and 5).

Many of the above problems can be minimized by using the right design, or a flexible one, and by having a detailed practical evaluation plan. Inexperienced evaluators and users need to consider these and other practical problems which are discussed in evaluation texts, but are often better described in different evaluation reports in the 'discussion of limitations' section. Checklists for assessing evaluations also alert evaluators and users to possible problems (see end of Chapter 9). The design and negotiation phases in an evaluation should look ahead to these possible problems and include different strategies for dealing with them.

## Responsibilities and roles in evaluation

Who is responsible for the failure of health personnel to give evaluators the data which they required, or for patients or services dropping out of the evaluation? One of the most common causes of practical problems arising in an evaluation is failure to agree the responsibilities of different parties, and this also delays action to respond to a problem once it has arisen. Evaluators, sponsors and others make assumptions about the roles and responsibilities of different parties in an evaluation which may not be justified, especially if they are unfamiliar with the type of evaluation which is being undertaken. In this section we consider how to clarify these issues and why we need to do so, and look at the role of the evaluator in more detail. After this we look at ways to deal with or minimize common problems and at the politics of evaluation.

This book shows the many different approaches to health evaluation and there are differences in the roles and responsibilities of the evaluator in each approach. If users and sponsors are not involved in the right way and do not agree their responsibilities, then misunderstandings, problems and conflict are more likely at different stages and can reduce the practical impact of the evaluation. People who are not evaluators are unlikely to be familiar with these differences, or to understand who is responsible for different tasks in a particular evaluation. The evaluator has a professional duty to raise questions in the planning phases about the roles and responsibilities of different parties, to seek agreement before the evaluation gets under way and continually to clarify expectations.

Some of the different tasks, responsibilities and roles in most evaluations follow.

♦ *Financial sponsors or their agent*: responsible for letting evaluators know when a decision will be made about whether to proceed, for providing finance of agreed amounts at agreed times in agreed ways and for giving agreed amounts of notice of any termination of financing. Sometimes responsible for publishing or making the findings available.
♦ *The steering group overseeing the evaluation*: a group responsible for giving advice and guidance to the evaluator during the evaluation, and

possibly for receiving and commenting on findings. This group may include stakeholders, and any rights to direct or overrule the evaluators on any issues need to be agreed in this group's terms of reference.

♦ *The evaluators (project leader and staff)*: the limits to their responsibilities need to be defined, together with a timetable for the evaluation and dates for reports and milestones, as well as budgetary and financial responsibilities.

♦ *Associated helpers (often health personnel)*: in some evaluations there is an agreement that health personnel or others will either cooperate or take an active role, possibly as full members of the evaluation team. The expectations of them and the time for which they are assigned need to be agreed and defined.

This list covers the minimum tasks for an evaluation study. However, in the concept of 'evaluation for action' (Chapter 1) this book proposed that, to maximize the impact of an evaluation, an evaluation study should be part of a larger evaluation process. This process involves more tasks and responsibilities than those in an evaluation study. Evaluations are not something which sponsors simply hand over to evaluators to complete, like placing an order for an item and awaiting delivery. Evaluation is a process which includes users and sponsors in deciding what to evaluate, agreeing value criteria and, in the later stages, drawing on findings from the evaluation study to decide action. The evaluation study carried out by evaluators is sandwiched within a larger evaluation process, which was described in Chapter 9 in terms of eight phases. Users and sponsors have a more active role at the beginning and end of this evaluation process. The evaluation process is itself part of a larger process of decision making and activity within health services, which precedes and continues after the evaluation.

We return to these points about the evaluation existing within an ongoing political and organizational context in Chapter 14, which considers the use and implementation of evaluations. The point here is that, if we are to maximize the use of the evaluation as well as to get cooperation from health personnel and others, then the evaluator needs to spend time agreeing roles and responsibilities beyond those in the evaluation team. There are many tasks to undertake in planning, carrying out and acting on an evaluation. Evaluators, sponsors and users need to agree who will do what, in relation to both the evaluation study and the evaluation process. There is a question here as to how much it is the responsibility of the evaluator to get sponsors and users to agree to responsibilities beyond the evaluation study – at least by raising these issues, the evaluator gets a better understanding of how or whether the evaluation study will be used.

## Responsibilities in each phase of the evaluation process

The underlying principle in clarifying roles and responsibilities is to consider the work and tasks to be done in deciding what to evaluate and how to evaluate, and in using the evaluation findings. To do this the evaluator needs a model of the evaluation process. The eight phases of evaluation described in Chapter 9 were based on such a model. Evaluators, sponsors and users who find this model suitable for their evaluation can use it to

*Table 10.1*  Responsibilities of different parties in each phase of an evaluation process

| Phase in the evaluation process | Division of responsibilities for one type of evaluation | | |
| --- | --- | --- | --- |
| | Sponsor/users decides or does the task | Consults, or does the task jointly | Evaluator decides or does the task |
| 1 *Initiation* Acting on a felt need to make a judgement of value about a treatment, service, policy or change. | The initiator may be a user, a sponsor, or the evaluator | | |
| 2 *Formulation* Deciding who the evaluation is for and which user perspectives to take, the primary questions and decisions it is to inform, the criteria for valuation and the comparisons which will be used in the evaluation. | | Jointly agreed | |
| 3 *Reviewing knowledge* Discovering and reviewing what is already known about the evaluated, or about similar things. | | | Evaluator responsibility |
| 4 *Finalizing evaluation design details* Finalizing design and the details about which data gathering methods to use, how to use them and how to analyse the data to give information about the criteria. | | | Evaluator responsibility may consult |
| 5 *Data collection* Gathering and recording data using qualitative or quantitative methods, or both. | | | Evaluator responsibility |
| 6 *Data analysis and reporting* Analysing the data, and reporting what was discovered about the evaluated in relation to the criteria. | | | Evaluator responsibility |
| 7 *Judging value and deciding action* Users judge value and decide what to do by drawing on the evaluation findings as well as other data, and by considering the options open to them. | User responsibility | Consults with evaluator | |
| 8 *Evaluator self-review* The evaluators review the lessons for them from the evaluation, and consider any methodological innovations or improvements which they might have developed. | | | Evaluator responsibility |

clarify the work to be done in different phases and to agree who will do different tasks. Table 10.1 gives a general illustration of how to use the model in this way to agree who makes which decisions and who is responsible for different tasks.

Table 10.1 shows the beginnings of a description of tasks and allocation of responsibilities for a typical developmental evaluation. This description would look different for other types of evaluations: for example, for a practitioner self-evaluation or peer evaluation, or for an experimental evaluation or managerial evaluation. In Chapter 14 we will consider the responsibility of the evaluator for action following from their evaluation. In the next section we raise this issue together with other practical issues which arise in the carrying out of an evaluation.

## Practice and politics

*Those who stand to lose from an evaluation are not as crude as to shoot the messenger – they just destroy the credibility of the message. An evaluation is never scientific enough for the losers. If there are no losers, then the evaluation probably has few practical consequences and is of little value.*

Evaluators need to understand the interests of different groups who could be affected by an evaluation in order to plan and conduct an evaluation, and to increase the chances of their work being acted on. In this section we discuss 'unacknowledged agendas', how to gain access and cooperation as an evaluator and issues of credibility, trust and confidentiality. We also consider how evaluators can best communicate their findings, and how evaluator ethics help to both minimize predictable problems and enhance validity. First, why do evaluators need to be aware of the 'politics of evaluation'?

This book emphasizes the practical purpose of evaluation and has proposed that an evaluation should not be carried out if no practical consequences would follow from it. The link between evaluation and action is closer than for other types of research. If there is no such link, then the evaluation has failed, at least in relation to one criterion of a successful evaluation. The practical consequences of evaluations are often change: practitioners change their practice, or finance is reallocated, or a policy is extended or cancelled. If there is a change then there are usually winners and losers, and a group of people who oppose a change and a group that wish it to happen.

If an evaluation does not raise objections, opposition or criticism from one group or another, then this could be a sign that the evaluation is of little value. Test this proposition: are there any useful evaluations which you know of which did not raise strong criticisms? The argument here is that, to some extent, the value of an evaluation is proportional to the criticism and opposition it attracts from groups which stand to lose from changes indicated by the evaluation. Whether the criticisms – for example of method or evidence – are valid is another important but different matter: a scientific rather than a political issue.

This is not to suggest that evaluation always leads to change, or should do so. Evaluation findings are one of many considerations which people take into account when deciding how to act. An evaluation may indicate that current practice should not be changed – but even then there is often a group who want change. The point is that both to carry out an evaluation and to maximize the chances of the findings being used evaluators need to recognize how different groups could be affected by an evaluation. This means understanding how different groups perceive the evaluation in terms of both how it affects them while the evaluation is being conducted and how the findings might affect them. Even evaluators who take a 'detached scientific' approach, and who do not accept that they have any responsibility for action, still have to recognize the interests of different groups because these groups can help and hinder their work in carrying out an evaluation.

Evaluators and users need to think ahead to the possible practical implications of different findings: those which show the evaluated to be ineffective, or which are negative, or which show it to be effective, in a positive light, or which give inconclusive or mixed findings. They need to understand who will gain, lose, be hurt or harmed by each of these types of findings. It is best to do this scenario analysis at the planning stage so as to build into the evaluation both practical and technical strategies which will help at later stages when one of the three scenarios happens. Attention to how an evaluation affects different people is not just for technical purposes – the evaluator has an ethical obligation to consider the impact of what she does, and an ethical approach also helps evaluators to negotiate their perilous path.

How do the interests and concerns of different parties affect how the evaluator carries out an evaluation? How does the evaluator anticipate and deal with the politics of evaluation in an ethical way and maintain integrity? In the following we consider some of the practical issues which arise in carrying out an evaluation.

*An evaluator needs to be 'street aware' without becoming a 'street person'*

## Unacknowledged agendas

There are often reasons why sponsors and others want an evaluation other than their stated reason. Evaluators need to be aware of 'hidden agendas' before undertaking an evaluation. This helps to think ahead about how to carry out the evaluation, and about how the findings will be used and sometimes misinterpreted or misused. Managers or others may commission an evaluation as a 'delay tactic' or to give the impression that something is being done while they consider the political options. The world does not stop for an evaluation: managers have both a right and a duty to consider options, and sometimes to start negotiations, before the results of an evaluation are available. This may affect the evaluation: for example, the willingness of some personnel to provide information. This does not mean that the evaluation is not of use when it is done, but that action may have already been 'framed' or even decided before the results are ready.

Other sometimes unacknowledged reasons for wanting an evaluation are to meet a financing requirement or to increase the chances of a proposal for a new service or intervention being successful. It is becoming more common that services or projects are financed on the condition that the service is evaluated externally or has built-in evaluation systems. Proposals are often more likely to be accepted by a financing body if they include a plan to evaluate the proposed project. In these instances the evaluation may be an irrelevant but irritating necessity for those who are successful in their bid to the financing body.

Alternatively, an evaluation may be requested because a manager or department has promised that a policy or service will achieve certain objectives, and others wish to check whether these promises were met. Evaluators may not know about such promises or commitments and only discover them during the evaluation. They may discover that the aim of one party is to prove the policy or service to be a failure or to show that promises were not met.

There are limits to how knowledgeable an evaluator can or should be about the motives and intrigues behind a proposed evaluation. In a few circumstances the evaluator should resolutely ignore and stand apart from these issues, as even being aware of them may bias the data gathering or findings. However, when evaluating services, policies or organizational interventions, in most cases the evaluator needs to ask questions in a diplomatic way about motives, and about who wants and does not want the evaluation.

---

**Looking good while avoiding change: advice to 'careful' managers**

Initiate an evaluation when:

♦ you have to do something but do not know what to do;
♦ you need time to negotiate in secret with key players;
♦ you want to bury the issue in complications while you make arrangements to move to your next job.

Never request an evaluation when:

♦ you know there will be enough finance to do a through evaluation;
♦ there is a chance that the evaluation will give specific practical recommendations that you will have to respond to.

If the evaluation looks like producing findings which are negative for you:

♦ make sure you change the intervention which they are evaluating during the evaluation;
♦ arrange for external changes to have an impact (e.g. get some of your key people promoted);
♦ explain any negative findings as 'welcome independent confirmation of what we had begun to address', or as biased because of the sample, inadequate controls, invalid statistical analysis or inaccuracies in the data provided by the service which the evaluators did not know about;
♦ always quote from the evaluation report selectively and out of context. Always get a preview of the report, and act before it goes public.

## Access and cooperation

Politics and motives can affect how easy it is for the evaluator to get access to and cooperation from personnel and patients. The ethical issues and ethical procedures for treatment evaluations are well documented in medical research texts (e.g. Pocock 1983). In service or policy evaluations, the evaluator will need access to service documentation, service statistics and service providers, to interview them. Access involves getting the formal agreement of the service manager, but getting cooperation is more difficult and more important. The evaluator must be seen as someone who understands the practical problems and work situation of people in the service, and is prepared to be flexible in scheduling interviews and visits. He or she also needs to be seen as persistent and as someone who stands up to those in the service whose cooperation is required but who see the evaluation as low priority or have something to hide.

A trusted, fair professional who 'speaks our language' is a model which an evaluator might aim for. Evaluators need to be aware of their 'image' on the informal work network or 'grapevine': in small organizations a new face is an important event, and myths and explanations of who the person is and her background will be rife and will affect access and cooperation. Fantasies will flower when the newcomer is known to be doing an evaluation. Cooperation can be damaged if the evaluator has not prepared the ground by being introduced in the right way, and by meeting and showing respect for formal and informal opinion formers and union representatives.

Cooperation is increased if the evaluator gives something back to those whose time and efforts have been given to the evaluation. This is also a matter of evaluation ethics, not just a technique to get cooperation. Discussions with sponsors and others at the planning stage need to consider how service personnel and patients will benefit from the evaluation while it is being carried out as well as after, and their contributions and roles need to be acknowledged. This can take the form of interim reports, but this is not possible in summative evaluations where evaluator-influenced change is to be minimized. Texts giving practical guidance for evaluation and for health service research discuss how to 'negotiate access' and present and introduce the evaluation to an organization (e.g. Fink 1993; Rossi and Freeman 1993; Breakwell and Millward 1995).

## Credibility and trust

Establishing trust and credibility is essential to a successful evaluation. Ethical evaluation practice helps to establish, and is essential to maintaining, trust. Trust and credibility have to be earned by the evaluator, and will be tested. Both are required in the evaluator's relationships with different parties, most notably with sponsors, users, service personnel and patients. Everyone will want to find out from the evaluator what has been learned so far, and to hear the latest 'inside' information, especially where organizational communications are poor. The more confidential the information, the more interested people will be, the faster it will be spread across the organization if the evaluator breaks confidence and the quicker the evaluator's credibility will be lost.

Trust takes time to establish and is a result of the evaluator balancing honesty and discretion. Credibility comes from proving one's competence but also from pointing out the limits to this competence. The proposal stage is where aspiring evaluators have to prove both their scientific and social competence by giving alternative designs, by being flexible in responding to sponsors' concerns and in the more conventional ways by showing their previous work and experience. Evaluators win trust by being cautious in their promises, and by honestly answering and predicting questions about finance, possible problems and the limits to their skills and resources.

To gain access to an organization, personnel and data, evaluators have to spend some time preparing the ground and introducing themselves. These introductory activities are especially important for gaining trust. Researchers are often not welcome because they 'get in the way' and 'create extra work', and are often treated with suspicion. 'So you have come to spy on us?' is a not uncommon welcome when one is being introduced, and it is not always a joking question. Evaluation is not a neutral activity, even if the idea of being a neutral scientist is important in many evaluations. It helps to be introduced by a respected member of the organization, but the evaluator must be prepared for and directly and honestly answer challenging questions, such as those which imply that the evaluation is not needed because a decision has already been made. They may be right.

## Confidentiality

A necessary precondition for gaining and maintaining access, cooperation and trust is to agree and make explicit how the information gathered for the information will be reported and made available. When negotiating access to patient records and service documents which are not public, the evaluator needs to agree with service providers which information can and cannot be reported to sponsors and users, or published (Øvretveit 1987a). This needs to be discussed at the planning stage with sponsors, as restrictions on access to and use of service records limit the data which can be gathered and shape the evaluation design. Evaluators should not discover partway into an evaluation that they cannot access essential data. These conditions and agreements need to be written down in the evaluation contract.

Confidentiality issues also arise in interviews with patients, service personnel and others. All interviews need to begin with the evaluator stating his or her understanding of the confidentiality rules which apply to the interview. Often it is best to give the interviewee a written statement of confidentiality rules which apply to the interview beforehand, together with a general explanation of the evaluation. The conditions need to state whether anything said in the interview will be attributed to the individual in a report, or repeated outside of the interview. One approach is for the evaluator to say that no individuals will be named or recognizable from the report, and that only general findings will be reported when they have been supported by evidence from more than one source.

Evaluators also need to state any circumstances under which their code of ethical practice requires them to break confidentiality, which is often the code of their 'home profession'. Some service providers feel that their only chance to report corruption, abuse, negligence or other activities is to the evaluator. Evaluators need to know what the usual channels are within the organization for dealing with such reports, and to decide and agree beforehand how to respond in these circumstances. Even with foresight, evaluators may be faced with weighing up how to act to cause the least harm and to uphold their integrity, even if this means jeopardizing the whole evaluation.

The question of the public or private status of the final evaluation report and of publication rights should also be agreed with sponsor and service providers at the beginning of the evaluation. There will be many people who will want to know what the evaluator found out, and evaluators need to agree who will make their report available and what they can and cannot say in public and in informal settings during and after the evaluation.

## The evaluation contract

Evaluators and sponsors can prevent many problems and misunderstandings by drawing up a contract which defines responsibilities and agreements about many of the items above. A good evaluation proposal should cover many of the above items in the design or in a separate heading about 'practical issues'. The proposal can serve as the contract, or additions can be made in a separate contract agreement. There are different views about whether the evaluator should draw up contracts with other parties in addition to the financial sponsor. In many cases a clear contract which describes responsibilities and expectations can enhance trust, rather than suggesting mistrust.

## Communicating evaluation findings

In recent years there has been increasing pressure on all scientists to communicate their work more widely and in more accessible ways. For evaluators, communication is not just a question of improving the public image of evaluation, but an integral part of their role and one of the phases of an evaluation. It is one of the things they are paid to do. Here we consider evaluators' responsibility for communicating their findings and the different ways in which they can do so.

Communication happens when the 'receiver' understands what the 'sender' intended to convey. Dialogue is a two-way exchange where both reach a new level of understanding. Dialogue is essential in the early phases of an evaluation to agree criteria, but communication is where the emphasis lies for evaluators when reporting their findings.

A well designed and conducted evaluation is wasted if users do not understand the findings and the limitations and significance of the findings. An evaluation can be harmful if users misunderstand the findings. It is arguable that evaluators have a greater ethical duty than other researchers to communicate clearly their findings, because an evaluation aims more directly than other types of research to change what people would otherwise do, and intends to have direct significant economic, social or health consequences.

Many users and evaluators agree that evaluators are often ill-equipped to make recommendations for action, in part because they often do not know all the factors which users have to consider. However, evaluators do have a duty to go beyond putting a report in the mail to the sponsor, or giving a simple presentation and then leaving. They have a duty to check that users have understood what the evaluation does and does not prove, but also a duty to resist being drawn into advising users about what they should do.

There are a number of ways to communicate findings to users: a verbal presentation to users or presentations at conferences; a workshop; a written report specifically for users or published in a 'users' journal'; putting the findings on a database or dissemination network which is accessed by users; informal discussions; and a press event such as a press release, a newspaper interview or a radio or television appearance. The most common ways are written or verbal presentations, but before evaluators decide to use these methods they need to think about exactly who their audience are, and the best way to communicate findings to them. Apart from the sponsor and other users agreed at the outset, the evaluation may have made discoveries which need to be communicated to other users, such as patients. An evaluator may only be familiar with communicating to researchers or academics, and may need advice or help to communicate the findings to users, and in some instances may need to hand over the communication to specialists.

Most general and practical texts on research give guidance about how to write a report, but most of this guidance is for an academic report or a scientific paper for publication. Writing a report for non-academic users such as health managers, practitioners, policy makers and the general public often follows similar principles and headings, but does require a different style and approach. For health evaluators reporting to health personnel, more useful guidance is given in two texts specifically for evaluators (Breakwell and Millward 1995: Chapter 6; Fink 1993: Chapter 8).

Guidance for written reports is given in the more practical health researcher texts, such as Sapsford and Abbott (1992: Chapter 15) and Edwards and Talbot (1994: Chapter 7), who also discuss differences between report writing for qualitative and quantitative studies. Breakwell and Millward (1995) emphasize analysing audience interests before deciding the medium for communication and the structure of a written or oral presentation. They note strengths and weakness of oral and written presentation and give practical guidance about using tables, graphs and figures. Evaluators can also benefit from general texts and guidance on presentation design and skills.

## Workshops for communicating and examining action options

The workshop format is rarely discussed as a vehicle for communication, but it is one of the most effective for enabling groups not only to understand but to work through the implications of findings. Such a format usually starts with the workshop facilitator (who may also be the evaluator) working with the group to identify questions which the group have in relation to the evaluation, and the practical concerns which the evaluation may be able to help with. The workshop can then include a short presentation by the evaluator of the study and findings, picking up audience concerns during the presentation and answering questions in the conventional way. Different formats are then possible, including group work and reports back, with the evaluator correcting or amplifying audience interpretations of the findings which are apparent from group discussions and reports back. Workshops also allow time for informal discussions between the evaluator and users during breaks – an effective and under-recognized way of communicating findings and of allowing evaluators to reflect on and consider what they might do differently in future evaluations.

An ethical evaluator will give a high priority to the phase of communication because sponsors have paid for users to become more informed, not just paid for an evaluation to be conducted. Evaluators have a duty to communicate clearly their findings, and to assist in exploring the implications. They have a duty to go to some lengths to ensure that users do not misinterpret the results. They need to know when and how to resist pressures to give advice about action. In communicating evaluation results it is wise to assume that everything will be misheard or misread, and that the report will not be studiously scrutinized, except by those who disagree with the results.

Evaluation ethics anticipates many of the above issues – ethical evaluation practice is not just something evaluators strive for in order to sleep easy at night, but something which enhances the validity of the findings, and is essential to the future reputation of evaluation as a practice and a discipline. The practical aims and the practice context in which evaluation is carried out create a greater potential for harm and conflict than many other types of research, and evaluation ethics are correspondingly more important. The ethical code of practice for researchers produced by the British Social Research Association is a good basis for many service and policy evaluations, and there are more detailed codes for US programme evaluation (JCSEE 1994) and specifically for medical research.

## Conclusions

♦ Technical knowledge is not enough to design and plan an evaluation, or to deal with practical problems when they do occur. Some problems are common and predictable, but others cannot be foreseen. Experienced evaluators try to reduce the chances of the unpredictable damaging the evaluation, and have a repertoire of tactics to deal with the more common problems.

♦ How the evaluator foresees and responds to practical problems which arise when one is carrying out an evaluation can significantly affect the validity and utilization of the findings.

♦ Predictable problems to consider when designing the evaluation and collecting data include: 'fuzzy' boundaries to the intervention; 'wobbly' interventions; 'ghostly goals' which are unclear or contradictory; the context may change; no 'baseline' measures; 'drop-outs'; the 'police car effect'; 'chalk and cheese' problems in making valid comparisons; and problems measuring outcome, especially 'distant outcomes'.

♦ The evaluation study made by evaluators is sandwiched within a larger evaluation process of eight phases, which involves users and sponsors in deciding what to evaluate, agreeing value criteria and, in the later phases, drawing on findings from the evaluation study to decide action. Users and sponsors have a more active role at the beginning and end of this evaluation process.

♦ The single most common cause of many problems is failure to agree the responsibilities of different parties. These responsibilities need to be agreed for each of the phases of the evaluation process. Evaluators have different views about whether they have any responsibility for encouraging the utilization of their evaluation study (discussed further in Chapter 14).

♦ Evaluators need to be aware of the politics of evaluation, unacknowledged agendas, likely problems in access and cooperation, how to build credibility and trust, and how best to communicate their findings.

♦ Ethics is more important to evaluation than to some other types of research because of the greater practical impact and potential for conflict and harm. Evaluation ethics anticipates and prevents problems, and contributes to the validity and utilization of findings.

Data gathering methods

*The most important things are always intangible and unmeasurable.*

*If it is important, then people notice it. If people notice it, then it can be measured.
If it is not counted, then it does not count.*

## Introduction

At the centre of an evaluation project is the work of collecting, recording and analysing data about the item being evaluated. Many of the methods are familiar to anyone with a research background. However, because evaluation is a broad subject it is likely that there are data which need to be collected which require us to use methods that we have not used before or may not even know about. Our 'home disciplines' favour particular data gathering methods which are suited to the subject of the discipline. We may be unfamiliar with or suspicious about the methods used by other disciplines which we may need to use in an evaluation. Evaluators need to be broad-minded about methods and knowledgeable about a number of ways to gather data. Users of evaluations need to understand how the data were produced and analysed in order to judge the validity of the conclusions.

How do you gather valid data about an intervention or the people who may be affected by it? Do you have to use measures in an evaluation? When should I use qualitative or quantitative methods? How can I collect qualitative information in a way that makes it easier to analyse it and is credible to others? These are some of the questions considered in this and the next chapter. Rather than giving instructions about how to use the methods, this chapter gives a simple introduction to five categories of method: observation, interviewing, questionnaires and surveying, specific measurement methods, and using already collected data such as statistics and service records. For more details the chapter refers the reader to general texts about research methods in health services, social sciences and nursing and medical research.

*Use existing data sources or validated methods if you can: the world does not need another 'quality of life measure'.*

The chapter will be of use to inexperienced evaluators, and shows them how they can use their existing skills and their knowledge of research methods. It will also be of use to evaluators who want a quick introduction to methods that they know little about. Users of evaluation will find this and the next chapter helpful for deciding how to interpret data presented in an evaluation.

The next chapter is more theoretical and looks at some of the conceptual and methodological issues which need to be considered when using these methods for data collection and when analysing the data produced. It highlights issues to consider in selecting and using a method in an evaluation, shows how to judge the quality of evidence reported in an evaluation and whether the evidence supports the conclusions, and gives ways to assess whether a proposal for an evaluation has chosen the best methods for the purpose. Both chapters refer readers who need further details to those texts which are particularly useful to evaluators and users of health evaluations.

## Data collection in the context of an evaluation

In this book 'data gathering' describes a part of the evaluation process where the evaluator identifies sources of data, gets access to these sources and collects data which are needed to judge the value of the evaluated. The term 'data gathering' describes a range of methods within the following categories.

- *Observation*: unobtrusive, participant or self-observation.
- *Interviews*: structured (e.g. questions), semi-structured, open or guided by a critical incident or vignette stimulus. Focus group interviews and nominal group techniques.
- *Questionnaire or survey*: small or large scale survey, with or without rating scales.
- *Measurement methods*: biophysical, subjective response or a pre-formulated measurement instrument such as disease-specific and quality of life measures.
- *Already collected data*: data collected for other purposes, by the service, by government departments, by others (e.g. newspapers), and other research on similar subjects, diary, minutes of meetings, case records.

---

**Typical subjects of data collection**

- People affected by or receiving a treatment, service or policy.
- People providing a treatment or service, or implementing a policy.
- Needs, inputs, processes or outcomes of the evaluated.

---

I use the term 'data gathering' because it does not imply that some methods are any more 'valid' than others or any hierarchy of methods, or that some data are 'hard' or 'soft'. The chapter does assume that some methods are better than others for certain purposes, and that some give more valid knowledge than others about particular phenomena. For example, if the aim is to understand how a particular person experienced a treatment, then an interview to explore his or her perceptions and feelings would give more valid data for these purposes than asking him or her to give a rating on a scale which the evaluator has selected, such as a painful–not painful 1–5 scale.

The terms 'data gathering' or 'data collection' do, however, imply that facts lie around waiting to be collected by a scientific 'vacuum cleaner', which is not the view taken here. This book takes the view that facts do not exist independently, but neither are facts entirely constructed by the mind of the observer – data 'production' and 'creation' are also slightly misleading terms. Facts are created in a relationship between the observer and the observed (interaction), and through relationships between observers who agree what is to be counted as fact and how to gather factual information (intersubjective agreement about procedures). Facts and evidence do not exist before or independently of the method for gathering or creating them. The approach taken here emphasizes that what is to be accepted as a fact and as evidence depends on the categories brought to bear by the evaluator in gathering data. Whether data are valid evidence also depends on the method being used in the right way, using techniques to maximize validity and reliability, and whether the data are related to the evaluation criteria.

The rest of this chapter describes each of the five categories of data collection methods. First we note some introductory points about how the methods are used within the context of a particular type of evaluation – these points and validity are discussed in more detail in the next chapter:

1 Data collection is a middle phase in the process of an evaluation: before data are collected, an evaluation will have clarified which data are required by deciding the criteria of valuation, and the decisions which the evaluation aims to inform, as described in the phases of evaluation in Chapter 9.
2 If the evaluation does not show links between the criteria of valuation and the data gathered, then the data are not valid for the evaluation. The validity of data for an evaluation depends on more than following procedures for data collection. An evaluator may collect valid data about an intervention, but if these data do not help to answer the evaluation questions or to judge the value of the evaluated or help users to make decisions, then they are not valid data for the evaluation.
3 The way a data gathering method is used depends on the perspective of the evaluation. An experimental paradigm will use data collection to test hypotheses. A developmental or qualitative evaluation will usually work more inductively, building up hypotheses out of the data. Both may use interviewing or observation, but will be using these data gathering methods in different ways.
4 For simplicity the chapter follows the traditional terminology of describing methods as qualitative and quantitative, but recognizes the limitations of this distinction and that the terms are best applied to data, not to methods. Some of the methods described are termed 'quantitative' because they assign numbers to an aspect of a person, organization or event. 'Qualitative data gathering methods', on the other hand, are methods for recording and understanding people's experiences and the meanings which they give to events, and their behaviour in natural settings.
5 Qualitative data are often gathered as part of an inductive approach, which seeks to build up categories of meaning out of the data, usually out of people's reported experiences and perceptions, or from observations of

their behaviour. In this way the evaluator defines categories after, rather than before, data collection. For some purposes this gives more valid data than quantitative methods, but they may be less reliable. 'Qualitative evaluations' are those which use only qualitative methods.

6 In general, experimental and economic evaluations gather data using quantitative methods, while descriptive and developmental evaluations tend to use 'qualitative methods'. Managerial evaluations use both. 'Qualitative methods' are more suited to certain evaluation subjects, such as policies and organizational changes, but are increasingly being used in treatment and service evaluations.

7 The method which the evaluator uses depends on the purpose of the evaluation and on how he or she conceptualizes the phenomenon in question. However, many data gathering concepts and principles discussed in the next chapter apply to all methods: for example, validity, or whether the method gathers data which are 'true representations' of the phenomenon (bias); and reliability, or whether the method does so consistently, regardless of who uses it and when (error).

8 The choice of data gathering method in part depends on which data are required. The needs-inputs process-outcomes model (Table 11.1) helps to clarify which data are needed and, from this, which methods are most suitable. The model is of most use in clarifying the different data required for an evaluation of a health service, but can also be used to clarify data required in some evaluations of policies and organizational changes.

With these points in mind we can turn to a simple summary of the different methods – the next chapter looks at the principles underlying these methods in more detail and at ways to assess evidence gathered using a particular method. The following describes methods that can be used to gather data in either a quantitative or a qualitative form, although the section on measurement only refers to quantitative data gathering. It describes observation, then interviewing, followed by questionnaires and surveying, then measurement methods and finally the use of already collected data.

*Table 11.1*   The needs-inputs-process-outcomes model

| *Needs* | *Inputs (or structure)* | *Process* | *Outcomes* |
|---|---|---|---|
| *The type, severity and urgency:* | *The amount and quality of:* | *Activities of care:* | *Change in health and patients attributed to care:* |
| The needs of different individuals. The needs of groups or sub-populations. The needs of communities or areas. | Buildings Equipment Staff: trained and grade Patients (selection) Information supplies | Assessment Choice of intervention Procedures for intervention Compliance with good practice | Patient satisfaction Medical outcome (+/−) |

## Observation

Observation methods are used to collect data about the behaviour of patients or the people who are the target of the evaluated (behavioural outcomes), or about the behaviour of the people providing the treatment or service or implementing the policy (behavioural features of process). 'Behaviour' here is used to describe what people do and say. 'Observation' is also used to describe analysing documents. Using existing data sources is a method which we consider later in the chapter.

Observation can be carried out by using a pre-structured coded observation form or by 'open' observation, and each of these methods may be used by an independent observer, or by a participant observer. One particularly useful method for gaining data about a service process is to observe and record what happens to a patient as the researcher follows him or her in the 'journey' from admission to discharge or beyond (a 'tracer-patient pathway study'; Øvretveit 1994e). This can be combined with interviewing the patient to gather his or her perceptions at different stages.

If used within a qualitative paradigm, 'open' observation allows evaluators skilled in this method to study what people do in a natural setting and to build up a conceptualization which reflects people's behaviour in this setting. The aim here is not to impose predefined categories and 'count' behaviour, as would be the approach using this method within an experimental paradigm, but to 'suspend' the observer's categories and to record carefully what is observed in 'field notes' during or shortly after. The aim is to observe and record as 'faithfully' and 'factually' as possible: for example, by recording the words used rather than summaries. This can mean video or audio recording, although this can influence people's actions even more than the presence of the observer.

'Participant observation' reduces the influence of the observer on people's behaviour but requires the 'participant evaluator-observer' to take part in everyday life for some time, sometimes without disclosing his or her role as an observer. This increases validity but still leaves a question as to whether a similarly trained observer would see and record the same things. There are also ethical problems with the participant observer role which are greater for an evaluator than for other researchers: for example, is it right that an evaluator does not disclose his or her role as a patient or as a staff member?

The strengths of observation are that it gives direct evidence of observed outcomes, rather than reported accounts, and can be used to develop theories about why a service or treatment works or fails. It also gives real examples for an evaluation report which capture the flavour of the setting. But while there are some uses for this method in evaluation, the two main threats to validity make it a less attractive method for many evaluators than for anthropologists or medical sociologists. First, the effect of the observer on what people would otherwise do is likely to be greater if the people know that the observer is an evaluator: every child knows that a teacher acts differently when the school inspector is there.

The second threat to validity applies to the use of this method within a qualitative paradigm, where the observer does not use preset categories. How do we know whether observers impose their categories or 'distort' what they observe? The observer has to have some categories or ways of seeing to decide what to observe and record – there is no such thing as 'open observation'. Qualitative researchers recognize this criticism and have a number of strategies to reduce observer bias and increase validity. They emphasize that the categories are built up inductively and stress the ideal of factual description. Second, records provide evidence which can be checked by others, including the participants ('participant validation'). Third, multiple observers or observation as one of multiple sources of data are required ('triangulation'; Jick 1983).

These and other problems and details of the observational method are described in outline in health settings by McConway (1994: 22–6), with examples from bedside medical teaching, and Pope and Mays (1995c) and in more detail in Sapsford and Abbott (1992: 127–35). Practical general accounts are given in Edwards and Talbot (1994: 76–85), and how to use pre-coded observation is described in Breakwell and Millward (1995). More detailed discussions can be found in general texts on social science methods such as Adams and Shavaneveldt (1991). How to analyse qualitative data from observation and from interviews is a subject considered in the next chapter.

## Interviewing

Interviewing gives the evaluator access to people's views, their recollected experiences, feelings and theories about causation. This method can be used to collect quantitative data, where the interviewer uses pre-structured categories and questions (e.g. a pre-coded questionnaire administered in an interview), or in a qualitative way, with open-ended questions or with a set of topics for open exploration and probing by the interviewer. Here we consider interviewing as a method for collecting qualitative data, used within a qualitative paradigm.

In-depth interviewing can be semi-structured with a set of topics, or unstructured where the interviewer is led by the person's concerns, and aims to discover what a person's views are and why he or she holds these views. Interviewing of this type is a skilled task, requiring the interviewer to demonstrate interest without becoming over-involved and biased, to gain trust, to appear neutral and non-judgemental to the person and to know when and how to probe when something of general interest to the evaluation arises. During some evaluations, interviewers may change their interview strategies so as to pursue topics and hypotheses which have emerged out of previous interviews.

Interviews are useful for gaining data about patients' experiences of outcome, in their own terms. Interviews can also find out patients' recollected experiences of processes, or of their situation and expectations before undergoing a treatment or a service. Where health service personnel or others are the target of an intervention, such as a training programme or new policy, interviews allow the evaluator to discover how they understood or responded to the intervention. These are important data for understanding how or why some policies work or fail – the perceptions of staff and their reasons for acting in the way they do can be useful data for all types of evaluation. A policy or change often has a meaning or symbolic importance which is not recognized by outsiders, but may be critical to the impact of an intervention – this is as true for interventions into health services as it is for health education programmes to particular groups. How 'targets' or health service personnel interpret change is important for understanding the effects, and interviews are the main way of gathering data about how people interpret and understand interventions. Evaluators can build theories about how an intervention works or fails, either by testing their own theories in interviews or by seeking out and refining participants' theories.

Thus qualitative interviewing is a method for discovering people's experiences, the meaning of events to them, their feelings or their 'lay theories'. But, as with observation, there are drawbacks and problems of validity and reliability which are often greater when these methods are used in an evaluation. Would a similarly trained interviewer have gathered the same data? Are the data different if the interviewer makes it clear that the data are to be used in an evaluation? How does one analyse pages of interview transcript, and how would an evaluation user judge whether the conclusions were really based on the interview data, or whether the interviewer biased the subjects' responses?

To some extent interviews create data in the sense that interviewees often have not thought about the issues which they are asked about. Interviewees usually do not simply report their experiences, but they create or make more explicit what they think during the interview. The skill of the interviewer is to enable the person to reflect on and develop his or her ideas, without introducing the interviewer's own biases. A second validity issue is that the interviewee may not recollect 'properly' or may have a selective view of the event. Golden (1992) describes work which shows that managers recollect with 'hindsight bias' and in ways which unconsciously maintain their own self-esteem – she describes methods to reduce this bias and emphasizes the need to acknowledge the limitations of such data.

A third validity issue is that interviewees may be more concerned with projecting the right image and with how they appear, rather than with representing 'the truth'. For example, men reported about 30 per cent higher levels of morbidity when they were interviewed by women than they did when interviewed by men (Nathanson 1978). As with observation, triangulation and corroboration can be used to increase validity, as well as probing where people give discrepant accounts, and 'respondent validation' to check emerging analyses with the people interviewed or with another group.

For more details of qualitative open interviewing in health settings the reader is referred to a summary in Britten (1995: 251–3); to Sapsford and Abbott 1992: 108–15) and McConway (1994: 27–30), who also introduces 'feminism and qualitative interviewing' in health care; and to Fitzpatrick and Boulton (1994: 107–8). Practical summaries are given by Edwards and Talbot (1994: 86–9) and Breakwell and Millward (1995: 67–73). The next chapter looks at methods for analysing data produced by these methods.

One interesting example of the use of semi-structured interviewing is given in a quality evaluation which sought older people's perceptions of care and problems (Powell *et al.* 1994). The in-depth interview method in organisational studies is described in Ghauri *et al.* (1995: 64–72). General social science methodology texts give extensive practical and theoretical discussion of the method. The social analytic interview technique in developmental evaluation is described in Øvretveit (1984, 1987a). Kvale (1994) gives a very readable and concise discussion of 'ten standard objections to qualitative research interviews'.

## Focus group interviews

The advantage of an 'interview' with a group rather than with individuals is the ability to gain a range of views more quickly and with fewer resources than a series of interviews. The focus group technique is one form of group interview where the 'facilitator-interviewer' leads a group of about eight people in a discussion of a particular topic. As with interviews, there may be an agenda, or the facilitator may allow the discussion to develop with little prompting or probing, or may ask for or give example situations (e.g. 'critical incidents') or 'vignettes' to stimulate views. If the group is of people with similar backgrounds they usually feel less inhibited, but this may mean that the evaluation will need many different focus groups to ensure that a range of views are captured.

When people are in a group with 'similar' people they are usually less intimidated by the interviewer and may speak more openly and stimulate each other to recall different incidents and express views. However, it is often less easy in a group to probe and follow up one person's views, and there may be a greater pressure to express views which a person thinks are acceptable to the group (group conformity). For example, Kitzinger (1995) notes,

> In group discussion with old people in residential care I found that some residents tried to prevent others from criticising staff – becoming agitated and repeatedly interrupting with cries of 'you can't complain'; 'the staff couldn't possibly be nicer'.

The quality of the data depends even more than with individual interviews on the skills of the facilitator, and detailed recording is more difficult, although video or tape recording may be possible. Summaries of focus group technique in health services can be found in Fitzpatrick and Boulton (1994: 108) and Kitzinger (1995: 299–302). More details are given in books on the subject by Morgan (1993) (e.g. when to use focus groups and why) and by Kreuger (1988). An example of focus group technique in peer service quality evaluation is given in Øvretveit (1991a), and its use in patient satisfaction evaluation in Øvretveit (1992c).

## Nominal group technique

A more structured method for gathering data from groups is the nominal group technique. In this method people in the group are asked first to make their own list in private of their views or feelings about the topic introduced to the group by the leader. A common list is created on a poster and people then discuss and rank the items in order of importance. This approach often leads to more considered responses, but loses the cross-stimulation of focus groups, although discussion can later reintroduce this factor. These techniques are useful to evaluators for developing standards or for defining criteria to be used in an evaluation (e.g. in consensus groups, where the group is given a description of a patient and then the possible procedures are listed and discussed). They are also useful for exploring people's expectations, experiences and feelings about process and outcome.

## Summary

Some of the strengths and weaknesses of qualitative observation and interviewing for evaluation were noted above. A strength is that the methods allow the evaluator to build up an understanding of the patients' and healthcare providers' experiences, meanings and feelings. They do this by understanding people in their own settings and own terms. This is particularly important for gathering data about outcomes and about how interventions may work where people's feelings are an important 'mediating variable'. We noted problems of validity – evaluators may impose their own biases and categories rather than represent those of the participants, interviews often create views as much as they reflect views, problems in reporting the analysis and conclusions, difficulties in knowing how general the findings might be and problems in reliability or replication.

Both observation and interviewing can be used to collect data in a quantitative or qualitative form. In the next chapter we consider methods for analysing these types of data. When choosing a data gathering method, evaluators need to consider how they will analyse the data and present them to users. One of the greatest weaknesses of qualitative observation and interviewing is the difficulty in analysing and presenting the data, especially to users who are unfamiliar with or sceptical of these methods for an evaluation.

## Surveying and questionnaires

Asking questions is one method to find out what people think about a particular topic, and we saw above how this could be done using a semi-structured interview method. Another method is through a self-completed questionnaire, which can be mailed to them or completed by people when they are in hospital, receiving care or at work. Examples of these methods include large scale population surveys with preset categories, and questionnaires designed to discover patients' expectations and experiences of treatment.

Questionnaires are used when evaluators want to collect data about specific topics and where the topics have the same meaning and are well understood by people in different settings or social groups. They are also less expensive than interviews, which are unnecessary where simple factual data are required or where people can easily and authentically express their ideas in terms of the categories used by the evaluator in the questionnaire.

Questionnaires can gather qualitative data by asking people to write descriptive accounts. More often questionnaires use one or more of a number of measurement scales which require subjects to express their views in the terms of a scale and thus provide quantitative data. The most well-known scale is the Likert five-item scale or the semantic differential scale (pairs of opposites, e.g. painful–not painful, usually with a seven-point scale: see Breakwell and Millward (1995: 64–6) for a simple summary). The issues involved in designing and using measurement scales are discussed below. The way the questions are worded and their order are important to validity. Of particular importance in design is to look ahead to how the analysis will be performed, and with quantitative questionnaires (e.g. with rating scales), issues such as sample size need to be considered if statistically valid inferences are to be drawn from the data.

The advantages of questionnaires are that they allow people time to think, and to respond anonymously. They are quick and easy to analyse (if there are few 'open questions' and they are pre-coded), and they can be given to many people at a low cost. The disadvantages include selective response rates – for example, responses only from those who feel particularly strongly about a topic – which can give misleading results if the evaluator generalizes the findings without noting this possibility. A proportion will often be part completed, some respondents may 'misuse' or misunderstand the categories or feel that they cannot express their view properly in the terms required, and some may under- or over-estimate in their replies. For example, McKinlay (1992) found that questionnaire respondents generally under-reported their alcohol consumption by about half, although he also notes that this under-reporting is even greater when respondents are interviewed. Much depends on the skill and experience of the questionnaire designer.

These and other issues are discussed in detail in general texts (e.g. Frankfort-Nachmias and Nachmias 1992) and for evaluation in Breakwell and Millward (1995: 58–67). Questionnaire design is summarized in overviews of the method in health care in Sapsford and Abbott (1992: 87–100), Edwards and Talbot (1994: 99–101), McConway (1994: 57–8). McKinlay (1992: 115–37) gives an excellent discussion of methods used for surveying older people. Surveys and questionnaires for organizational evaluations are discussed in Ghauri et al. (1995: 58–64).

There is a fine dividing line between a questionnaire survey and standard measurement instruments such as the General Health Questionnaire (Bowling 1992). The difference is that the latter are usually constructed on the basis of an explicit conceptual model and have been extensively tested and often validated, whereas questionnaires and surveys are usually developed for the specific purpose of the evaluation and might have little pilot testing or no validation.

## Measurement methods

The design of controlled experimentation has been refined to a science that is within the grasp of any researcher who owns a table of random digits and recognizes the difference between blind and sighted assessments. However, the measurement of outcome seems to have been abandoned at a primitive stage of development. . . . A superfluity of instruments exists, and too little is known about them to prefer one to another.

(Smith *et al.* 1980)

This critical view of outcome measures is an extreme one, and measures have advanced considerably since 1980. However, it is still true that evaluations sometimes do not choose the most appropriate measure for the purpose. The fourth category of data collection methods considered here are measurement methods. When used as a general term, 'measurement' describes any method of data collection – questionnaires are sometimes described as measures. Here the term is used in a specific sense to mean only methods for collecting data in a numerical or 'quantified' form. In this sense we may measure people's attitudes by asking them to express their views in terms of a number on a rating scale, or measure their temperature using a thermometer.

Measurement is itself evaluation because it is quantifying something by comparison with something else. Measures are often used in evaluation to quantify needs and outcome, but also to quantify inputs (e.g. costing) and processes (e.g. time, the number of defined activities). Measurement is an efficient way to communicate evidence and describe things, and, if the evaluation is well designed and conducted, can be used to discover and prove causation.

Measures of patient outcomes used in treatment and service evaluations include measures of physiological functioning (temperature, blood pressure, haemoglobin value, erythrocyte sedimentation rate, glucose levels etc.), measures of physical function (e.g. activities of daily living, ability to walk, range of motion), measures of psychological functioning (e.g. response rate, cognitive abilities, depression, anxiety) and measures of social functioning (e.g. social skills, ability to participate in employment, community participation).

This section does not describe these different measures in detail because they are well described in general research texts such as Bowling's text on measuring disease (Bowling 1995) and her review of quality of life measures (Bowling 1992), as well as in evaluation texts such as St Leger *et al.* (1992) Fink (1993), Rossi and Freeman (1993), and Breakwell and Millward (1995). Chapter 13 describes some methods used in measuring health service quality.

## Concepts and theories underlie measures

When we measure, we or our subjects assign a number to a category: for example, age or a rating of 4 on a scale of 1 to 5. Or we read off a number from a measuring instrument such as a clock, thermometer or EEG machine. The numbers do not pre-exist our measurement, but are created by us, our subjects or our machines according to certain procedures. These procedures depend on a concept about the phenomenon. The concept of age is one which is commonly agreed, and can be measured directly – it is easy to 'operationalize' the concept in the measure of time since birth, and everyone knows what it means. Note that this measure itself depends on other concepts and the measure of time. Note also that when we considered qualitative data gathering above we also faced issues of operationalization: for example, difficulties in defining a term in such a way that people understood the same thing (e.g. 'illness' or 'quality programme').

Many concepts in evaluation are difficult to operationalize – for example, 'health' – and we use indicators or proxy measures where the link between the concept and the measure is less direct than for concepts such as age. This is the first of many issues which the evaluator has to consider when presenting results, defining the concept and then the link between this concept and the measure used so as to justify the validity of the measure.

In many evaluations we use numerical data from measures to describe or to explain. Numbers are efficient for describing phenomena and allow us to see patterns when they are presented in a visual or graphical way: for example, in a pie chart, histogram or scattergram. We can also describe by showing features of the numbers (which we hope 'represent' features of the phenomenon measured), such as average and spread (e.g. standard deviation, variance, interquartile range). We can see quickly, for example, how many people who received the treatment were within different age ranges, or what proportion of the costs of a service were personnel costs. Numbers can also allow us to discover and prove causation – we consider statistical analysis in the next chapter.

Generally, most numerical data gathering assumes that:

♦ the quality or property is sufficiently important to be measured;
♦ the method of measurement can distinguish in a useful way different amounts of the property;
♦ the property of one item at one time that we measure can be compared to the property at another time or of another item;
♦ the difference between, for example, '2' and '3' is equal in amount to the difference between '13' and '14', if we are using an interval or ratio scale.

---

**Some common measurement terms**

*Sample*: a smaller number of a larger population.

*Prevalence*: at a particular time, the number of existing cases identified in a population.

*Incidence*: over a period of time, the number of new cases or events identified or arising in a population, e.g. 1 year.

*Rate*: the proportion of a population with a particular problem or characteristic, often expressed by age or by sex. *Prevalence rate* is the proportion of cases in a population at a particular time (e.g. 26 in 100,000). *Incidence rate* is the proportion of new cases which arise over a period of time. *Death or mortality* rate is the proportion of a population who die – but who die during a defined time period!

In summary, when using measurement methods the evaluator moves from concepts about the evaluated to operational categories which can be used to gather data in a numerical form. To put it another way, the evaluator moves from ways of conceptualizing needs, inputs, processes and outcomes, to operational categories for measuring the intervention and its effects. Assigning items to categories is one type of measure ('classification'), as is 'ranking', but measurement is more often thought of as assigning a number using an interval or ratio scale. The next chapter discusses methods for analysing numbers collected in the ways described above so as to discover causes and to explain associations. This is the main use to which measures are put in an experimental evaluation.

## Using existing data sources

*The palest ink is clearer than the best memory.*

(Chinese proverb)

Do not collect data which someone else has already collected. However, before you use already collected data, be careful to check how these data were collected and whether you can use them for the evaluation you are carrying out. This fifth and last category of data gathering methods describes methods for finding and then using data which have already been collected and recorded for purposes other than the evaluation. Examples are methods for abstracting and using data recorded in government statistics, patient case records, minutes of meetings or data reported in other research.

### Finding data sources

The first step is to identify possible sources of already collected data ('secondary sources'). This, as with all data collection methods, depends on being clear as to which types of evidence are required to answer the evaluation question and which would give evidence in relation to the evaluation criteria. Is evidence needed about the outcomes of the treatment, service, policy or organizational change? Or about processes, or about inputs? And what type of evidence: patient perceptions, staff perceptions, economic or other types of evidence? Over what time scale is the evidence required? Answers to these questions help to suggest possible sources of existing data.

There are different methods for searching for sources. The simplest is to ask service providers or clerical staff if there are records, statistics and other sources which might give the data needed for the evaluation. Sometimes it is easier to ask patients what they think service providers might have recorded, or whether any patients have kept a diary. The evaluator can also look at public or private indexes or registers of documents held by institutions. For identifying data published in research reports and journals there are a variety of databases and search methods, such as MEDLINE and Social Science Citations Indexes. Search methods are well described in Gray (1997).

Most national governments collect data about populations and about public services for a variety of purposes. St Leger *et al.* (1992) describe sources of data in the UK, which include a 10-year national population census carried out since 1801 (apart from 1941), details about a 1 per cent sample of this census, population 'deprivation' measures, national interview surveys such as the General Household Survey, health statistics such as births and deaths, occupational mortality and morbidity indicators. These sources are similar to those in the Nordic countries, but in the latter there are also national disease registers (e.g. cancer registers) and other registers, some of which are run by medical specialities (Garpenby and Carlsson 1994).

Service statistics include data about inputs and processes such as bed numbers, admissions, staffing and sometimes outcomes. Health service activity and performance data include numbers referred, numbers using the service, number discharged, age and sex and other patient characteristics, types of needs/diagnoses, types and numbers of treatments provided, through-put, bed utilization, average length of treatment, waiting lists, waiting times, unit costs, staffing numbers/grades, absenteeism, sickness and turnover. Some countries also have national or local statistics on number of patients for the major diagnostic-related groups. Chapter 8 considers performance measures in more detail.

There are also individual patients' case records: these are used for some types of evaluation, such as some quality assurance procedures or audit. Medical and other types of audit reports are also useful data sources for some evaluations (e.g. NCEPOD 1987, 1989, 1993).

## Assessing data sources

The second step in this method is to assess the data for the purposes of the evaluation. This means applying the same tests to these 'already' 'recorded-data' which one applies to data gathered using a direct method, such as an interview or questionnaire. The tests include validity, reliability, sampling and tests of appropriate analysis if the data are already presented as composite measures. Note, however, that these tests should be for the use of the data for the purpose of the evaluation. These tests are described in chapter 12. The general validity and reliability of some specific secondary sources are discussed in Gissler *et al.* (1995) (data quality after restructuring the Finnish 'medical birth registry') and of Swedish medical registers in Garpenby and Carlsson (1994). The poor quality of the few data on inpatient maternity care in the UK is discussed in Middle and Macfarlane (1995). It is always worth checking to find out if a validation study has been carried out on data from a particular source.

A separate but important issue to consider in assessing the potential use of the data source is the question of confidentiality. There are usually strict rules to ensure patient confidentiality which researchers will need to understand and respect. Some evaluators have found that these rules are even stricter for evaluations. Evaluators may be allowed access to the data, but can they publish them, or what changes would be required to allow publication? Who owns data which are not already public?

## Using existing data sources

The third step is to abstract from the data sources those data which are needed for the evaluation, and to analyse these abstracted data. The data may be qualitative, as, for example, in descriptions in case records, or minutes or agenda of meetings. If so, the evaluator uses coding or other methods of abstraction and data analysis for qualitative data, always bearing in mind that the text was recorded for purposes other than the evaluation. Often the evaluator will be using already collected quantitative data and will analyse them using statistical and other methods, which take account of the known limitations of the data.

In my experience the detective work involved in discovering already collected data is well worth the effort, especially if these data pass the assessment described above. Sometimes finding that there are no collected or recorded data is itself important. For example, in an evaluation of total quality programmes in five Norwegian hospitals, one finding was that there was little documentation of the quality projects which were running, and few of these projects were using measures, despite the fact that documentation, reporting and measurement were generally agreed to be essential features of such programmes (Øvretveit 1996b). Finding that there are recorded data, but that they are not available to the evaluator, or cannot be made public, can also be useful information for an evaluation.

In the next chapter we consider how to analyse and interpret data produced by using the methods described above: it finishes with a checklist for assessing the evidence produced in an evaluation.

## Conclusions

♦ Because of the broad range of subjects and user questions they are faced with, health evaluators need to be aware of a wide range of data gathering methods. They need to be able to choose the most cost-effective method for the purpose of the evaluation.

♦ Users of evaluations need to have some understanding of the methods used to gather data in order to interpret the data presented in an evaluation, to judge the validity of the conclusions and to judge the suitability of the methods proposed in a plan for an evaluation.

♦ Data for an evaluation can be collected by methods within the five categories of observation, interviewing, questionnaires and surveys, measurement methods and methods for using already collected data.

♦ The choice of data gathering method should follow from the evaluation design and questions to be answered, rather than design and the questions answered following from the data gathering method with which the evaluator is most familiar.

♦ Data gathering methods are not 'scientific vacuum cleaners' for collecting facts. Facts are created through a relationship between the observer and the observed, and through relationships between observers who agree what is to be counted as fact and how to gather factual information.

♦ Methods for analysing quantitative data are better understood in the health sector than methods for analysing qualitative data.

♦ It is often more difficult to judge the validity of conclusions from a qualitative evaluation using participant observation or interview methods than from an evaluation using a validated rating scale or measurement instrument.

Some important points to remember are:

♦ Define what data you need and how those data will help to answer the evaluation question and judge the value of the intervention.
♦ Consider existing data sources: what information is already collected, how valid is the information for the purposes of the evaluation and how accessible is it?
♦ Never develop a new data collecting instrument without checking whether you could use an existing and validated instrument (the world does not need another quality of life measure).
♦ If possible, combine methods to make up for each method's weaknesses.
♦ Always estimate the time and costs – and then double them (to test the method, to collect the data and to analyse the data).
♦ There are no good or bad methods for gathering data, just those which are most suited to the subject and cost-effective for the purpose and questions of the evaluation.

When choosing a method, look ahead to how the data will be analysed – one of the subjects of Chapter 12.

# Data gathering concepts, analysis and interpretation

*Reality resides neither with an objective external world nor with the subjective mind of the knower, but within the dynamic transaction between the two.*

(Barone 1992)

## Introduction

In Chapter 11 we looked at methods for collecting data within the five categories of observation, interviewing, questionnaires and surveying, measurement and already collected data sources. How do we analyse and interpret the data collected in order to answer the evaluation questions? One of the purposes of this chapter is to encourage evaluators and users to ask this question before collecting data, and to plan ahead.

This chapter looks in more depth at data gathering concepts and principles. Users of evaluations need to understand these concepts in order to judge whether the conclusions of an evaluation report are justified by the data presented in the report, and also to judge whether the methods in a proposal are the most cost-effective for the purpose of the evaluation. Evaluators with a research background will be familiar with concepts such as reliability and validity, but may not have considered how these concepts apply to methods which they have not used before, or how to ensure that the data gathering methods are related to the criteria of valuation.

First we consider the concepts of reliability, validity, sensitivity, specificity and sampling which apply to most data gathering methods. These concepts are important for deciding the validity of evidence in an evaluation, but so is using a particular method within the context of a particular evaluation perspective, and in relation to earlier phases in an evaluation which have determined which data are required. After placing these data gathering methods in the context of the evaluation perspective and process, we then consider methods for analysing quantitative and qualitative data. Understanding the methods of analysis is as important to interpreting the results as understanding how the data were gathered. We then summarize these ideas in a list of questions which help to choose and use one or more data gathering methods.

## Data gathering concepts

Surprisingly, there has been little research in health settings to evaluate different methods of data collection: whether, for example, there are differences in people's estimates of the effects of a treatment when asked in interview compared to a questionnaire, and when asked, and by whom, in different contexts. There has, however, been considerable research into and validation of different health and disease measures (Bowling 1992, 1995). In the following we note ways to judge the value of a data gathering method for a particular evaluation, and note techniques which are used as part of a data gathering procedure to ensure the quality of the data which are collected.

Validity, reliability, sensitivity and other concepts are part of a language which is used to describe features of data gathering methods and of data. Such terms are used to describe both quantitative measures and qualitative methods and to discuss which methods are most suitable for gathering the kind of information required in an evaluation. When we are planning and carrying out an evaluation, these concepts help us to devise practical strategies to improve the quality of the data: for example, knowing about principles of reliability helps us to think about the best ways to train interviewers to ensure a standard approach.

### Reliability

Reliability is the extent to which a data gathering method will give the same results when repeated (i.e. consistency). It refers to the amount of random or systematic error (bias) or variance in data which the method gives, either between times (e.g. one interviewer at different times) or between units (e.g. between interviewers or target populations). A measure may be unreliable because it is difficult for the subject to understand (e.g. ambiguous questions) or because the setting or method of administration affects the measure (e.g. a hospital patient is given a satisfaction questionnaire by a nurse and asked to return it to the nurse).

Unstructured interviewing as a data gathering method can sometimes be unreliable: unless certain precautions are taken, such as careful training, different interviewers are likely to elicit and collect different data. This is not to suggest that qualitative methods are always less reliable than quantitative methods, just that each method includes different techniques to increase reliability (e.g. ensuring that all interviewers are skilled). For example, Olympic judges use techniques in their assessments which have been found to have a higher reliability than some psychology tests. The three main concepts of reliability are:

♦ *Inter-rater reliability*: the extent to which two or more observers give the same value to the thing that they measure at the same time.
♦ *Intra-rater reliability*: the same observer gives the same value at different times, if the thing that he or she observes is the same.
♦ *Stability* of a measure refers to its ability to give the same scores at different times if nothing has changed (e.g. satisfaction). This is sometimes called 'test–retest reliability'.

By analogy, if we think of people shooting at a target, an 'unreliable' shooter is one whose shots are randomly spread across the target – and beyond. A 'reliable' shooter will produce a concentration of shots in one area, but this area may be way off centre. A 'valid' shooter will produce a concentration of shots in the centre of the target. In evaluation as in other types of research, the aim is to reduce random errors by using a reliable measure, and to reduce additional and 'built-in' systematic errors (bias) by using a valid measure.

## Validity

The reliability of a method is a necessary condition for producing valid data, but it is not a sufficient condition. Validity is the extent to which a measure or piece of data 'reflects' what it is supposed to measure or give information about. Accuracy is similar, but refers to the amount of average deviation of a measure from the true value. Thus a measure may be very accurate, but may not be a valid measure of a particular thing (this is where our 'target shooter' analogy breaks down). One can only describe the validity of a data collection method by referring to the thing or phenomenon which the method is supposed to yield data about. Note that there are different philosophical views about whether the thing or phenomenon really does have an independent objective status or is 'created' by our method of data collection (the 'is a red rose red in the dark?' debate) – our philosophical position on this affects how we view validity. Five different ways of describing or assessing the validity of a data gathering method are:

- *Face validity*: the data gathering method appears to measure what it claims to measure (a simple test of face validity is to ask someone knowledgeable about the phenomenon if he or she thinks that the measure represents the phenomenon).
- *Criterion validity*: the data gathering method or measure produces data which correlate with data from another method which are accepted as a valid measure of the thing studied (i.e. its consistency with alternative measures or data gathering methods).
- *Predictive validity*: the ability of the method to predict an event.
- *Content validity*: the measure comprehensively covers the things it is intended to measure (e.g. an exam covers all of a course, a quality of life measure covers all aspects of quality of life). Often linked to a conceptual model of the thing being measured.
- *Construct validity*: the measure distinguishes between people who do and people who do not have the thing being measured.

These terms are sometimes used in different ways in different disciplines.

Qualitative methods can give more valid data than quantitative methods – for example, about the meanings which people give to events or experiences – but can be less reliable than quantitative methods. Validity in qualitative studies is increased by triangulation and respondent validation. Triangulation is gathering data from different sources, sometimes using different methods. Respondent validation is cross-checking information by asking a number of people.

Questions to ask to assess the validity of evidence collected by the methods described in Chapter 11 include the following. How large and representative a sample of people and settings was examined (see below under 'sampling')? Are 'raw' data available and open to inspection by others (e.g. field notes, tapes, records)? Were multiple sources of data used and were findings cross-checked and corroborated in different ways? Were conclusions purporting to represent people's views or feelings fed back to these people and were their comments used to revise the conclusions?

Finally, we need to bear in mind that a method may give valid data about something, but can be invalid for the evaluation. Validity in evaluation refers to whether the data are relevant for judging value – it does not just refer to whether the data give a valid representation of some aspect of the evaluated or its effects. A patient's view is valid information about a treatment, but it is invalid information for an evaluation which does not have patients' views as one criterion for valuation.

## Sensitivity and specificity

Sensitivity describes the ability of a method to identify correctly something or an event, such as a disease or a person with a particular characteristic: sensitivity is how well the measure detects the health problem or thing it is intended to measure (sometimes termed 'responsiveness'). 'Specificity' is used to describe how well a measure identifies those without a particular health problem or who do not exhibit the characteristic being assessed.

In evaluation, when we are comparing people's state before and after an intervention, the sensitivity of the measure we use before and after is important if we are to detect any change effected by the intervention. Specificity is important when we select people for a controlled trial. We would need a measure which identified people who did not have certain characteristics so that we could exclude them from the study. Here we are considering the sensitivity and specificity of data gathering methods, but note that specificity is also an important feature of a health screening technique and a criterion which we would use in an evaluation of one.

## Sample

Questions of sampling arise in the use of nearly all types of qualitative and quantitative methods. One sampling question arises in some service evaluations: how do we choose a service for a comparative evaluation. Some evaluations deliberately choose (sample) a particular service or groups of services because these exemplify a feature which is of interest (e.g. are considered successful or innovative). This is 'purposive' or 'systematic' sampling for case studies.

However, the more common sampling questions are, how many people and of which type should we select as targets for the intervention we are evaluating? If the evaluation looks at effectiveness or seeks to interview personnel, it is likely to have to deal with 'statistical sampling' issues which are concerned with representativeness.

We can rarely get data from every member of a 'population' (as in a 'census'), such as all the people who received a treatment, or who work in a service, or who live in an area and are the target of a health policy. If we use a smaller sample, we need to know how representative this sample is of a larger population. The sample may be the item to be evaluated (e.g. three organizations) or the targets of the intervention (such as the people receiving a treatment or health personnel within an organization). Care in deciding and selecting a sample before gathering data is necessary for both the 'internal validity' of an experimental evaluation, and in order to be able to make generalizations and valid inferences later ('external validity')

There are a number of sophisticated methods for sample design and statistical analysis. Generally the options are 'random sampling' (each person has a random chance of being selected, as in 'randomized trials'), 'cluster sampling' (selecting at random a cluster from within a selected sample of areas or organizations) or 'quota sampling', which selects 'quotas' of the population that represent one or a few features of the larger population (e.g. a certain number of the same age and sex as the larger population). A minimum total number in a sample is also important for some statistical tests of significance. Short summaries of sampling in health care are given in Sapsford and Abbott (1992: 89–93), St Leger *et al.* (1992: 164–9) and Edwards and Talbot (1994: 33–4). A related issue which is important to validity is response rate or ratio, where data are actually recorded from a group that is smaller than the sample (e.g. completed questionnaires are received from 67 per cent of the people who were sent a questionnaire). McConway (1994: 58–61) gives a simple discussion of the issues involved, as do St Leger *et al.* (1992: 167–9).

Note that 'theoretical sampling' is a specific technique for qualitative analysis. This technique is used during or after data collection within qualitative research and grounded theory approaches – it is a very different method from the 'subject sampling' discussed above. Glaser and Strauss (1968) use the term to describe how the researcher reflects on data, develops concepts and hypotheses out of the data, and then tests these ideas against the data or in further data collection. More details about data gathering concepts and issues for health service evaluation are provided in St Leger *et al.* (1992: Chapter 11), and a comparison of qualitative and quantitative methods is given in Najman *et al.* (1992), who also give an excellent discussion of the validity and reliability of qualitative methods.

## Data gathering methods in context

We can use the concepts outlined above to decide which method to use and how to assess the data gathered by the method. However, which data gathering method evaluators choose and how they use the method also depends on the perspective which they bring to the evaluation. In this section we consider how the assumptions underlying the experimental and developmental perspectives affect the choice and use of a data gathering method. We also note that data gathering is one of eight phases in an evaluation and the decisions made before data gathering influence which data gathering method is used and how it is used. First we consider what the terms 'qualitative' and 'quantitative' mean when they are used to describe data, data gathering methods and types of evaluation.

Some of the methods described in Chapter 11 were termed 'quantitative' data gathering methods because they assign numbers to an aspect of a person, organization or event. All methods in the category of 'measurement' are of this type. Qualitative data gathering methods, on the other hand, are methods for recording and understanding people's experiences and the meanings they give to events and behaviour. This can be confusing because some people assume that interviewing or observation methods only ever gather data in a qualitative form. In part this is because many descriptions of these methods are by social science researchers committed to a 'qualitative philosophy' who are arguing for an approach to research rather than dispassionately describing the uses of a data gathering method. In fact these methods can be used to gather numerical data if the observer or interviewer starts with predefined categories which he or she or the subject then uses to assign a number: for example, the interviewer asks the subject to give a rating from one to five on a scale which is then described to the subject. However, interviewing and observation are often used within a 'qualitative perspective' and in an inductive way to build up categories of meaning out of the data, usually out of people's reported experiences and perceptions or observed behaviour.

Thus we can characterize data as either qualitative or quantitative in form, and many methods can gather data in either form. 'Quantitative methods' only collect data in numerical form – these are measurement methods. These methods are often used within an experimental perspective which seeks to test hypotheses. 'Qualitative methods' is a slightly misleading term, because most methods can collect qualitative or numerical data. However, the term is often used to convey the idea that the method is used in research which is carried out in a different way from experimental research – where the method is used to discover people's feelings in their own terms and the meanings people give to events. The heated debates which innocent readers may encounter are usually debates about the philosophical perspective within which a method is used, rather than the method itself.

Finally, 'qualitative evaluation' refers to evaluations which use methods to gather only qualitative data and which are carried out within a developmental perspective or a 'descriptive-ethnographic' paradigm (i.e. the writing down (graphy) of facts about collections of people (ethno)). Likewise, 'quantitative evaluation' is an evaluation which uses only quantitative methods (Greene 1994). These are usually evaluations within the experimental paradigm which 'impose' preset categories before data gathering and use data gathering to quantify events. Quantitative methods define categories before data collection: for example, a rating scale of 'painful' to 'no pain'. Thus 'qualitative' and 'quantitative' are terms used to describe three things: data, data gathering methods and the philosophical assumptions underlying an evaluation.

## Methods in context: is the evaluator's choice of method set by their philosophy?

Why do different perspectives have a preference for different data gathering methods? Is it a preference, or is the choice of method based on a fundamentally different philosophical world view? The answers to these questions have implications for how flexible an evaluator can be in choosing the data gathering method. This book has proposed that there are different perspectives in evaluation, with different assumptions. It has also proposed a flexible approach to choosing data gathering methods, and one which goes beyond traditional disciplinary preferences. Are these two propositions contradictory: how can an evaluator working within a particular perspective choose a method which does not 'fit' within that perspective, or can all methods be used within each perspective?

Chapter 2 described some of the underlying assumptions of different perspectives about the nature of the many different social and physical entities and phenomena which are evaluated in the health sector. These include assumptions about how to gain valid knowledge about these interventions and their targets. We noted that treatments, services, policies and organizational change are all very different in their nature, as are the targets of these interventions. We drew a distinction between the experimental evaluation perspective, which tended to involve positivist conceptions about facts and fact gathering, and a developmental evaluation perspective, which explored and developed participants' conceptions, meanings and understandings of the evaluated, often during the evaluation. The evaluation perspective influences both the choice and the use of the method. But in what way, and how?

Generally, experimental evaluations tend to use methods to gather data in a quantitative form, and developmental evaluations tend to use methods which gather qualitative data. Experimental evaluations form hypotheses before gathering data and 'test' these hypotheses using a few specific measurement techniques. Developmental evaluations often use methods to build up and test concepts and hypotheses in an inductive way and draw on people's interpretations and experience using the terms which people ordinarily use. Many developmental evaluations are based on phenomenological philosophical assumptions about both the people who are the targets of an intervention and health providers. They are usually undertaken within a 'qualitative paradigm'.

The ways in which data gathering methods are used thus depend on the evaluation perspective. For example, how a patient pain rating scale measure is used depends on the evaluation perspective. As a method, there are some aspects of the use of this measure which are independent of the perspective, but there are other aspects which depend on whether it is used within an experimental or developmental evaluation. However, these distinctions are not clear cut. Developmental evaluations often use evidence from more than one source ('triangulation') and may use quantitative data gathered using a measurement method such as a patient rating scale. Further, qualitative methods often involve quantitative analysis, as, for example, when interview transcripts are coded and the items which arise are quantified. They also use the principle of hypothesis testing before, during and sometimes after interviews or observation. Experimental evaluations can use qualitative data to test a specific hypothesis: a randomized controlled trial can use qualitative unstructured interviews as one method of data collection in addition to others.

There is a further point to be made here about putting the method in a broader context. This is that, in the developmental perspective, there is not such a clear distinction between the phases of data gathering, recording and analysis. The concepts and theories are often built up in interaction with the data, sometimes during the interview, sometimes when recording and often when deciding the next parts of the data gathering phase, e.g. using 'progressive focusing' in the grounded theory approach (Glaser and Strauss 1968). The evaluator will often feed back and test emerging findings with users at intervals (Øvretveit 1987a). Further, the evaluation report and presentation in a developmental evaluation will be different from reports of an experimental evaluation and give more of a narrative than a traditional report.

The decision about which data to collect also depends on the work carried out in earlier phases of the evaluation process, which was described in Chapter 9. We have seen that evaluation is different from other types of research in involving criteria and comparisons which allow judgement of value. Before the data gathering phase the evaluator will have worked with users to clarify the purpose and criteria to be used, and to finalize the design. The discussion of methods in Chapter 11 assumed that the evaluator has worked through these phases and knows which type of data are needed to provide evidence in relation to the value criteria which have been selected.

## Evidence in evaluation

To finish this discussion about assumptions underlying data gathering methods we need to consider what we mean by evidence in an evaluation. Chapter 11 proposed that facts do not exist independently of the observer, but neither are facts entirely constructed by the mind of the observer. Facts are created in a relationship between the observer and the observed, and through relationships between observers who agree what is to be counted as fact and how to gather factual information (consensus). In one sense facts and evidence do not exist separately from the method for 'gathering' or 'creating' them.

We have noted the assumptions of different perspectives about what is a fact and how to create facts. In evaluation, whether a fact is considered significant evidence also depends on the criteria of valuation, which decide what the evaluator will look for. Thus an evaluation may produce evidence about the evaluated, which everyone agrees is true, but which is not related to the evaluation criteria and which is irrelevant for the evaluation purposes and for judging value. Whether the methods described above produce valid evidence for the evaluation does not just depend on using the method in the right way and understanding the assumptions of the method – it depends on how the data relate to the criteria of valuation.

This suggests that the evaluation criteria are always preset, and that data collection is limited to collecting data about these criteria. Is there then no room for inductive or grounded theory approaches in evaluation, where concepts and theories are built up out of the data? Is 'discovery' in evaluation only discovering the presence or absence of data which are related to the valuation criteria? The view of evaluation as using criteria to decide which evidence to collect is not incompatible with qualitative methods or with grounded theory and progressive focusing techniques. First, 'criteria' is a general term for different dimensions against which the evaluated is to be judged. Criteria could be the effectiveness of the evaluated, the degree to which it achieved objectives or met standards, or met needs, or the resources used, or all of these, depending on which allows the user to assign value.

However, evaluation users or sponsors may want to include criteria which other people use to judge value, such as those of patients, but may not know these criteria. Qualitative and grounded theory approaches can be used to understand and create theories about how certain groups evaluate the evaluated. The main purpose of some evaluations may be to do only this, while some may use this criterion clarification as part of the evaluation process and follow it with data gathering (e.g. some patient satisfaction evaluations).

Qualitative and grounded theory methods can be used to help users to define or refine their own criteria, again as part of an evaluation or as the sole aim of the evaluation. Finally, qualitative and grounded theory methods can also be used during an evaluation to develop theories about what it is about the evaluated which produces success or failure or about influences or causes of effects. These theories can be those of the evaluators, or evaluators eliciting and representing the theories of providers or patients. Thus it does not follow that the view of evidence only being valid in relation to criteria presumes an experimental paradigm, or a strict set of phases in succession.

Readers who wish to look into these issues in more detail will find general overviews of 'qualitative methods' in a health setting given in McConway (1994: Chapter 3), Fitzpatrick and Boulton (1994), Jones (1995) and Pope and Mays (1995a; 1995c), and discussion in general texts such as Sapsford and Abbott (1992), Edwards and Talbot (1994), Ghauri, *et al.* (1995: Chapter 8) and St Leger *et al.* (1992). Greene (1994) describes 'qualitative programme evaluation', as does Patton (1980, 1987). The scientific rigour of 'qualitative methods' is discussed in Najman *et al.* (1992) and in Pope and Mays (1995b).

## Analysis and interpretation

Much of the time the data are not in dispute, except where errors of observation or measurement are suspected, but it is their potential alternative interpretations which are of concern. Irrespective of the methods used, if the researcher fails to consider alternative interpretations of the findings and to discuss the merits of these alternatives, then there remain questions which serve to limit the confidence which one might have in the conclusions the author derives.

(Najman *et al.* 1992)

In this section we look at methods for analysing and interpreting data. To do so we follow the distinctions noted previously between quantitative data expressed in numerical form, and qualitative data which are usually expressed as text descriptions. Data could be gathered in a qualitative or quantitative form by a method included in the categories of observation, interviewing, questionnaires and surveying, and already collected data.

First, we concentrate on concepts and principles which mostly apply to methods within the category of measurement, and then we look at analysing qualitative data. It is important to understand some of the principles which apply to these types of data in order to decide how to gather, analyse and interpret the data. Looking ahead to how to analyse the data allows us to plan to ensure that valid inferences can be drawn from the data so as to answer the questions that users raised in the early phases of the evaluation.

## Analysing quantitative data

### *Types of measure*

There are four main ways of assigning a number to a conceptual item or phenomenon. Evaluators and users need to know the difference between them in order to design and interpret an evaluation.

♦ *Classification*: assigning an item to a category and giving the category a number. Examples are when coding a questionnaire, calling groups 'group 1', 'group 2' etc., or categorizing different descriptions of health states and asking people to choose one or more. When we classify we usually assign the items to categories which cover all the items (collectively inclusive), and to categories which are mutually exclusive, and do so according to one or more features of the item. We cannot assume any numerical relationship between the numbers. A classification of this type is called a 'nominal scale', and is not really considered a 'real measure' by many lay people.

♦ *Ranking*: assigning items in a rank order, according to some feature: for, example, self-ratings of health as 'very poor', 'poor' etc. on a five-point Likert scale. We can only say that items in one category are the same in respect of that feature, and are greater or less than those in another category, but we cannot say by how much they are greater or less. Some health status and disability measures use ranking scales.

♦ *Interval scaling*: this is like ranking, but quantifies the difference in the amount by which items are greater or less than each other, in respect of the feature measured. An example is the common temperature scale: 5 °C is 5 °C less than 10 °C (but note that it is not half as warm). We can quantify the difference between items in categories using measures of this type, and can also use 'parametric' statistical methods to describe the data (e.g. to calculate the average, mean and variances).

♦ *Ratio scaling*: if we assign numbers to items using a ratio scale we use a scale with an absolute zero, such as age, height, weight or serum glucose levels. With numbers assigned in this way we can say that one item is half the amount of another.

Most lay people do not make these distinctions and think of measurement as interval or ratio scaling. Dictionary definitions reflect this common view: to measure is to 'ascertain the extent or quantity of something by comparison with a fixed unit or with an object of known size' (*Concise Oxford Dictionary*). However, these distinctions are important for deciding how to analyse the data and how to judge the validity of evaluation conclusions, and some evaluations have made mistakes by analysing ranking measures as if they were interval scaling or ratio scaling measures.

The evaluator can help users to clarify further what they mean by using distinctions proposed by Jaques (1982), who suggests that the term measurement is used confusingly for four different procedures in relation to entities (entities being objects, events or episodes, which are objective in the sense of being socially shareable).

♦ *Counting* a number of entities.
♦ Using a *yardstick* to measure an objectively specifiable property of an entity (length, weight, temperature, time).
♦ A *judgement of preference* or valuation about an entity, which is a personal feeling that varies between people and in the same person over time.
♦ A *judgement of probability*.

Jaques proposes that the term 'quantification' be used to refer to the general process of assigning numbers to entities, properties, preferences and probabilities. He suggests counting the number of entities, measurement of the objectively definable properties of entities, rating by individuals of the preferences or utility they attribute to entities and quantified judgement of the probability of the outcome of the as yet unknown.

The distinctions help to clarify what we want to quantify in an evaluation, and help users to explain what they want when they ask an evaluator to, for example, 'measure the effectiveness' or 'quality' of their service.

## Statistical analysis

The section on validity, reliability and sampling above noted ways to make sure that the data collected give 'true' information about the evaluated or its effects. Each method of data collection described in Chapter 11 has procedures for ensuring validity and reliability which form part of the method. In the following we assume that a quantitative data collecting method has been used in the proper way and with attention to sampling. How, then, do we analyse these data?

Any data produced using measures will have errors. Some of the errors will be produced by the measurement method, and may be chance errors or may be systematic bias. Increasing the sample size will not reduce systematic bias in the measuring method. However, some variation is inherent in the item being studied, and is not an artefact of the method. Statistical techniques are used to minimize variation and to analyse data which include variation. Techniques for calculating statistical significance and confidence intervals help evaluators and users to make inferences about associations and causes.

In many quantitative evaluations we have two sets of numbers: for example, before and after sets, or outcomes from two interventions. Statistical significance testing helps to show whether or not any differences between the two sets really represent true differences in the populations from which the samples were drawn. It is based on the idea that any difference between the two sets is caused by a real difference as well as by differences arising from random and systematic error introduced by the measurement method. It involves proposing a null hypothesis that there is no difference between the sets, and examining whether any difference shown is greater than that expected by chance. The significance level is the level of probability at which we decide to reject the null hypothesis.

Phillips *et al.* (1994) give a useful and simple summary of the main statistical methods for analysis by distinguishing different stages of analysis. The first is to describe and summarize the data by representing each numerical value in a pie chart or bar chart, by calculating the averages (the mean, median and mode), the range (the difference between the smallest and largest values in a data set) and the standard deviation (how much the data values deviate from the average). The second stage is to define the generalizability of the data by stating how much confidence we would have of finding the results from the sample in the general population. This is done by calculating the 'confidence interval'. A third 'hypothesis testing' stage involves using data to confirm or reject a hypothesis. A type I error is to reject a null hypothesis when it is in fact true, and the analysis calculates the probability of having a type I error – called the significance level. A fourth stage is to calculate the strength of the association between two variables using chi-squared tests, calculating a correlation coefficient or carrying out a regression analysis.

Giving a short listing of these statistical methods makes them look more complicated than they are. There are now a number of texts which give simple summaries with examples. Techniques for deciding significance levels and other details of measurement, sampling and statistical analysis in health evaluation are described in summary in St Leger *et al.* (1992: Chapter 11), Edwards and Talbot (1994: Chapter 6) and McConway (1994: Chapters 5 and 6). A simple general practical overview of 'describing and summarizing data' and of drawing inferences in evaluation is given in Breakwell and Millward (1995: 80–96). Wilkin *et al.* (1992) describe measurement of need and outcome, as does Bowling (1992, 1995). A more detailed and comprehensive text for clinicians is Gardner and Altman (1989).

## Analysing and interpreting qualitative data

Perhaps the greatest problem in using qualitative data in an evaluation – usually gathered using observation or interview methods – is analysing the data. The challenge does not stop there: there are related problems of how to display qualitative data or summaries of these data and to convince users and other scientists that the conclusions are justified by the data. There are two issues. The first is how to use the techniques of analysis which are generally agreed by qualitative researchers in order to reach conclusions which other scientists using these methods would accept. The second is how to present the conclusions and analysis to those who are unfamiliar with these techniques.

Many people in health services are familiar with methods for analysing and presenting quantitative data, but not with those for qualitative data. Indeed, one researcher proposed developing 'a kind of hierarchy in qualitative research design as evidence based healthcare researchers have done'. This was in the context of a paper arguing that health promotion 'needs to develop an approach to evaluation and effectiveness that values qualitative methodologies' (Macdonald *et al.* 1996) (the hierarchy of evidence model is reproduced in Table 14.1). In my view difficulties in data analysis and presentation and lack of familiarity with the methods are significant problems in using qualitative data in a health evaluation.

Data analysis is one of the most difficult, time-consuming, but also creative, tasks in using observation and interviewing methods within a qualitative paradigm. Analysis can be made after the data collection phase, but within the qualitative paradigm some analysis is made during data collection. We noted this technique when describing interview methods – where an interviewer decides to follow up a subject of interest, or where the interviewer formulates a hypothesis and explores it through probing and testing within the interview. A similar process of analysis is where the interviewer or team carries out an analysis after an interview and uses the 'results' in subsequent interviews, these results being categories of experience or hypotheses which can be tested in other interviews. We can represent a common approach to qualitative data analysis by the following steps.

1  Interview or observation.
2  Text (a write-up of the interview, field notes or a transcript of a tape).
3  Code or classify (according to 'emergent' themes or patterns).
4  Further analysis (recoding or hypothesis testing, often by returning to the original text or other texts to compare views or settings for similarities and differences).
5  Conclusions/results: categories of experience or feelings of the subjects, meanings subjects give to events, explanatory models and concepts or generalizations.

Qualitative analysis is inductive, building and testing concepts in interaction with the data or the subjects. It is also usually iterative: the analyst forms categories from the data and then returns to the data to test their generalizability.

These techniques of data analysis are complex and are not easy to describe in evaluation reports for readers unfamiliar with the techniques, but then this is also true for methods for analysing quantitative data. However, examples from the original data give vivid illustrations, and also 'ring true' with users. A comprehensive and detailed account of qualitative data analysis is given in Miles and Huberman (1984), but simpler and shorter summaries are provided in Edwards and Talbot (1994: 102–5), Fitzpatrick and Boulton (1994: 110–11), and Sapsford and Abbot

(1992: 117–25). A discussion specifically for evaluation is given in Patton (1987). A discussion of different qualitative methods is given in Van Maanen *et al.* (1982).

---

**Assessing evidence from an evaluation: a checklist**

The above concepts and discussion of methods can be summarized in terms of a set of questions which both users and evaluators can use to assess the evidence produced in an evaluation. The questions apply to data gathered by either qualitative or quantitative methods.

♦ *How reliable are the data?* Could there be consistency errors in the data (random bias) which are introduced by the data gathering method? What is the general reliability of this method, and what precautions were used in the evaluation to ensure and maximize reliability (e.g. interviewer training)? Would others using the same methods have collected the same data?

♦ *How valid are the data?* What are the concepts which define the type of data required (e.g. personnel costs, health, knowledge retention)? Are the theoretical links between the concepts and the measure or data described (discussion of 'operationalization' of concepts)? What are the techniques for ensuring validity which are usually used for this data gathering method, and were these used in the study?

♦ *How well are the data related to the criteria of valuation?* Does the evaluation describe the criteria of valuation used to judge the intervention? Does it explain the relationship between these criteria and the data presented?

♦ *How was the sample selected?* Was the sampling method justified? What are the assumptions made when generalizing from this sample?

♦ *Is the method of analysis described?* What are the usual methods of analysis used for this type of data for the type of evaluation questions asked? How well were these analysis methods applied?

♦ *Are raw data presented or available for inspection?*

♦ *What type of explanations for the discovered effects are proposed* (e.g. influences, associations, or causes)? If causal statements are made, are alternative hypotheses considered and confounding variables discussed (e.g. were the right statistical tests used and in the right way, are differences statistically significant)?

♦ *If the evidence points to necessary changes, will it be credible to the people who have to change?*

♦ *Were the data collected and reported in an ethical way* (For example, were patients anonymous, documents public or 'cleared'?

---

In conclusion, both this chapter and Chapter 11 proposed that evaluators need to be able to choose from a variety of different data gathering and analysis methods. This flexible approach to data gathering and analysis is itself part of a multidisciplinary and broad perspective of evaluation which is proposed in this book as one that is necessary for evaluations in the health sector. This is not to suggest that evaluators should or could become expert in all the methods described. While disciplinary prejudices have no place in health evaluation, disciplinary expertise is more necessary than ever, both for those evaluations which do require specific skills and focus, and for broad and multidisciplinary evaluations. Maintaining disciplinary expertise while developing multidisciplinary approaches is a real challenge in health evaluation, which requires both conceptual and practical managerial skills.

We questioned whether gathering either qualitative or quantitative data was merely a matter of preference and familiarity on the part of the evaluator, or was part of a more fundamental world view. This chapter did not fully answer this question, but it did point out that the choice of data gathering method needs to be viewed in relation to the perspective used in an evaluation and to the questions and purpose of the evaluation. It is not simply a question of choosing an 'off-the-shelf' data gathering procedure: deciding which method to use and how to use it depends on how validity and reliability are understood and assured within an evaluation perspective. Evaluators need to know enough about the strengths and weaknesses of different methods to be able to choose the best for the purpose. But a flexible and pluralist approach to methods may mean that the evaluator has to ask others who are more skilled and knowledgeable to advise about, or to carry out, data collection.

## Conclusions

♦ Principles of validity, reliability, sensitivity, specificity and sampling apply to most data gathering methods.

♦ For evaluators, these concepts help to decide which methods to use for a particular evaluation, to devise ways to ensure the quality of the data and to devise new methods, as well as helping to define the limitations of the results.

♦ For users of evaluations, these concepts help to assess the suitability of the data gathering methods put forward in an evaluation proposal, to judge how well the data were collected, and whether the conclusions are justified by the evidence presented.

♦ The validity of the conclusions of an evaluation depend on more than the validity of the data gathering methods which were used – they depend on links made in the evaluation between the criteria of valuation, the design and the data.

♦ Deciding which method to use to collect data depends on having clarified the purpose of the evaluation and the questions to be answered: data gathering comes after the work of deciding criteria of value and deciding which information is required.

♦ The method to be used and how it is used also depend on the evaluation perspective: for example, measurement methods are not appropriate in some descriptive or developmental evaluations.

♦ Data may be described as quantitative (numerical) or qualitative, but to describe data gathering methods in these terms can be misleading, as many methods can be used to gather data in either form.

♦ The methods for analysing, presenting and interpreting numerical data are better known than those for qualitative data. Evaluators using qualitative data are not able to draw on widely understood conventions. They need to describe their methods clearly, and pay attention to how they present their results and to showing how they derived their results from the data.

♦ To choose the best data gathering method, the evaluator needs to consider:

   ♦ The nature of the subjects about which data are required, e.g. people (attitudes, meanings or behaviour), physiology, organizations, organizational change.
   ♦ The questions, purpose and criteria of valuation of the evaluation.
   ♦ Their own skills and knowledge about using different methods of analysis.
   ♦ The evaluation perspective to be used and how a data gathering method is used within this perspective.
   ♦ The time and resources available.
   ♦ Whether data gathering is retrospective, prospective or both.
   ♦ The timing, frequency and duration of the data gathering (when, how often, and for how long?).
   ♦ Sampling issues, as well as the validity and reliability of possible methods.
   ♦ Whether data have already been collected which could be used.
   ♦ The possibility of using already developed or validated questionnaires or other methods rather than developing and testing a new one.
   ♦ How to analyse the data and how to relate the findings to the evaluation questions.
   ♦ Ethical issues, such as honesty about the use of data for an evaluation, confidentiality and publication rights.

# Evaluating quality

*The evaluator's nightmare is being asked by a roomful of people representing different interest groups to evaluate the quality of a health service. Each person means something different by quality. Even if the evaluator could get agreement about what to measure, there would be disagreement about the significance of the actual performance. If the evaluator includes comparisons with other services, or with the same service over time, the scope for disagreement will increase with objections about the validity of the comparisons.*

*The evaluator will be blamed for causing confusion, conflict and dissent where there was none. Their crime was to make explicit the different conceptions and ways of valuing and attempting to measure 'the intangible'. The nightmare ends when someone says that the service already evaluates quality with its own quality assurance system: 'With all this evaluation, who will have any time to see patients?'*

*More than other types of evaluation, quality assessments have a reputation of being 'no-win evaluations' for evaluators.*

## Introduction

Of all the many concepts in health, quality is one of the most 'evaluative', and second only to health itself in the variety of meanings which people bring to the term. Apparently 'objective' definitions of quality have been used by different professions to advance their interests. Quality is political, and, perhaps more than in any other type of evaluation, the evaluator needs to define clearly for whom the evaluation is being made, the criteria being used and how these criteria are derived. This book takes the view that any definition or category is socially created and sustained and is connected with the values and aspirations of individuals and of interest groups. This is especially so with definitions of quality, and even more so with evaluation of quality. As Rodriguez (quoted in Ellis and Whittington 1993) points out, what we mean by quality depends 'on who is assessing it – and what values and consensus are used in evaluation – and by what implicit or explicit standards or gauges it is being objectively or subjectively evaluated.'

There are different views about the purpose and methods of quality evaluation. Some argue that quality evaluations should act for taxpayers or patients and carry out a 'watchdog' or inspection function, exposing and representing quality and especially those aspects of quality which patients cannot assess. This view holds that whether providers use the evaluation should be of no concern to the evaluators, whose only task is to measure and report the quality of a service. Reporting will put extra pressure on service providers to improve quality, and providers are in the best position to know what to do to improve their own quality. Others argue that quality evaluations should give service providers data and ideas about how to improve quality, should be more developmental in aim, and, in some cases, confidential to the providers. This tension between inspection and development is one which exists in other types of evaluation, but is particularly marked within the field of quality evaluation.

The subject of this chapter is how to evaluate the quality of a service, which is different from, but includes how to measure, quality and outcome. The purpose of the chapter is to outline different approaches to evaluating quality in order to help both evaluation users and practitioners to choose which approach is most suited to their purposes. It concentrates on quality evaluations carried out by external evaluators, rather than on quality evaluation as one task which service providers carry out as part of quality assurance. We first consider the variety of types of 'quality evaluation' in the health sector, and for whom we evaluate quality and why. The chapter then considers different definitions of quality which are suitable for different types of quality evaluations. The core of the chapter describes methods for measuring quality and a model to guide quality evaluation. We finish with a discussion of internal quality evaluation and of how to evaluate quality programmes and quality systems which are interventions to organizations and one of many 'management technologies' on healthcare which need to be evaluated (Øvretveit 1997c).

## Evaluating quality: the variety

'Quality evaluation' describes a variety of activities undertaken by different people. A quality evaluation can be carried out by people who provide a service ('self-evaluation'), as, for example, in many clinical audits, or by an external group, which can sometimes be colleagues from another service as in an 'external peer audit', and the evaluation may be a routine or special exercise.

External evaluators are increasingly being asked to evaluate the system which a service itself uses to assure quality, or to evaluate a quality programme. This is different from evaluating the quality of the service directly because the subject of the evaluation is the quality assurance system or the programme, not the service. Examples of external evaluations of quality systems are evaluations of medical and clinical audit (Walshe and Coles 1993; Kogan and Redfern 1995), of organizational audit (Edgren 1995), of total quality management (Joss and Kogan 1995; Øvretveit 1996b, 1997b) and also routine evaluations of an organization's quality assurance system which are carried out for accreditation purposes (Scrivens 1995).

The different quality evaluations examine different things. Some consider only outcomes and do not examine service process and what the service might be doing internally. Examples are evaluations of patient satisfaction and functioning after leaving the service – these 'quality evaluations' are often outcome measurement exercises. A second type consider service processes and these are of more help to providers because they assess the aspects of the service which are thought to produce quality outputs and outcome, and give ideas to service providers about the changes which they might make. A third type is an experimental evaluation for the purpose of assessing whether certain features of the service really do cause high or low quality outcomes – understanding the complex links between service processes and outcomes. This third type can be carried out by external evaluators with rigorous controls, or by providers themselves using small scale continuous improvement methods (Berwick *et al.* 1990). Each of these three types of evaluation would be designed and conducted in very different ways: the first is a quality output and outcome measurement evaluation, the second is often an audit-type evaluation and the third is an experimental evaluation. All three could be carried out internally or externally.

Even these distinctions between internal and external, routine and special, and outcome, process and cause evaluations over-simplify the variety of types of quality evaluations. The following notes some of the other different ways of evaluating quality in a set of questions for users and evaluators which help to clarify which type of evaluation is wanted.

♦ *What is to be evaluated?* patient quality, carer quality, professional quality, management quality, of inputs, process or outcome, of one aspect or part of a service or of the whole service.
♦ *Who makes the evaluation?* external quality inspectors, providers for an internal self-review, quasi-independent development staff, external consultants or academics.
♦ *When?* routinely, special studies, in response to a crisis or a complaint.
♦ *Why?* for accountability, to protect patients, to give information to patients or purchasers, to help continual self-improvement or as an integral part of quality assurance.
♦ *For whom?* for taxpayers, patients or patient associations, government, owners, managers, health personnel or scientific purposes.
♦ *How?*: using ready-made standards and systems, deriving and using users' and stakeholders' criteria, deriving and using professionals' and managers' criteria or using evaluators' criteria.
♦ *Design*: patients' perceptions after the service, expectations compared to experiences, trends over time for one service, service quality comparisons.

**One definition of quality**

Health service quality is meeting the health needs of those most in need at the lowest cost, and within regulations.

(Øvretveit 1992a)

## Why evaluate quality?

The short answer is that someone wants an evaluation carried out, by an outsider or by an insider. Who might want a quality evaluation, and for what purposes? To what uses will they put a completed quality evaluation – what could they do differently as a result of having a quality evaluation?

In the past, patients or patient associations rarely asked for or sponsored service quality evaluations, but this is changing. When asked to evaluate quality, professionals often do not include a patient perspective, but concentrate on their own criteria of quality. (Notable exceptions to this generalization are the quality audits of surgical services carried out by the UK Royal College of Surgeons.) Patients now want independent quality evaluations because they cannot judge the quality of all aspects of a service, and because they want the work of professionals to be judged according to patients' criteria of value – patients appear to be less trusting that professionals always put patients' needs first or that public services will assure quality. Sometimes the motive is an instance of poor care, and patients want to know if the instance is more general or could happen again, and want to judge whether it could happen to them before they undergo care. Examples are instances of neglect in care homes for older people, poor aftercare or questionable deaths after surgery, all of which may move patients to call for a quality evaluation of one or more services. Other motives are that patients want information about quality in order to be able to make an informed choice of provider, where they do have such a choice (Øvretveit 1996a).

*Who sponsors and initiates quality evaluations for the voiceless and disempowered?*

Another reason to assess quality is that some patients or clients are less able to express their views, to choose a service or to act when they experience poor quality. People with dementia, very disabled people and homeless people are often ignored or not heard, but they have equal rights and should be treated as equal human beings. There are many patients who rarely make their views about quality heard to service providers or to others. Service providers often do not have the time, expertise or incentives to find out how people without power or a voice value their service. Quality evaluations are even more necessary than other types of evaluation for upholding social values of equity and respect for persons in public services. Such evaluations can use techniques to find out how people value a service when these people have difficulty or are reluctant to express their views. It is all too easy for evaluators and others to impose their own criteria rather than eliciting and using those of such patients, at least as one set of criteria in the evaluation.

Professionals are a second interest group who want service quality evaluations, and for a number of purposes. First are professional pride and professional vocation. Most professions declare that a duty of their members is to evaluate their own practice, and to take part in evaluations to improve services and maintain standards. This in turn derives from professionals' espoused principle of 'service' and intent to put the interests of patients above all others. Many professions themselves run quality evaluation programmes for their members, and have done so for many years. However, more recently another reason has led professionals to be involved in quality evaluations. In health services in many countries there is now a requirement that professionals take part in quality assurance, or cooperate with external quality evaluations: for example, recent laws passed in Norway and Sweden. A further reason has become more important for professionals in the 1990s: evaluating quality helps to monitor the impact of cuts to finance or changes in a service on the quality of the service. Generally, the purpose of evaluating quality from the professional perspective is self-improvement, and this can be carried out through either self-evaluation or external evaluation.

A third set of reasons for evaluating quality come from the management perspective, and from health managers at different levels. There are three answers to 'why evaluate quality?' from this group. The first is that because health managers are responsible for ensuring that taxpayers' money is well spent, they cannot restrict their attention to the costs and quantity of services, but also need to assess quality – the 'value-for-money' triangle (Øvretveit 1994d). Second, health managers have a responsibility to all of the population served by a service, not just to those 'passing through' it. They need to assess its availability and access for all of the population, and some definitions of quality include these more comprehensive features of a service ('population quality'). The third is more political and rarely stated: to increase managers' power over and control of professionals, who claim exclusive ability to assess and regulate their own quality. Independent quality evaluation can provide management with credible data to justify their plans to make service changes.

This third set of management reasons overlaps with those of government. In addition to ensuring value for money, governments have a duty to protect citizens from harm which may come from citizens' inability to assess professional quality – this applies to any service. Governments have additional responsibilities as owners and providers of public services to reduce unacceptable or preventable risks for patients and service personnel. A final set of reasons for evaluating health service quality are to contribute to scientific knowledge, rather than to any immediate and direct practical purpose. Little is known about the relationships between outcome and processes, and the methods of evaluation have much to contribute to understanding the causes of high and low quality outcomes from systems of care.

---

**Why evaluate quality?**

♦ For patients to be able make informed choices about which service to use, or whether to undergo a treatment.
♦ To ensure that the quality judgements of people who have little power or voice are recognized.
♦ For professionals to improve their practice and monitor the effects of service changes on their quality of practice.
♦ For managers to assess value for money, ensure that all patients' interests are served and increase control over professionals.
♦ For governments to protect the public.
♦ To contribute to scientific knowledge about the causes of high and low quality outcomes from systems of care.

> **Quality terms**
>
> *Quality assurance (QA)*: a general term for activities and systems for monitoring and improving quality. QA involves measuring and evaluating quality, but also covers other activities to prevent poor quality and ensure high quality.
>
> *Audit*: most medical and clinical audit is setting standards or protocols, comparing practice with standards and changing practice if necessary. Audits are usually carried out internally for self-review and improvement. Peer audit can use already existing standards or practitioners can develop their own.
>
> *Organizational audit*: an external inspection of aspects of a service, in comparison to established standards, and a review of an organization's arrangements to control and assure the quality of its products or services. Audits use criteria (or 'standards') against which auditors judge elements of a service's planning, organization, systems and performance.
>
> *Continuous quality improvement*: an approach for ensuring that staff continue to improve work processes by using proven quality methods to discover and resolve the causes of quality problems in a systematic way.
>
> *Quality accreditation*: a certification through an external evaluation of whether a practitioner, equipment or service meets standards which are thought to contribute to quality processes and outcomes.

## What is quality?

This section of the chapter considers definitions which are relevant for evaluating quality. We will look at definitions suitable for a formal external evaluation of service quality for a defined user of the evaluation. Many of the definitions are also useful for services or purchasers who wish to establish a system for routine quality evaluation.

Why consider 'expert' definitions of quality: surely the definition of quality should come either from the people who use a service or from the users of the evaluation? Certainly patients' and clients' views about quality and their definition of quality are important in a quality evaluation, but we also need to consider other definitions of quality. Another reason for considering experts' definitions is that many sponsors often do not have clear definitions which can be used as value criteria or operationalized in an evaluation. Users of the evaluation may want to know how interest groups other than patients understand and rate quality, so that they can make a more informed judgement of value. If the evaluator has a number of different definitions, then he or she can work with the user to agree the definition and criteria of quality to be used in the evaluation. Where users want to leave the decision to the evaluator, these definitions can give a start for the evaluator to decide the criteria and what would constitute useful evidence of quality for a particular service and population.

## Definitions of service quality for evaluation purposes

While simple definitions of quality are necessary for an organization's quality programme in order to communicate an idea to employees, they are of little use for a quality evaluation. An example is: 'quality is the ability of a service to satisfy customers'. In commercial services the customer pays directly for the service and judges quality in relation to price. In public health services quality and price are separated and patients are less able to use price as one comparator for assessing quality. Another drawback is that patients cannot judge professional quality, which may only become apparent years after, or if a post mortem is conducted. Simple commercial definitions also do not recognize the variety of 'customers' whose requirements have to be met (e.g. purchasers or funders, referrers, patients/clients and carers). They do not recognize the range of government and other regulations, and that population needs have to be met, as well as public health aims. 'Conformance definitions are also problematic, for example, 'quality of service is the degree to which it conforms to present standards of care' (Gray 1997). The standards might not be based on knowledge of what people want or need, but could be based on providers' out of date knowledge.

Quality evaluations need definitions which are suited to public health services and which help evaluators and users to focus on specific criteria: below we consider a number of 'dimensional' definitions which are helpful for these purposes. Donabedian's conceptualization of structure, process and outcome is not a definition of quality as such – his other definitions are more useful for deriving criteria for quality evaluation. Three aspects of quality are defined by Donabedian (1980): the goodness of technical care, of interpersonal relationships and of the amenities of the setting of care. He also distinguishes four types of definitions of quality: the 'individualized' type defines quality in relation to patients' views; the 'social' in relation to benefits for the population; 'absolutist' definitions in relation to the best balance between risks and benefits; and a fourth type of definition which specifies that the 'primary function of medical care is to advance the patient's welfare'. Another 'dimensional' definition of quality which is helpful for deriving criteria for a quality evaluation is that of Maxwell (1984), who defines the following dimensions.

♦ Accessibility: distance, time, social barriers.
♦ Relevance to need: 'appropriateness'.
♦ Equity: equal services for equal needs, unequal services for unequal needs.
♦ Social acceptability: what is provided and the manner in which it is provided is acceptable.
♦ Effectiveness: produces the desired effect in everyday conditions.
♦ Efficiency: for example, produces the desired effect with the least waste, such as at a low cost and in an economical way.

Maxwell's definition is comprehensive (too broad for some) and covers areas of interest to different evaluation users. It is useful for defining the quality of purchasing (Øvretveit 1994d). It is similar to that of the Joint Commission for Accreditation of Healthcare Organizations (JCAHO), which adds 'continuity', gives a different emphasis to some of the dimensions and links them.

- Efficacy: is the treatment useful?
- Appropriateness: is it right for this patient?
- Accessibility: if it is right, can the patient get it?
- Effectiveness: is it carried out well?
- Efficiency: is it carried out in a cost-effective way?
- Continuity: did the treatment progress without interruption, with appropriate follow-up, exchange of information and referral?

However, in both these definitions the usual emphasis on quality as patient satisfaction has been lost. Note also that one feature of quality is its holistic nature. Our perception of quality is not the sum total of all the elements – the elements combine to give a perception which is greater than the sum of the elements. This 'system' feature of the perception of quality is also a feature of how quality is created: quality assurance and quality programmes have to ensure that different quality activities link to create an impact which is more than the sum of the activities. This is an important aspect of quality to bear in mind in a quality evaluation, and something which dimensional or reductionist definitions rarely capture.

The next definition is one which informs the discussion in the rest of the chapter about how to measure different aspects of quality for a quality evaluation. This is the definition of quality as 'meeting the health needs of those most in need at the lowest cost, and within regulations' (Øvretveit 1992a), which breaks down to a three-dimensional definition.

---

**Definition of the three dimensions of health service quality**

*Patient quality*: whether the service gives patients what they want.

*Professional quality*: professionals' views of whether the service meets patients' needs as assessed by professionals (outcome being one measure), and whether staff correctly select and carry out procedures which are believed to be necessary to meet patients' needs (process).

*Management quality*: the most efficient and productive use of resources to meet client needs, within limits and directive set by higher authorities.

---

Which of these or other definitions the evaluator uses depends on the purpose of the evaluation and whom it is for. Some definitions are more suited to primary healthcare services, to primary services with a range of social and other services, to complex secondary or tertiary specialist care services, to support or diagnostic service, to evaluating the quality of financing organizations (Øvretveit 1994d), and some to health promotion. The evaluator needs to be familiar with these and other definitions in order to help users who are not sure what they mean by quality to decide exactly what they want the evaluation to look for and for which purposes.

## The difference between quality, outcome and performance evaluation

In this section we distinguish quality evaluation from related and overlapping activities, and introduce a model for evaluating the quality of a health service.

### Evaluating quality is different from evaluating outcome and performance

An evaluation of service outcome is different from an evaluation of service quality. Outcome evaluations measure end results which are thought to be produced by a service, and may measure the resources used. Many measure these end results to find out about the effectiveness of the service. Most quality evaluations also measure outcomes, but usually concentrate on patient satisfaction and certain types of medical outcomes. Having said this, some continuous quality improvement programmes use a wide range of outcome measures, as well as resource consumption (e.g. Batalden and Stoltz 1993).

The main difference is that quality evaluations usually measure aspects of process as well as, or even instead of, measuring outcome. Aspects of process includes patients' experiences while they are receiving the service, whether certain procedures are followed by professionals, the time between stages of a process and error rates within a process. There are two reasons for measuring aspects of process. Outcome alone is not a reliable measure of quality: for example, a procedure might not have been followed and by chance some people may survive or experience a good outcome. A second reason is that knowing the outcome alone rarely helps service providers to know what to change or keep constant so as to improve quality: we rarely know what caused good or bad outcome and we often get the knowledge many months or years afterwards.

Evaluating performance is also different from evaluating quality, but often includes an assessment of quality – service quality is one aspect of an organization's performance. Evaluating performance involves a range of measures such as progress towards objectives, capacity utilization and financial performance. However, the wider the definition of service quality we use, the closer it gets to describing organizational performance in general. Note also that an organization's performance measurement and reporting system often includes one or more quality measures: for example, waiting times and complaints rates. Further discussion of the relation between service quality, performance and productivity is given in Edvardsson et al. (1994).

### Evaluating quality is different from measuring quality

As we saw in the discussions of measurement in Chapters 11 and 12, measurement is quantifying the amount of an item. In one sense measurement does not involve a judgement of value: we can measure health by rating a person's state of health according to a defined scale. However, the value we give to that state of health can differ and depends on many considerations. This is not to suggest that measurement is not without value judgements: what is selected for measurement involves a judgement of value that this selected phenomenon is important in some way. Evaluation, however, involves an explicit judgement of value.

Evaluating quality involves measuring quality, but is different because the evaluation framework shapes which particular quality measures are to be used, and it is within this context that the measures allow the users of the evaluation to judge value. The evaluation framework also decides which types of comparison are of most help to users for them to judge the value of the evaluated. For example, one measure of quality is how patients rate their satisfaction with a service on a seven-point scale. A quality evaluation would decide which measures of quality were of most use to enable users of the evaluation to judge value and take action, and which comparisons would help them to do so. If the evaluation users were patients, then measures of patient satisfaction might be of interest, but of more help to patients for deciding whether to use the service are satisfaction scores compared to last year or compared to similar services. Evaluating quality thus includes measuring quality, but also an explicit judgement of the value of the quality attained, usually through making a comparison.

Note that some people would call 'auditing a service' carrying out a quality measurement because the auditors use a set of standards to 'measure' the service against. Other people might call the same thing a 'quality evaluation'. In this book evaluation includes making a judgement of value, so if the audit involved a judgement of value, as it does in some accreditation systems, then it would be termed here an evaluation. We look now at two features of a quality evaluation which distinguish it from a quality measurement project – this also shows some of the different ways of carrying out a quality evaluation.

## Valuation through comparison

Judging value can only be done by making a comparison. A key part of an evaluation design is the type of comparison to be made, which will allow this judgement of value. In designing an evaluation, the quality evaluator has a choice of the type of comparison which will be of most help for users to judge value. The type of comparisons can be any of the following:

♦ Comparing the service's statement of quality objectives with the levels of quality which have been achieved. (Has the service translated the quality objectives into measurable targets? Is the service already measuring performance against these targets?) For example, type 2 evaluation design, as described in Chapter 3.
♦ Comparing the service's quality performance with the levels of performance achieved by other services using a standard set of quality measures (e.g. type 2 design).
♦ Comparing patients' expectations with their experiences after receiving the service (e.g. type 3 before–after design).
♦ Comparing quality changes over time for the same service (trends) (e.g. a variant of the type 3 design).

♦ Comparing similar services on the quality measures selected for the evaluation (type 4 design).

Different types of quality evaluations will use different designs: these are discussed in the penultimate section of this chapter.

## Criteria for valuation

The second element to evaluation is the criteria for valuation which are to be operationalized to allow data collection. In quality evaluations these criteria depend on the definition of quality adopted and the comparison design. Note that in quality evaluations there are primary criteria and secondary criteria. Primary criteria are those of the users of the evaluation: for example, purchasers may want the focus to be on standards set by government departments and the extent to which the service meets patients' expectations. The secondary criteria are the criteria which key groups who are not the evaluation users apply to judge quality: for example, patients' quality criteria, if patients will not be users of the evaluation.

It is quite common for evaluation users to define criteria for valuation (primary criteria) that include those of other groups (secondary criteria), and to require the evaluation to find out these criteria and measure the service against these criteria. In some evaluations, users will ask for an evaluation to be carried out using preset criteria: for example, using an organizational audit or award system (Øvretveit 1994a).

## From criteria to operational measures

Once criteria are defined, they need to be operationalized so that the evaluator can decide which sources of data to seek out and the methods for gathering the data. Criteria can be the quality objectives of the service, the quality outcome performance or quality standards which are already formulated in a quality system or in an audit or award framework, or which are unique to the evaluation users and to be formulated by the evaluator with the users.

Drawing on these ideas, we can now turn to methods for measuring quality for an evaluation and to a general model which helps to decide which types of data to collect.

## Measuring quality for an evaluation – methods and framework

*If in doubt, ask 'how many', 'how often', and 'for how long'?*

Data gathering is a central part of a quality evaluation, as it is for all types of evaluation. The section above emphasized that how we measure quality in a quality evaluation depends on who the users are, their criteria of valuation and the purposes of the evaluation. We also noted that some types of quality evaluation called quality audits use ready-formulated standards against which to measure the service. To illustrate methods for measuring quality for an evaluation, this section uses the three-dimensional quality evaluation model described in Figure 13.1.

This model is helpful for most types of quality evaluation to clarify the types and sources of evidence, and for thinking about possible data gathering methods. Examples of evaluations using this framework are an evaluation of primary care (Øvretveit 1991a) and an evaluation of a family care service for people with a learning disability (Øvretveit 1988) In the following we consider methods for measuring patient, professional and management quality, and how to combine these measures for a comprehensive quality evaluation. Note, however, that there are other approaches to measuring quality, and users may, for example, want only an evaluation of outcome from the patient's perspective.

Generally, it is easier to discover and measure poor quality than it is to measure adequate or high quality, but doing so can lead to an evaluation being viewed as a punitive and negative exercise, rather than one which also shows the strengths of a service.

| | **Inputs**<br>The right amount and quality of: | **Process**<br>Activities of care | **Outcomes**<br>Change in patient's experience, health and resources that can be attributed to the service's actions. |
|---|---|---|---|
| **Patient quality**<br>What patients say they want, or what is necessary in inputs, process or outcomes to give patients what they want. | *e.g. Well qualified and experienced health personnel; clean and attractive buildings and facilities.* | *e.g. Polite and friendly treatment by health personnel; the right amount of information at each stage of the treatment; no unnecessary pain; quick service when required.* | *e.g. Patient satisfaction; pain reduction or elimination; return to activities.* |
| **Professional quality**<br>*(a)* Professionals' views about whether the service meets patients' needs (b) whether staff correctly select and carry out procedures which are believed to be necessary to meet patients' needs. | *e.g. Well trained and cooperative practitioners; the right patients are referred; sufficient information about patients is provided; the right equipment; access to efficient support services.* | *e.g. Correct diagnosis; correct choice of intervention; compliance with procedures; fast support services; good interprofessional communication.* | *e.g. Good health outcome; no negative outcomes.* |
| **Management quality**<br>The most efficient and productive use of resources to meet client needs within limits and directive set by higher authorities. | *e.g. Sufficient resources; good external services and information.*<br>(Similar to 'structure': Donabedian 1980) | *e.g. No waste, error or delays; compliance with higher-level regulations.* | *e.g. Lowest costs per patient; fewest resources consumed.* |

**Figure 13.1** A model for evaluating quality (combining Donabedian 1980; Øvretveit 1992a)

## Measuring patient quality

There are many methods for measuring patients' perceptions of service quality and for evaluating services from a patient's perspective. The following presents three popular methods, and then some principles to bear in mind when choosing a method. Note that most measures assume a link between how people judge quality and their behaviour: for example, that high satisfaction means that they will use the service again. In health services more than in other services, such a relation between perceptions, attitudes and behaviour may not apply because people may have no alternative but to use the service. As with all types of evaluation, the evaluator and users need to be clear about what information is required to evaluate service quality. The following list helps to clarify this. Decide whether you need to find out:

♦ the type of service which people want, expect and need;
♦ features of service which are important to them and the relative importance of these features;
♦ their view of the level of quality achieved on each feature of service;
♦ their actual experience of what happened to them (e.g. 'did the doctor explain the risks of the treatment?')
♦ their knowledge or ignorance of the services provided and how to access a service;
♦ the benefits (and disbenefits) they gain from receiving the service;
♦ their good and bad experiences of the service;
♦ problems caused by the way the service is delivered;
♦ whether customers are prepared/want to pay more for a better service/less for a lower service, have choices of level/price;
♦ who is not using the service and why.

### Counting complaints

The first data gathering method is counting complaints over a given period and categorizing by type of complaint. It is a simple and inexpensive method for getting data which indicate some patients' perceptions, and evaluators can usually get these data from service records. However, there are drawbacks. The volume of complaints depends, in part, on how easy it is to complain. No complaints may mean patients do not know how to register their complaint, are discouraged from doing so, find it too much effort or are afraid of the consequences. In England simply calling it a complaint will discourage some patients from using it. Even in commercial services, only a small percentage of dissatisfied clients will complain. TARP (1980) found that, on average, 96 per cent of dissatisfied customers do not complain. For each complaint 26 customers had problems, and at least six had 'serious' problems.

In addition, this method does not distinguish the importance to customers of different causes of complaint, or the importance of the complaint for those services which have to compete. It is also not a measure of patient satisfaction: the absence of complaints does not mean that service quality is high, but only that there are no records of dissatisfaction. It takes different things to produce satisfaction and to avoid dissatisfaction (e.g. a clean health service environment is necessary to avoid dissatisfaction, but rarely produces satisfaction). Having said this, any quality evaluation would be limited if it did not seek out evidence of dissatisfactions. Counting complaints is one important measure of poor quality and can suggest subjects for quality improvements. Much depends on to whom patients register their complaints, when and how easy it is to complain.

### Rating service attributes

The second and now common approach to measuring patients' perceptions of service is to invite patients to express their judgements of different 'features' of service (or 'attributes') in terms of a rating scale (e.g. a five-point Likert scale). Rating questions are usually asked after the patient received the service, and through a questionnaire or a 'comments card', or by an interviewer, with all the strengths and limitations of these data gathering methods, which were described in Chapter 11.

There are criticisms of the surveys used by some services: for example, poorly phased questions, the context in which the questions are asked and fewer responses from patients who do not have strong feelings. There is also a gratitude factor in health services and especially in public health services (Øvretveit 1992a). There is an extensive literature on the technicalities of designing and analysing service quality survey tools, some of which is not well known by health service researchers (e.g. Denton 1989; Zemke and Bell 1989; Albrecht and Bradford 1990; Heskett et al. 1990). Evaluators need to consider whether to use surveys carried out by the service, or to use their own survey, and if the latter, whether to develop their own or to use an already developed or validated patient satisfaction questionnaire. Another alternative is to contract a specialist agency to do it. Many computer-based systems now make it quite feasible to do an independent survey.

### Identifying critical patient quality features

Patient satisfaction surveys only have a chance of yielding useful information if the quality features are important in some way to the patient who is rating them. This is something to bear in mind if the evaluator is using the results of a survey done by others. If evaluators are to develop their own then they need to do research to find out which are the most important features to most patients of the type who are served by the service in question. A good example is the approach used in an evaluation of maternity services in Dublin (Gavin et al. 1996).

Special methods are used to discover these quality features and to find out the importance or 'weighting' of each to patients. People do not remember features as such, but do remember critical incidents. The methods which are suitable for this research are focus groups (Parasuraman et al. 1985), critical incident technique (Flanagan 1954), Kelly repertory grids (Kelly 1955), process-flow tracer studies (Øvretveit 1990a, 1994e) and multi-attribute utility techniques (Edwards and Newman 1988). Not only is it necessary to use special methods to help specify the features and their relative importance or 'weighting', but care has to be taken to find out in what way these features are 'important'.

---

**Questions for evaluators to answer in designing or using a patient satisfaction questionnaire**

♦ *Whom* to interview/survey (sample).
♦ *What* to ask them (do you know what is important to them, or is the survey to find this out?).
♦ *Where* to interview/survey them (at which point in their experience of the service process?).
♦ *When* or how often to interview/survey them.
♦ *How* to interview or survey them (e.g. by telephone, by questionnaire, by interviewer).

But most important of all,

♦ *Why* you are interviewing/surveying them (the specific details of how the information will be used and why it is needed).

---

As with all data gathering methods, design and piloting research is expensive and takes time. Some quality evaluators or services use a questionnaire which has been developed elsewhere from previous research to find out which attributes were valued by one set of patients. The risk is that the patients or the customers of the services studied for the questionnaire design research are not sufficiently similar to those using the service.

### The SERVQUAL method

These risks are reduced in the third popular approach, the SERVQUAL questionnaire and variations of this method (Parasuraman *et al.* 1988; Zeithaml *et al.* 1990). The research on which the SERVQUAL method is based suggests that customers of different services all view the same features as being important (Parasuraman *et al.* 1985). Part of the popularity of the SERVQUAL method with researchers is because it is founded on a sound conceptual basis. The method is based on research which found that customers' perceptions of service depend on the gap between the service they expected, and their perception of the service which they got. The SERVQUAL questionnaire method gets customers to rate what they expect from the service on a set of attributes, and then to rate their perception after receiving the service. The gap between the two on each attribute is calculated, and the total gives an index of service quality.

However, there are weaknesses with this method, especially for public health services. The method does not put weights to the relative importance of different attributes. It is likely that customers of different services value some attributes more than others (e.g. health patients would value 'capability' more highly than fast-food customers). In competitive markets the type and weight of attributes will change significantly every year. Further, people from different ethnic groups and cultures are likely to value different attributes of service, and people also assess service quality at different times, not just before and after. Their assessments may be important for their participation, and they may also withdraw. These criticisms suggest caution in using the method and in interpreting results. If the strengths and limitations are understood, the method can be of use in some situations (see Babakus and Mangold 1992).

### Satisfaction, experience and other quality concepts

To enable evaluators to decide which method to use to measure patients' perceptions of service quality, the following notes some key points from marketing, psychology and other disciplines, some of which are not well known within the health services research and evaluation community.

*Thresholds*. Most customers only become aware of an aspect of service if it is particularly good or bad in some respect about which they carried an assumption or implicit expectation. The critical incident technique is one method for finding out these features, which may generate different features from focus group, interview and other methods. Whether patients will communicate their perception of the service depends on:

♦ how easy it is for them to do so (for example, a patient may not have any particular comments to make, but when helped in discussion, especially by making comparisons with other services, may become more aware of his or her underlying perceptions of service);
♦ whether they think that staff really want to know;
♦ how strongly they feel;
♦ their social background (e.g. cultural or class);
♦ their personality;
♦ their personal state at the time (tired, harassed or relaxed);
♦ their wish to make things better for other patients.

*Valued attributes are ordered hierarchically, and change with competition*. Once a service performs well on one set of factors, another set becomes more important as the lower order set becomes taken for granted. In competitive markets, a once innovative or 'luxury' feature becomes expected, and a qualifier for market entry (e.g. TV in each room).

*Choice is a constructive process*. Research into decision making shows that people do not always know their values or attitudes, and are not always reliable predictors of their actions. Preferences are constructed, not merely revealed, in the elicitation process, and depend on the method of elicitation, the framing of the options and the context of choice (Tversky 1991). A finding of relevance to choice of service is that risky decisions are more likely where there is nothing to lose, whereas if people fear losing something they value low-risk options more highly.

*Services are processes*. Patients' perceptions change as they experience the service over time. In some services their final perception is less important than their perceptions during the service process, especially in long-term services, where withdrawal is a possibility and patient participation is important (e.g. chronic health problems). Service quality evaluations thus may need to gather data about patient perceptions at different stages of the treatment or service.

These and other issues in measuring quality are discussed in Øvretveit (1993c), including methods for measuring quality using 'cost-to-patients' techniques. In concluding, evaluators should note that there are a variety of other methods for getting feedback from patients which they could use, or which a service might already use and record. These include:

- talking to staff or patients about what clients like and dislike about the service;
- routine patient group or liaison meetings;
- a letter sent to a sample of patients asking them to fill in an enclosed sheet of paper which is headed 'What I think about X service . . .';
- mystery patient (secret visit or use of service by an assessor);
- comments cards;
- free telephone 'hot line' for comments and complaints;
- observation against checklist (internal or external observer);
- objective indicators of patient satisfaction (e.g. demand, drop-out rate, patient-cancelled appointments, a variety of service time intervals and waiting times, temperature, noise).

## Measuring professional quality

There are two related components to the professional quality of a service.
- *Professional quality outcome*: whether the service meets the professionally assessed needs of its patients.
- *Professional quality process*: whether the service correctly selects and carries out the techniques and procedures which professionals believe will meet the needs of patients.

The first component is judged by assessing outcomes which can be attributed to the service. Chapter 11 described ways of measuring the treatment and service outcomes of which patients may not be aware. These methods range from one or more professionals' judgements of the effects of the service, to one or more of a range of physiological, functional and quality of life measures. The key problem is knowing to what extent the outcome is attributable to the service rather than to other factors.

The second, and 'process', aspect of the definition is concerned with how well professionals carry out assessments, interventions, treatments and other procedures. It also refers to the efficacy ('does it work?') and effectiveness ('does it work in everyday practice?') of these interventions: the phrase 'techniques and procedures which professionals *believe* meet the needs of clients' refers to the fact that many service interventions or treatments and based on professional experience and tradition – many have not been scientifically evaluated. This part of the definition recognizes that a service may carefully follow procedures and set standards for interventions which are actually of unproven benefit, or proven to be ineffective or even harmful. It recognizes that the quality of many services would be significantly improved by a more rigorous evaluation of techniques, and by developing interventions or treatments on a more scientific basis (Appleby *et al.* 1995; Sackett *et al.* 1996). Quality evaluations should assess whether there are mechanisms for enabling professional staff to incorporate new knowledge of techniques and procedures into their practice through guidelines and 'evidence-based medicine' methods, and whether these mechanisms are successful.

Many services do not, or will not, have sophisticated routine outcome measures or evaluated interventions. Hence this second part of the definition recognizes that the best thing to ensure the right professional outcomes is to apply properly the assessment techniques and interventions which are believed to be the most effective. Note that many medical and clinical audit approaches which focus on the professional aspects of care will use measures of professional quality as part of the audit approach to evaluating and improving care. A broader quality evaluation of a service may be able to use such measures as a data source for the evaluation (e.g. a service may have done an audit of pressure sores, or of unscheduled patient returns to the operating room). Measures of professional quality are of three types: of input, of process and of outcome.

### Input measures

These are measures of inputs to the process which contribute to service quality. Common measures are of staff competence, or of supplies, information or other services which are necessary to the process. Examples are the time it takes to request and receive a patient record which a service provider needs, missing file rates or error rates. Some professional services have to rely on measures of input where it is difficult to define and measure both the outcome and the type of intervention, or where the type of intervention needs to be frequently changed. Some services or types of treatment can be standardized in order to develop process measures.

### Process measures

To develop professional process quality measures a service needs to be able to identify, map and specify key processes. Evaluators need to examine whether a service has maps of patient pathways and of their key process, and consider the professional quality dimension of a patient's progress through the service (Øvretveit 1993a, 1994e).

If the key processes are mapped then evaluators can assess whether a service identifies common professional quality problems at different stages, and also whether it specifies standards or requirements about what should happen at certain stages (e.g. procedures, protocols or policies). They can check if the service has methods for monitoring and documenting variations from standards or procedures (compliance or variation from standards measures) and for measuring common professional quality problems (e.g. how often a professional reports not having the skills or time to respond safely to a patient's needs). A drawback with this approach is that it is difficult for evaluators who are not from the profession to judge whether professionals use the right guidelines or have well mapped processes.

### Outcome measures

Most quality evaluations need measures of outcome to assess professional quality, but these can be the most difficult to develop or to choose from the range of measures which exist. The simplest measure is a rating by a professional provider or by a professional referrer of the change in the patient's condition which, it is judged, can be ascribed to the intervention made by the service. This approach is cost-effective but might not be valid or reliable.

One mistake made by small scale evaluations (and services) looking for more objective yet cost-effective measures is to use a method developed for scientific research. Many measures used for research into effectiveness and causation, such as some health status or quality of life measures, are not appropriate for routine quality evaluations or small scale single evaluations. Even a well funded quality evaluation has to distinguish between measures of professional outcomes which indicate the quality of the service and measures which are suitable for a full scientific outcome evaluation. Evaluators need to ask whether an evaluation of quality is required, or a comprehensive and detailed evaluation of outcome, possibly including looking for causal explanations.

As with patient and management quality measures, quality evaluators are often able to use data from measures already used by the service, after investigating the validity and reliability of these existing data sources. When looking at professional quality, evaluators are usually able to draw on data gathered by professionals for different forms of audit or quality assurance, and these data often have a higher validity and reliability than other existing administrative data or service statistics.

## Measuring management quality

The third and most neglected of the three dimensions of service quality is management quality, defined as:

*The selection and deployment of resources in the most efficient way to meet patient needs, without errors and delays, and within higher-level limits and directives.*

High management quality is achieved by:

♦ designing the simplest and most efficient combination and 'flow' of the elements needed to meet patients' needs (e.g. information supplied in the right way, in the right place and on time, efficient transport and other support services);
♦ identifying and avoiding problems which cause delays, mistakes and waste;
♦ increasing productivity at the same time as cutting costs;
♦ ensuring that the service operates within laws and regulations for public health services.

One reason for looking at management quality separately from the other dimensions is to assess whether a service is making cost savings unskilfully in ways which reduce both quality and productivity. Examples are making savings by employing fewer administrative staff and giving clerical work to expensive professionals, or by 'making do' with equipment that breaks down or is unsuitable. The poor management quality of a service may be shown by comparing the costs of a service to one which is known to have a high management quality. It may also be shown by a public service not being available to those people who need it, because the service does not properly prioritize whom it serves, or uses resources poorly, or does not follow higher-level policy requirements. The most important way to measure management quality is to calculate the cost consequences of things which are not done correctly the first time, which is one part of the cost of poor quality (the other part is lost patients or 'external quality costs'). A quality evaluation which does not examine this dimension of the quality of a service is only a partial evaluation.

There are two main types of measures of management quality. The first is of whether the service complies with 'higher-level' operating requirements. The second is process measures of poor resource usage and error rates, especially certain quality cost measures.

### Monitoring standards and policy requirements: compliance monitoring and measurement

All organizations and their sub-units have 'higher-level operating requirements' with which they have to comply to be a quality service. Some of these are basic professional standards discussed above. Others include meeting health and safety at work standards, employment regulations, priorities or policies set at local or national levels and other laws and regulations. Some are requirements which funders or purchasers specify in contracts, which are not patient or professional quality requirements, such as a requirement that a service is open at certain hours.

This first type of management quality can often be measured by simple monitoring methods which judge and record whether or not the service has met the regulation or complied with the policy. The evaluator can assess whether the service, for example, has up-to-date checklists completed by supervisors to check fire regulation compliance, or measures of staff turnover required by purchasers. Note, however, that many purchaser and higher-level requirements are not to do with service quality, but are part of more general performance requirements or objectives set for the service: for example, keeping within budget, or meeting project targets on time.

### Quality costing measures

The second type of management quality is to do with how well the service uses resources. Poor management quality shows in wasted resources and inefficiencies, and is measured by utilization rates, unit costs, error rates and certain measures of quality cost. An evaluator can develop measures of this type in two ways. The first is by selecting 'in-process measures' of poor management quality. This is done by using methods to map and describe the service process, as noted above for professional quality. Then the evaluator can list with staff or others the common quality problems in each phase which waste resources needlessly, or incur unnecessary costs. Having selected the problems which are the most costly, or the least expensive to solve, the evaluator can then develop measurement methods to quantify the problem. The second type of measure is of the current total cost of poor internal and external quality in the service process. This measure includes the estimated cost of patients lost to the service and of dealing with complaints (Øvretveit 1991b, 1993c).

Unfortunately (and inexplicably) quality costing is rarely used in quality evaluations, although some services are beginning to use this method. It is noted here because it can give evaluation users an idea of the comparative size of each quality problem and of the potential savings if the quality problem is resolved. It also makes it possible to compare problems to decide which problems to address, to compare services and to judge and track the impact and cost-effectiveness of different changes. There are four categories of quality costs which we consider below:

1  The cost of 'external failure' and lost income.
2  The cost of 'internal failure' due to inefficiencies.
3  The cost of preventing specific quality problems.
4  The cost of assessing the current level of quality (including calculating costs) and of assuring quality.

*External failure costs.* These are the costs of dealing with complaints and negligence claims, and the cost of 'patients' lost to the services where this results in a loss of income. To calculate the first type, evaluators can estimate the time staff take to deal with complaints and the costs of 'making good' service errors. Then they can make an estimate of the cost of defending negligence claims and paying for those awarded against the service – some services have to pay for these claims out of annual income. This is a difficult cost even to estimate – one approach is to estimate a range from 'worst case' scenarios to an 'ideal' outcome of the claim for the service.

Calculating the cost of lost custom depends on the range of alternative services which referrers and patients could use. However, it would be a mistake to say that there is no cost if there are no alternatives. Some people would rather suffer than use a service which is poor, or which they think is poor. Further, people can be dissatisfied and still use the service, but as soon as an alternative becomes available they will try it. Thus, for some quality evaluations it is important to make an estimate of actual or potential lost custom, even if there is no competition at present. Øvretveit (1991b) describes ways of estimating these costs by extrapolating from recorded complaints using rates from research carried out into commercial services.

*Internal failure costs.* These are the costs to the services of the waste, duplication, delays and usual everyday errors. These are revealed by using quality methods to analyse the service process. The assumption is that there is a right way to do things and that things can always be done correctly (the cost of making sure that this happens is estimated later). The best way for evaluators to estimate internal failure costs if the service has not already done so is first to construct a diagram of the flow of patients (or orders), from their selection of the service, through entry, assessment, intervention, to closure and beyond. Looking at each part of the process, they can list all the problems which commonly happen and which incur unnecessary cost to the service. Often it is problems at early stages of the service which are most costly – problems such as poor assessment, poor selection of the service by a referrer, or poor designs of buildings, or of the type of services for the population served.

The 'internal costs' of poor quality are the cost consequences to the service of all these problems – or the money saved if these problems did not occur. Usually it is a high proportion of annual operating costs. Whether a service needs to focus on the most costly problems depends on whether the cost of resolving the problem is comparatively low in relation to the expected savings: there may be a higher return on investment for dealing with other problems, and this would be revealed by estimating 'prevention costs'.

*Prevention cost.* This is the cost of preventing the 'internal failure' problems and complaints. Evaluators can assess the prevention costs by taking each problem and gathering ideas about possible causes. Data are then gathered to find out which causes do in fact contribute the most to causing the problem, and the cost of removing the main causes is calculated.

*Appraisal and assurance costs.* These are the overall and continuing costs of running quality systems, training and other activities which generally contribute to maintaining high quality and preventing problems. They include surveys, audit, quality costing, time in problem solving and any other quality costs which are not included under prevention costs.

## Measuring quality for a quality evaluation: concluding point

This section of the chapter discussed different ways of measuring service quality by thinking of three dimensions of quality and looking at data gathering in relation to each dimension for inputs, processes and outcomes. In concluding this section on measurement we need to note that the evaluator is likely to find that data about quality already exist for the service in question, and, if not, other research is likely to have considered how to measure the quality of the service in question. We saw in Chapter 11 that direct data gathering is not the only way to collect data for an evaluation although it is the most expensive way. There are three types of sources of data for an external quality evaluation. Primary direct data are data which the evaluator collects directly and independently from the service. Secondary indirect data are data which the service collects for its own purposes and which can be used by the evaluator, depending on their validity and reliability. Tertiary published data are data about the service which are published: for example, in government statistics or outcome reports. The use of secondary and tertiary data for quality evaluation for purchasers is discussed in Øvretveit (1994d) and a quality evaluation using secondary data is reported in Øvretveit (1988).

One thing which can make quality evaluations easier than other types of evaluations is that there may well be a considerable amount of already collected quality data for the service which the evaluation can use. Another is that others may have already evaluated a service of the type which is the subject of the evaluation, and the evaluator may be able to build on the research methods and techniques which others have used and which are published in the growing number of quality journals.

## Audit, accreditation and evaluating quality programmes

The first part of this chapter noted the many different types of quality evaluation carried out in health services, and we then considered at length methods for measuring quality used in external evaluations. In this section we change emphasis to look at internal quality evaluation and participatory and developmental quality evaluations, as well as how to evaluate a quality programme.

Audit, accreditation, quality programmes and many other 'quality initiatives' are in fact examples of a broader category of 'management technologies' which include project management, organization by objectives, and performance-related pay, to name but a few. Many management technologies have been imported into health-care without evaluation – one reason why they are regarded with scepticism by clinicians. Quality initiatives however, are different in that they stress the importance of measurement, facts and evaluation in making systematic quality improvement. It it therefore even more important that these methods are evaluated, and the lack of valid evidence of their effectiveness is even more striking.

### Audit: a note on terminology

Chapter 8 noted the increase in the number and type of monitoring activities in health services and the need to draw a dividing line between routine monitoring and evaluation, even though this line is somewhat arbitrary. Here we consider audit evaluations of clinical practice, usually carried out by practitioners on their own practice or with peers ('clinical audit' or clinical quality assurance') as well as organizational audit and accreditation.

There is a confusing use of terms in this area. Traditionally, quality evaluation has been undertaken by professionals and in relation to their own practice (practitioner self-evaluation), or through local or national colleague peer review. In Europe these types of quality evaluations have been termed 'quality assurance', although this term also describes other activities (Ellis and Whittington 1993; Shaw 1993). Many health services have 'internal quality audits' and auditors in their own quality departments to monitor, prove and improve their quality systems. A service may have introduced a quality system because it has to, or it believes this to be the best way to assure service quality in order to compete, or to show purchasers or public regulators that it has a systematic approach to controlling and assuring quality.

In the UK, professional self-evaluation has been termed professional audit, although it is also sometimes called professional quality assurance. Below we consider medical audit in the UK, which exemplifies many of the features of self and peer evaluation carried out in other countries (Øvretveit 1997a).

### Medical and clinical audit

Following a critical report from the UK National Audit Office in December 1995, it was reported that:

> The Department of Health is still unable to assess the benefits of clinical audit five years after it was first set up in the health service, the NHS chief executive admitted last week . . . Some MPs expressed astonishment that the NHS executive has still not measured the outcome of the estimated 100,000 clinical audits carried out by Trusts, health authorities and GPs. A labour MP demanded to know how the NHS could justify spending £279m to data on clinical audit in hospitals – equivalent to recruiting 1,500 doctors a year.
>
> (*Health Services Journal*, 21 March 1996: 7)

The term 'audit' means to give an account of actions and to check actions against expectations. From 1990 all doctors in the UK NHS were required to take part in medical audit, which can be broadly defined as the systematic use of data and methods by doctors to select and solve priority problems in providing medical care. Medical audit is used to describe a variety of activities, most of which are concerned wholly or partially with evaluating the quality of diagnosis, treatment and care. Audits are carried out at national and local levels: national and regional medical audits are carried out by doctors in a medical speciality, and concentrate on comparisons and encouraging the introduction of proven techniques of care (e.g. NCEPOD 1987, 1989, 1993); locally, doctors in a speciality audit their own care by focusing on particular problems or assessing trends, and sometimes will carry out audit projects which cross specialities or providers (e.g. 'shared care' for diabetics).

The purposes of medical audit include professional education and self-development, research into effectiveness, increasing the local effectiveness of medical care, proving local medical quality to purchasers or the public, improving the local quality of medical care, reducing and preventing poor medical quality and reducing the costs of medical care. There are three predominant models for audit. The first is an 'audit cycle' which defines standards and procedures, monitors care against standards, identifies divergencies and makes corrections (Shaw 1989; Øvretveit 1992a). The second is the 'research model', where audit is used to describe a research project. The third is the 'continuous quality improvement' model, which focuses on processes of care and uses experimental techniques to run small scale experiments (Berwick 1996). Black (1992) discusses the relations between audit, research and education.

The relevance of medical audit to the topic of quality evaluation is that it is a particular type of quality evaluation, where professional practitioners are both the evaluators and users of the evaluation. Medical audit can draw on techniques used in evaluation, such as qualitative evaluation methods, and evaluation can also learn from successful medical audits and draw on data collected for medical audit. In some instances evaluators may be asked to help practitioners to develop an auditing technique. Two examples are the quality peer review techniques developed in collaboration with practitioners and patients in primary care (Øvretveit 1991a) and in services for people with a learning disability (Øvretveit 1988).

Medical audit often uses the results of treatment and service evaluations: the evidence-based medicine movement views medical audit as one means of encouraging clinicians to make greater use of effectiveness research by taking it as a basis for audit standards and guidelines (Sackett *et al.* 1996, Gray 1997). Evaluations of medical and clinical audit (i.e. interprofessional audit) in the UK are reported in Kerrison *et al.* (1993), Walshe and Coles (1993) and Kogan and Redfern (1995). The politics of audit and its significance in the managerial–professional relationship are discussed in Pollitt (1987, 1990).

## Organizational audit and accreditation

We noted earlier that one method for quality evaluation is to use pre-existing standards and assess the service against these: one such approach is that of organizational audit (Brooks and Pitt 1990; Brooks 1992). An organization quality audit is an examination of an organization's arrangements to control and assure the quality of its products or services. Audits use criteria (or 'standards') against which auditors judge elements of a service's planning, organization, systems and performance. The criteria are based on a quality framework which highlights areas of an organization which quality experts believe to be essential to the organization's ability consistently to provide a quality service. As Brooks and Pitt (1990) put it, 'Whilst it cannot guarantee the quality of clinical care, it is a good measure of a hospital's ability to sustain a quality clinical service.'

As with medical audit, organization audit can be used for inspection and accountability, or as a developmental method, although whether it can serve both purposes at once is questionable. In the UK, organizational audit has become a method of accreditation, although still voluntary. It can be a useful quality development tool in that the process requires service personnel first to assess themselves against the set of standards, before the auditors visit and do an external assessment. An effective balance is where colleagues from another service do a peer review of each other's service using the standards. The system used by the US Joint Commission for Accreditation of Healthcare Organizations has shifted from a focus on inputs and processes to more emphasis on outcomes and outcome comparisons (JCAHO 1991), and also tries to incorporate a continuous quality improvement philosophy.

Audit and quality award frameworks have been painstakingly developed by experts to cover areas which are thought to be important in producing quality outcomes, and some include measures of outcome trends over time. The use of these for evaluating health services is discussed in Øvretveit (1994a). The strengths are that audit frameworks provide a ready made and comprehensive set of standards and a method for a quality evaluation, or can be used as a basis for discussions with users about which aspects to evaluate, and they can allow comparative evaluations. The main weakness is that no evaluative research has been done to assess whether high scores on the input and process standards do in fact result in high quality outcomes.

## Evaluating a quality programme

The last type of quality evaluation which we will consider in this chapter is an evaluation of a quality programme. Many health service organizations are starting programmes to introduce quality systems and to train personnel to use quality methods. A part of some quality programmes is an evaluation of the programme itself in order to check the progress of the programme and to replan it. There have also been regional or national initiatives to try out total quality management (TQM) in health services which have then been evaluated: for example, the evaluations of the UK NHS TQM programme (Joss et al. 1994; Joss and Kogan 1995), the Norwegian TQM programme (Øvretveit 1996b, 1997b, in press) and an evaluation of TQM in primary care in the former Oxford Region in the UK (Lawrence and Packwood 1996).

How would an external or internal evaluator carry out an evaluation of a quality programme? If we consider the quality programme as an intervention to organization, there are at least six different ways to evaluate the programme, depending on for whom we are doing the evaluations and for which purposes. The first approach is to describe the programme and its history using a type 1 design, as discussed in Chapter 3. The features to be described would depend on the evaluation user's questions and criteria of valuation – common management questions are, 'What is the value of the programme to health service personnel? What do we need to do to increase people's motivation to work on quality improvement?'

A second approach is to study the service providers who are the target of the programme and ask them what they think of the programme, its progress and impact (the main method used by Lawrence and Packwood 1996). A third approach is to take the service's quality plan and objectives and compare these to what had actually been done in the service. Unfortunately for evaluators who wish to use this approach, not many services have plans or objectives which are useful for an evaluation, or any at all. However, showing the lack of evaluable plans and objectives can itself help to develop the programme by drawing attention to the absence of this necessary feature of a quality programme.

A fourth approach is to compare what the service has done to a prescriptive model of what a service should do to pursue a successful quality programme. There is no lack of such prescriptions in the quality literature, but not many are suitable for public health services and most also emphasize the importance of adapting the model to a particular service. One option is for evaluators to develop their own model by drawing on the quality literature (e.g. Joss and Kogan 1995; Øvretveit 1996b). A fifth approach is to measure directly the quality of the service before and at different intervals during the quality programme. In theory this is what the service should do, and it may be possible to draw on measures collected by the service as well as making independent direct measures. In practice few services have measures of quality before they started the programme, and ask for the evaluation some time after the programme has been running. A sixth approach is to use a framework of key choices which all services face when pursuing a quality programme and compare the service's choices to those of other services (Øvretveit 1996b).

More details about methods for internal and external evaluations of quality programmes in health services are discussed in Joss et al. (1994), Joss and Kogan (1995) and Øvretveit (1996b, 1997c, in press). The methods are of wider interest becasue they can be used to evaluate other 'management technologies' and changes to health services.

## How to evaluate quality

To summarize this chapter the following draws together some key points to bear in mind when planning a quality evaluation. The design, methods and steps for an evaluation of quality depend on four main factors. The first is for whom the evaluation is to be carried out (users), and the valuation criteria which they and the evaluator agree. The users may be practitioners who evaluate their own practice, or a service as part of a self-improvement process (which may be in response to an external requirement that they do so). Users may also be patients or patient associations, local or central government, or service managers or purchasers. Often there are multiple users, which may mean that the evaluator has to prioritize between primary and secondary users.

---

**Types of quality evaluations**

♦ *External formal single evaluation*, by an independent contracted organization such as a university evaluation centre or private consultants (e.g. 'an evaluation project').
♦ *Quasi-external formal single evaluation*, by a government department or a separate unit within an organization (e.g. Norwegian county medical departments evaluating the quality or the quality system of a provider).
♦ *Internal formal single evaluation*, by an individual or unit within the organization that also manages the service (a special evaluation study of a department performed by a quality coordinator employed by the same service).
♦ *Routine external evaluation*, by an independent contracted organization such as an accreditation or auditing agency.
♦ *Routine quasi-external evaluation*, by a government department or a separate unit within an organization which provides routine quality monitoring.
♦ *Routine internal evaluation*: routine self-monitoring for quality assurance and improvement, by practitioners or quality units.

---

The second factor is whether users have already defined criteria. If users are not clear then the evaluator can work with them to develop criteria by showing them examples of quality criteria which may be suitable for the evaluation (e.g. organizational audit criteria), or different definitions of quality. The third factor which affects how the evaluation is carried out is whether it is to be a special single evaluation – for example, for management users to help them to design a quality programme – or a routine quality evaluation. If the latter, is the purpose of the evaluation to test different systems which could be used for routine quality evaluation? The fourth factor is who carries out the evaluation. Is it to be an external evaluator independent of the organization, a quasi-external evaluator or an internal evaluator?

The following gives one outline of steps which are suitable for formal external single evaluations of service quality, where there are no predefined criteria.

> **Steps in evaluating quality**
>
> 1  Clarify whom the evaluation is for. Who is asking for and/or paying for the evaluation and who will be the main users of the findings?
> 2  Clarify the decisions and action which could follow from the evaluation. What do they want the evaluation for?
> 3  Clarify evaluation criteria. How do they define and judge quality, which other perspectives do they want included, which perspectives does the evaluator think should be included and what are the criteria of valuation of quality?
> 4  Define the service, the questions to be answered and the purpose of the evaluation.
> 5  Design and plan the quality evaluation.
> 6  Collect data which will allow users to judge the quality of the service.
> 7  Analyse and report findings which allow users to judge quality and to make better informed decisions.

## Conclusions

As a subject within the field of evaluation, service quality has features which make it unique:

♦ what we mean by the quality of a service is more value-laden and closely shaped by the interests of a social group than other criteria which we use to evaluate a service;
♦ the services which we evaluate themselves carry out quality evaluation as a part of their own quality assurance and improvement activities;
♦ evaluators are sometimes asked to evaluate both the quality of a service and the quality system which a service is using;
♦ services use reported evaluations of treatments and of service effectiveness to improve the quality of the service (for example, by using research findings to formulate guidelines).

♦ Outcome evaluations are different from quality evaluations because they do not assess the quality of service processes. Performance evaluations may include quality as one aspect of the performance of a service.

♦ Evaluators need to be careful to distinguish the evaluation users' criteria for valuation (primary evaluation criteria) from criteria which other people use to assess quality (secondary criteria). Users may decide to include or wholly adopt others' criteria, but they should choose to do so in the early phases of the evaluation process, rather than being given a report which has adopted others' criteria and which may be of little use to them in making decisions.

♦ Evaluators need to clarify whether users want an evaluation of a service, an evaluation of a quality programme or an evaluation of the system which the service itself uses to evaluate quality as part of the service's own quality assurance arrangements.

♦ There are many ways to evaluate quality, and many ready made systems and standards which an evaluator could use. They may be tempted to pick such a system too quickly and without properly examining what the users of the evaluation need, the purpose of the evaluation and the criteria of valuation to be used.

♦ Because of the political nature of quality, there is more scope for 'confusion' than in other types of evaluation, and it is the task of the evaluator to be clear and explicit about the terms and purposes, not to compound the confusion or become an unwitting ally to a particular interest group.

♦ A framework which has been found useful for evaluating service quality is:

|  | Input | Process | Outcomes |
|---|---|---|---|
| *Patient quality* | | | |
| *Professional quality* | | | |
| *Management quality* | | | |

# 14 ▶ Making more use of evaluation

*One experienced evaluator warns that, 'The chances of an evaluation study being judged successful are not high'.*

(Parlett 1981: 220)

*Judging the value of something is only a start towards doing something. Evaluators are naive if they assume that others will only use evaluation information to judge value, and that judging value then automatically leads to action.*

## Introduction

If evaluation studies are so practical and useful, why are they not used more in health services and policy making? There is already knowledge from evaluations which health practitioners or policy makers could use in their decisions and everyday actions. Knowledge is increasing but the gap between this knowledge and our use of it has never been wider. This gap will not be narrowed significantly by easier access to the knowledge and better information technology or by insisting that everyone practises 'evidence-based healthcare'.

Do we really need more evaluations or rather more knowledge about how to make use of evaluations and about how to carry out change? Are we concentrating our attention and resources on evaluating the treatments, services and policies which really need to be evaluated? Should we be carrying out evaluations in a different way to make sure they are acted on? Should we also be evaluating methods for implementing the results of evaluations? This chapter considers answers to these questions and how to make evaluations more useful.

This book described the practical value of evaluation, and also proposed an approach which places users' questions and their decisions to be informed at the centre of evaluation – encapsulated in the concept of 'evaluation for action' which was outlined in Chapter 2. However, even evaluations which are closely linked to users' questions and needs are often not acted on. There are many reasons for this, some of which we consider in this chapter when we look at the use of evaluations, first by policy makers and managers, and then by clinicians.

Responsibility for action and change and the limits to the role of the evaluator are two of the subjects of this chapter. Do evaluators have a responsibility to maximize the chances of their findings being acted on? This chapter argues that they share a responsibility with sponsors and users, and that there are steps which evaluators can take in each phase of an evaluation to maximize the use of the evaluation. Evaluators should not be resigned to their work having little impact. Evaluators and users now have a considerable amount of knowledge from empirical studies of the utilization of research and from theories of power, change and implementation which they can use to plan evaluations and subsequent action. They also need to evaluate different methods used to try to change people's clinical or management practice.

## Who is responsible for action?

*Evaluators should not worry about whether the results of their evaluation are implemented. This is only the concern of users, who will have other things to consider in deciding whether or how to act.*

*The evaluator has a duty to maximize the use value of the evaluation. Evaluators know better than many users how to ensure that the evaluation is designed and conducted in a way which will yield actionable results. The role they take in different phases of the evaluation will be critical in ensuring that users act on the evaluation.*

At one extreme there are those evaluators who take a detached and 'pure science' approach. They see their role as to take the brief set by the sponsor, design and conduct the evaluation and deliver a report – the 'mail order' role. Whether the sponsor or anyone uses the report is of no interest. There is no detailed dialogue or negotiation in the early phases about evaluation criteria, and the evaluator does not advise about how to use the evidence to judge the value of the evaluated.

At the other extreme are evaluators who see their role as to support and assist sponsors and other users in their decision making and action. The 'committed participatory evaluator' works with users at every phase of the evaluation process to help them focus their questions, to help them define criteria, feeding back data as it is gathered, interpreting findings, advising how to use the findings to judge value and helping to implement changes.

The view taken in this book is that what evaluators do to increase the utilization of their evaluation depends on the type of evaluation which they are carrying out and the perspective which they are using – their role will be different in an experimental evaluation of a treatment from that in a developmental evaluation of a health policy. However, all evaluators have responsibility to maximize the chances of their work being used. They need to make more use of the research into utilization of evaluations to decide how best to increase these chances in ways which are compatible with the type of evaluation approach they are using. We can also learn from evaluations which have had too great an impact: how and why were the results acted on so quickly and extensively when they should have been examined in more detail and when issues other than the evaluation findings should have been considered before action?

## Improving the use value and utilization of evaluations

> In 1601 James Lancaster showed that lemon juice was effective (in pre-
> venting scurvy), but it was not until 1747 that James Lind repeated the
> experiment, and the British navy did not fully adopt the innovation
> until 1795 (not until 1865 in the case of the merchant marine).
>
> (Haines and Jones 1994)

The question of how to increase the utilization of evaluations of treatments, services, policies and organizational interventions is part of a more
general subject of increasing the utilization of research. Financial constraints and other factors have led to more attention being paid to making
a greater use of research to improve health services, to selecting which
research to sponsor and to encouraging the use of effectiveness and economic research. However, much of this effort has not made use of lessons
from policy and organizational research into change. Some attempts to use
research still involve simplistic rational planning and implementation
assumptions. Theories of rational planning have been questioned as an
adequate description of or prescription for change in healthcare. What are
the lessons for evaluators and for the 'evidence-based healthcare movement' from the empirical and theoretical studies of the utilization of evaluations, and of research generally?

### Evidence about the utilization of evaluations

There is some evidence which supports the general impression that evaluation, and indeed most research, has not had a great practical impact
(Booth 1988; HERG 1994). Utilization has probably been discussed in
relation to economic evaluations (Coyle 1993; Salked et al. 1995), policy
formulation and implementation (e.g. Walt 1994a,1994b) and clinical practice (e.g. Haines and Jones 1994). A common theme is the time it takes for
the findings of evaluations to change clinical practice, or to affect policy or
managerial decision making, if such an influence can be traced at all (Goodwin and Goodwin 1984; Coyle 1993; Haines and Jones 1994).

Some of the early assessments of the utilization of evaluation looked at
their direct impact on decisions to expand or reduce services. Shadish et al.
(1991) noted that 'discontinuing programmes based on evaluation results
is virtually unheard of', and that, at least in the short term, evaluations
rarely affect the size of a programme budget, although they can change
internal programme priorities such as which population groups to target,
and ways in which a service is provided.

Later assessments took a broader view of utilization. One example is a
study which described five categories of 'research payback': (a) knowledge;
(b) research benefits, such as better targeting of future research and
researcher development; (c) political and administrative benefits; (d) health
and social service sector benefits, such as cost reduction in providing existing services, qualitative improvements, increased effectiveness and health
and more equity; and (e) broader economic benefits, such as commercial
exploitation. This study also described a seven-stage model for assessing

payback, (HERG 1994). Coyle (1993) also proposed a model, after reviewing the utilization of economic evaluations, which describes causes of and lessons for non-utilization in each of the four 'impact' stages of dissemination, recognition, understanding and utilization.

If we look more closely at what we mean by utilization and impact, then the less than startling impact of evaluation can look less depressing for eager and earnest evaluators with a mission to make the world a better place. It can also help us to make better use of evaluations. Utilization refers to how evaluations are used by different parties in the short and long term to influence decisions and actions and in other more diffuse ways. The use value of an evaluation is its value to different parties such as health practitioners, managers, citizens, policy makers and health researchers. Use value implies potential utilization, but is a broader concept and is a necessary but not sufficient condition for actual utilization. For example, high scientific validity gives an evaluation high use value to many users, but utilization depends on much more than this.

Discussions of impact have recognized that there are different impacts for different parties, and that impact occurs over different timescales and in diverse and complex ways. Weiss (1978) describes a 'knowledge-driven model' of the use of evaluation which starts with scientists identifying a problem and developing solutions, and these 'find their way' into application. Another model of use is the 'problem solving model', which starts with a practical problem and then scientists develop solutions which are applied in practice: for example, in action research. A 'tactical model' is where research is financed and used primarily as part of a political and adversarial system of policy making.

In contrast to these and other sequential models, Weiss proposed an 'interactive model', where research is used to conceptualize and define problems, and where research findings and other considerations mix in a complex process which also includes policy and researcher meetings and networks. Closely related to this model is the 'enlightenment model', which Weiss proposed after research into decision making:

> All the decision makers whom we interviewed reported a much more common mode of research use, which is the diffuse and undirected influence of research ideas into their understanding of the world . . . It is not planned and conscious use, not directed toward immediate applications, but the research information and ideas that percolate into their stock of knowledge represent a part of their intellectual capital upon which they draw in the regular course of their work.
>
> (Weiss and Bucuvalas 1980: 263)

Walt (1994a), in asking 'how far does research influence policy?', also draws attention to models other than rational-linear models for understanding how research is used. Walt describes policy changes occurring as a result of the accumulation of scientific evidence, but also notes ways to 'accelerate the process of diffusion' by using a 'policy analysis approach'. Using such an approach helps one to understand the barriers to research being recognized and utilized in policy. It is to this subject that we now turn – later we will consider models of utilization which apply to clinical practice.

## Why are evaluations not used more?

What are the lessons for evaluators and others from work examining the utilization of evaluation, and of research generally? This work is of two broad types: empirical research into how evaluations have been used or not used, and theoretical discussions about how to increase utilization, some of which draw on empirical research and some of which draw on theories of change and of the policy process.

An early study in the health sector was that reported by Patton *et al.* (1977), which looked at the impact of 20 US federal evaluations of health policies and programmes. This study found that the evaluations had not had a significant impact, and for a variety of reasons: the findings were inconclusive and open to interpretation, evaluators put more effort into academic communication and quality than into ensuring practical relevance and impact, decision makers had little ability to control decision making and tended to pursue their own objectives regardless, the evaluations were too late to affect decisions, as well as encountering problems in collecting the data which they needed.

There have been a number of studies of the use made of economic evaluations and of how their utilization could be increased (e.g. Drummond *et al.* 1987; Coyle 1993; Salked *et al.* 1995). A UK study of researchers by Ludbrook, and a report by Ludbrook and Mooney (1984) which also drew on a workshop with decision makers, concluded that there was a need to educate the users about how to assess and implement the results of evaluations. One finding was that some clinicians found economic evaluations a threat to clinical freedom and did not understand how they were conducted and could be used. The study recommended that economic evaluation should be included in management training and in managers' responsibilities, and that there should be incentives for and requirements to use economic evaluations.

The HERG (1994) report on 'assessing payback of health research' reviewed a number of empirical and theoretical studies of utilization and concluded that six main factors were associated with high payback: continuing support from sponsors; liaison with stakeholders; the appropriateness and quality of the research; brokerage; appropriate dissemination; and ongoing programmes which provide a context for specific projects. This review, however, did not consider in detail the large body of research into the utilization of research in clinical practice, which is discussed later in this section.

We can summarize some of the lessons from empirical research into the use of service and policy evaluations as follows.

♦ Policy makers do not use or notice research when it conflicts with or contradicts their ideology (e.g. the UK 'Black report' on poverty and health; Walt 1994b).
♦ There are many factors apart from information from an evaluation which affect how policy makers and clinicians act (e.g. Patton *et al.* 1977; Klein 1989).
♦ The public's conception of risk may be low and difficult to change, and this affects policy makers' interest in some research (Walt 1994b).

♦ The findings of one or even a number of evaluations are rarely conclusive enough in themselves to justify change – 'scientific uncertainty' is common (Lindblom and Cohen 1979; Weiss and Bucuvalas 1980).
♦ There is considerable resistance to change in health services even when there are no vested interests, owing to 'administrative inertia' and findings not fitting current paradigms (e.g. 'the tomato effect'; Goodwin and Goodwin 1984).
♦ Research evidence is often not available at the time or place where decisions have to be made.
♦ Research is poorly communicated.
♦ Those who will need to change should be involved in the evaluation process.

## Selecting what to evaluate: backing the winners?

One approach to increase utilization has been to select carefully which interventions to evaluate, so as to choose those where the chances of change are high and where change would have the highest impact in terms of cost savings and health improvement. In the field of treatment and technology evaluation, models and guidelines have been developed to enable research funding bodies to be more systematic in their selection of studies to finance (e.g. DoH 1994).

One example is a computer-based model for 'technology assessment priority setting' (Eddy 1989). This was developed for the US Institute of Medicine (IoM), which later proposed a seven-criteria method for selecting which interventions to evaluate, the first three being quantitative and the remaining four based on qualitative judgements:

♦ the prevalence of the health condition;
♦ the unit cost of the existing technology;
♦ variation in the rate of use of the technology;
♦ the burden of illness of the condition on the individual;
♦ the potential for changing health outcomes which the evaluation could have;
♦ the potential for changing costs which the evaluation could have;
♦ the potential for informing ethical legal or social issues which the evaluation could have (IoM 1992).

Another model for deciding which interventions to evaluate is that proposed by HERG (1996), which also describes four stages involving different types of evaluation. The model also describes methods for combining economic assessments with different experimental and quasi-experimental evaluations.

## Theories of implementation, change and power

Some of the literature reviewed above noted that both researchers and policy makers often held questionable assumptions about decision making and how change was effected. While some writers have highlighted the inadequacy of rationalist and other implementation models, few have drawn on recent research into organization, change and policy making to propose alternative models for increasing the use of evaluations. In the following we note only a few of the theories from the literature on these subjects. There are different issues for policy makers and their advisors from those for managers at different levels or for practising clinicians. How to apply theories of change also depends on the type of organization and culture within which the evaluation findings could be used. The following is intended only to illustrate how these theories can help to plan how to make the best use of an evaluation.

Early research into policy implementation separated policy formulation from execution and saw both as a rational and sequential process. Policy formulation and goal setting was viewed as the task of politicians and their advisors, and implementation was viewed as something carried out by managers and health personnel. In this 'planning and control model' the implementation problems are how to choose between alternative implementation plans, and how to ensure that local politicians, managers or health personnel carry out the plan. Some users and evaluators assume that health policy is formulated and carried out in this way. They see the role of evaluation being mainly to help formulate policy, or to assist implementation: for example, by making sure that managers and health personnel know that evaluators were comparing their achievements to goals and plans.

More sophisticated models of policy implementation in the 1970s and early 1980s were influenced by social science research, and by the same theories which led to the 'interactional' models of research utilization noted above. In part this also reflected changes in health services and decentralization of decision making, especially in the Nordic countries. Research discovered what most managers knew: that policy makers and planners were often not aware of practical constraints, and could never be aware of all the different circumstances under which a policy might be implemented locally. This and other discoveries of research into 'the policy process' led to increasing recognition of the role of local managers and others, not only in shaping how policies were implemented, but also in 'acting upwards' to adapt or change policies. The theories which arose from this research saw the stated policy as only a starting point for policy formulation through 'realization in practice'. Some models saw policy plans and goals as 'resources' which managers and others used in their local political intrigues.

In a review of 'top-down' and 'bottom-up' approaches to implementation research, Sabatier (1986) noted criticisms of each approach and argued that both neglected power. Work since has developed more sophisticated models, although there has not been sufficient recognition of the differences between health and other contexts, or difference between implementation issues in different types of health context or types of policy. A useful summary of other models, such as 'backward and forward mapping', is given in Joss and Kogan (1995).

These models can be termed 'interactive' or 'political' models of implementation, and view policies and goals as changing during implementation. The models do not separate formulation from implementation but view them in interaction, or 'implementation as evolution' (Majone and Wildavsky 1979). Evaluators can judge whether such models describe the policy process within which their evaluation might fit. It may be that there is more opportunity for evaluation findings to have an impact if they are made available to local managers at the right times, rather than findings being aimed only at formal policy makers and at what is believed to be the time when formal policy is decided.

### Theories of decision making, change and power

A related but different subject to that of implementation is decision making. Research into and theories of decision making can help both evaluators and users of evaluation to make a greater use of evaluation findings. It is important, however, not to over-generalize from decision making in one context to another. Descriptions and models of decision making in health policy contexts may not apply to operational managerial decision making, or to clinical contexts, and clinical decision making in a hospital emergency department may be very different from that in radiology or primary care.

St Leger *et al.* (1992) review theories of decision making and choice which are relevant to evaluation. They draw attention to how many decisions are confused or overturned (persistence may succeed owing to the 'disorder phenomenon'), to political and non-rational factors (e.g. decisions having a 'symbolic' rather than functional significance) and to the tendency to seek a satisfactory solution ('satisficing') rather than the best of the possible alternatives ('optimizing').

Other theories which help to plan how to make more use of evaluation are those of power and conflict in organizations (Morgan 1988) and in policy making (Walt 1994a). These theories also help evaluators to understand better how they are perceived and to carry out their role (Breakwell and Millward 1995). A further category of relevant research is from the field of organizational and behavioural change (French and Bell 1995, Burnes 1992). We note research from the latter field in the next section when looking at the utilization of evaluation in clinical practice.

## Towards evidence-based healthcare?

Whether savings are large or small, we simply cannot justify inflicting ineffective procedures on patients, nor omitting to do things which have been shown to be effective. . . . We will not be able to change practice if patients do not know that the procedure is ineffective or inappropriate for them.

(Stocking 1996)

When evidence is inadequate clinicians should support the need for appropriate research rather than uncontrolled use of unproven interventions.

(Haines and Jones 1994)

In this section we consider clinicians' use of the results of evaluation studies in clinical practice, as well as clinicians' use of evaluation methods as a routine part of clinical practice: for example, in clinical audit. One set of issues concerns choosing which treatments and services to evaluate and evaluating them in ways which produce useful results which are credible with clinicians. Another set of issues concerns how to ensure that clinicians make use of results from evaluations and how to encourage changes in practice where appropriate.

Assuming that the right evaluation research has been carried out in the right way, how might this research be better utilized in health services? This is one of the questions addressed by work undertaken under the heading of 'evidence-based medicine' (EBM), which has been defined as 'the conscientious, explicit, and judicious use of current best evidence in making decisions about the care of individual patients. The practice of EBM means integrating individual clinical expertise with best available external clinical evidence from systematic research' (Sackett *et al.* 1996). Others have proposed that similar principles need to be applied to decision making in policy formulation ('evidence-based policy making'; Ham *et al.* 1995), in 'evidence-based purchasing' and in operational health service management when deciding whether to use a 'management technology' such as a particular type of quality assurance method (Øvretveit 1997c). In the following we concentrate on using evaluations within clinical practice.

Davids *et al.* (1996) propose that EBM is founded on five related ideas: that the best available evidence should inform clinical decisions; that the type of evidence sought should be determined by the clinical problem; that epidemiological and statistical methods should be used to find the best evidence; that this evidence is only useful if put into action in treating patients; and that practice should be continually evaluated. The advantages of EBM for doctors are summarized by Rosenberg and Donald (1995), who describe a systematic process of clarifying the question, searching the literature, assessing the evidence and applying conclusions in medical practice. A 'hierarchy of evidence model' is used in formal reviews and also forms the

*Table 14.1* The Hierarchy of Evidence Model (Canadian Task Force on the Periodic Health Examination (1979))

| | |
|---|---|
| Level 1 | Evidence obtained from at least one properly designed randomized controlled trial. |
| Level 2–1 | Evidence obtained from well designed controlled trials without randomization. |
| Level 2–2 | Evidence obtained from well designed cohort or case–control analytic studies, preferably from more than one centre or research group. |
| Level 2-3 | Evidence from comparisons between times and places with or without the intervention, and dramatic results in uncontrolled experiments. |
| Level 3 | Opinions of respected authorities, based on clinical experience, descriptive studies or reports of expert committees. |

basis for models suggested for clinicians to use to assess evidence. We note this model here because it shows which types of evaluations and evidence carry credibility with most clinicians, and is a model and set of assumptions which many also apply, erroneously in my view, to evaluations of services and non-treatment interventions.

The ideas behind EBM have provoked much debate, including challenges to the assertion that 80 per cent of medical treatments are of unproven value. One study of general medical services in the UK John Radcliffe Hospital found that 82 per cent of treatments were based on evidence (Ellis *et al.* 1995). A study in surgery found 91 per cent and 65 per cent of treatments in psychiatry were found to be based on RCTs. There is also concern about the potential misuse of EBM – for example, drawing the wrong conclusions from poor evidence – and about reducing clinician discretion. Letters following the Rosenberg and Donald (1995) paper in the *British Medical Journal* note other objections.

One, perhaps extreme, example of this movement is a proposal that treatments which cannot be evaluated should not be financed (Roberts *et al.* 1996). (Note that this is different to the general principle advanced by Cochrane that all effective treatment should be free). This paper is of general interest to evaluators because it is based on one model of experimental evaluation, which it proposes as the only valid way to evaluate treatments and services, and it derives criteria from this model to judge whether a treatment or service can be evaluated. The paper proposes that, before evaluating an intervention, it is necessary to judge whether an assertion about the intervention is testable, according to the following criteria:

1 Does the intervention have a single component or multiple components?
2 Will the intervention be targeted at a single, well defined population or multiple poorly defined populations?
3 Is the intervention a single or multiple process?
4 Is the intended health benefit a single outcome or a multiplicity of outcomes?
5 Are the intended outcomes easy or difficult to measure?

Roberts *et al.* (1996) propose that an assertion that a specified service is effective is untestable if one or more of these criteria are not met, or if two or more are partially met. Their concern is that 'The impact of EBM will be undermined if a practical solution to untestability is not found, for there is a danger that undue attention will be paid to testable assertions, most of which are in the acute hospital sector.' They argue that claims for the effectiveness of many health visiting, health promotion, alternative therapies, community mental health teams and other community services are untestable.

If this approach was applied rigorously, it would lead to financing only a small range of services which are testable according to these criteria. These criteria derive from the experimental perspective and are based on the randomized controlled trial as the ideal, the criticisms of which were outlined in Chapter 5. The proposal is that these criteria should be applied to all interventions and, by implication, that evidence-based healthcare should not use evidence from other types of evaluations.

## Lessons for increasing the use of evaluation findings in clinical practice

Roberts *et al.* (1996) and other work which can be classified in the EBM movement are of general interest for evaluators. Not only do they highlight different views about the nature of evidence and approaches to evaluation, but they usefully focus issues, problems and solutions in increasing the utilization of evaluations in clinical practice. We have noted some of the issues in selecting which subjects to evaluate and how to judge the evidence, but following the criteria discussed above is no guarantee that an evaluation will be acted on. The question of change is one which is increasingly being addressed, and here we note some of the research into change in clinical practice.

A review of 36 studies which assessed the effect of statistical information on clinical care concluded that information alone had little effect (Mugford *et al.* 1991). Although this review is of the effect of information from clinical and administrative data systems on clinical practice, it is suggestive of how evaluation findings could also inform practice: the study proposed that information feedback 'most probably influences clinical practice if it is part of an overall strategy which targets decision makers who have already agreed to review their practice. Information feedback is likely to have a more direct effect on practice if presented close to the time of decision making.' This study and others emphasize the potential for computer prompting and information at the time of consultation, or to assist other types of decision making.

There has been a considerable amount of work on methods for clinical implementation of evaluations using guidelines, protocols and criteria (e.g. converting guidelines into specific criteria for reviewing practice; Baker and Fraser 1995). EBM has also led to practical methods for clinicians to use to judge the quality of evidence (based on the hierarchy of evidence model). This work is considered by Grimshaw and Russel (1994), who review previous research into guideline development and impact. They propose a three-step process for: (a) developing guidelines; (b) dissemination, e.g. through education; and (c) implementation, noting the effectiveness of patient specific reminders at the time of consultation.

Haines and Jones (1994) consider guidelines as one of a number of approaches for 'implementing the findings of research'. They propose an integrated strategy for speeding up implementation, which includes systematic reviews of research findings, guidelines, continuing medical education and audit, as well as a greater role in implementation for professional organizations, educational bodies, providers, purchasers, the public and policy makers. Davis *et al.* (1995) gives a review of RCTs of different methods of continuing medical education, and Gray (1997) gives a more recent overview of the issues. Some of these ideas are also of use for developing ways to help managers make more use of evaluation findings.

We can summarize the lessons from research into making use of evaluations to improve clinical practice in the following way:

♦ The need for clinicians to be able to identify easily the information which they need and access the available evidence.

♦ Authoritative reviews and data sources, e.g. the York UK Centre for the Review and Dissemination of the Results of Health Research, the Effective Health Care Bulletins and the Cochrane Database of Systematic Reviews (Long *et al.* 1993; Sheldon and Chalmers 1994; Freemantle *et al.* 1995).

♦ The need to educate clinicians about how to assess the evidence and to decide how to act on it (Rosenberg and Donald 1995).

♦ Working with clinicians to help them change their routines to increase their use of evidence (Davis *et al.* 1995)

♦ Converting evaluation findings into protocols and behavioural guidelines, making clear where clinical discretion is and is not necessary (Grimshaw and Russel 1994; Baker and Frazer 1995).

♦ Educate patients about effective practice (Davis et al. 1995).

♦ Developing and implementing guidelines using a variety of proven techniques (Haines and Jones 1994).

Developments which have followed from these ideas are national and local databases, computer systems to provide information and prompts at the right time in the right place, local projects such as the UK Anglia and Oxford Region's Getting Research into Practice and Purchasing Project (Stocking 1996) and systems for providing information to patients (Øvretveit 1996a).

One of the important issues which the EBM movement raises is the evidence basis for many health management decisions, and for health policies and reforms. Clinicians may justifiably draw attention to the money wasted by unevaluated management technologies and health policies, even though decisions about these should be influenced by considerations other than effectiveness and costs alone. We note, however, that where such interventions have been evaluated, the type of evidence produced is often more difficult to draw conclusions from and the methods to assess this evidence are not so well developed. Some of the methods of evidence-based medicine carry a limited and inappropriate view of evidence when applied to some interventions.

Another issue is patient access to evaluation findings. Apart from the ethical issues of patients' rights to evaluation information about treatments (Øvretveit 1996a), there is some evidence that providing information to the public is an effective way to change practice, although some research from the USA suggests that the impact is not as much as expected. One of the few studies on this subject was of two areas in Switzerland (Ticino and Berne), where the rate of surgery for hysterectomy was compared in one area to that in the other. This comparison was made after the high rate rates of surgery in Ticino compared to Norway and the UK had been publicized and discussed in the media for nine months. The rate in Ticino dropped significantly as a result, but in Berne, where there was no publicity, the rate remained constant (Domenighetti, *et al.* 1988). Publicizing the results of evaluations beyond the healthcare community is one of a number of methods for increasing the impact of evaluations.

## More useful evaluations

The brief review above proposed ways in which evaluators and users could plan ways to maximize the use of an evaluation. However, the review was in general terms and only made a simple distinction between impact on policy and impact on management and clinical practice: it said little of the many different types of policy, management and clinical decisions and practice which evaluations do and could influence. It also noted, but said little about, the different tactics for increasing the impact of economic evaluation, as distinct from tactics suitable for experimental, developmental and managerial evaluations.

Methods to maximize the use of an evaluation depends so much on who the users are, their decision and practice situation and the type of evaluation. A problem for evaluators and users is to find the research into the utilization of evaluations which is most appropriate for their type of evaluation and situation, and to draw lessons from this work in order to decide how best to influence practical decisions. In doing so, they also need to look at the history of change, or lack of it, in the organization with which they are concerned, to understand how decisions were made in the past and why past changes failed and succeeded.

Evaluators and users also operate within a context which may or may not encourage the use of evaluation. For example, in most countries and for some time there have been requirements to evaluate new drugs, but now in Australia there is a requirement to give cost–effectiveness data before a drug can qualify for state reimbursement (HERG 1996), and there are growing pressures in many countries to give evaluation evidence before introducing new technologies. These wider requirements and cultural changes affect whether and how evaluations are used.

We can summarize this chapter in a set of proposals for increasing the utilization of evaluations. In drawing on the research reviewed above, we need to be cautious about generalizing from one type of evaluation or situation to another type, but many of the following suggestions would increase the impact of most types of evaluation.

*The planning stages*
♦ Clarify sponsors' and users' questions and concerns, the decisions which the evaluation should influence, when the information is needed and in which forms.
♦ Plan how to involve those who may use the evaluation, or who may need to change their behaviour.
♦ Plan ways to maximize the impact of the evaluation, by drawing on relevant theories of change and decision making and on knowledge about the fate of previous proposals for change in the setting in question.
♦ Understand the formal and informal process of decision making within which the results of the evaluation will be considered.
♦ Consider with users and sponsors at least three finding scenarios and anticipate the consequences if: (a) the evaluation confirms current practice or does not suggest change; (b) the evaluation suggests that significant change is necessary or the results should have a significant influence on a decision; (c) the evaluation is inconclusive.
♦ Consider how best to disseminate the findings, and which people other than the evaluators could help to communicate the results.
♦ Agree a 'contract' with sponsors and others about what they will do to help to disseminate and increase the utilization of the evaluation findings.

*When conducting the study*
- Involve users in appropriate ways, giving interim reports if possible and if appropriate.
- Note different ideas about how to enable change which may arise during the study.
- Prepare dissemination channels.

*After the study*
- Recognize that different channels will be required for academic communication to those for communicating with decision makers.
- Communicate findings in the right way, to the right people, at the right time, and get advice or help to do this.
- Present findings to users clearly and simply, show the certainties and limitations, and give easy access to the details of the study for those who want to assess the evidence and methods.
- Get the advice and assistance of formal and informal 'opinion formers' about how to influence decision making.
- Consider direct communication to the public, with the agreement of sponsors and others.
- Assess the impact of the evaluation and the lessons for increasing the impact of future studies.

In conclusion, this book has given a broad overview of different approaches to evaluation in the health sector. The aim was to show how evaluation can help us to promote health, prevent and cure illness, improve our work organizations and make the best use of our resources. The health problems which we as clinicians, managers and policy makers have to respond to are many and various, and there are numerous types of interventions which we could use at different times and in different ways. Because of this variety we need different perspectives and methods to assess the value of different interventions, and even for one intervention we often need a multidisciplinary approach.

The book emphasized the practical and action orientation of evaluation, and the role of values: in deciding what to evaluate, in defining the criteria of valuation, the values of the evaluator and those of the people who may need to change as a result of the evaluation. Health personnel are now routinely using evaluations as well as making more use of evaluation methods in everyday settings. As we noted in the opening chapter, the questions are no longer whether to use or make an evaluation, but how well we use one or carry one out. I hope that this book will help you to make better use of finished evaluations, improve your own evaluations and stimulate you to look further into this fascinating subject.

# Conclusions

- Evaluators have different views about whether they have any responsibility for encouraging the utilization of their evaluation study. Some take a 'mail order supplier' role and have little interest in what the sponsor or other users do with their 'product' after 'delivery'. Others take a 'committed' and 'participatory' role, and view lack of action as a failure on their part. There is a place for both approaches, but all evaluators can do more to increase the use value of their evaluations.

♦ The use value of an evaluation is its value to different parties, while utilization refers to how evaluations are used in making decisions. Use value implies potential utilization, but is a broader concept and is a necessary but not sufficient condition for actual utilization. Scientific validity may give an evaluation high use value, but utilization depends on more than this.

♦ Evaluation findings influence decision making and policy making in a variety of ways. Studies have shown different impacts for different parties, and impact occurs over different timescales and in diverse and complex ways.

♦ Encouraging practitioners to use evaluation principles in everyday practice is one way of both introducing the results of evaluations into clinical practice and stimulating practitioners to carry out evaluations.

♦ Evaluators and users can increase the utilization of an evaluation by drawing on empirical research into and theories of implementation, organizational change and power.

♦ Although there are some general guidelines for maximizing the utilization of most evaluations, evaluators and users need to decide a strategy which is suited to the subject of the evaluation, the type of decision or policy which it aims to influence and the culture and history of a health organization or system which is to be changed.

♦ Some of the assumptions of the evidence-based healthcare movement are questionable when applied to assessing evaluations of services, alternative therapies, and some health policies. More attention needs to be paid to methods for evaluating techniques for changing clinical and managerial practice.

# Appendix 1: Definitions

**Action research**: a systematic investigation which aims to contribute to knowledge as well as solve a practical problem (some action research is a type of evaluation – much 'developmental evaluation' is action research).

**Audit**: an investigation into whether an activity meets explicit standards as defined by an auditing document. The auditing process can be carried out by external auditors or internally for self-review, and can use external ready made audit standards or internally developed standards. Medical and clinical audit is using pre-existing standards or setting standards, comparing practice with standards and changing practice if necessary, and is usually carried out internally for self-review and improvement. Peer audit can use already existing standards, or practitioners can develop their own, but usually practitioners adapt existing standards to their own situation.

**'Blinding', single-blinded trial**: the people in the control and experimental groups (subjects) do not know which group they are in.

**'Blinding', double-blinded trial**: neither the subjects nor the service providers know which group is the experimental and which is the control.

**The 'box'**: the boundary around the intervention, which defines what is evaluated. Includes inside the box a specification of the key features of the intervention.

**Case study**: 'an empirical inquiry that investigates a contemporary phenomenon in its real-life context, especially when the boundaries between context and phenomenon are not clearly evident' (Yin 1989).

**Case control study**: a retrospective observational study of people or organizations with a particular characteristic ('cases') compared to those which do not have this characteristic ('controls') to find out possible cases or influence which could explain the characteristic.

**Cohort**: a group of people, usually sharing one or more characteristics, who are followed over time.

**Confounding factors or variables**: something other than the intervention which could influence the measured outcome.

**Continuous quality improvement**: an approach for ensuring that staff continually improve work processes by using proven quality methods to discover and resolve the causes of quality problems in a systematic way.

**Control group or control site**: a group of people or an organization which do not get the intervention. The evaluation compares them to the experimental group or site, which gets the intervention. People are randomly allocated to either group, or, if this is not possible, the control group or site is 'matched' with the experimental group or site.

**Cost description**: measurement of the costs of one thing, or of more than one, in a way which allows an explicit or implicit comparison of costs. (A 'partial' economic evaluation looks at only one intervention and does not make an explicit comparison.)

**Cost-benefit**: valuing the consequences of a programme in money terms, so as to compare the assessed value with the actual costs. A range of benefits are valued in money terms.

**Cost-effectiveness**: the effectiveness or consequences, as shown on one measure, for the cost (e.g. lives saved, cases of diseases avoided or years of healthy life). No attempt is made to value the consequences – it is assumed that the output is of value. Used to compare the different costs of different ways to achieve the same end result.

**Cost minimization**: assumes that the differences in outcome produced by the alternatives are not significant, and calculates the cost of each alternative with the purpose of discovering which is the lowest cost.

**Cost–utility**: considers the utility of the end result to the patient for the cost. Often uses the quality-adjusted life years measure. Measures consequences in time units adjusted by health utility weights (i.e. states of health associated with outcome are valued relative to each other). More complex than cost-effectiveness.

**Criterion**: a comparison against which we judge the evaluated: effectiveness is often such a criterion.

**Evaluated**: the item or intervention which is evaluated – the subject of the evaluation (otherwise termed 'the intervention').

**Evaluation**: a comparative assessment of the value of an intervention, in relation to criteria and using systematically collected and analysed data, in order to decide how to act (other definitions are given at the end of this appendix).

**Evaluator**: the person doing the evaluation.

**Evidence-based medicine**: 'the conscientious, explicit, and judicious use of current best evidence in making decisions about the care of individual patients. The practice of EBM means integrating individual clinical expertise with best available external clinical evidence from systematic research' (Sackett *et al.* 1996).

**External evaluators**: research or consultancy units not directly managed by and independent from the sponsor and user of the evaluation.

**Internal evaluators**: evaluation and development units that are internal to the organization, and evaluate treatments services or policies carried out by the organization or one of its divisions.

**Matching**: ensuring that people (or organizations) in the experimental and control groups (or sites) are the same in all the characteristics which could affect the outcome of the intervention which is given to the experimental group or site.

**Monitoring**: continuous supervision of an activity to check whether plans and procedures are being followed (audit is a sub-type of the wider activity of monitoring).

**Operationalize**: converting something general (e.g. a criterion) into something specific, usually into something which can be measured.

**Organizational audit**: an external inspection of aspects of a service, in comparison to established standards, and a review of an organization's arrangements to control and assure the quality of its products or services. Audits use criteria (or 'standards') against which auditors judge elements of a service's planning, organization, systems and performance.

**Outcome measure**: a measure of an important predicted effect of the intervention on the target person or population. Outcome: the difference an intervention makes to the person, population or organization which is the target of the intervention.

**Placebo**: something which the subjects of the intervention think is an intervention, but which has no known 'active ingredient' (used to control for effects which may be caused only by subjects thinking that they are receiving an intervention).

**Police car effect**: when people think they are being evaluated they follow regulations more closely than when they think that they are not being evaluated.

**Prospective evaluation**: designing an evaluation and then collecting data while the intervention is happening, and usually also before and after the intervention.

**Quality**: meeting the health needs of those most in need at the lowest cost, and within regulations (Øvretveit 1992a).

**Quality accreditation**: a certification through an external evaluation of whether a practitioner, equipment or service meets standards which are thought to contribute to quality processes and outcomes.

**Quality assurance**: a general term for activities and systems for monitoring and improving quality. Quality assurance involves, but is more than, measuring quality and evaluating quality.

**Randomization**: allocating people in a random way to an experimental or a control group. The purpose is to try to ensure that the people (or organizations) with characteristics which might affect the outcome have an equal chance of being allocated to either group. This is because there are many known and unknown characteristics which may influence outcome. Randomization allows the evaluators to consider any differences between the two groups which are more than chance differences as significant, and avoids the need for matching.

**Randomized controlled trial**: an experiment where one group gets the intervention and another group does not, and people are assigned to both groups in a random way. A control group is a group of people who do not get the intervention but get a placebo, or in some trials, get another native intervention.

**Research – basic or pure**: the use of scientific methods which are appropriate to the subject for discovering valid knowledge of a phenomenon for the purpose of contributing to scientific knowledge about the subject.

**Retrospective evaluation**: looking into the past for evidence about the intervention ('concurrent' means at the same time).

**Review**: a single or regular assessment of an activity, which may or may not compare the activity to an explicit plan, criteria or standards (most audits or monitoring are types of review; many 'managerial evaluations' are reviews or monitoring).

**Self-evaluation**: practitioners or teams evaluate their own practice so as to improve it.

**Sponsors**: those who initiate or pay for the evaluation.

**Standard**: a pre-defined level of performance on a defined measure (e.g. 'no more than ten minutes after arrival').

**Target**: the part or whole of the person or population which the evaluated aims to have an effect on (not the target of the evaluation).

**Users**: those who make use of or act on an evaluation.

**Validity, external**: the ability of an evaluation experiment to show that the findings would also apply when the intervention is applied in another setting.

**Validity, internal**: the validity of an evaluation experiment, e.g. in being able to show whether or not the intervention has an effect or the size of the effect.

**Variable, dependent**: the outcome variable or end result of a treatment, which might be associated with, or even caused by other (independent) service or policy variables. The study tests for associations between the dependent (outcome) variable and the independent variables. (Examples: cancer mortality, patient satisfaction, resources consumed by a service).

**Variable, independent**: a variable whose possible effect on the dependent variable is examined (something which may cause the outcome and which is tested in the research).

**Variable(s), mediating**: other variables which could affect the dependent variable or outcome, which the research tries to control for in design and in statistical analysis (e.g. outcome).

**Variable(s), extraneous**: variables not considered in the theory or model used in the study.

## Evaluation: some different definitions

A systematic way of learning from experience and using lessons learnt to improve current activities and promote better planning by careful selection of alternatives for future action.

(WHO 1981)

Any scientifically based activity undertaken to assess the operation and impact of public policies and the action programmes introduced to implement these policies.

(Rossi and Wright 1977)

Evaluation research is the systematic application of social research procedures for assessing the conceptualisation, design, implementation, and utility of social intervention programs.

(Rossi and Freeman 1993)

The process of determining the merit, worth and value of things, and evaluations are the products of that process.

(Scriven 1991)

Any activity that throughout the planning and delivery of innovative programmes enables those involved to make judgments about the starting assumptions, implementation processes and outcomes of the innovation concerned.

(Stern 1990)

Program evaluation is a diligent investigation of a program's characteristics and merits. Its purpose is to provide information on the effectiveness of projects so as to optimize the outcomes, efficiency, and quality of healthcare.

(Fink 1993)

Program evaluations aim to provide convincing evidence that a program is effective. The standards are the specific criteria by which effectiveness is measured.

(Fink 1993)

The critical assessment, on as objective a basis as possible, of the degree to which entire services or their component parts (e.g. diagnostic tests, treatments, caring procedures) fulfil stated goals.

(St Leger *et al.* 1992)

# Appendix 2: Framework for analysing an evaluation and assessing evidence

**Title of the evaluation**

**Type of evaluation**

*Design*: type 1 (descriptive); type 2 (audit); type 3 (outcome); type 4 (comparative experimental); type 5 (randomized controlled experimental); type 6 a or b (intervention to service provider (a) impact on providers, (b) impact on patients).
*Intervention*: treatment; service; health promotion; intervention to provider; policy; reform.
*Perspective*: experimental, economic, developmental, managerial.

## 1 Target of the intervention

*Who or what does the intervention which is evaluated aim to change? (e.g. patients, population, providers)*

## 2 Description of the intervention

*Are the elements of the intervention precisely described, and the boundaries of the intervention defined? (What is 'in the box', and what is not evaluated?)*

## 3 Users

*Who was the evaluation done for, or who might be users of the evaluation?*

## 4 Value criteria and perspective

*Are explicit criteria used to judge the value of the intervention, or are these implied?*

*What are the criteria used to judge the value of the intervention? From whose perspective is the intervention evaluated? What are the comparisons which are used to judge the value of the intervention?*

## 5 Evaluation question(s) or hypotheses for testing

## 6 Type of evaluation design (draw it)

*Note in the diagram*:
Data gathering or measures of *the target* of the intervention:

◆ any measures or data gathering of *outcome*, and when and how often these were made (timing and frequency);
◆ any *'before'* measures or data gathering, and when and how often these were made (timing and frequency);
◆ any measures or data gathering of the target *during* the time the target received the intervention;
◆ how many people or providers (targets) began undergoing the intervention and how many people completed? (any 'drop-outs'?);

What else was measured or data gathered about (e.g. about health workers, or about the intervention)?

## 7 Data sources and collection methods – details

*When in the design were data collected, from whom or what did the data come (data sources), which methods were used to collect data from these sources and what did these data describe?*

### Validity

*Are valid connections made between the criteria of valuation and the things about which data are collected (discussion of 'operationalization' of concepts)? How good are the measures as representations of the phenomena or things they are supposed to measure? Did the study use accepted techniques for ensuring validity for the data gathering method which was used?*

### Reliability

*Would others using the same methods get the same results?*
*Could there be errors in the data (systematic bias or random) introduced by the data gathering method or design? What is the general reliability of this method, and what precautions were used in the evaluation to ensure and maximize reliability (e.g. interviewer training)?*

## 8 Validity of conclusions

*Did the evaluation prove that the intervention did or did not make any difference to the targets of the intervention, if that was one of the purposes of the evaluation? Is there sufficient evidence to support the conclusions?*

## 9 Practical conclusions and actions resulting from the evaluation

## 10 Strengths and weakness for the purpose

*Is it clear or implied who is the actual or intended user of the evaluation?*
*Is it clear which decisions and actions the evaluation is intended to inform?*
*Strengths and weaknesses of the <u>design</u> for the purpose.*
*Was there bias in the sample, in selection before and in the population measured after (i.e. drop-outs)?*
*Would the study have detected possibly important unintended effects?*
*What changes might the evaluation itself have produced which reduce the validity or reliability of the findings?*
*Strengths and weaknesses of the data gathering methods/measures for the purpose?*
*Were all the limitations described?*
*Were the conclusions justified by the results?*
*Could some people be misled by the report?*
*Would the conclusions be credible to the audience for the evaluation (users)?*
*Were there any unethical aspects?*
*Could the purpose have been achieved with fewer resources or in a shorter time?*
*What can we learn from this example about how to do and not to do an evaluation?*

**Strengths**

**Weaknesses**

## 11 Other comments

# Appendix 3: Six evaluation designs – 'empty' formats

Copy the relevant 'blank' format and write notes on it about an evaluation you are reading or planning

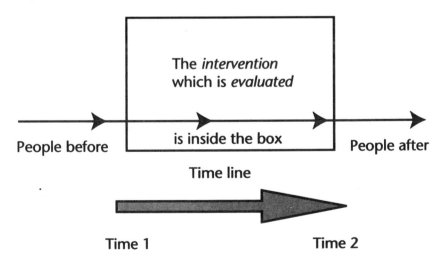

Drawing an evaluation design
*If you cannot draw it, then it is not clear or understood*

**Descriptive (Type 1)**

Evaluators observe and select features
of the intervention which they describe
*(and may describe the people receiving the intervention)*

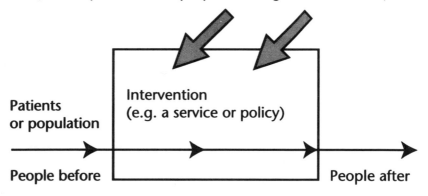

Patients
or population

Intervention
(e.g. a service or policy)

People before

People after

('Targets' of the intervention)

Features which the study describes:

**Audit (Type 2)**

Written standards, procedures or objectives

Evaluator compares what the service does, with what
it should do or was intended

Patients
or population

Intervention
(e.g. a service or policy)

**Outcome (Type 3)**

The before–after comparison (single case quasi-experimental design).

How people were selected:

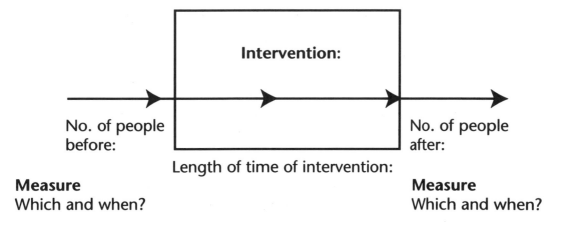

Confounding variables and controls:
(what, apart from the intervention, could have
produced the change in the measures?)

## Comparative-experimental (Type 4)

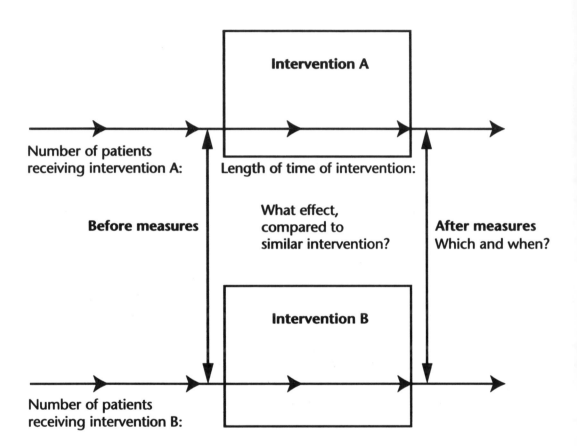

Number of patients
receiving intervention A:

**Before measures**

Length of time of intervention:

What effect,
compared to
similar intervention?

**After measures**
Which and when?

Number of patients
receiving intervention B:

How people were selected
for each intervention:

**Randomized controlled experimental (Type 5)**

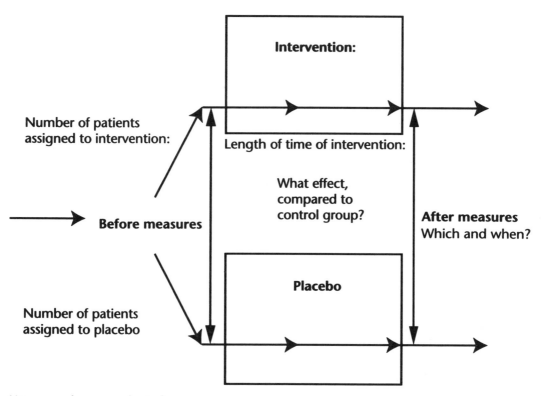

Number of patients
assigned to intervention:

Intervention:

Length of time of intervention:

Before measures

What effect,
compared to
control group?

After measures
Which and when?

Number of patients
assigned to placebo

Placebo

How people were selected
(before random allocation):

**Intervention to a service (Type 6a): Impact on providers**

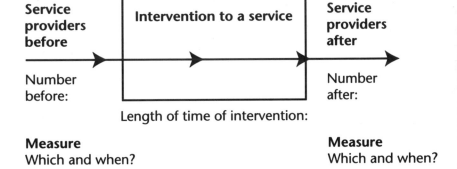

Length of time of intervention:

**Measure**                                               **Measure**
Which and when?                                           Which and when?


*Confounding variables and controls:*
*(what, apart from the intervention, could have*
*produced the change in the measures?)*

**Intervention to a service (Type 6b): Impact on patients**

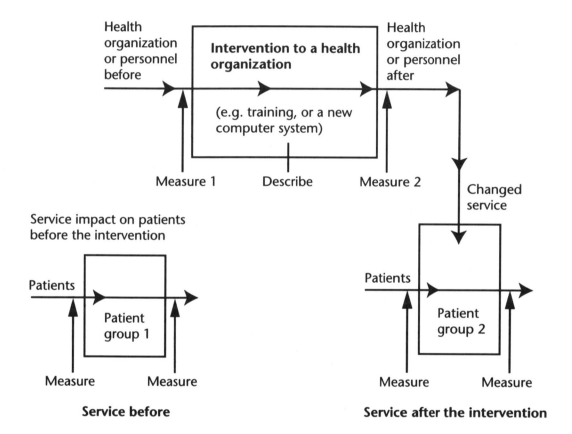

Health organization or personnel before

**Intervention to a health organization**

(e.g. training, or a new computer system)

Health organization or personnel after

Measure 1          Describe          Measure 2

Changed service

Service impact on patients before the intervention

Patients

Patient group 1

Measure          Measure

**Service before**

Patients

Patient group 2

Measure          Measure

**Service after the intervention**

*What was the intervention which was evaluated?*
*What were the criteria of valuation?*

# Appendix 4: Ten learning exercises

## Introduction

This appendix contains learning exercises which may be used by a reader of this book or by groups in courses. The exercises have been tested and refined for distance learning programmes and for short or residential courses which are based on a 'learning by doing' philosophy. Teachers are encouraged to copy and adapt those exercises which they think would help to develop the skills and understanding of their learners. No acknowledgement or permission is necessary. The exercises are:

1 Defining my learning needs and objectives.
2 'Apply and digest' (a general exercise to apply ideas to a work setting).
3 Summarizing an evaluation.
4 Assessing your colleagues' analysis and presentation.
5 Assessing the evidence used in an evaluation.
6 Data gathering methods – strengths and weaknesses.
7 Assessing quality of life outcome measures.
8 Colleague listening and consultation group (a learning discussion of an evaluation which a colleague is planning, doing or managing).
9 Practise designing and planning an evaluation.
10 Assessing a proposal for an evaluation.

## Exercise 1: Defining my learning needs and objectives

*Application*: for individuals to clarify their learning needs and objectives. This exercise can also be used as a basis for course participants introducing themselves at the beginning of a course (the questions can be sent beforehand, or completed at the beginning of a course)

1 My name, work title and the organization I work for:

2 The evaluation subjects which I need to know more about, and the skills which I need for my work and career:
(Tick your selection of the following)
   (a) the different purposes of evaluation (Chapter 1);
   (b) history and theory of evaluation (Chapter 1);
   (c) evaluation perspectives (Chapter 2);
   (d) basic concepts and designs (Chapter 3);
   (e) to read and assess an evaluation report quickly (Chapter 4);
   (f) experimental evaluation – different types and strengths and weaknesses (Chapter 5);
   (g) economic evaluation – different types and strengths and weaknesses (Chapter 6);
   (h) developmental evaluation (social research and action evaluations) – different types and strengths and weaknesses (Chapter 7);
   (i) managerial evaluations – different types and strengths and weaknesses (Chapter 8);
   (j) how to manage an evaluation and the different phases in an evaluation project (Chapter 9);
   (k) practical problems in carrying out an evaluation (Chapter 10);
   (l) different methods for gathering data (Chapter 11);
   (m) data gathering principles, analysis, and assessing evaluation findings (Chapter 12);
   (n) evaluating quality and outcomes (Chapter 13);
   (o) how to increase the use and impact of an evaluation study (Chapter 14).

3 The specific questions which I need to find answers to are:

4 I will be disappointed if, after having read this book (or completed this course), I have not

   ◆ answered these questions:

   ◆ found out more about:

   ◆ learned how to:

   ◆ gained help for the following task which I have to do or may have to do:

## Exercise 2: 'Apply and digest' – The implications for my work

*Application*: for groups or individuals to apply the ideas from a reading or a course presentation to their own work and to deepen their understanding of the subject.

*Instructions*: for groups, agree a chairperson, agree the task and the times to finish and, for each part of the task, agree a 'cuckoo clock' who speaks the times you agree for each part of the exercise, and agree a scribe if the group has to report back.

You must *leave five minutes* for the chairperson to summarize three main points or themes of the discussion before finishing.

*Task*: on your own for 15 minutes, write your answers to the questions below. Then in turn share each person's answer to the first question with others in the group. Then do the same with question 2, each person in the group sharing the answer to question 2 etc.

1 Write down what you think were *three of the main points or themes* which the author or presenter made and would want you to remember.

2 What did you think was *very true* or a very important point?

3 Did they say anything which *helped you or which you could use* in your work? What was it?

4 What *surprised* or *excited* you about what they said – I was surprised (or excited) that they said . . . ?

5 What did you *disagree* with or thought might not be correct?

6 What did you *not understand*, or want to *find out more* about?

## Exercise 3: Summarizing an evaluation

*Application*: for groups or individuals to analyse and summarize an evaluation.

Which types of evaluation do you need to be able to analyse and critically assess? Choose a report of an evaluation of this type and work through the following:

1 Which of the six types of evaluation design did the evaluation use (Chapter 3 and Appendix 3). *Draw a diagram* of the evaluation showing:

   ◆ What was the *intervention* which was evaluated?
     (Be very precise. Say what is, and what is not clear inside or outside of the box)
   ◆ Which *measures* of the outcome of the intervention were made (i.e. the dependent variable)?
   ◆ When and how often were they made?
   ◆ Which methods were used to *collect data*, and from which sources?
   ◆ How *long* did the evaluation take (start to finish)?

2 *Who* carried out the evaluation and how many *resources* did the evaluators have (people, time, money, help from others etc)?

3 Are the *conclusions justified by the evidence* presented? Could anything reported *mislead* an average reader, and what might be the consequences?

4 What actual *practical decisions and actions* by practitioners, managers, policy makers or citizens/patients did the evaluation help to inform, or could have done?

5 What are *the strengths and weaknesses* of the study compared to the ideal way to carry out such an evaluation?

6 How could the evaluation have been *better carried out with the same time and resources*? (Related question: was the evaluation cost effective?) What specific improvements would you recommend?

## Exercise 4: Assessing your colleagues' analysis and presentation

*Purpose*: for your colleagues to learn more from the experience of presenting a summary of an evaluation to you. Your comments will help them if your comments are respectfully truthful.

*Circle the number nearest to your view*:

**1** The presentation gave a *clear and understandable explanation* of the study

| *I fully understood the evaluation which they were explaining* | *They could have explained the study a bit more clearly* | *They did not explain some things about the study* | *I had some difficulty understanding the study from their explanation* | *The presentation did not explain the study at all well* |
|---|---|---|---|---|
| 5 | 4 | 3 | 2 | 1 |

**2** The *style of presentation* was lively and interesting and kept my attention

| *Knockout!* | *Very good* | *Quite good* | *Could have been better* | *Dreary and deadly* |
|---|---|---|---|---|
| 5 | 4 | 3 | 2 | 1 |

**3** The group identified and explained *all possible weaknesses* in the study (what was bad)

| *Yes, every one* | *Most, missed one or two* | *Missed a few weaknesses* | *Should have identified one (or more) major weaknesses of the study* | *Hardly said anything about weaknesses – very uncritical* |
|---|---|---|---|---|
| 5 | 4 | 3 | 2 | 1 |

**4** The group identified and explained *all possible strengths* in the study (what was good)

| *Yes, every one* | *Most, missed one or two* | *Missed a few weaknesses* | *Should have identified one (or more) major strengths of the study* | *Hardly said anything about* |
|---|---|---|---|---|
| 5 | 4 | 3 | 2 | 1 |

**5** They gave good *proposals for how the evaluation could have been done better* (better for the purpose and people that the evaluation was intended to serve)

| *Excellent and realistic ideas* | *Some good ideas* | *One or two ideas for improvement* | *They gave ideas for improvements, which I did not think were very good* | *They did not propose how it could have been better* |
|---|---|---|---|---|
| 5 | 4 | 3 | 2 | 1 |

**6** To do a better analysis and presentation next time I think the group should (give suggestions about how to do it better)

## Exercise 5: Assessing the evidence reported in an evaluation

The purpose of this exercise is to practise using concepts for data gathering and analysis to assess the evidence presented in an evaluation report and the suitability of the data gathering methods for the purpose of the evaluation. The questions apply to data gathered by either qualitative or quantitative methods.

Choose an evaluation which gives a description of the data gathering methods and presents the data which were collected. Then answer the following questions:

1 How reliable are the data?
(Could there be consistency errors in the data (systematic bias or random) which are introduced by the data gathering method? What is the general reliability of this method, and what precautions were used in the evaluation to ensure and maximize reliability (e.g. interviewer training)? Would others using the same methods have collected the same data?)

2 How valid are the data?
(What are the concepts which define the type of data required (e.g. personnel costs, health, knowledge retention)? Are the theoretical links between the concepts and the measure or data described (discussion of 'operationalization' of concepts)? What are the techniques for ensuring validity which are usually used for this data gathering method, and were these used in the study?)

3 How was the sample selected, was the sampling method justified and what are the assumptions made when generalizing from this sample?

4 Is the method of analysis described, what are the usual methods of analysis used for this type of data for the type of evaluation questions asked and how well were these analysis methods applied?

5 Are raw data presented or available for inspection?

6 What type of explanations for the discovered effects are proposed (e.g. influences, associations or causes), and, if causal statements are made, are alternative hypotheses considered and confounding variables discussed (e.g. were the right statistical tests used and in the right way, are differences statistically significant)?

7 If the evidence points to necessary changes, will the evidence be credible to the people who have to change?

8 Were the data collected and reported in an ethical way (e.g. patients anonymous, were documents public or 'cleared')?

## Exercise 6: Data gathering methods – strengths and weaknesses

*Purpose*: To decide the advantages and disadvantages of different methods for gathering data about the criteria of valuation used in a particular evaluation study (e.g. equity, cost, satisfaction).

*Instructions*: agree a chairperson, agree the task and the times to finish and, for each part of the task, agree a cuckoo clock, and agree scribe if the group has to report back. Follow the group guidelines. You must *leave five minutes* for the chairperson to summarize three main points or themes of the discussion before finishing.

*Task*: the group is to fill in the following chart and write it on a flip-chart. Then the group hang up the flip chart in the main room and look at what the others wrote on their charts.

   Write down the general advantages and disadvantages of each data gathering method, for the purpose of gathering data for an evaluation. The task is easier if you think about examples of an evaluation which used the method, and what were the strengths and weaknesses of that method for the purpose of that type of evaluation. Your 'criteria for valuation' of the method should be: suitability for the purpose, reliability, validity, sensitivity and specificity, cost-effectiveness and 'ethicality' – but only if you know what these terms mean for each particular method. Remember that each type of data gathering method itself has sub-types, so what might be true for one might not be true for all methods in this type category.

|  | *Advantages* | *Disadvantages* |
|---|---|---|
| **Observation:**<br>unobtrusive, participant<br>or self-observation |  |  |
| **Interviews:** structured (e.g.<br>questions),<br>semi-structured, open<br>or guided by a critical incident or<br>vignette stimulus.<br>Focus group interviews |  |  |
| **Questionnaire or survey:**<br>small or large scale survey, with<br>rating scales<br>without rating scales |  |  |
| **Measurement methods:**<br>biophysical,<br>subjective response,<br>a pre-formulated measurement<br>instrument such as<br>disease-specific and quality of life<br>measures |  |  |

*Advantages* *Disadvantages*

**Already collected data**: data
collected for other purposes,
by the service, by government
departments, by others,
diary, minutes of meetings, case
records

**Other data gathering methods**:

## Exercise 7: Assessing Quality of Life outcome measures

*Purpose of the group*: to deepen your understanding of quality of life outcome measures and when to use a particular quality of life (QoL) measure.

*Instructions*: agree a chairperson, agree the task and the times to finish and, for each part of the task, agree a 'cuckoo clock', and agree scribe if the group has to report back. Follow the group guidelines. You must *leave five minutes* for the chairperson to summarize three main points or themes of the discussion before finishing.

*Task*: the task of the group is *not* to discuss each person's ideas about what is good quality of life, but to assess critically the advantages and disadvantages of QoL measures as an outcome measure for an evaluation.

*Discuss*:

1 What are some of the *assumptions* underlying QoL measures?

2 For which types of evaluation might you use a QoL measure? In what circumstances?
3 Why? Would it give information which are relevant to any criteria of valuation which was being used in this evaluation?

4 What are the advantages and disadvantages of different QoL measures? (Estimate the cost to get and analyse QoL data from 100 people, two times (one year interval) for each type of measure.)

| *Name of specific QoL measure* | *Advantages* | *Disadvantages* |
|---|---|---|
| | (good) | (bad) |

## Exercise 8: Colleague listening and consultation group

*Purpose*: The primary aim is to help the person presenting the problem, concern or task to understand it better and to decide what he or she should do. The secondary aim is for other group members to learn from the person presenting and from other people in the group as a result of the discussions.

*Minimum ground rules*: No one interrupts the presenter during their allocated time. Everyone gives full attention to the presenter during their time. Confidentiality: no names of people or organizations mentioned are repeated outside the room. The chairperson's decisions are final, as long as they have consulted the group.

*Method*: The group agrees a chairperson to agree and uphold the rules of the group, to ensure the group sticks to its two purposes and to ensure the group spends 15 minutes before the end listing five key conclusions. The group also agrees a 'cuckoo clock' to speak the times which the group decides to give to different activities and to breaks and finishing times.

An agreed amount of time is decided for the person to give a presentation. The person gives the presentation, finishing with a statement of exactly what he or she would like the group to help and advise on.

The work of the group members is to give their full attention to listening and understanding the presentation without interruption.

After the presentation, group members can ask questions of facts and clarification.

The general discussion aims to help the person to understand the issues, to clarify different courses of action for the future and to decide which to carry out.

*Key points to remember*: The purpose of the presentation is not to impress the others or to give fully formed ideas, but to describe the facts and your and others' interpretations, thoughts and feelings about these facts.

The purpose of the discussion is to help the presenter. To do this you will first have to listen extremely hard to understand what he or she is saying in the presentation. Then you will have to use theories, concepts, and known research to help him or her to understand better the issues and to see different ways forward. You will also share your own and others' practical experiences, when these are relevant.

Leave time to summarize and draw conclusions.

## Exercise 9: Practise designing and planning an evaluation

Look at your self-assessment of your learning needs. Use this to decide an intervention which you might evaluate, and work through the following to create a design and a plan for the evaluation. (Your plan could be assessed by your peers later.)

Choose from the following types of health interventions: a treatment, a service, a health programme, a policy, a health reform or an intervention or change to an organization, such as a teaching programme for health personnel or a quality system.

### Task

1 Decide:

- ♦ whom the evaluation is for;
- ♦ what decisions they make or need to make which your evaluation can help them to make;
- ♦ possible designs;
- ♦ data gathering methods, making maximum use of existing data which are relevant and of adequate quality;
- ♦ the budget you will need between $50,000 and the limit of $150,000, recognizing that the proposal will be assessed in terms of the value of the results for the cost of the study and lower cost designs are much more likely to get funding (this is not a research council but an evaluation funding council).
- ♦ a practical work plan for the resources (you estimate the number of part- or full-time researchers and other costs, what help you can expect from health personnel and the time length of the evaluation, i.e. when will the results be available).

2 In your proposal or presentation draw a diagram for your design and draw a time chart showing the phases and milestones of the evaluation. Say what are the strengths and weaknesses of the design.

3 List the main likely practical, scientific and ethical problems which you expect will make it difficult to complete the design as planned, and ideas for overcoming these problems. List the strengths and weaknesses of the proposal.

4 If your proposal is to be assessed, make sure that you know the criteria to be used for the assessment and make sure your presentation covers these.

5 If you are presenting this plan to others, finish by saying the advice you would like from them and questions to them.

## Exercise 10: Assessing a proposal for an evaluation

To: Members of an imaginary 'Council for Health Evaluation Financing'

*Re: Our special meetings to assess the evaluation proposals*

Members are asked to use the following guidelines to rate a proposal and to make their final decision

Name of proposal:

During the time for questions ask the evaluators: 'If you had half this time and money what would you propose?' If they cannot prioritize at this stage, then be warned that they will have more difficulty doing so as the data builds up in the middle of the evaluation. Unless evaluators are very experienced, their ambitions are likely to exceed what they are actually able to deliver.

*Proposals should cover each of these areas.* Give a rating which expresses your judgement about how well the proposal addresses each area. Ask questions about each of these areas if they did not give the information in the presentation.

1 *Whom* is the evaluation for

| Clear | | | | Unclear |
|---|---|---|---|---|
| 5 | 4 | 3 | 2 | 1 |

2 *Questions* the evaluation aims to answer

| Clear | | | | Unclear |
|---|---|---|---|---|
| 5 | 4 | 3 | 2 | 1 |

3 *Definition of the intervention* to be evaluated (boundary and elements inside 'the box')

| Clear | | | | Unclear |
|---|---|---|---|---|
| 5 | 4 | 3 | 2 | 1 |

4 *Design* of the evaluation was not clearly described, or is not a good one for the purpose

| Clearly described | | | | Not described |
|---|---|---|---|---|
| Good design | | | | Bad design |
| 5 | 4 | 3 | 2 | 1 |

5 *Data gathering methods*: are these 'appropriate', according to the following criteria. Clearly described and justified as the most cost effective for the purpose? An appropriate number of data-gathering methods used for the purposes and resources available?

| Entirely | | | | Not at all |
|---|---|---|---|---|
| appropriate | | | | appropriate |
| 5 | 4 | 3 | 2 | 1 |

6 Costs, time and other resources needed are described and realistic for the project

| Described and | | | | Not described or |
|---|---|---|---|---|
| realistic | | | | unrealistic |
| 5 | 4 | 3 | 2 | 1 |

7 *Value of the benefits* of the evaluation to the user of the evaluation, if achieved
*High value*                                                                                   *No real value*
   5                          4                          3                          2                          1

8 *Strengths* and *weaknesses* of the proposed evaluation are well described
*All are described*                                                                            *None described*
   5                          4                          3                          2                          1

9 *My gut feeling* about whether we should back this one:
*Yes!*                                                                                                    *No!*
   5                          4                          3                          2                          1

*Comments on back of sheet*:

# References

Adams, G. and Shavaneveldt, J. (1991) *Understanding Research Methods*. New York: Longman.

Alban, A. and Christiansen, T. (eds) (1995) *The Nordic Lights: New Initiatives in Health Care Systems*. Odense: Odense University Press.

Albrecht, K. and Bradford, L. (1990) *The Service Advantage*. Irwin, IL: Dow Jones.

Albrecht, K. and Zomke, R. (1985) *Service America: Doing Business in the New Economy*. New York: Warner.

Aldridge, D. (1988) Single-case research designs. *Complementary Medical Research*, 3(1), 37–46.

Appleby, J., (1993) Health and efficiency. *Health Services Journal*, 6 May, 20–2.

Appleby, J., Smith, P., Ranade, W., Little, V. and Robinson, R. (1994) Monitoring managed competition. In R. Robinson and J. Le Grand (eds) *Evaluating the NHS Reforms*. London: King's Fund Centre, 24–35.

Appleby, J., Walshe, K. and Ham, C. (1995) *Acting on the Evidence: a Review of Clinical Effectiveness – Sources of Information, Dissemination and Implementation*. Birmingham: NAHAT.

Auditor General (1991) *Administration of the Medicare Benefits Schedule*. Canberra: Department of Community Services and Health, AGPS.

Axelsson, L. and Svensson, P.G. (1994) Setting goals and targets for performance standards within the Swedish health care system. *Health Policy and Planning*, June, 217–33.

Babakus, E. and Mangold, W.G. (1992) Adapting the SERVQUAL scale to hospital services: an empirical investigation. *Health Services Research*, 26(6), 767–86.

Bagenal, S., Easton, D., Harris, E., Chilvers, C. and McElwain, M. (1990) Survival of patients with breast cancer attending Bristol Cancer Help Centre. *Lancet*, 336, 606–10.

Baker, R. and Fraser, R. (1995) Development of review criteria: linking guidance and assessment of quality. *British Medical Journal*, 311, 370–3.

Bardsley, M. and Coles, J. (1992) Practical experiences in auditing patient outcomes. *Quality in Health Care*, 1, 124–30.

Barer, M. (1981) *Community Health Centres and Hospital Costs in Ontario*. Toronto: Ontario Economic Council.

Barlow, D. and Hursen, M. (1984) *Single Case Experimental Designs: Strategies for Studying Behaviour Change*. New York: Pergamon.

Barone, T. (1992) On the demise of subjectivity in educational inquiry. *Curriculum Inquiry*, 22, 25–38.

Batalden, P. and Stoltz, P. (1993) A framework for the continual improvement of healthcare. *Journal of the Joint Commission for Accreditation of Healthcare Organisations*, 19(10), 424–45.

Beecher, H. (1955) The powerful placebo. *JAMA*, 159, 1602–6.

Benson, H. and Epstein, M. (1975) The placebo effect: a neglected asset in the care of patients. *Journal of the American Association*, 232, 1225–7.

Benson, H. and McCallie, D. (1979) Angina pectoris and the placebo effect. *New England Journal of Medicine*, 300, 1424–9.

Berwick, D. (1996) Improving healthcare. *British Medical Journal*, 312, 605–18.

Berwick, D., Enthoven, A. and Bunker, J. (1992) Quality management in the NHS: the doctor's role, parts I and II. *British Medical Journal*, 304, 235–9 (part I), and 304, 304–8 (part II).

Berwick, D., Godfrey, A. and Roessner, J. (1990) *Curing Healthcare: New Strategies for Quality Improvement*. San Francisco: Jossey-Bass.

Black, N. (1992) Research, audit and education. *British Medical Journal*, 304, 698–700.

Booth, T. (1988) *Developing Policy Research*. Aldershot: Gower.

Bowling, A. (1992) *Measuring Health: a Review of Quality of Life Measures*. Buckingham: Open University Press.

Bowling, A. (1995) *Measuring Disease: a Review of Disease-specific Quality of Life Measurement Scales*. Buckingham: Open University Press.

Breakwell, G. and Millward, L. (1995) *Basic Evaluation Methods*. Leicester: British Psychological Society Books.

Britten, N. (1995) Qualitative interviews in medical research. *British Medical Journal*, 311, 251–3.

Brooks, R. (1986) *Scaling in Health Status Measurement*. Lund: The Swedish Institute of Health Economics.

Brooks, T. (1992) Success through organisational audit. *Health Services Management*, Nov/Dec, 13–15.

Brooks, T. and Pitt, C. (1990) The standard bearers. *Health Services Journal*, 30 August, 1286–7.

Brunel University Faculty of Social Sciences (1984) Evaluation of management advisory and performance review trials in the NHS. Report prepared for the King's Fund, London.

Bruster, S., Jarman, B., Bosanquet, N. *et al.* (1994) National survey of hospital patients. *British Medical Journal*, 309, 1542–6.

BSI (1987) *BS 5750 Quality Systems part 1: Specification for Design/Development, Production Installation and Servicing*. London: British Standards Institute.

BSI (1992) *BS 5750 for Services*. London: BSI.

Buck, N., Devlin, H. and Lunn, J. (1987) *Report of a Confidential Enquiry into Perioperative Deaths*. London: Nuffield Provincial Hospitals Trust.

Burnes, B. (1992) *Managing Change*. Pitman: London.

Buxton, M. (1992) Scarce resources and informed choices, AMI conference paper, HERG, Brunel University, November.

Campbell, D. (1969) Reforms as experiments. *American Psychologist*, 24, 409–29.

Campbell, D. (1970) Considering the case against experimental evaluations of social innovations. *Administrative Science Quarterly*, 15, 110–13.

Campbell, D. and Stanley, J. (1966) *Experimental and Quasi-experimental Designs for Research*. Chicago: Rand-McNally.

Canadian Task Force on the Periodic Health Examination (1979) The periodic health examination. *Canadian Medical Association Journal*, 121, 1139–254.

CEPPP (1991) *Evaluation of TQM in the NHS: First Interim Report*. Uxbridge: CEPPP, Brunel University.

Chassin, M., Brook, R., Part, R., Keesey, J., Fink, A., Kosecoff, J., Kahn, K., Merrick, N. and Solomon, D. (1986) Variations in the use of medical and surgical services by the Medicare population. *New England Journal of Medicine*, 314, 285–9.

Cheetham, J., Fuller, R., McIvor, G. and Petch, A. (1992) *Evaluating Social Work Effectiveness*. Buckingham: Open University Press.

Chen, H. (1990) *Theory-driven Evaluation*. London: Sage.

Cleary, P., Edgman-Levitan, S., Walker, J. and Delbanco, T. (1993) Using patient reports to improve medical care: a preliminary report from 10 hospitals. *Quality Management in Health Care*, 2(1), 31–8.

Cochrane, A. (1972) *Effectiveness and Efficiency*. London: Nuffield Provincial Hospitals Trust.

Cochrane, A. and Blythe, M. (1989) *One Man's Medicine*. BMJ Books.

Cohen, S., Weinberger, M., Hui, S., Tiernay, W. and McDonald, C. (1985) The impact of reading on physicians' nonadherence to recommended standards of medical care. *Social Science and Medicine*, 21, 909–14.

Cook, T. and Campbell, D. (1979) *Quasi-experimentation: Design and Analysis Issues in Field Settings*. Chicago: Rand-McNally.

Coyle, D. (1993) Increasing the impact of economic evaluations in decision-making. Discussion Paper 108, Centre for Health Economics, University of York.

Craig, N. and Walker, D. (1996) Choice and accountability in health promotion: the role of health economics. *Health Education Research*, 11, 355–60.

Crombie, I. (1996) *The Pocket Guide to Critical Appraisal*. BMJ Books: London.

Cronbach, L. (1980) *Towards Reform of Program Evaluation*. San Francisco: Jossey-Bass.

Crosby, P. (1979) *Quality Is Free*. New York: Mentor.

Crosby, P. (1985) *Quality without Tears*. New York: Mentor.

Cummings, S., Rubin, S. and Oster, G. (1989) The Cost-effectiveness of counseling smokers to quit. *JAMA*, 261(1), 75–9.

Dale, A. and Wooler, S. (1988) *SOS-Strategy and Organisation for Service: a Content and Process Model for Decision-making*. Uxbridge: BIOSS, Brunel University.

Daley, J., McDonald, I. and Willis, E. (eds) (1992) *Researching Health Care: Designs, Dilemmas, Disciplines*. London: Routledge.

Dam, H., Molin, J., Bolwig, T., Wildschiødtz, G. and Mellerup, E. (1993) Development of winter depression and the effect of light therapy. *Nordic Journal of Psychiatry*, 48, 75–8.

Davidow, W.H. and Uttal, B. (1989) *Total Customer Service*. London: Harper and Row.

Davids, F., Hayes, B., Sackett, D. and Smith, R. (1995) Evidence based medicine, *British Medical Journal*, Vol. 310, 1089–1096.

Delamothe, T. (ed.) (1994) *Outcomes into Clinical Practice*. London: BMJ Publishing.

Deming, W.E. (1986) *Out of the Crisis*. Cambridge, Mass: MIT.

Demone, H. and Gibelman, M. (eds) (1989) *Services for Sale*. London: Rutgers University Press.

Denton, D.K. (1989) *Quality Service*. London: Gulf Publishing.

Denzin, N. and Lincoln, Y. (eds) (1993) *Handbook of Qualitative Research*. London: Sage.

DesHarnais, S., Laurence, F., McMahon, M. Jr and Wroblewski, R. (1991) Measuring outcomes of hospital care using risk-adjusted indexes. *Health Services Research*, 26(4), 425–45.

DHHSPHS (1995) *Performance Improvement 1995: Evaluation Activities of the Public Health Services*. Washington, DC: US Department of Health and Human Services.

Dixon, P. and Carr-Hill, R. (1989) *The NHS and Its Customers III. Consumer Feedback: a Review of Current Practice*. York: Centre of Health Economics, University of York.

DoH (1989a) *Report on Confidential Enquiries into Maternal Deaths in England and Wales 1982–84*. London: HMSO.

DoH (1989b) *Working Paper 6 – Medical Audit*. London: HMSO.

DoH (1989c) *Medical Audit in the Family Practitioner Services*. London: HMSO.

DoH (1989d) *Working for Patients*. London: HMSO.

DoH (1990) *The National Health Service and Community Care Act 1990*. London: HMSO.

DoH (1991a) *Medical Audit in the Hospital and Community Health Services*. HC(91)2, January.

DoH (1991b) *The Patient's Charter*. London: HMSO.

DoH (1992) *The Health of the Nation*. London: HMSO.

DoH (1993) *Managing the New NHS*. London: HMSO.

DoH (1994) *Standing Group on Health Technology: 1994 Report*. London: HMSO.

Domenighetti, G., Luraschi, P., Gutzwiller, F., Pedrinis, E., Casabianca, A., Spinelli, A. *et al.* (1988) Effect of information changes by the mass media on hysterectomy rates. *Lancet*, ii, 1470–3.

Donabedian, A. (1980) *Exploration in Quality Assessment and Monitoring Volume I. Definition of Quality and Approaches to Its Assessment.* Ann Arbor: Health Administration Press, University of Michigan.

Drummond, M. (1987a) Economic evaluation and the rational diffusion and use of health technology. *Health Policy*, 7, 309–24.

Drummond, M. (1987b) *Economic Appraisal of Health Technology in the European Community.* Oxford: Oxford University Press.

Drummond, M., Stoddard, G. and Torrence, G. (1987) *Methods for the Economic Evaluation of Health Care Programmes.* Oxford: Oxford Medical Publications.

Dubinsky, M. and Ferguson, J. (1990) Analysis of the National Institutes of Health Medicare Coverage Assessment. *International Journal of Technology Assessment in Health Care*, 480–8.

Eddy, D. (1989) Selecting technologies for assessment. *International Journal of Technology Assessment in Health Care*, 5, 485–501.

Eddy, D. and Billings, J. (1988) The quality of medical evidence. *Health Affairs*, 7(1), 19–32.

Edgren, L. (1995) *Evaluation of the SPRI Version of Organisational Audit at Lund University Hospital.* Goteborg: The Nordic School of Public Health (summary in English).

Edvardsson, B., Øvretveit, J. and Thomasson, B. (1994) *Service Quality – a TQM Perspective.* London: McGraw-Hill.

Edwards, W. and Newman, J. (1988) *Multiattribute Evaluation.* Newbury Park, CA: Sage.

Edwards, A. and Talbot, R. (1994) *The Hard-pressed Researcher.* Harlow: Longman.

Edwards, N. (1996) Lore unto themselves. *Health Services Journal*, 12 September, 26–7.

EFQM (1992) *The European Quality Award 1992.* Brussels: European Foundation for Quality Management.

Ellis, R. and Whittington, D. (1993) *Quality Assurance in Health Care: a Handbook.* London: Edward Arnold.

Ellis, J., Mulligan, I., Rowe, J. and Sackett, D. (1995) Inpatient medicine is evidence based. *Lancet*, 346, 407–9.

Emery, F. and Trist, E. (1969) Socio-technical systems. In F.E. Emery (ed.) *Systems Thinking.* Harmondsworth: Penguin.

Engelkes, E. (1993) What are the lessons from evaluating PHC projects? A personal view. *Health Policy and Planning*, 8(1), 72–7.

Eyler, J. (1979) *Victorian Social Medicine: the Ideas and Methods of William Farr.* Baltimore: Johns Hopkins University Press.

Fink, A. (1993) *Evaluation Fundamentals.* London: Sage.

Firth-Cozins, J. (1995) Looking at effectiveness. *Quality in Health Care*, 5, 55–9.

Fitzpatrick, R. and Boulton, M. (1994) Qualitative methods for assessing health care. *Quality in Health Care*, 3, 107–13.

Flanagan, J. (1954) The critical incident technique. *Psychological Bulletin*, 5, 327–58.

Forss, K. and Carlsson, J. (1997) The quest for quality: or can evaluation findings be trusted, paper presented to the 1997 European Evaluation Society Conference, Stockholm.

Fowkes, F. and Fulton, P. (1991) Critical appraisal of published research: introductory guidelines. *British Medical Journal*, 302, 1136–40.

Frankfort-Nachmias, C. and Nachmias, D. (1992) *Research Methods in Social Sciences*, 4th edn. London: Edward Arnold.

Franklin, B. (1941) Letter to John Pringle (1757). In I. Cohen (ed.) *Benjamin Franklin's Experiments.* Cambridge, MA: Harvard University Press.

Freemantle, N., Grill, I., Grimshaw, J. and Oxman, A. (1995) Implementing the findings of medical research: the Cochrane Collaboration and effective professional practice. *Quality in Health Care*, 4, 45–7.

French, W. and Bell, C. (1995) *Organisational Development*. Prentice Hall: London.

Fuchs, B. (1990) *Medicare's Peer Review Organizations*. Washington, DC: Congressional Research Service.

Gardner, M. and Altman, D. (1989) *Statistics with Confidence*. London: BMJ Books.

Garner, P., Thomason, J. and Donaldson, D. (1990) Quality assessment of health facilities in rural Papua New Guinea. *Health Policy and Planning*, 5(1), 49–59.

Garpenby, P. and Carlsson, P. (1994) The role of national quality registers in the Swedish health service. *Health Policy*, 29, 183–95.

Gavin, K., Conway, J., Glynn, W., Turner, M. and Brannick, T. (1996) Designing a measurement instrument for evaluating quality in the maternity services: a composite view involving internal and external customers. In B. Edvardsson *et al.* (eds) *Advancing Service Quality: a Global Perspective*. New York: ISQA, St John's University.

Gerard, K. and Mooney, G. (1993) QALY league tables: handle with care. *Health Economics*, 2, 59–64.

Ghauri, P., Grønhaug, K. and Kristianslund, I. (1995) *Research Methods in Business Studies*. London: Prentice-Hall.

Giddens, A. (1974) *Positivism and Sociology*. London: Heinemann.

Gissler, M., Teperi, J., Hemminki, E. and Merilainen, J. (1995) Data quality after restructuring a National Medical Registry. *Scandinavian Journal of Social Medicine*, 23(1), 75–80.

Glaser, B.G. and Strauss, A.L. (1968) *The Discovery of Grounded Theory: Strategies for Qualitative Research*. London: Weidenfeld and Nicolson.

Glennerster, H., Matsaganis, M., Owens, P. and Hancock, S. (1994) *Implementing GP Fundholding*. Buckingham: Open University Press.

Golden, B. (1992) The past is the past – or is it? The use of retrospective accounts as indicators of past strategy. *Academy of Management Journal*, 35(4), 848–60.

Goodwin, J. and Goodwin, J. (1984) The tomato effect. *JAMA*, 251(18), 2387–90.

Gray, M. (1997) *Evidence-based healthcare*. Churchill Livingstone: London.

Greene, J. (1994) Qualitative program evaluation. In N. Denzin and Y. Lincoln (eds) *op. cit.*

Greenhalgh, J., Long, A., Brettle, A. and Grant, M. (1996) The value of an outcomes information resource. *Journal of Management in Medicine*, 10(5), 55–65.

Grimshaw, J. and Russel, I. (1994) Achieving health gain through clinical guidelines II: ensuring guidelines change medical practice. *Quality in Health Care*, 3, 45–52.

Gronroos, C. (1991) Facing the challenge of service competition: costs of bad service. Papers from Conference on Quality Management in Services, EIASM.

Gummesson, E. (1987) *Quality – the Ericsson Approach*. Stockholm: Ericsson.

Guyatt, G., Sackett, D., Adachi, G. *et al.* (1988) A clinician's guide for conducting randomised trials in individual patients. *Canadian Medical Association Journal*, 139, 497–503.

Guyatt, G., Sackett, D., Taylor, D., Chong, J., Roberts, R. and Pugsey, S. (1986) Determining optimal therapy: Randomised trials in individual patients. *NEJM*, 314, 889–92.

Haines, A. and Jones, R. (1994) Implementing findings of research. *British Medical Journal*, 308, 1488–91.

Ham, C. and Woolley, M. (1996) *How Does the NHS Measure up? Assessing the Performance of Health Authorities*. Birmingham: National Association of Health Authorities and Trusts.

Ham, C., Hunter, D. and Robinson, R. (1995) Evidence based policy making. *British Medical Journal*, 310, 71–2.

Harper, J. (1986) Measuring performance – a new approach. *Hospital and Health Services Review*, January, 26–8.

Harrison, S., Hunter, D. and Pollitt, C. (1990) *The Dynamics of British Health Policy*. London: Unwin Hyman.

Hart, E. and Bond, M. (1996) *Action Research for Health and Social Care.* Buckingham: Open University Press.

Haycox, A. (1994) A methodology for estimating the costs and benefits of health promotion. *Health Promotion International,* 9(7), 5–11.

Helman, C. (1994) *Culture, Health and Illness,* Butterworth Heinemann: London.

Henkel, M. (1991) *Government, Evaluation and Change.* London: Jessica Kingsley.

HERG (1994) *Assessing Payback from Department of Health Research and Development.* Uxbridge: Health Economics Research Group, Brunel University.

HERG (1996) *Economic Evaluation in Healthcare Research and Development: Undertake It Early and Often.* Uxbridge: Health Economics Research Group, Brunel University.

Heron, J. (1979) *Peer Review Audit.* Guildford: University of Surrey Human Potential Research Project, University of Surrey.

Heron, J. (1981) Self and peer assessment for managers. In T. Boydell and M. Pedler (eds) *Handbook of Management Self-development.* London: Gower.

Heron, J. (1986) Critique of conventional research methodology. *Complementary Medical Research,* 1(1), 14–22.

Heskett, J.L. (1986) *Managing in the Service Economy.* Cambridge, MA: Harvard Business School Press.

Heskett, J.L., Sasser, W.E. and Hart, C. (1990) *Service Breakthroughs.* New York: Free Press.

Hoey, J., McCallum, H. and LePage, E. (1982) Expanding the nurse's role to improve preventative service in an outpatient clinic. *Canadian Medical Association Journal,* 127, 27–8.

Holland, W. (ed.) (1983) *Evaluation of Health Care.* Oxford: Oxford University Press.

House, E. (1980) *Evaluating with Validity.* Beverly Hills, CA: Sage.

Hunter, D. (1992) Rationing dilemmas in health care. NAHA & T Paper 8, Birmingham.

IoM (1992) *Setting Priorities for Health Technology Assessment: a Model Process.* Washington, DC: National Academy Press.

Jackson, C. (1997) *Evaluation of the Exercise by Prescription Programme.* Harrogate: North Yorkshire Health Authority.

Jaques, E. (1982) *The Form of Time.* London: Heinemann.

Jaques, E. (1989) *Requisite Organization.* Arlington, VA: Casson Hall.

JAMA (1993) User's guides to the medical literature: how to use an article about therapy or prevention, 1. *JAMA,* 270, 2598–601.

JCAHO (1991) *Transitions: from QA to CQI – Using CQI Approaches to Monitor, Evaluate and Improve Quality.* Oakbrook Terrace, IL: Joint Commission on Accreditation of Healthcare Organizations.

JCSEE (1994) *The Programme Evaluation Standards: How to Assess Evaluations of Educational Programs,* 2nd edn. Thousand Oaks, CA: Sage.

Jick, T. (1983) Mixing qualitative and quantitative methods: triangulation in action. In J. Van Maanen (ed.) *Qualitative Methodology.* Beverly Hills, CA: Sage.

Johannessen, H., Launsø, L., Gosvig Olsen, S. and Staugård, F. (eds) (1994) *Studies in Alternative Therapies, 1: Contributions from the Nordic Countries.* Odense: Odense University Press.

Johannessen, T. (1991) Controlled trials in single subjects. *British Medical Journal,* 303, 173–4.

Johnson, S. and Mclaughlin, C. (1996) Simulating alternative quality improvement methods. In B. Edvardsson *et al.* (eds) *Advancing Service Quality: a Global Perspective.* New York: ISQA, St John's University.

Johnston, N., Narayan, V. and Ruta, D. (1992) Development of indicators for quality assurance in public health medicine. *Quality in Health Care,* 1, 225–30.

Jones, J. and Hunter, D. (1995) Consensus methods for medical and health services research. *British Medical Journal,* 311, 376–9.

Jones, R. (1995) Why do qualitative research? *British Medical Journal,* 311, 2.

Joss, R. and Kogan, M. (1995) *Advancing Quality*. Buckingham: Open University Press.

Joss, R., Kogan, M. and Henkel, M. (1994) *Final Report to the Department of Health on Total Quality Management Experiments in the National Health Service*. Uxbridge: Centre for Evaluation of Public Policy and Practice, Brunel University.

Jost, T. (1990) Assuring the quality of medical practice, King's Fund Project Paper No. 82, London.

Kazdin, A. (1982) *Single Case Research Design: Methods for Clinical and Applied Settings*. Oxford: Oxford University Press.

Keen, J. (1994) Evaluation: informing the future not living in the past. In J. Keen (ed.) *Information Management in Health Services*. Buckingham: Open University Press.

Kelly, G. (1955) *A Theory of Personality*. New York: Norton.

Kerrison, S., Packwood, T. and Buxton, M. (1993) *Medical Audit: Taking Stock*. London: King's Fund.

Kinston, W. (1995) *Working with Values*. London: Sigma Centre.

Kirk, J. and Miller, M. (1986) *Reliability and Validity in Qualitative Research*. London: Sage.

Kitzinger, J. (1995) Introducing focus groups. *British Medical Journal*, 311, 299–302.

Kleijnen, J., Knipschild, P. and ter Riet, G. (1991) Clinical trials of homeopathy. *British Medical Journal*, 302, 316–23.

Klein, R. (1989) Research and the health policy process: a UK perspective. In *Research and the Health Policy Process: Proceedings of the Second Annual Policy Conference*. Center for Health Economics and Policy Analysis, McMaster University.

Klein, R. and Scrivens, E. (1993) The bottom line – Accreditation in the UK. *Health Services Journal*, 25 November, 25–6.

Kogan, M. and Redfern, S. (eds) (1995) *Making Use of Clinical Audit: a Guide to Practice in the Health Professions*. Buckingham: Open Univeristy Press.

Kreuger, R. (1988) *Focus Groups: a Practical Guide for Applied Research*. London: Sage.

Kvale, S. (1994) Ten standard objections to qualitative research interviews. *Journal of Phenomenological Psychology*, 1–28.

Lawrence, M. and Packwood, T. (1996) Adapting total quality management for general practice: evaluation of a programme. *Quality in Health Care*, 5, 151–8.

Lewin, K. (1947a) Group decision and social change. In T. Newcomb and E. Hartley (eds) *Readings in Social Psychology*. New York: Holt, Rinehart and Winston.

Lewin, K. (1947b) Frontiers in group dynamics: (1) Concept, methods and reality in social sciences: social equilibria and social change; (2) Channels of group life, social planning and action research. *Human Relations*, 1(1, 2), 5–41, 143–53.

Lindblom, C. and Cohen, D. (1979) *Usable Knowledge: Social Science and Social Problem Solving*. New Haven, CT: Yale University Press.

Lockwood, F. (1994) *Exercise by Prescription in York and Selby*. Harrogate: North Yorkshire Health Authority.

Long, A., Dixon, P., Hall, R., Carr-Hill, R. and Sheldon, T. (1993) The outcomes agenda. *Quality In Health Care*, 2, 49–52.

Ludbrook, A. and Mooney, G. (1984) *Economic Appraisal in the NHS: Problems and Challenges*. York: Northern Health Economics.

McConway, K. (ed.) (1994) *Studying Health and Disease*. Buckingham: Open University Press.

Macdonald, G., Veen, C. and Tones, K. (1996) Evidence for success in health promotion: suggestions for improvement. *Health Education Research*, 11(3), 367–76.

Macfarlane, A. (1996) Trial would not answer key question, but data monitoring should be improved. *British Medical Journal*, 312, 754–5.

McKenna, M., Maynard, A. and Wright, K. (1992) *Is Rehabilitation Cost-effective?* York: Centre for Health Economics, University of York.

McKinlay, J. (1992) Advantages and limitations of the survey approach – understanding older people. In J. Daley *et al.* (eds) *op cit*.

Mahaparatra, P. and Berman, P. (1994) Using hospital activity indicators to evaluate performance in Andra Pradesh, India. *International Journal of Health Planning and Management*, 9, 199–211.

Majeed, F. and Voss, S. (1995) Performance indicators for general practice. *British Medical Journal*, 311, 209–10.

Majone, G. and Wildavsky, A. (1979) Implementation as evolution. In G. Pressman and A. Wildavsky (eds) *Implementation*, 4th edn. Berkeley: University of California Press.

Marks, S. *et al.* (1980) Ambulatory surgery in an HMO. *Medical Care*, 18, 127–46.

Maxwell, R. (1984) Quality assessment in health. *British Medical Journal*, 288, 1470–2.

Mays, N. and Pope, C. (1995) Observational methods in health care settings, *British Medical Journal*. 311, 192–4

Mercer, G., Long, A. and Smith I. (1995) Researching and Evaluating Complementary Therapies. Leeds: Nuffield Institute for Health.

Middle, C. and Macfarlane, A. (1995) Recorded delivery. *Health Services Journal*, 31 August, 27.

Miles, M. and Huberman, A. (1984) *Qualitative Data Analysis: a Source Book of New Methods*. Beverly Hills, CA: Sage.

Morgan, D. (ed.) (1993) *Successful Focus Groups*. London: Sage.

Morgan, G. (1988) *Images of Organisation*. London: Heinemann.

Mugford, M., Banfield, P. and O'Hanlon, M. (1991) Effects of feedback of information on clinical practice: a review. *British Medical Journal*, 303, 398–402.

Najman, J., Morrison, J., Williams, G. and Anderson, M. (1992) Comparing alternative methodologies of social research. In J. Daley *et al.* (eds) (1992) *op cit*.

Nathanson, C. (1978) Sex roles as a variable in the interpretation of morbidity data: a methodological crtique. *International Journal of Epidemiology*, 7(3), 253–62.

NCEPOD (1987, 1989) *The Report of a National Confidential Enquiry into Perioperative Deaths*. London: King's Fund.

NCEPOD (1993) *Report of the National Confidential Enquiry into Perioperative Deaths, 1991/92*. London: NCEPOD.

Newell, D. (1992) Randomised controlled trials in health care research. In J. Daley *et al.* (eds) *op. cit.*

NHSCR&D (1996) *Undertaking Systematic Reviews of Research on Effectiveness: CRD Guidelines for Carrying out or Commissioning Reviews*. York: NHS Centre for Reviews and Dissemination.

Nichol, K., Lind, A., Margolis, K., Murdoch, M., Mcfadden, R., Hauge, M., Magnan, S. and Drake, M. (1995) The effectiveness of vaccination against influenza in healthy, working adults. *New England Journal of Medicine*, 333(14), 889–93.

Nightingale, F. (1863) *Notes on Hospitals*, 3rd edn. London: Longman, Green, Longman, Roberts and Green.

NIST (1990) *The Malcolm Baldrige National Quality Award 1990 Application Guidelines*. Gaithersburg, MD: National Institute of Standards and Technology.

Nordberg, E., Oganga, H., Kazibwe, S. and Onyango, J. (1993) Rapid assessment of an African district health system. *International Journal of Health Planning and Management*, 8, 219–33.

Oakland, J. (1989) *Total Quality Management*. Oxford: Heinemann.

Odegård, K. (1995) Lex Maria – from punishment to prevention? A study of medical errors reported to the National Board of Health and Welfare. Masters thesis, The Nordic School of Public Health, Goteborg.

Olsen, J. (1995) Aiming at what? The objectives of the Norwegian health services. In A. Alban and T. Christiansen (eds) *op. cit.*

Olsen, J. and Donaldson, C. (1993) Willingness to pay for public sector health care programmes in Northern Norway. HERU Discussion Paper, Univerity of Aberdeen.

Ong, B. (1993) *The Practice of Health Service Research*. London: Chapman and Hall.

Øvretveit, J. (1984) Is action research scientific? Social analysis and action research. Unpublished master thesis, Brunel University, Uxbridge.

Øvretveit, J. (1986) *Improving Social Work Records and Practice*. Birmingham: BASW Publications.

Øvretveit, J. (1987a) Social analytic evaluation research. BIOSS Research document, Brunel University, Uxbridge.

Øvretveit, J. (1987b) Volunteers in drugs agencies: an evaluation of supervision arrangements. BIOSS Working Paper, Brunel University, Uxbridge.

Øvretveit, J. (1988) A peer review process for developing service quality. BIOSS Working Paper, Brunel University, Uxbridge.

Øvretveit, J. (1990a) Quality health services. BIOSS Research report, Brunel University, Uxbridge.

Øvretveit, J. (1990b) What is quality in health services? *Health Service Management*, June, 132–3.

Øvretveit, J. (1990c) Improving primary health care team organisation. BIOSS Research report, Brunel University, Uxbridge.

Øvretveit, J. (1991a) Primary care quality through teamwork. BIOSS Research report Brunel University, Uxbridge.

Øvretveit, J. (1991b) Quality costs – or does it? *Health Service Management*, August.

Øvretveit, J. (1992a) *Health Service Quality*. Oxford: Blackwell Scientific Press.

Øvretveit, J. (1992b) Maps-Qual quality audit software. *Quality News*, 18(3), 116–17.

Øvretveit, J. (1992c) Towards market-focused measures of customer/purchaser perceptions. *Quality Forum*, 19(3), 21–4.

Øvretveit, J. (1993a) *Coordinating Community Care: Multidisciplinary Teams and Care Management in Health and Social Services*. Buckingham: Open University Press.

Øvretveit, J. (1993b) Quality awards and auditing for purchasers of services: towards partnership contracting. *International Journal of Service Industry Management*, June.

Øvretveit, J. (1993c) *Measuring Service Quality*. Aylesbury: Technical Communications Publications.

Øvretveit, J. (1994a) A comparison of approaches to quality in the UK, USA and Sweden, and of the use of organisational audit frameworks. *European Journal of Public Health*, 4(1), 46–54.

Øvretveit, J. (1994b) *Evaluation of a Community Mental Health Resource Centre*. Uxbridge: Mental Health Unit, Hillingdon Hospital Trust.

Øvretveit, J. (1994c) Quality in health services purchasing. *Journal of the Association of Quality in Health Care*, 2(1), 9–22.

Øvretveit, J. (1994d) *Purchasing for Health*. Buckingham: Open University Press.

Øvretveit, J. (1994e) A framework for cost effective team quality and multiprofessional audit. *Journal of Interprofessional Care*, 8(3), 329–33.

Øvretveit J. (1996a) Informed choice? Patient access to health service quality information. *Health Policy*, 36, 75–93.

Øvretveit, J. (1996b) *The Quality Journeys of Five Norwegian Hospitals*. Oslo: Norwegian Medical Association.

Øvretveit, J. (1997a) Learning from quality improvement in Europe and beyond. *Journal of the Joint Commission for Accreditation of Healthcare Organisations*, 23(1), 7–22.

Øvretveit, J. (1997b) *Evaluation of the Norwegian Total Quality Programme – Second Report*. Oslo: Norwegian Medical Association.

Øvretveit, J. (1997c) Evidence-based management technologies. *Journal of Health Gain*, Autumn, 1–5.

Øvretveit, J. (in press) *Six Norwegian Hospitals' Experience with Total Quality Management*. Oslo: Norwegian Medical Association.

Packwood, T., Keen, J. and Buxton, M. (1991) *Hospitals in Transition: the Resource Management Experiment*. Milton Keynes: Open University Press.

Parasuraman, A. *et al.* (1985) A conceptual model of service quality and its implications for future research. *Journal of Marketing*, 49, 41–50.

Parasuraman, A. *et al.* (1988) SERVQUAL: a multiple item scale for measuring consumer perceptions of service quality. *Journal of Retailing*, Spring, 12–40.

Parlett, M. (1981) Illuminative evaluation. In P. Reason and J. Rowan (eds) *op. cit.*

Parlett, M. and Hamilton, D. (1976) Evaluation as illumination. In G. Glass (ed.) *Evaluation Studies Review Annual, Volume 1.* Beverly Hills, CA: Sage.

Parlett, M. and Dearden (1977) *Introduction to Illuminative Evaluation: Studies in Higher Education.* California: Pacific Soundings Press.

Patel, M. (1987) Problems in the evaluation of alternative medicine. *Social Science and Medicine,* 25, 669–78.

Patton, M. (1980) *Qualitative Evaluation Methods.* London: Sage.

Patton, M. (1987) *How to Use Qualitative Methods in Evaluation.* London: Sage.

Patton, M. *et al.* (1977) In search of impact: an analysis of the utlisation of federal health evaluation research. In C. Weiss (ed.) *op. cit.*

Pearce, K. (1996) Show a leg. *Health Service Journal,* 2 May, 33.

PHCCCC (1992) *Hospital Effectiveness Report.* Harrisburg: Pennsylvania Health Care Cost Containment Council.

Phillips, C., Palfry, C. and Thomas, P. (1994) *Evaluating Health and Social Care.* London: Macmillan.

Pocock, S. (1983) *Clinical Trials: a Practical Approach.* Chichester: John Wiley.

Pollitt, C. (1987) Capturing quality? The quality issue in British and American health policies. *Journal of Public Policy,* 7(1), 71–91.

Pollitt, C. (1990) Doing business in the temple. *Public Administration,* 68(4), 435–52.

Pollitt, C. (1992) The politics of medical quality: auditing doctors in the UK and the USA. Unpublished draft, Dept of Government, Brunel University.

Pope, C. and Mays, N. (1995a) Reaching the parts other methods cannot reach: an introduction to qualitative methods in health and health services research. *British Medical Journal,* 311, 42–5.

Pope, C. and Mays, N. (1995b) Rigour and qualitative research. *British Medical Journal,* 311, 109–12.

Pope, C. and Mays, N. (1995c) Observational methods in health care settings. *British Medical Journal,* 311, 182–4.

Powell, J., Lovelock, R., Bray, J. and Philp, I. (1994) Involving consumers in assessing service quality using a qualitative approach. *Quality in Health Care,* 3, 199–202.

RCP (1989) *Medial Audit – A First Report. What, Why and How?* London: Royal College of Physicians of London.

Reason, P. and Rowan, J. (eds) (1981) *Human Inquiry.* London: John Wiley & Sons.

Richardson, J. (1992) Cost–utility analyses in health care: present status and future issues. In J. Daley *et al.* (eds) *op. cit.*

Roberts, C., Lewis, P., Crosby, D., Dunn, C. and Grundy, P. (1996) Prove it. *Health Services Journal,* 7 March, 32–3.

Roberts, H. (1990) *Outcome and Performance in Health Care.* London: Public Finance Foundation.

Robertson, A. and Gandy, J. (1983) Policy Practice and Research: An Overview, in Gandy, J. *et al* (1983) *Improving Social Intervention: Changing Social Policy and Social Work Practice Through Research.* London: Croom Helm.

Robinson, R. and Le Grand, J. (1994) *Evaluating the NHS Reforms.* London: King's Fund Centre.

Robson, M., France, R. and Bland, M. (1984) Clinical psychologists in primary care: controlled and economic evaluation. *British Medical Journal,* 288, 1805–8.

Rooney, E.M. (1988) A proposed quality system specification for the national health service. *Quality Assurance,* 14(2), 45–53.

Rooney, E.M. (1989) *A Quality Management System for the NHS and a Strategy for Training.* Bristol: NHS-Training Authority.

Rosenberg, W. and Donald, A. (1995) Evidence-based medicine: an approach to clinical problem-solving. *British Medical Journal,* 310, 1122–6.

Rossi, P. and Freeman, H. (1993) *Evaluation – a Systematic Approach.* London: Sage.

Rossi, P. and Wright, S. (1977) Evaluation Research: An assessement of theory, practice and politics, *Evaluation Quarterly* 1, 5–52.

Rowbottom, R. and Billis, D. (1977) Stratification of work and organisational design. In E. Jaques (ed.) *Health Services*. London: Heinemann.

Russell, I., Fell, M., Devlin, H., Glass, N. and Newell, D. (1977) Day case surgery for hernias and haemorrhoids – a clinical, social and economic evaluation. *Lancet*, **i**, 844–7.

Sabatier, P. (1986) Top-down and bottom-up approaches to implementation research: a critical analysis and suggested synthesis. *Journal of Public Policy*, 6(1), 21–48.

Sackett, D., Haynes, R., Guyatt, G. and Tugwell, P. (1991) *Clinical Epidemiology: a Basic Science for Medicine*. Boston: Little Brown.

Sackett, D., Rosenberg, W., Gray, J., Haynes, R. and Scott-Richardson, W. (1996) Evidence-based medicine: what it is and what it isn't. *British Medical Journal*, 312, 71–2.

Sacks, H., Chalmers, T. and Smith, H. (1982) Randomized versus historical controls for clinical trials. *American Journal of Medicine*, 72, 233–40.

St Leger, A., Schienden, H. and Walsworth-Bell, J. (1992) *Evaluating Health Service Effectiveness*. Buckingham: Open University Press.

Salked, G., Davey, P. and Arnolda, G. (1995) A critical review of health-related economic evaluations in Australia: implications for health policy. *Health Policy*, 31, 111–25.

Sapsford, R. and Abbott, P. (1992) *Research Methods for Nurses and the Caring Professions*. Buckingham: Open University Press.

Sasco, A., Day, N. and Walter, S. (1986) Case–control studies for the evaluation of screening. *Journal of Chronic Diseases*, 39, 399–405.

Schein, E. (1987) *The Clinical Perspective in Fieldwork*. London: Sage.

Schelesselman, J. (1982) *Case–Control Studies: Design, Conduct, Analysis*. Oxford: Oxford University Press.

Schwartz, D., Flamant, R. and Lellouch, J. (1980) *Clinical Trials*. London: Academic Press.

Schyve, P. (1995) Models for relating performance measurement and accreditation. *International Journal of Health Planning and Management*, 10, 231–41.

Scott, A. and Hall, J. (1995) Evaluating the effects of GP remuneration: problems and prospects. *Health Policy and Planning*, 31, 183–95.

Scriven, M. (1967) The methodology of evaluation. In R. Tyler *et al.* (eds) *Perspectives of Curriculum Evaluation*. Chicago: Rand-McNally.

Scriven, M. (1972) The methodology of evaluation. In C. Weiss (ed) *Evaluating Action Programmes: Readings in Social Action and Education*. Boston: Allyn and Bacon

Scriven, M. (1973) Goal-free evaluation. In E. House (ed.) *School Evaluation: the Politics and the Process*. Chicago: University of Chicago Press.

Scriven, M. (1980) *The Logic of Evaluation*. Inverness, CA: Edgepress.

Scriven, M. (1991) *Evaluation Thesaurus*. London: Sage.

Scrivens, E. (1995) *Accreditation: Protecting the Professional or the Consumer?* Buckingham: Open University Press.

Sechrest, L., Perrin, E. and Bunker, J. (eds) (1990) *Research Methodology: Strengthening Causal Interpretations of Non-experimental Data*. Washington, DC: US Department of Health and Human Services.

Senge, P. (1992) *The Fifth Discipline*. London: Random House.

Shadish, W., Cook, T. and Leviton, L. (1991) *Foundations of Programme Evaluation: Theories of Practice*. London: Sage.

Shapiro, D. and Firth, J. (1987) Prescriptive vs exploratory psychotherapy. *British Journal of Psychiatry*, 151, 790–9.

Shaw, C. (1989) *Medical Audit: a Hospital Handbook*. London: King's Fund Centre.

Shaw, C. (1993) Quality assurance in the UK. *Quality Assurance in Health Care*, 5(2), 107–18.

Sheldon, T. and Chalmers, I. (1994) The UK Cochrane Centre and the NHS Centre for Reviews and Dissemination. *Health Economics*, 3, 201–3.

Sibley, J., Sackett, D., Neufeld, V. *et al* (1982) A randomised controlled trial of continuing medical education, *New England Journal of Medicine*, 302, 511.

Silagy, C. (1993) Developing a register of randomised controlled trials in primary care. *British Medical Journal*, 306, 897–900.

Sinclair, C. and Frankel, M. (1982) The effect of quality assurance activities on the quality of mental health services. *Quality Review Bulletin*, July, 78–89.

Sivestro, R., Johnston, R., Fitzgerald, L. and Voss, C. (1990) Quality measurement in service industries. *International Journal of Service Industry Management*, 1(2).

Sketris, I. (1988) *Health Service Accreditation – an International Overview*. London: King's Fund Centre.

Smith, G. and Cantley, C. (1985) *Assessing Health Care: a Study in Organizational Evaluation*. Milton Keynes: Open University Press.

Smith, J. (1992) Ethics and health care rationing. *Journal of Management in Medicine*, 26–8.

Smith, M., Glass, G. and Miller, T. (1980) *The Benefits of Psychotherapy*. Baltimore: Johns Hopkins University Press.

Spitzer, W., Kergin, D., Yoshida, M. *et al.* (1973) Nurse practitioners in primary care. *Canadian Medical Association Journal*, 108, 1006–16.

Spitzer, W., Sackett, D., Sibley, J., Roberts, R., Gent, M., Kergin, D., Hackett, B. and Olynich, A. (1974) The Burlington randomized trial of the nurse practitioner. *New England Journal of Medicine*, 31 January, 252–6.

SSI (1989) *Homes Are for Living in*. London: HMSO.

SSSSG (1994) Randomised trial of cholesterol lowering in 4444 patients with coronary heart disease. *Lancet*, 344, 1383–9.

Stern, E. (1990) *Evaluating Innovatory Programmes*. London: The Tavistock Institute.

Stern, E. (1993) The challenge of 'real-time' evaluation. In *The Tavistock Institute Review 1992–93*. London: The Tavistock Institute.

Stocking, B. (1996) The art and science of medicine. *The IHSM Network*, 3(6), 3.

Strauss, A. and Corbin, J. (1990) *Basics of Qualitative Research*. London: Sage.

TARP (1980) *Consumer Complaint Handling in America: Summary of Findings and Recommendations*. Washington, DC: White House Office of Consumer Affairs.

Thomson, R., Cook, G., Elliott, P., Baket, I. and Goodwin, R. (1993) Audit and the purchaser/provider interaction. Report of a working group of the regional medical audit co-ordinator's committee and conference of colleges' audit working group members. NHSME, Leeds.

Tolley, K., Buck, D. and Godfrey, C. (1996) Health promotion and health economics. *Health Education Research*, 11(3), 361–4.

Townsend, J., Piper, M., Frank, A., Dyer, S., North, W. and Meade, T. (1988) Reduction in readmission of elderly patients by a community based hospital discharge team: a randomised controlled trial. *British Medical Journal*, 297, 544–7.

Tukey, J. (1962) The future of data anlaysis. *Annals of Mathematical Statistics*, 33, 13–14.

Tversky, A. (1991) Winner Takes All? *The Psychologist*, June, 268.

Unell, J. (1996) *The Carers Impact Experiment*. London: King's Fund Centre.

Van Maanen, J., Dabbs, J. and Faulkner, R. (1982) *Varieties of Qualitative Research*. Beverly Hills, CA: Sage.

Walshe, K. and Coles, J. (1993) *Evaluating Audit: a Review of Initiatives*. London: CASPE Research.

Walt, G. (1994a) *Health Policy: an Introduction to Process and Power*. London: Zed Books.

Walt, G. (1994b) How far does research influence policy? *European Journal of Public Health*, 4(4), 233–5.

Webb, E., Campell, D., Schwarz, R. and Sechrest, L. (1966) *Unobtrusive Measures: Nonreactive Research in the Social Sciences*. Chicago: Rand-McNally.

Weiss, C. (ed.) (1977) *Using Social Research in Public Policy Making*. Lexington, MA: Lexington Books.

Weiss, C. (1978) Improving the linkage between social research and public policy. In L. Lynn (ed.) *Knowledge and Policy: the Uncertain Connection*. Washington, DC: National Academy of Sciences.

Weiss, C. and Bucuvalas, M. (1980) *Social Science Research and Decision-making*. New York: Columbia University Press.

WHO (1981) *Health Programme Evaluation*. Geneva: World Health Organization.

WHO (1994) Implementation of the global strategy for health for all by the year 2000 – second evaluation. Eighth report of the world health situation. World Health Organization, Geneva.

Wholey, J. (1977) Evaluability assessment. In L. Rutman (ed.) *Evaluation Research Methods: A Basic Guide*. Beverly Hills, CA: Sage.

Wholey, J. (1983) *Evaluation and Effective Public Management*. Boston: Little, Brown.

Wilkin, D., Hallan, L. and Dogget, M. (1992) *Measures of Need and Outcome for Primary Health Care*. Oxford: Oxford Medical Publications.

Wilson, D. (1992) Assessment of an intervention in primary care: counseling patients on smoking cessation. In F. Tudiver, M. Bass, E. Dunn, P. Norton and M. Stuart (eds) *Assessing Interventions*. London: Sage.

Yin, R. (1981) The case study: some answers. *Administrative Science Quarterly*, 26(1), 58–65.

Yin, R. (1989) *Case Study Research: Design and Methods*. Beverly Hills, CA: Sage.

Zeithaml, V.A., Parasuraman, A. and Berry, L.L. (1990) *Delivering Service Quality*. London: Macmillan.

Zemke, R. and Bell, C.R. (1989) *Service Wisdom: Creating and Maintaining the Customer Service Edge*. Minneapolis: Lakewood Books.

# Index

Entries in italics refer to tables, diagrams or figures.